9-11

DC COMICS

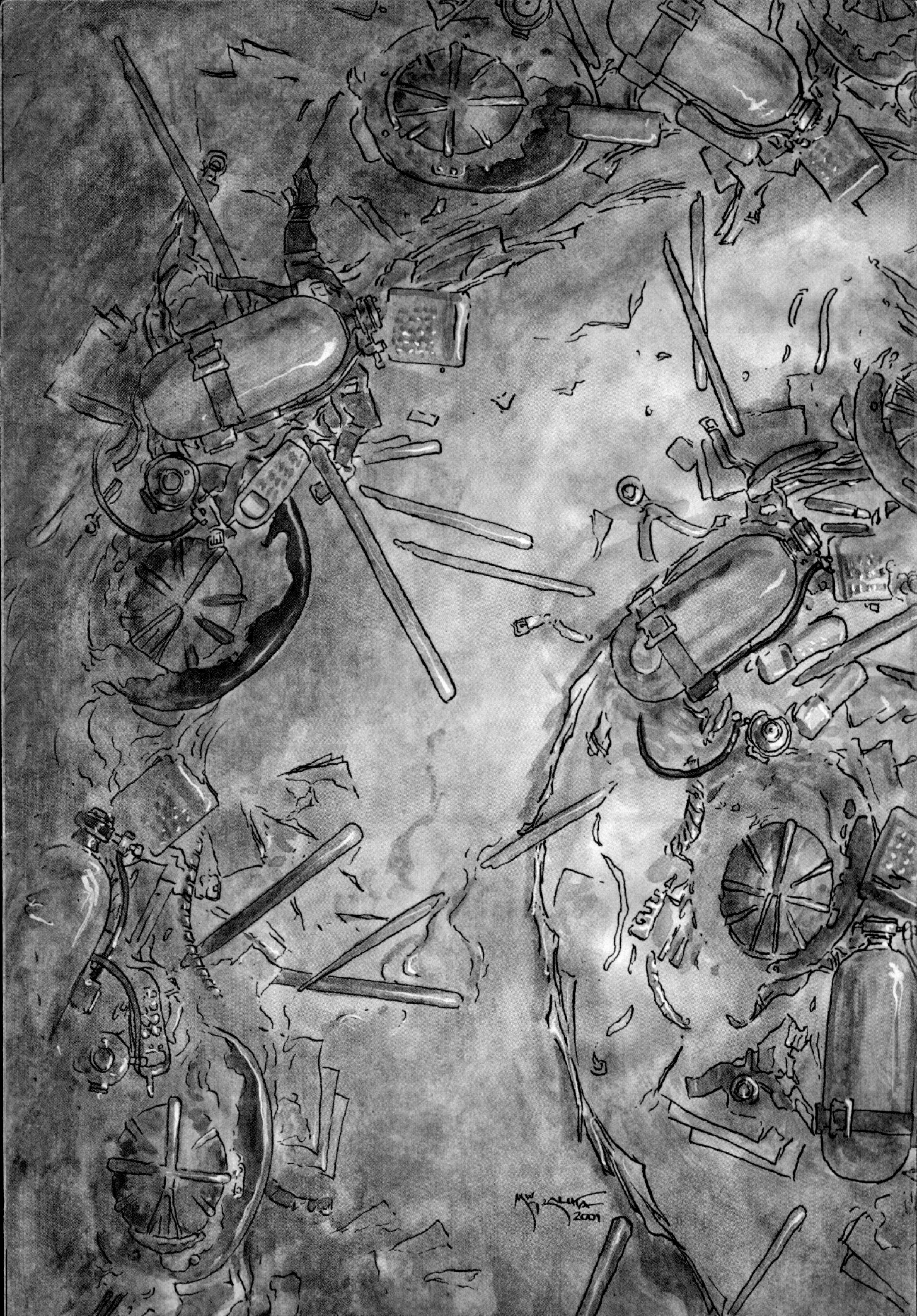
MW ZALUKA 2001

THE WORLD'S FINEST COMIC BOOK WRITERS

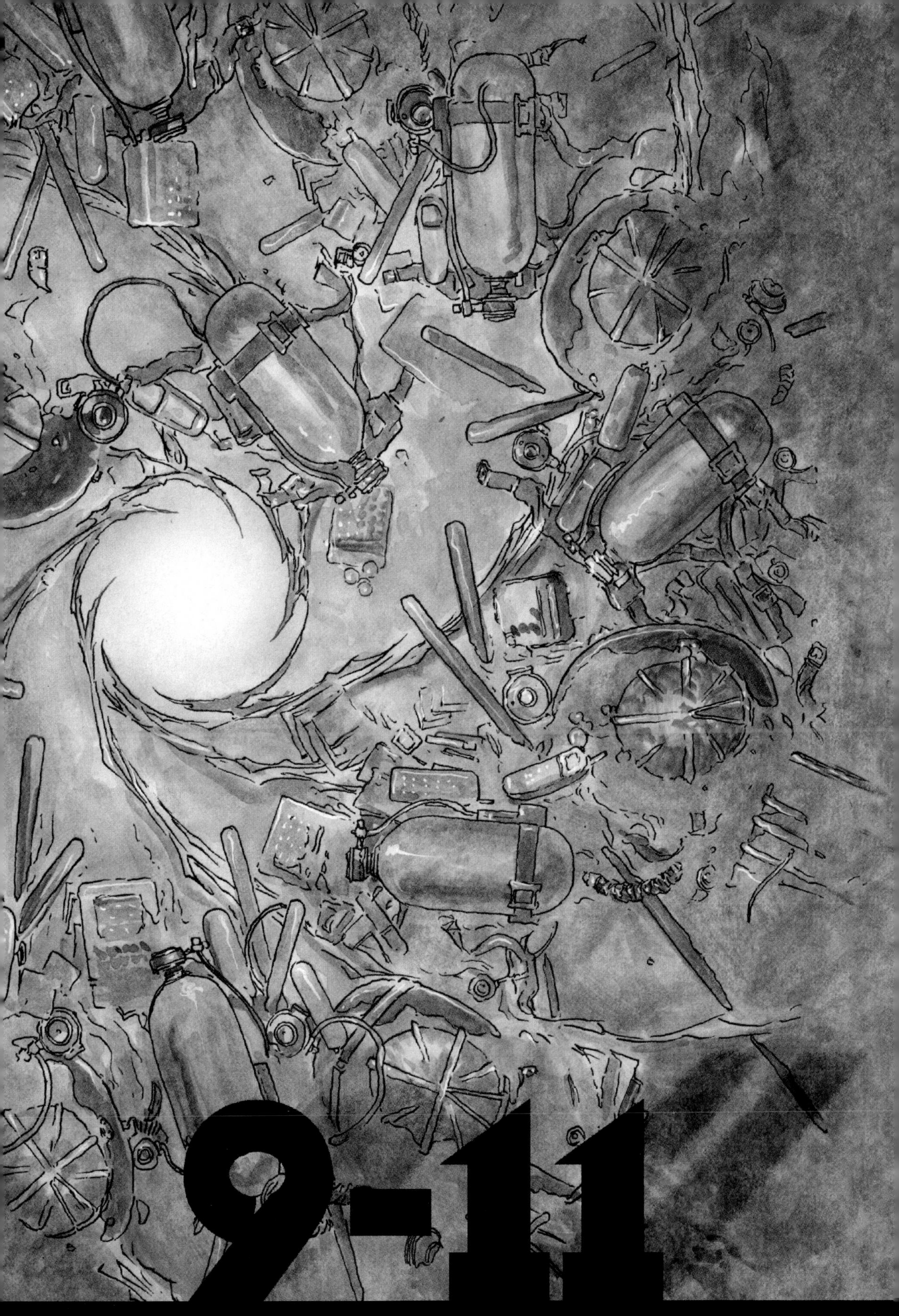
9-11

AND ARTISTS TELL STORIES TO REMEMBER

ISBN: 156389-878-0

DC Comics
1700 Broadway, New York, NY 10019

CONTENTS

11 INTRODUCTION

Section 1: Nightmares

13 *Introductory art by* Glenn Fabry

14 *art by* Kieron Dwyer

15 "UNREAL" . . . . *story by* Steven T. Seagle
. . . . *art by* Duncan Rouleau *and* Aaron Sowd

17 "THE REAL THING" . . . . *story and art by* Will Eisner

19 "WAKE UP" . . . . *story by* Joe Kelly
. . . . *art by* Scott Kolins *and* Dan Panosian

24 *art by* Danijel Zezelj

25 "THE WALK" . . . . *story by* James Denning
. . . . *art by* Guy Davis

29 Static Shock: "WEDNESDAY AFTERNOON"
. . . . *story by* Dwayne McDuffie
. . . . *art by* Denys Cowan *and* Prentis Rollins

38 *art by* Richard Corben

39 "GEMINI FALLING" . . . . *story by* Jo Duffy
. . . . *art by* Todd Nauck *and* Jaime Mendoza

42 *art by* Dave Gibbons

43 "HAVE YOU SEEN..?" *story by* Dan Abnett & Andy Lanning
. . . . *art by* David Lloyd

45 "TRADITION" . . . . *story by* Paul Levitz
. . . . *art by* Joe Staton *and* Bob Smith

46 *art by* Klaus Janson

47 UNTITLED . . . . *story and art by* Tom Mandrake

48 *art by* Brian Stelfreeze

Contents

Section II: Heroes

51 *Introductory art by* Greg *and* Tim Hildebrandt

52 *art by* Alex Horley

53 Astro City: "SINCE THE FIRE"...... *story by* Kurt Busiek
.... *art by* Brent Anderson

59 UNTITLED................ *story and art by* Gary Fields

60 I, PAPARAZZI.................. *story by* Pat McGreal
.... *art by* Stephen John Phillips *and* Steven Parke

63 "THE JOB"..................... *story by* Josh Krach
.... *art by* Scott McDaniel *and* James Pascoe

68 *art by* Steve Scott *and* Eman Torre

69 "HUMAN VALUES"....... *story and art by* Darwyn Cooke

70 *art by* Tim Sale *from an idea by* Chuck Kim

71 "A HARD DAY'S NIGHT"........... *story by* Jeph Loeb
.... *art by* Carlos Pacheco *and* Jesús Meriño

74 "THE FIRSTS DIVISION".......... *story by* Hilary Bader
.... *art by* Sergio Cariello

78 "I NEVER THOUGHT OF MYSELF AS A HERO"........
.... *story by* Rick Veitch
.... *art by* Sergio Aragonés

85 Hellblazer: "EXPOSED".......... *story by* Mike Carey
.... *art by* Marcelo Frusin

88 *art by* Cliff Wu Chiang

89 "SOLDIERS"................... *story by* Beau Smith
.... *art by* Val Semeiks *and* Romeo Tanghal

95 *art by* Enrique Breccia

Contents

Section III: Recollections

97 *Introductory art by* John Bolton

98 "PRIORITIES" . . . . *story by* Ashley-Jayne Nicolaus
. . . . *art by* Rick Burchett

99 "WALKING THE WILLIAMSBURG BRIDGE TO WORK"
. . . . *story and art by* Mo Willems

104 UNTITLED . . . . *story by* Don McGregor
. . . . *art by* José Luis García-López

105 Scene of the Crime: "STILL LIFE" . . . *story by* Ed Brubaker
. . . . *art by* Michael Lark

111 "DUST" . . . . *story by* Keith Giffen
. . . . *art by* William Wray

114 *art by* Phil Jimenez

Contents

Section IV: Unity

117 *Introductory art by* John Van Fleet

118 *art by* John Lucas

119 "9:00 E.S.T." . . . . *story by* Dan Abnett & Andy Lanning
. . . . *art by* Yanick Paquette *and* Jim Royal

120 "FOR ART'S SAKE" . . . . *story by* Brian K. Vaughan
. . . . *art by* Pete Woods *and* Keith Champagne

125 "NO SALE?" . . . . *story by* Jennifer Moore
. . . . *art by* Jill Thompson

127 "THE CALL" . . . . *story by* Eddie Berganza
. . . . *art by* Kyle Baker

128 "A TALE OF 2 AMERICANS" . . . . *story by* Ben Raab
. . . . *art by* Roger Robinson *and* Dennis Janke

132 "AMERICA'S PASTIME" . . . . *story by* Brian Azzarello
. . . . *art by* Eduardo Risso

134 "SILVER LININGS IN A BIG DUST CLOUD" . . . .
. . . . *story and art by* Amanda Conner *and* Jimmy Palmiotti

136 "WHAT WE LEARNED TODAY" . . *story by* Eddie Berganza
. . . . *art by* Kyle Baker

137 "THIS, TOO, SHALL PASS" . . . . . . *story by* Marv Wolfman
. . . . *art by* Barry Kitson *and* Rich Faber

141 *art by* Paul Pope

142 UNTITLED . . . . *story by* Peter Gross
. . . . *art by* Darick Robertson

Contents

Section V: Dreams

147 *Introductory art by* Christopher Moeller

148 *art by* Ariel Olivetti

149 "IF ONLY" . . . . *story by* Dan Jurgens
art by Alan Davis, Robin Riggs, Mike Collins *and* Mark Farmer

153 "ASCENDING" . . . . *story by* J.M. DeMatteis
. . . . *art by* Michael Zulli

159 "THE AMERICAN DREAM" . . . . *story by* Paul Levitz
. . . . *art by* Jim Lee

165 "SPIRIT" . . . . *story by* Alex Simmons
. . . . *art by* Angelo Torres

169 "TALL BUILDINGS" . . . . *story by* Chris Sequeira
. . . . *art by* Tom Grummett *and* Tom Palmer

172 *art by* Steve Leialoha

173 *art by* Phil Noto

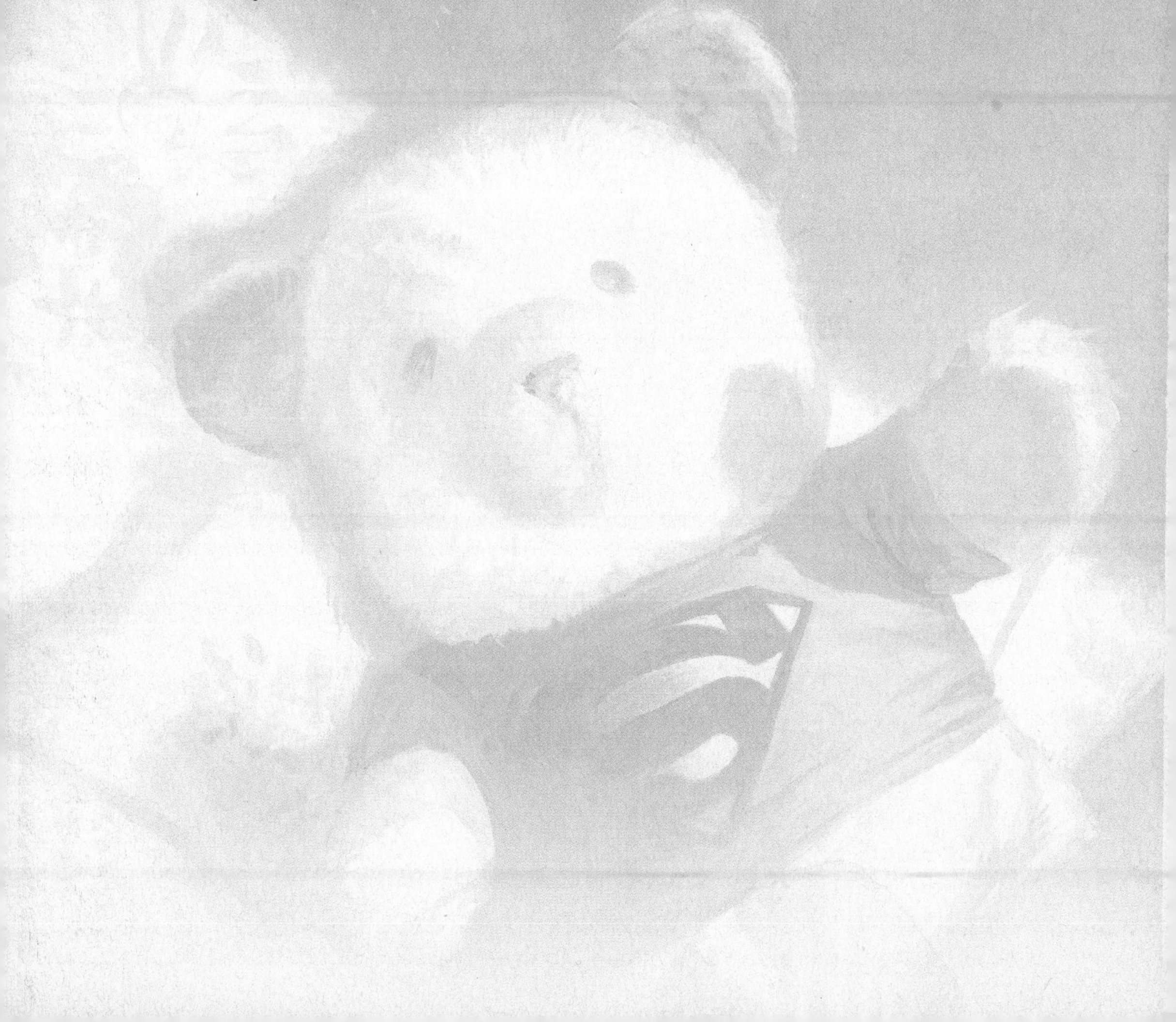

Section VI: Reflections

175 *Introductory art by* Dave McKean

176 "FIRST THINGS FIRST" . . . . *art by* Neal Adams

177 "THE SLEEPING GIANT" . . . . *story by* Stan Lee
. . . . *art by* Marie Severin

181 "THE WHEEL" . . . . *story by* Neil Gaiman
. . . . *art by* Chris Bachalo

186 "CHILD'S PLAY" . . . . *story by* Jamie Delano
. . . . *art by* Goran Sudžuka

189 "A BURNING HATE" . . . .
. . . . *story by* David S. Goyer & Geoff Johns
. . . . *art by* Humberto Ramos *and* Sandra Hope

195 "BLITZ KID" . . . . *story by* Michael Moorcock
. . . . *art by* Walter Simonson *and* Bob Wiacek

200 "CAREFUL" . . . . *story by* Andy Helfer
. . . . *art by* John Cebellero

202 "WARNINGS" . . . . *story by* Denny O'Neil
. . . . *art by* Phil Hester *and* Ande Parks

207 "THERE WERE TEARS IN HER EYES"
. . . . *story and art by* Sam Glanzman

211 *art by* Lee Bermejo

212 "WHAT OF TOMORROW" . . . . . *story and art by* Joe Kubert

216 CONTRIBUTORS

223 CAUSES

Cover by Alex Ross (after THE BIG ALL-AMERICAN COMIC BOOK by Kubert, Hibbard, Mayer and others)

Logo by Richard Bruning

Additional art by Colleen Doran, Paul Gulacy, Dave Johnson, Michael Wm. Kaluta and Bill Sienkiewicz

Color separations by Mark Chiarello, American Color, Digital Chameleon, Heroic Age and WildStorm Productions

Batman created by Bob Kane

Raven created by Marv Wolfman & George Pérez

Static created by Dwayne McDuffie, Derek T. Dingle, Denys Cowan & Michael Davis

Superman created by Jerry Siegel & Joe Shuster

Wonder Woman created by William Moulton Marston

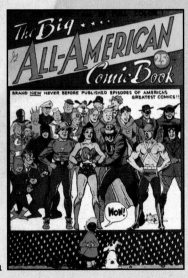

INTRODUCTION

This is for us, and this is for you. As creative people confronted by an astounding day of willful destruction and death, we needed to express ourselves, and reach out to you. We had stories to tell and images to share, in the hope that they will help you to remember September 11th and to ease the pain you lived through that day. We needed to lift our

pens, measure them against the swords of vengeance and the crumpled steel of anger. We hope this helps you, and we know producing it has helped us.

All the creative talent whose work comprises this volume have donated their time and efforts, bringing together one of the most accomplished arrays of talent ever assembled in our field. To make this possible, they did some of their best work against the short deadlines, while continuing their regular projects. Their work speaks for itself, but you can learn a little more about them on page 216.

We have been joined in this effort by Quebecor World Montréal (our printer), UPM-Kymmene, and Kruger Inc. (our paper manufacturers), Sun Chemical Inc. (our ink supplier), Diamond Comic Distributors and AOL Time Warner Trade Publishing Group (our distributors), and the publishers of Volume One, Chaos! Comics, Dark Horse Comics and Image Comics. All of the profits from this project will be going to 9-11 charitable funds, and you can learn more about that on page 223. We thank them all for their donations.

Most of all, we thank you for being our audience.

Paul Levitz
DC Comics

NIGHTMARES

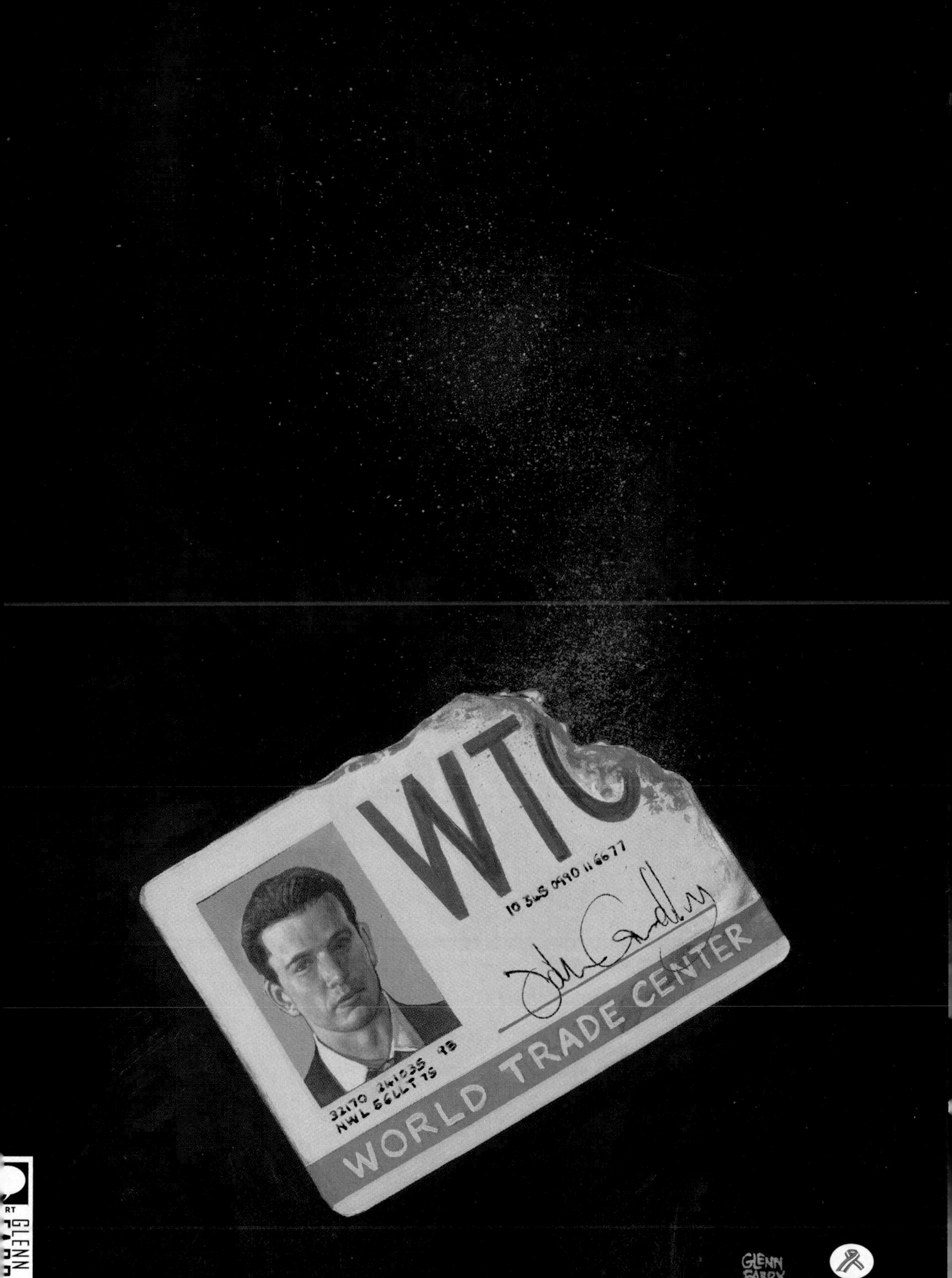
WTC
10 345 0990 116677
32170 241035 93
NWL 66LLT 19
WORLD TRADE CENTER
WORLD TRADE CENTER
GLENN FABRY

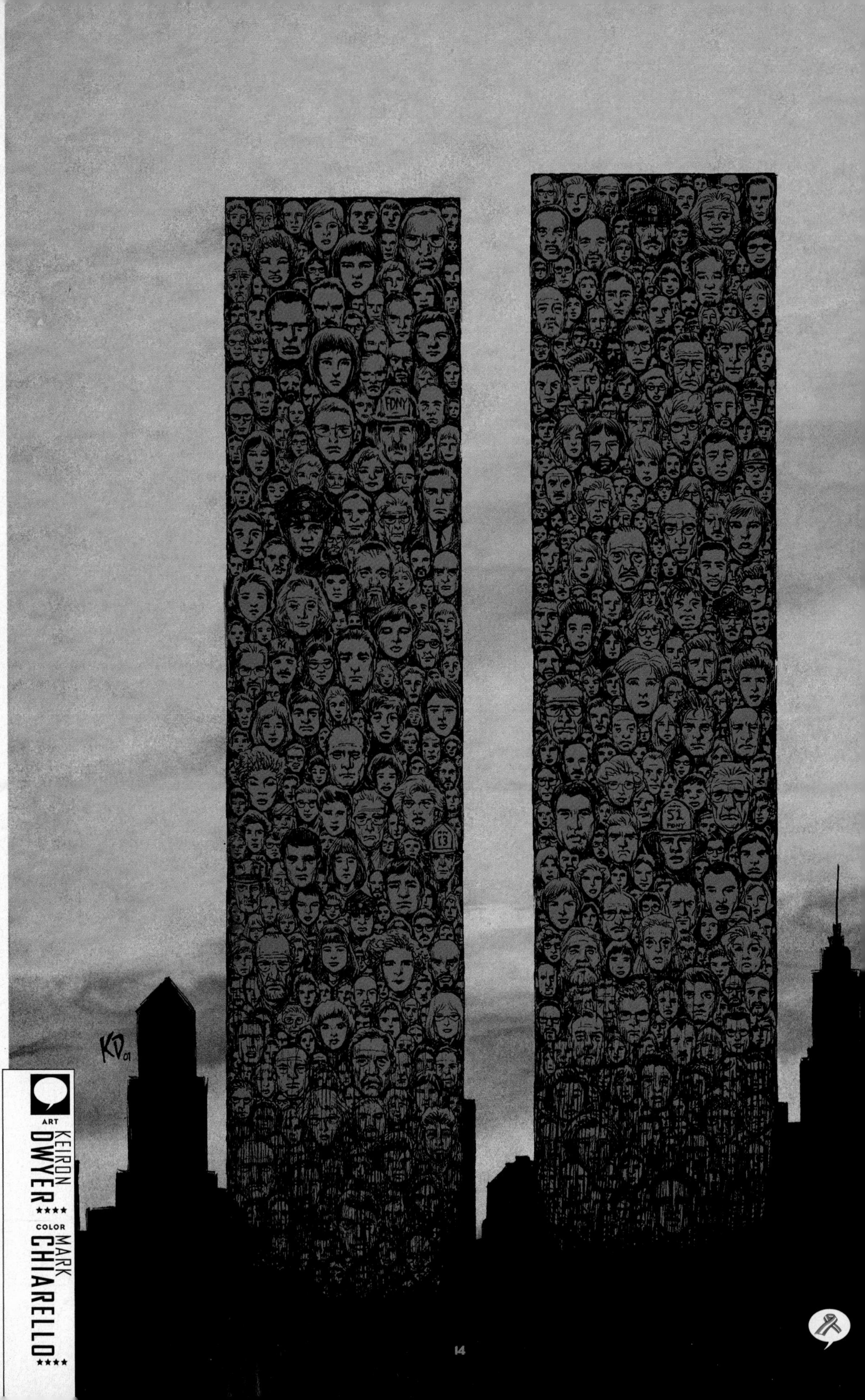
FDNY
13
51
FDNY
KD 01

ART
KEIRON DWYER

COLOR
MARK CHIARELLO

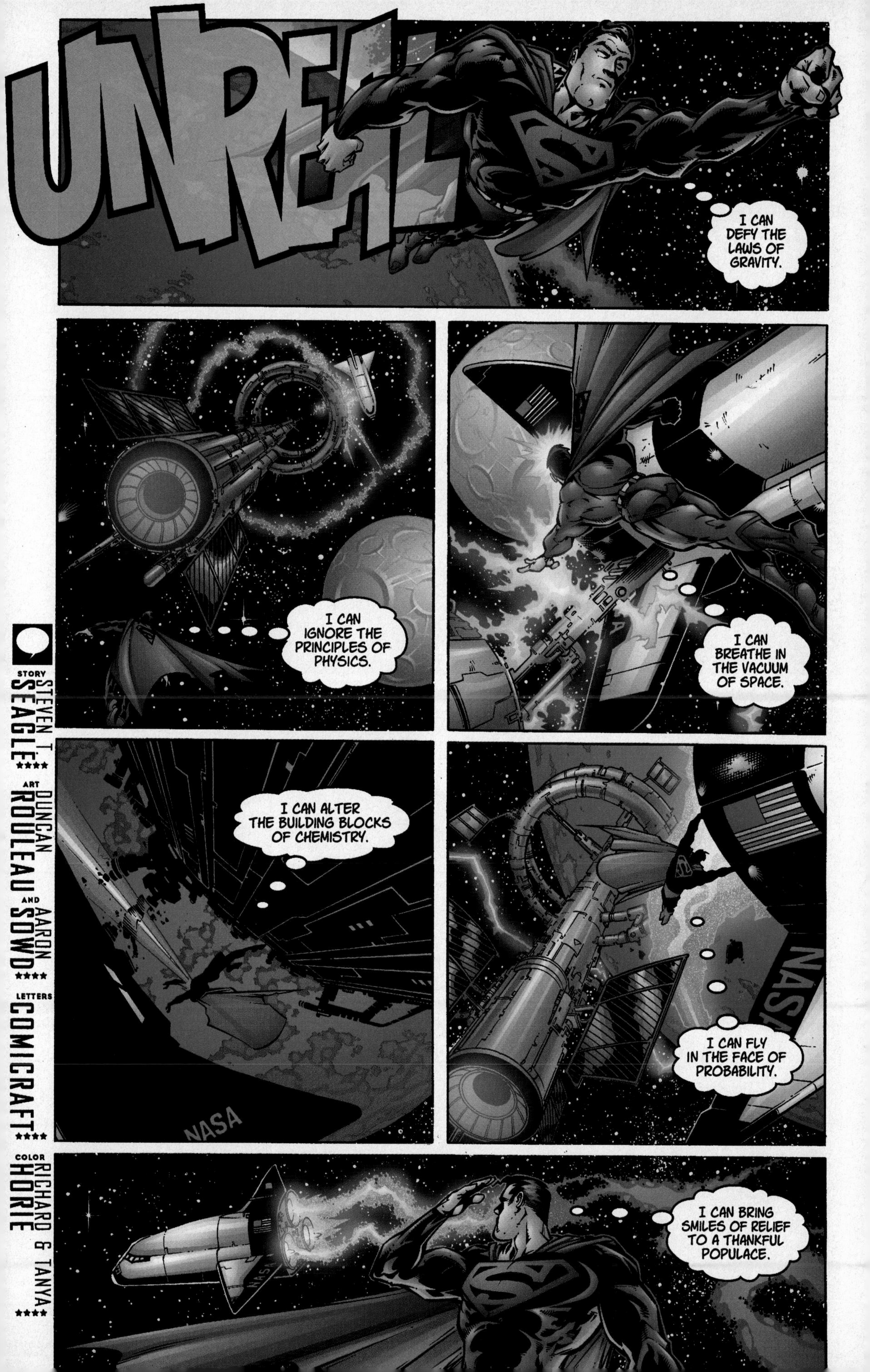
UNREAL
I CAN DEFY THE LAWS OF GRAVITY.
I CAN IGNORE THE PRINCIPLES OF PHYSICS.
I CAN BREATHE IN THE VACUUM OF SPACE.
I CAN ALTER THE BUILDING BLOCKS OF CHEMISTRY.
I CAN FLY IN THE FACE OF PROBABILITY.
I CAN BRING SMILES OF RELIEF TO A THANKFUL POPULACE.
NASA
STORY STEVEN T. SEAGLE
ART DUNCAN ROULEAU AND AARON SOWD
LETTERS COMICRAFT
COLOR RICHARD & TANYA HORIE

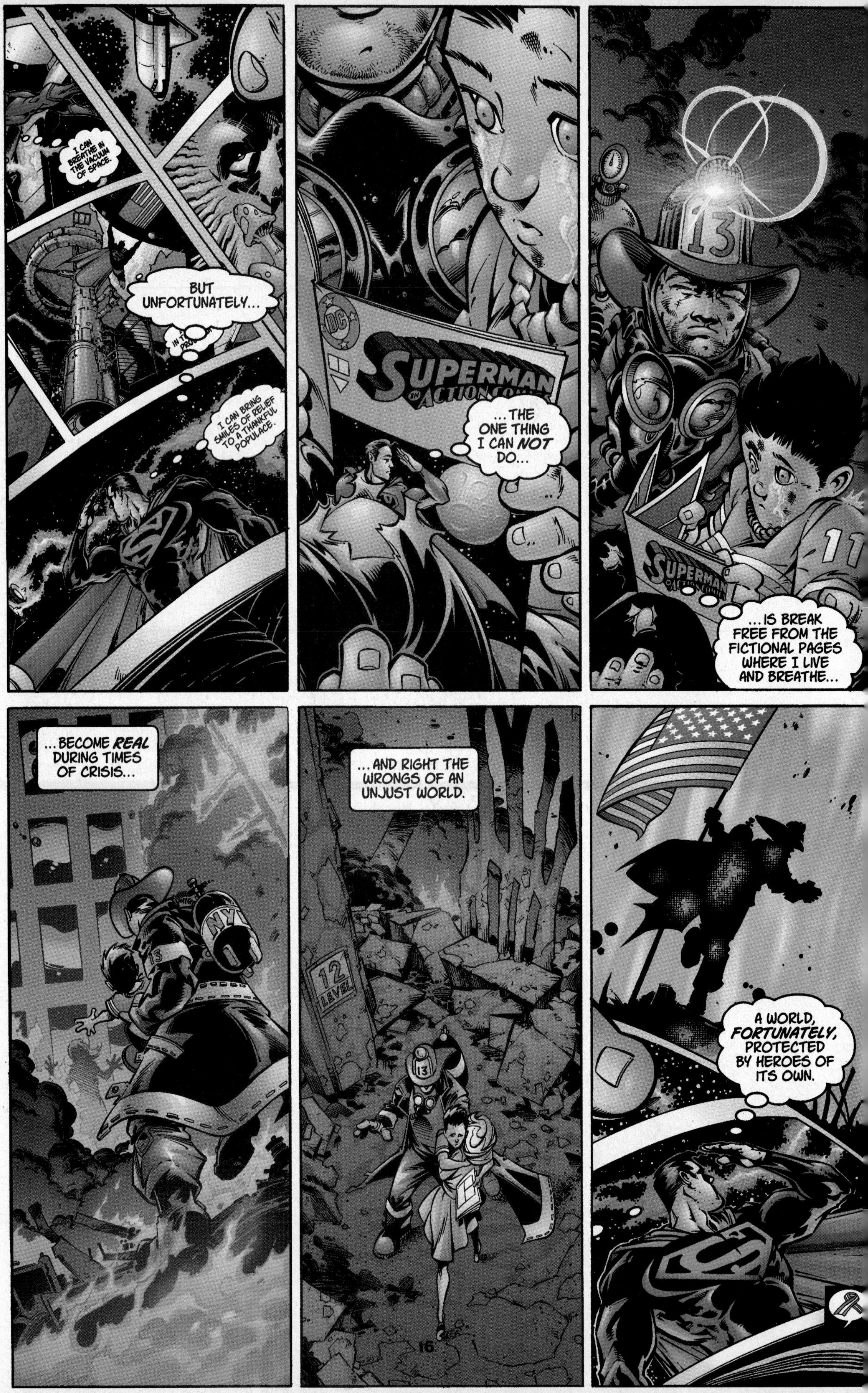
I CAN BREATHE IN THE VACUUM OF SPACE.
BUT UNFORTUNATELY...
I CAN BRING SMILES OF RELIEF TO A THANKFUL POPULACE.
SUPERMAN
...THE ONE THING I CAN *NOT* DO...
13
...IS BREAK FREE FROM THE FICTIONAL PAGES WHERE I LIVE AND BREATHE...
...BECOME *REAL* DURING TIMES OF CRISIS...
...AND RIGHT THE WRONGS OF AN UNJUST WORLD.
12 LEVEL
A WORLD, *FORTUNATELY*, PROTECTED BY HEROES OF ITS OWN.

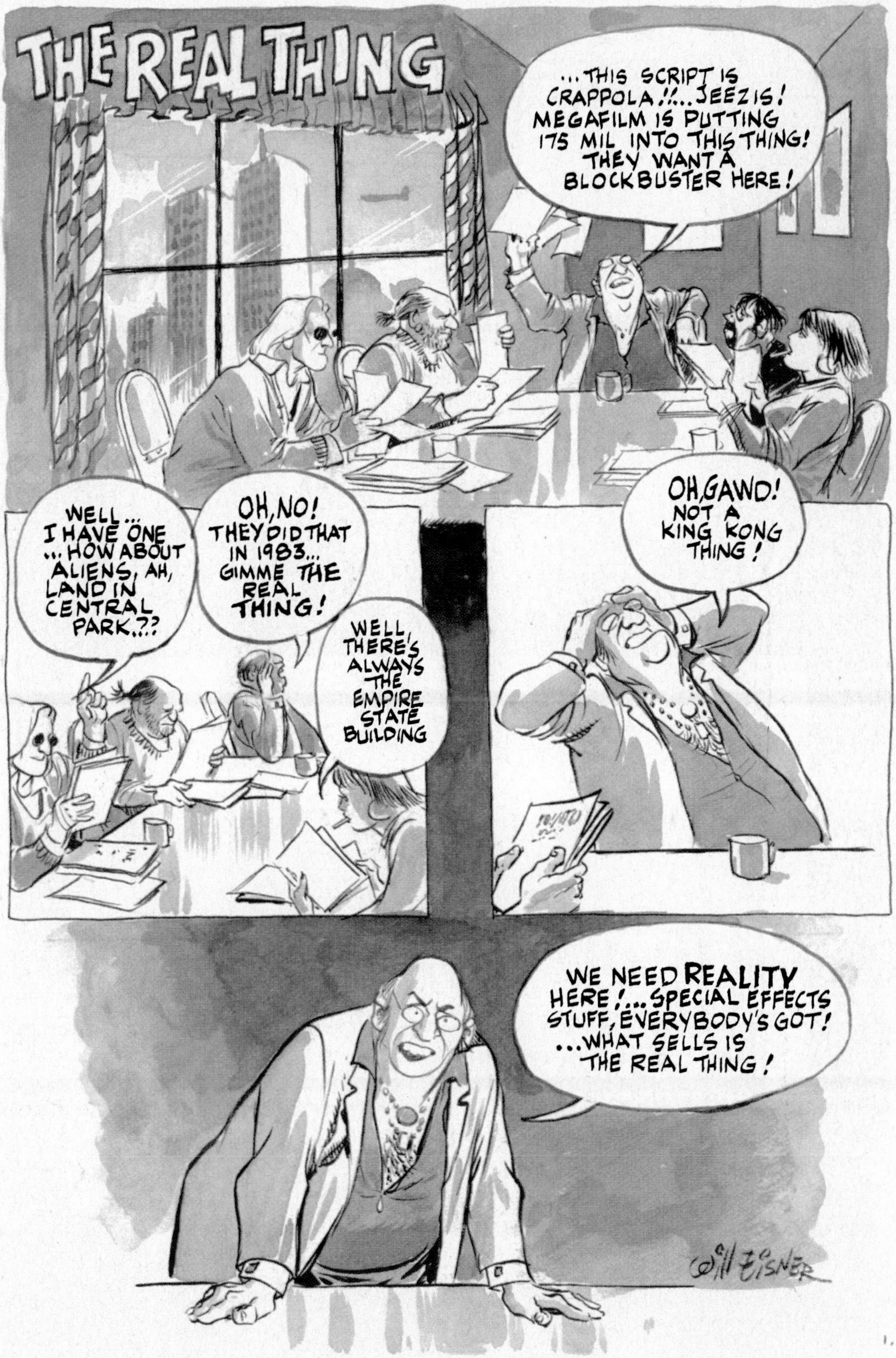
THE REAL THING
...THIS SCRIPT IS CRAPPOLA!!...JEEZIS! MEGAFILM IS PUTTING 175 MIL INTO THIS THING! THEY WANT A BLOCKBUSTER HERE!
WELL... I HAVE ONE ...HOW ABOUT ALIENS, AH, LAND IN CENTRAL PARK..??
OH, NO! THEY DID THAT IN 1983... GIMME THE REAL THING!
WELL, THERE'S ALWAYS THE EMPIRE STATE BUILDING
OH, GAWD! NOT A KING KONG THING!
WE NEED REALITY HERE!...SPECIAL EFFECTS STUFF, EVERYBODY'S GOT! ...WHAT SELLS IS THE REAL THING!
Will Eisner

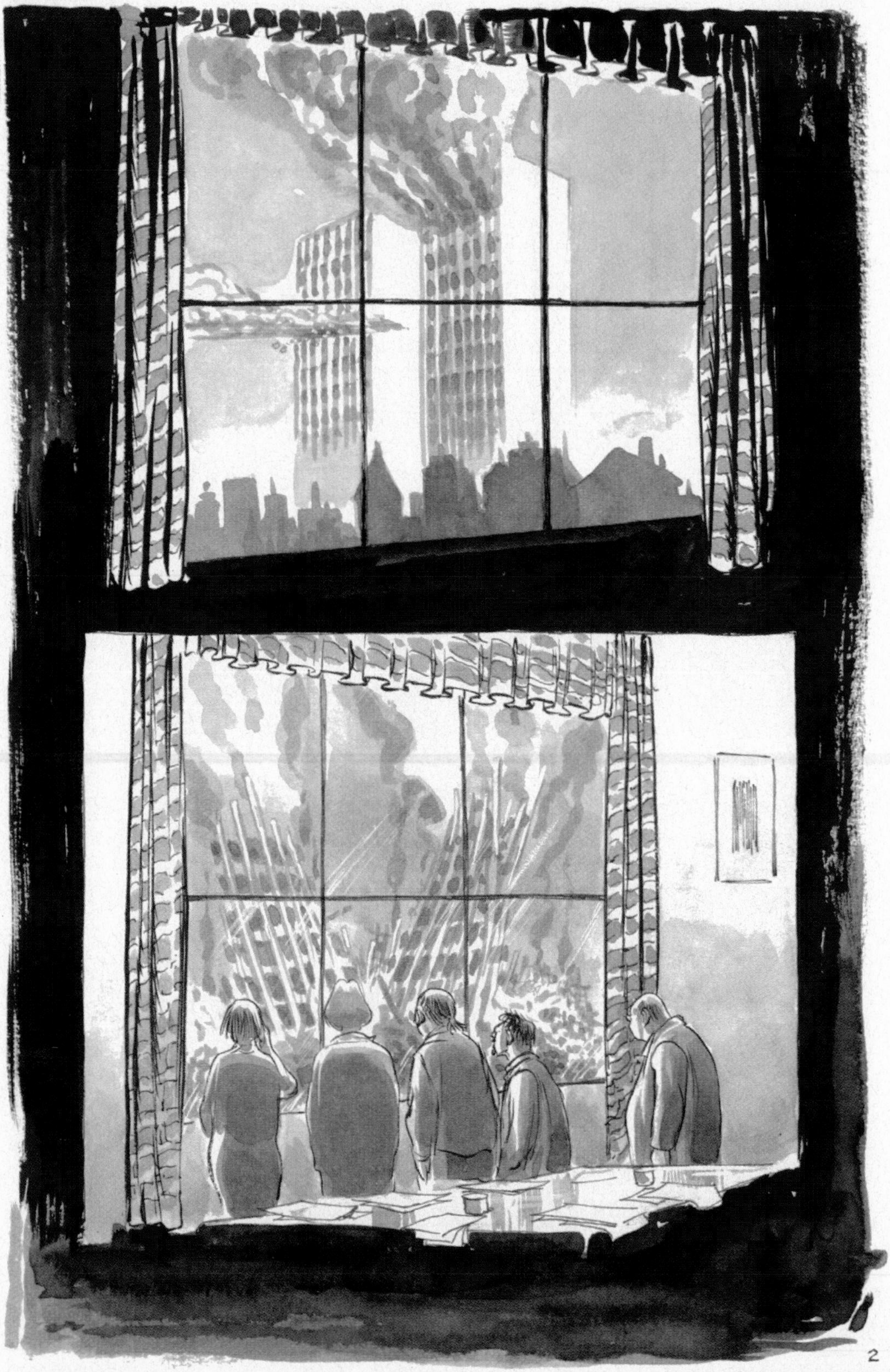

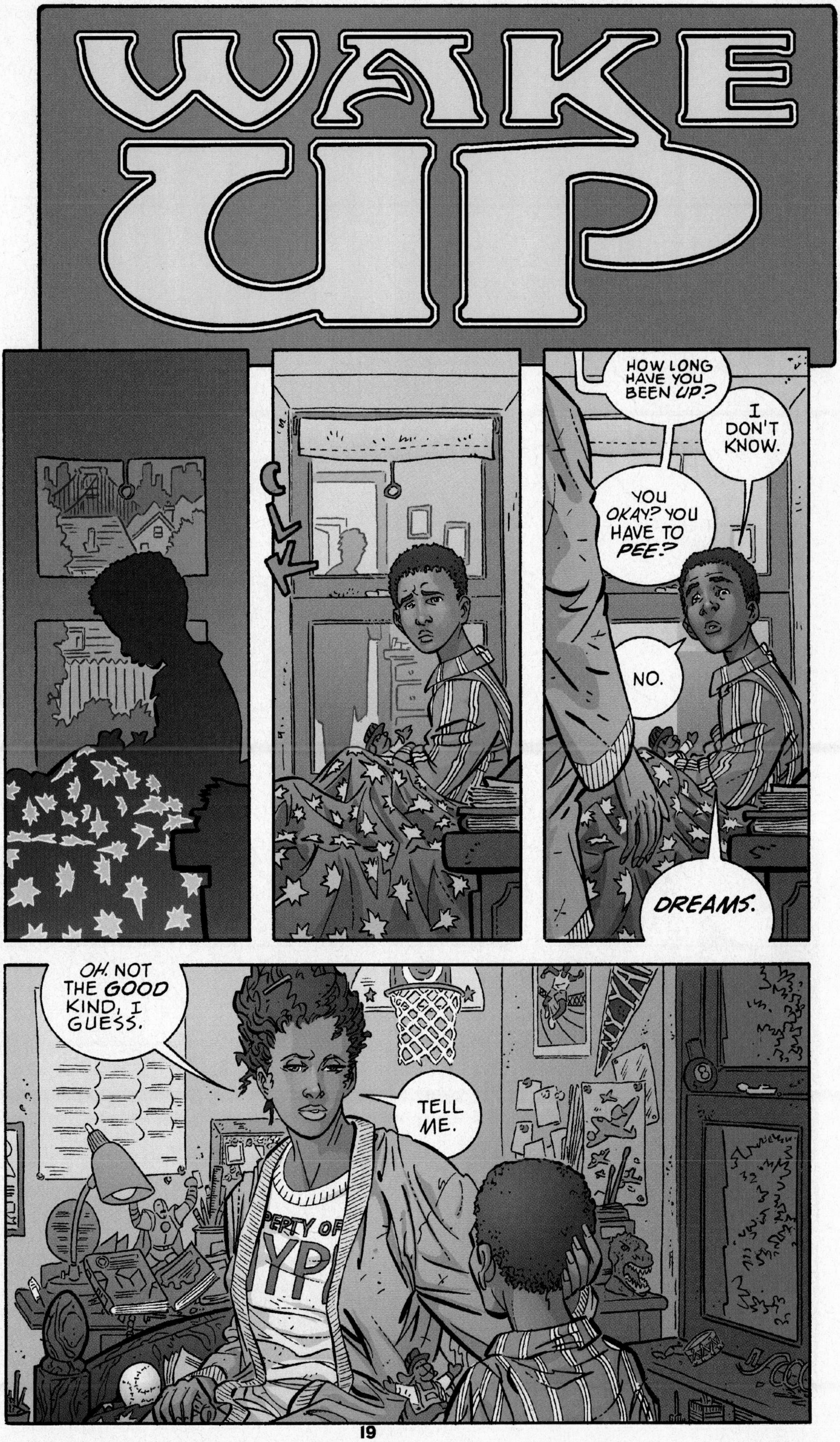
WAKE UP
HOW LONG HAVE YOU BEEN *UP?*
I DON'T KNOW.
YOU OKAY? YOU HAVE TO *PEE?*
NO.
DREAMS.
OH. NOT THE *GOOD* KIND, I GUESS.
TELL *ME.*

STORY JOE KELLY
ART SCOTT KOLINS AND DAN PANOSIAN
LETTERS JOHN WORKMAN
COLOR WILDSTORM

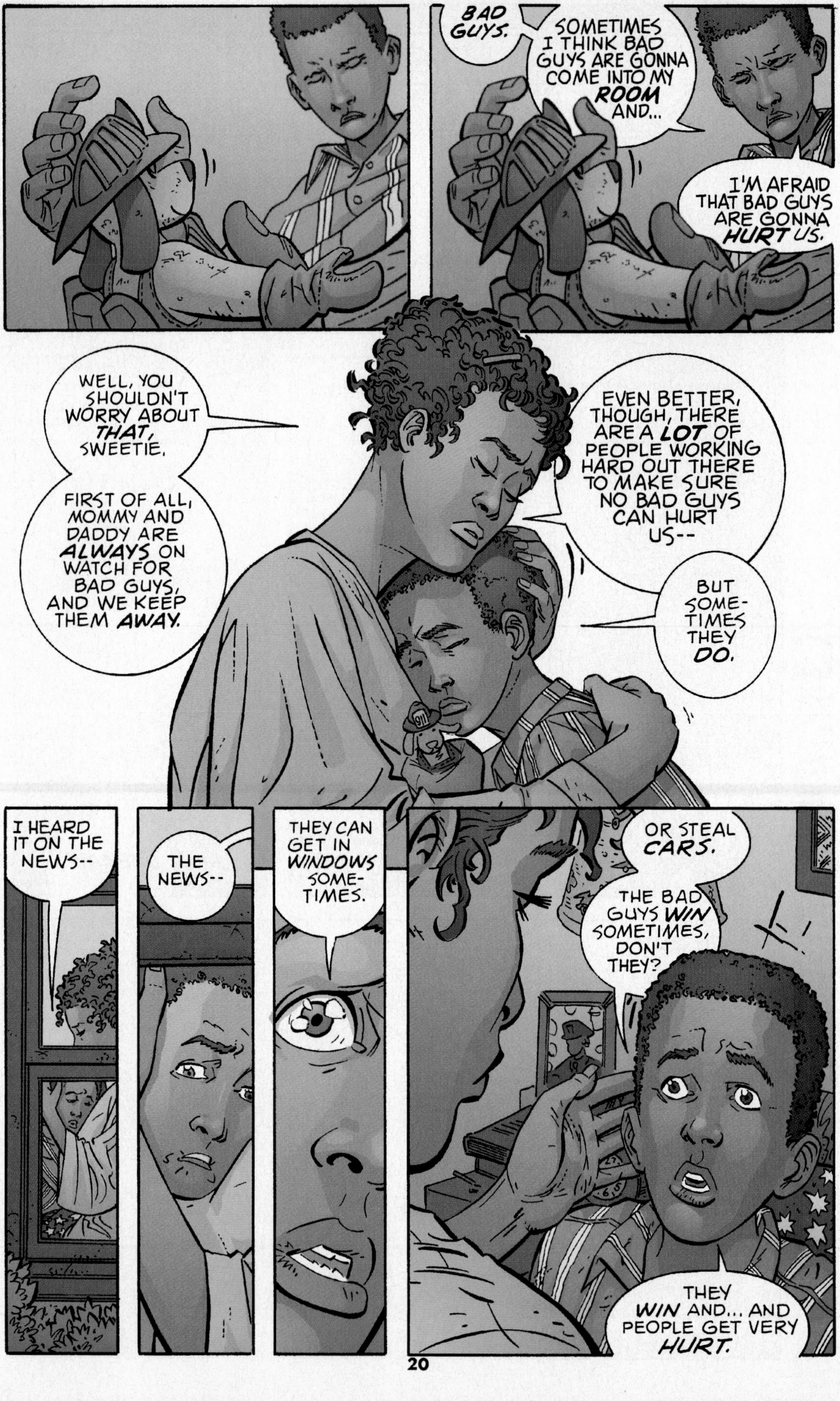
BAD GUYS.
SOMETIMES I THINK BAD GUYS ARE GONNA COME INTO MY ROOM AND...
I'M AFRAID THAT BAD GUYS ARE GONNA HURT US.
WELL, YOU SHOULDN'T WORRY ABOUT THAT, SWEETIE.
FIRST OF ALL, MOMMY AND DADDY ARE ALWAYS ON WATCH FOR BAD GUYS, AND WE KEEP THEM AWAY.
EVEN BETTER, THOUGH, THERE ARE A LOT OF PEOPLE WORKING HARD OUT THERE TO MAKE SURE NO BAD GUYS CAN HURT US--
BUT SOME-TIMES THEY DO.
I HEARD IT ON THE NEWS--
THE NEWS--
THEY CAN GET IN WINDOWS SOME-TIMES.
OR STEAL CARS.
THE BAD GUYS WIN SOMETIMES, DON'T THEY?
THEY WIN AND... AND PEOPLE GET VERY HURT.

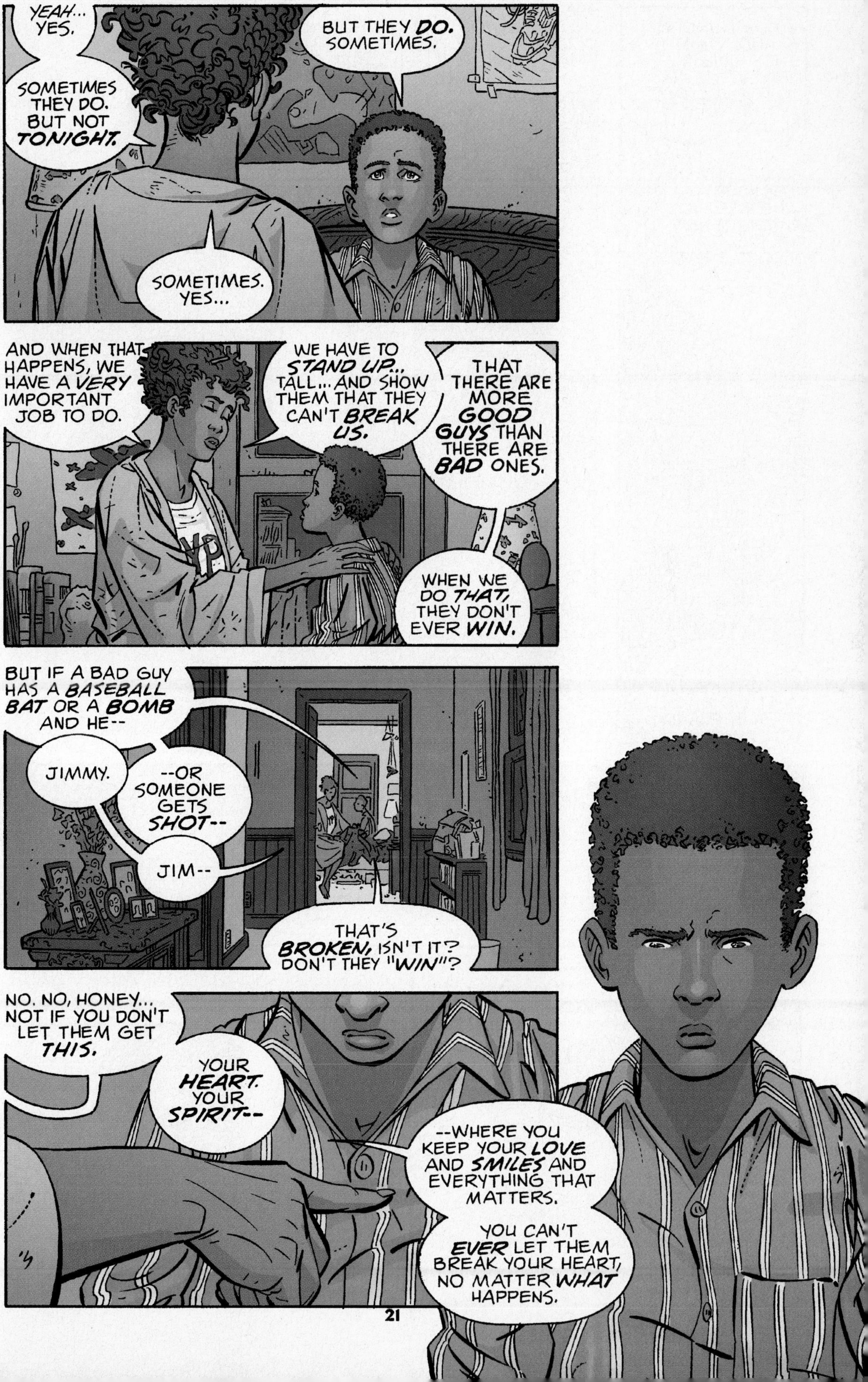
YEAH... YES.
SOMETIMES THEY DO. BUT NOT TONIGHT.
BUT THEY DO. SOMETIMES.
SOMETIMES. YES...
AND WHEN THAT HAPPENS, WE HAVE A VERY IMPORTANT JOB TO DO.
WE HAVE TO STAND UP... TALL... AND SHOW THEM THAT THEY CAN'T BREAK US.
THAT THERE ARE MORE GOOD GUYS THAN THERE ARE BAD ONES.
WHEN WE DO THAT, THEY DON'T EVER WIN.
BUT IF A BAD GUY HAS A BASEBALL BAT OR A BOMB AND HE--
JIMMY.
--OR SOMEONE GETS SHOT--
JIM--
THAT'S BROKEN, ISN'T IT? DON'T THEY "WIN"?
NO. NO, HONEY... NOT IF YOU DON'T LET THEM GET THIS.
YOUR HEART. YOUR SPIRIT--
--WHERE YOU KEEP YOUR LOVE AND SMILES AND EVERYTHING THAT MATTERS.
YOU CAN'T EVER LET THEM BREAK YOUR HEART, NO MATTER WHAT HAPPENS.

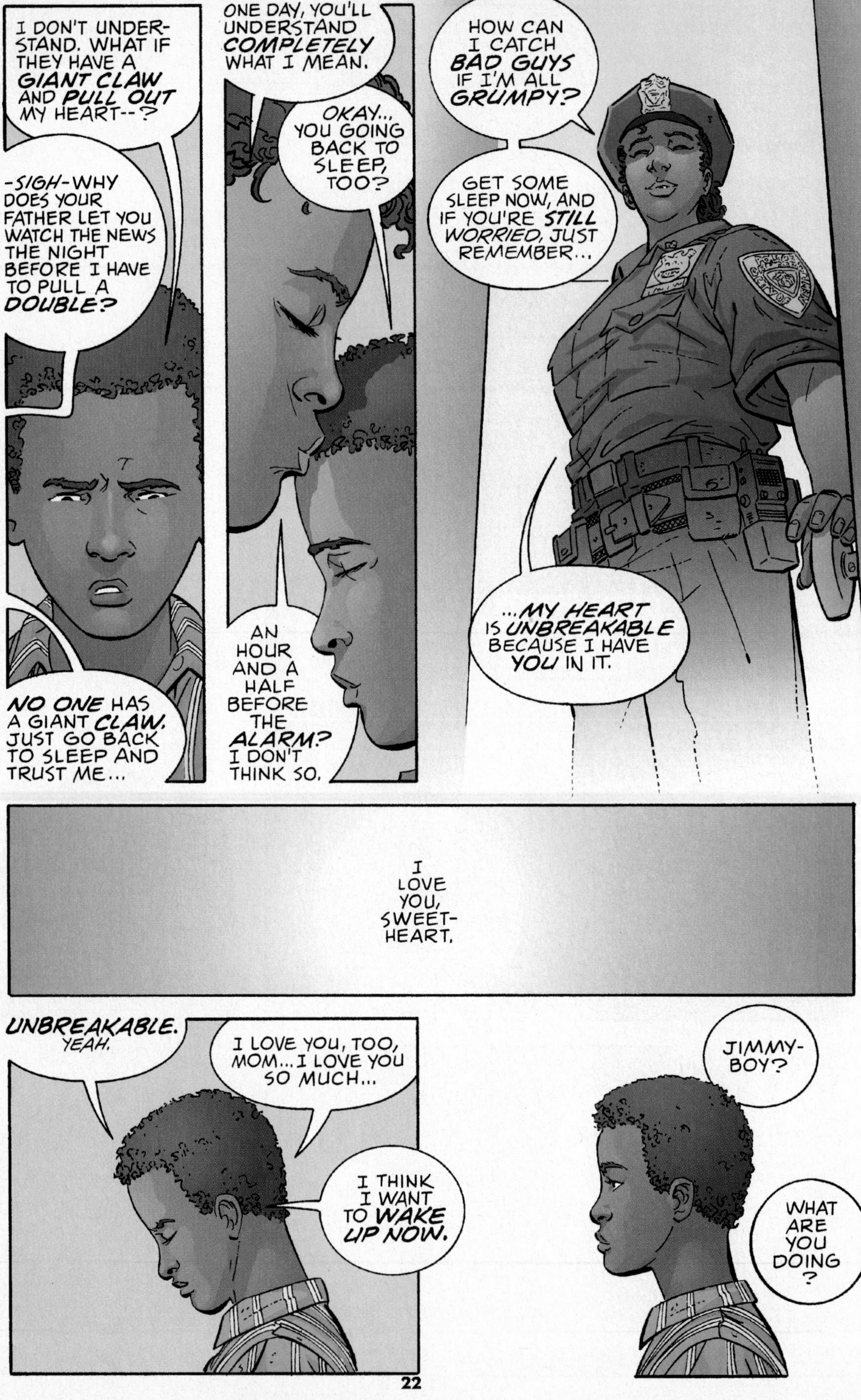
I DON'T UNDERSTAND. WHAT IF THEY HAVE A GIANT CLAW AND PULL OUT MY HEART--?
-SIGH- WHY DOES YOUR FATHER LET YOU WATCH THE NEWS THE NIGHT BEFORE I HAVE TO PULL A DOUBLE?
NO ONE HAS A GIANT CLAW. JUST GO BACK TO SLEEP AND TRUST ME...
ONE DAY, YOU'LL UNDERSTAND COMPLETELY WHAT I MEAN.
OKAY... YOU GOING BACK TO SLEEP, TOO?
AN HOUR AND A HALF BEFORE THE ALARM? I DON'T THINK SO.
HOW CAN I CATCH BAD GUYS IF I'M ALL GRUMPY?
GET SOME SLEEP NOW, AND IF YOU'RE STILL WORRIED, JUST REMEMBER...
...MY HEART IS UNBREAKABLE BECAUSE I HAVE YOU IN IT.
I LOVE YOU, SWEETHEART.
UNBREAKABLE. YEAH.
I LOVE YOU, TOO, MOM... I LOVE YOU SO MUCH...
I THINK I WANT TO WAKE UP NOW.
JIMMY-BOY?
WHAT ARE YOU DOING?

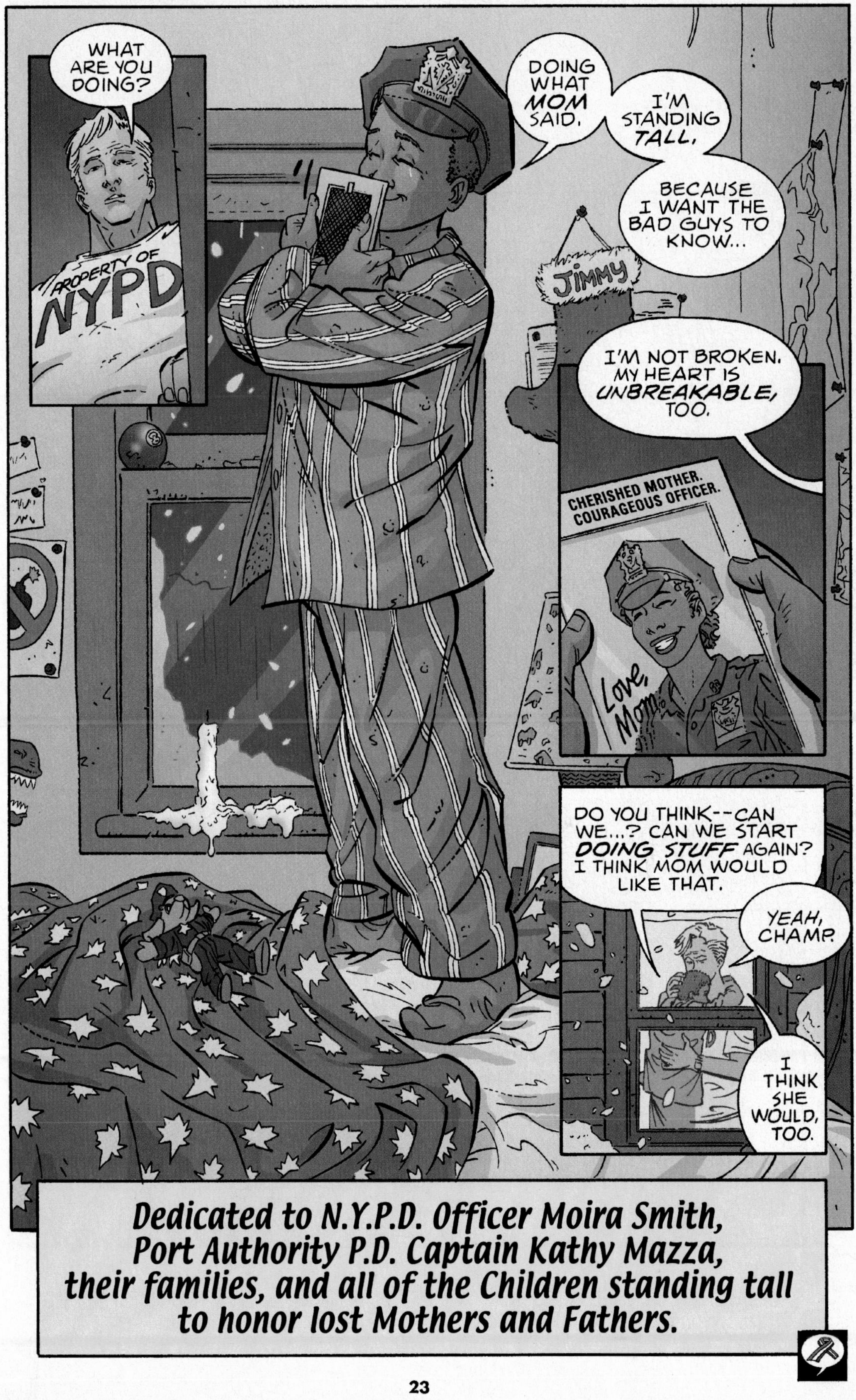
WHAT ARE YOU DOING?
DOING WHAT *MOM* SAID.
I'M STANDING *TALL*,
BECAUSE I WANT THE BAD GUYS TO KNOW...
PROPERTY OF NYPD
JIMMY
I'M NOT BROKEN. MY HEART IS *UNBREAKABLE*, TOO.
CHERISHED MOTHER. COURAGEOUS OFFICER.
Love, Mom
DO YOU THINK--CAN WE...? CAN WE START *DOING STUFF* AGAIN? I THINK MOM WOULD LIKE THAT.
YEAH, CHAMP.
I THINK SHE WOULD, TOO.

Dedicated to N.Y.P.D. Officer Moira Smith,
Port Authority P.D. Captain Kathy Mazza,
their families, and all of the Children standing tall
to honor lost Mothers and Fathers.

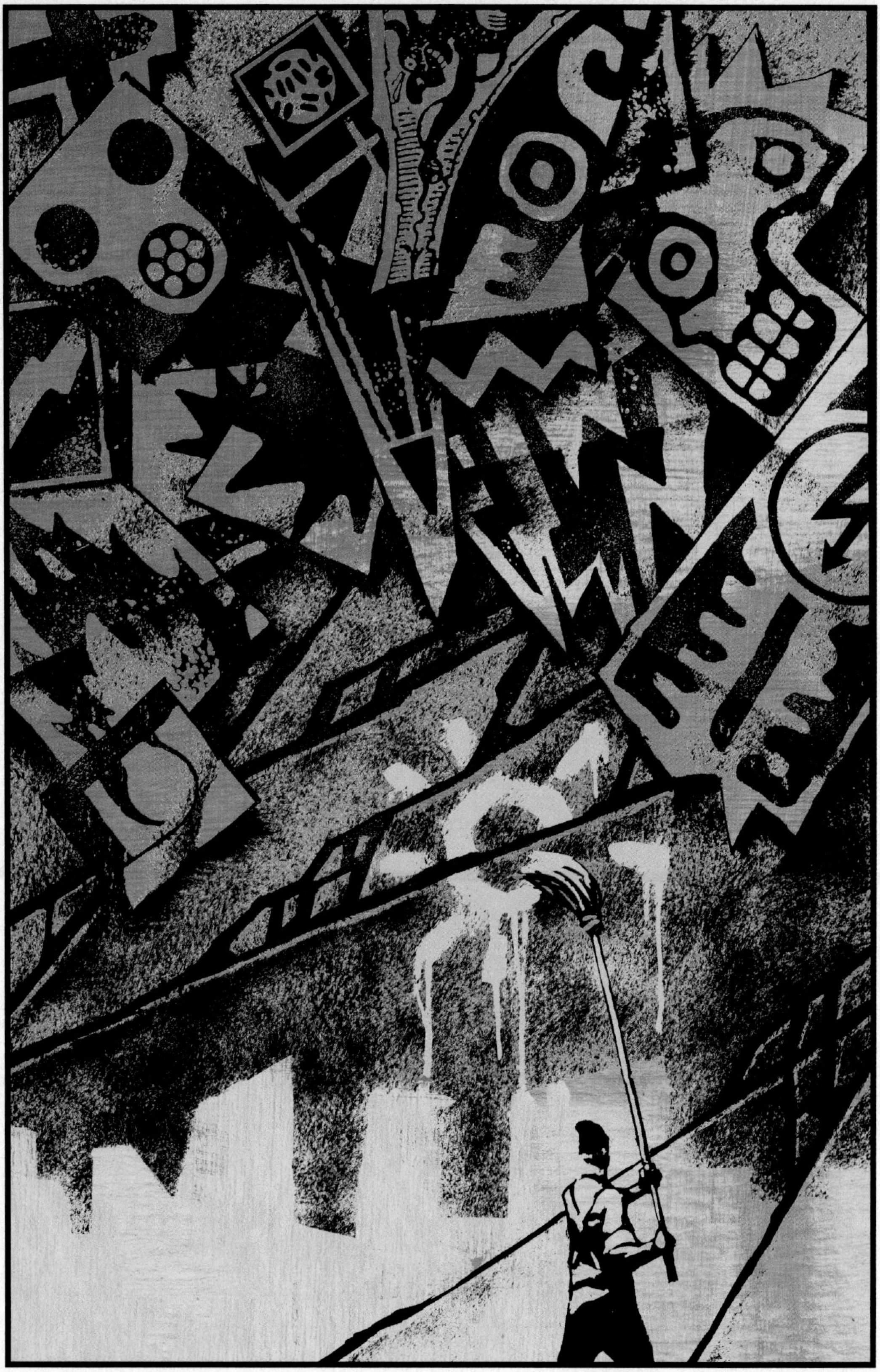

ART
DANIEL ZEZELJ

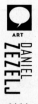

WALK

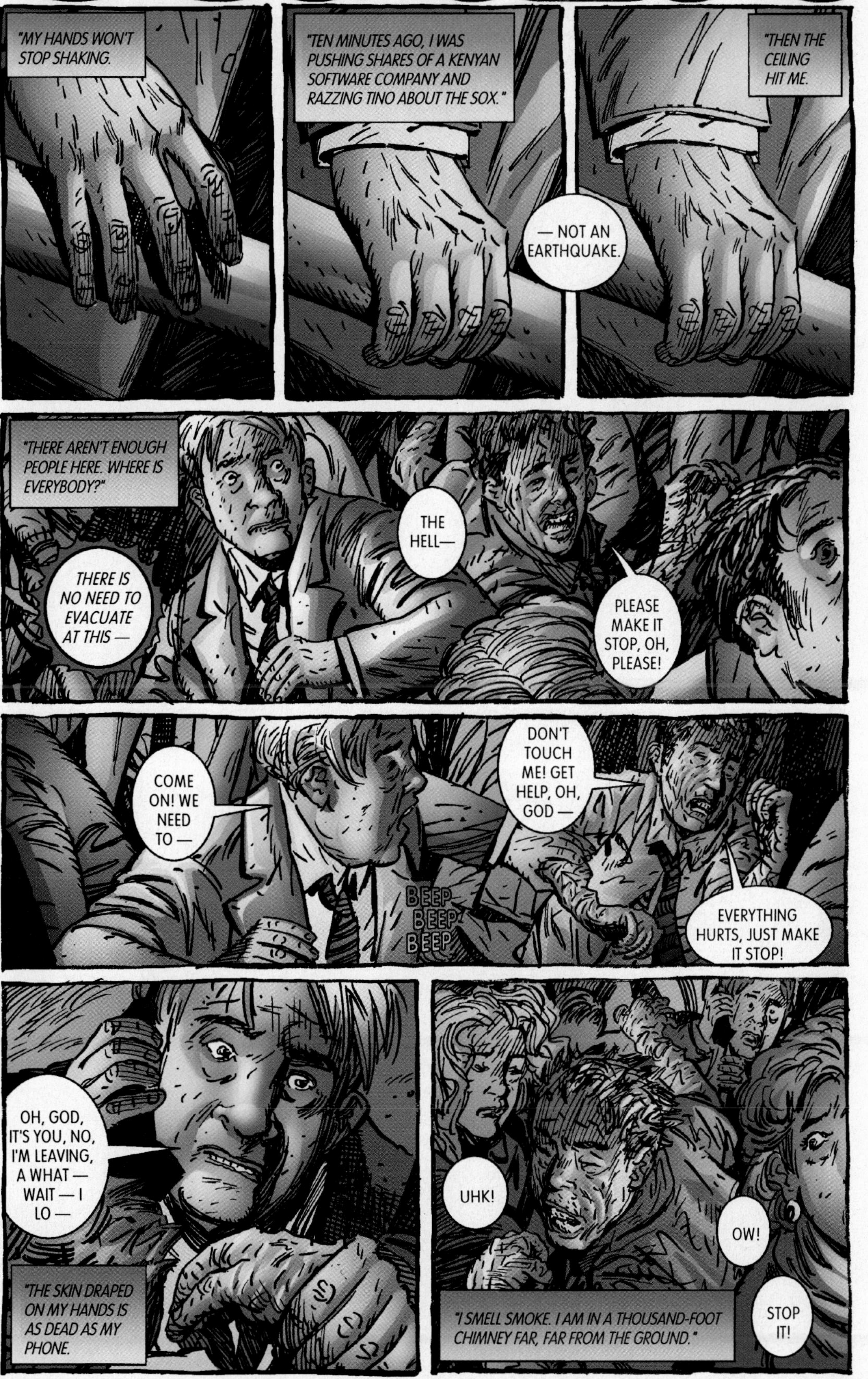

"MY HANDS WON'T STOP SHAKING.
"TEN MINUTES AGO, I WAS PUSHING SHARES OF A KENYAN SOFTWARE COMPANY AND RAZZING TINO ABOUT THE SOX."
— NOT AN EARTHQUAKE.
"THEN THE CEILING HIT ME.
"THERE AREN'T ENOUGH PEOPLE HERE. WHERE IS EVERYBODY?"
THERE IS NO NEED TO EVACUATE AT THIS —
THE HELL—
PLEASE MAKE IT STOP, OH, PLEASE!
COME ON! WE NEED TO —
BEEP BEEP BEEP
DON'T TOUCH ME! GET HELP, OH, GOD —
EVERYTHING HURTS, JUST MAKE IT STOP!
OH, GOD, IT'S YOU, NO, I'M LEAVING, A WHAT — WAIT — I LO —
"THE SKIN DRAPED ON MY HANDS IS AS DEAD AS MY PHONE.
UHK!
OW!
"I SMELL SMOKE. I AM IN A THOUSAND-FOOT CHIMNEY FAR, FAR FROM THE GROUND."
STOP IT!

STORY JAMES DENNING
ART GUY DAVIS
LETTERS JOHN WORKMAN
COLOR WILDSTORM

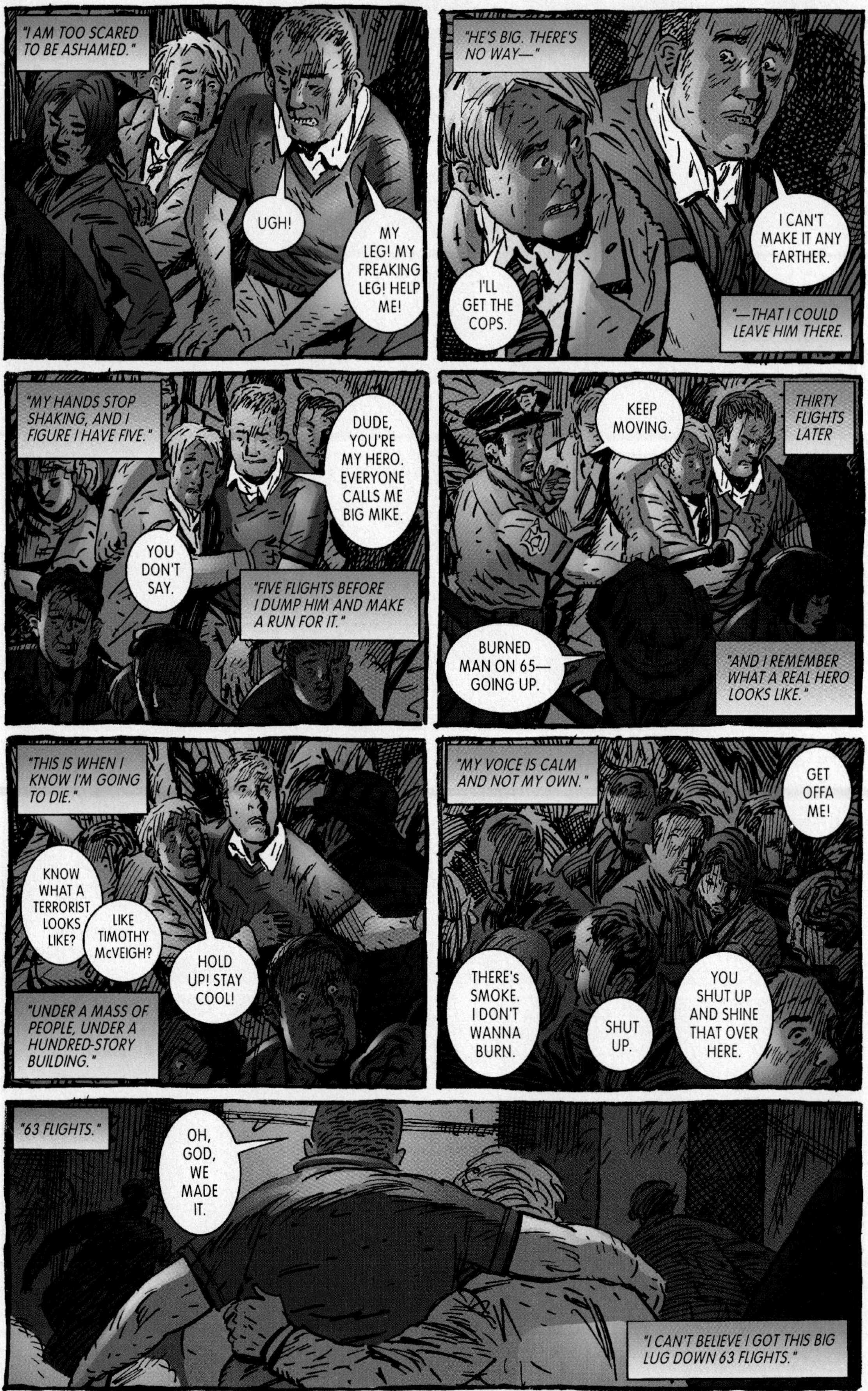
"I AM TOO SCARED TO BE ASHAMED."
UGH!
MY LEG! MY FREAKING LEG! HELP ME!
"HE'S BIG. THERE'S NO WAY—"
I'LL GET THE COPS.
I CAN'T MAKE IT ANY FARTHER.
"—THAT I COULD LEAVE HIM THERE.
"MY HANDS STOP SHAKING, AND I FIGURE I HAVE FIVE."
DUDE, YOU'RE MY HERO. EVERYONE CALLS ME BIG MIKE.
YOU DON'T SAY.
"FIVE FLIGHTS BEFORE I DUMP HIM AND MAKE A RUN FOR IT."
THIRTY FLIGHTS LATER
KEEP MOVING.
BURNED MAN ON 65— GOING UP.
"AND I REMEMBER WHAT A REAL HERO LOOKS LIKE."
"THIS IS WHEN I KNOW I'M GOING TO DIE."
KNOW WHAT A TERRORIST LOOKS LIKE?
LIKE TIMOTHY McVEIGH?
HOLD UP! STAY COOL!
"UNDER A MASS OF PEOPLE, UNDER A HUNDRED-STORY BUILDING."
"MY VOICE IS CALM AND NOT MY OWN."
GET OFFA ME!
THERE's SMOKE. I DON'T WANNA BURN.
SHUT UP.
YOU SHUT UP AND SHINE THAT OVER HERE.
"63 FLIGHTS."
OH, GOD, WE MADE IT.
"I CAN'T BELIEVE I GOT THIS BIG LUG DOWN 63 FLIGHTS."

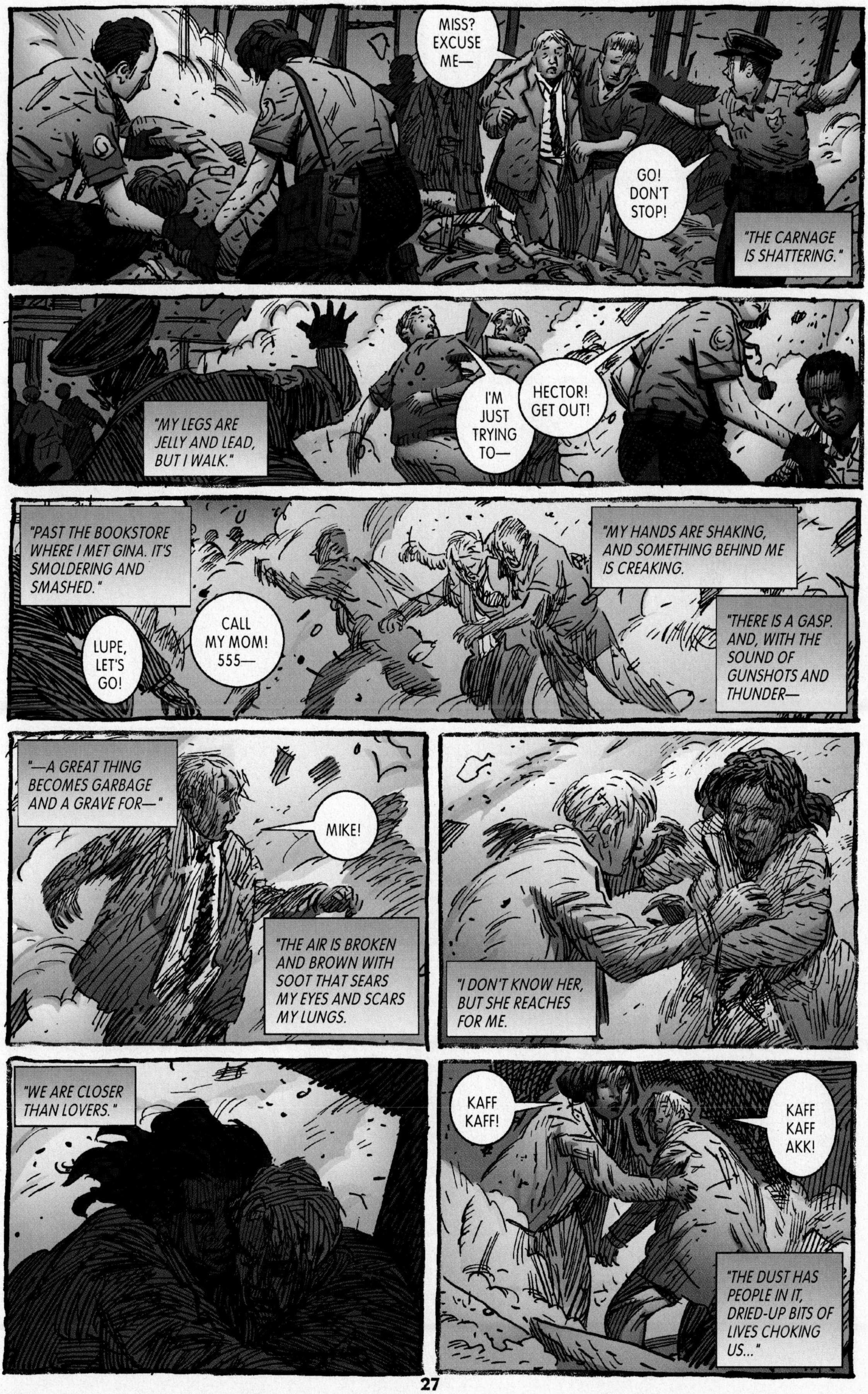

MISS? EXCUSE ME—
GO! DON'T STOP!
"THE CARNAGE IS SHATTERING."
"MY LEGS ARE JELLY AND LEAD, BUT I WALK."
I'M JUST TRYING TO—
HECTOR! GET OUT!
"PAST THE BOOKSTORE WHERE I MET GINA. IT'S SMOLDERING AND SMASHED."
LUPE, LET'S GO!
CALL MY MOM! 555—
"MY HANDS ARE SHAKING, AND SOMETHING BEHIND ME IS CREAKING.
"THERE IS A GASP. AND, WITH THE SOUND OF GUNSHOTS AND THUNDER—
"—A GREAT THING BECOMES GARBAGE AND A GRAVE FOR—"
MIKE!
"THE AIR IS BROKEN AND BROWN WITH SOOT THAT SEARS MY EYES AND SCARS MY LUNGS.
"I DON'T KNOW HER, BUT SHE REACHES FOR ME.
"WE ARE CLOSER THAN LOVERS."
KAFF KAFF!
KAFF KAFF AKK!
"THE DUST HAS PEOPLE IN IT, DRIED-UP BITS OF LIVES CHOKING US..."

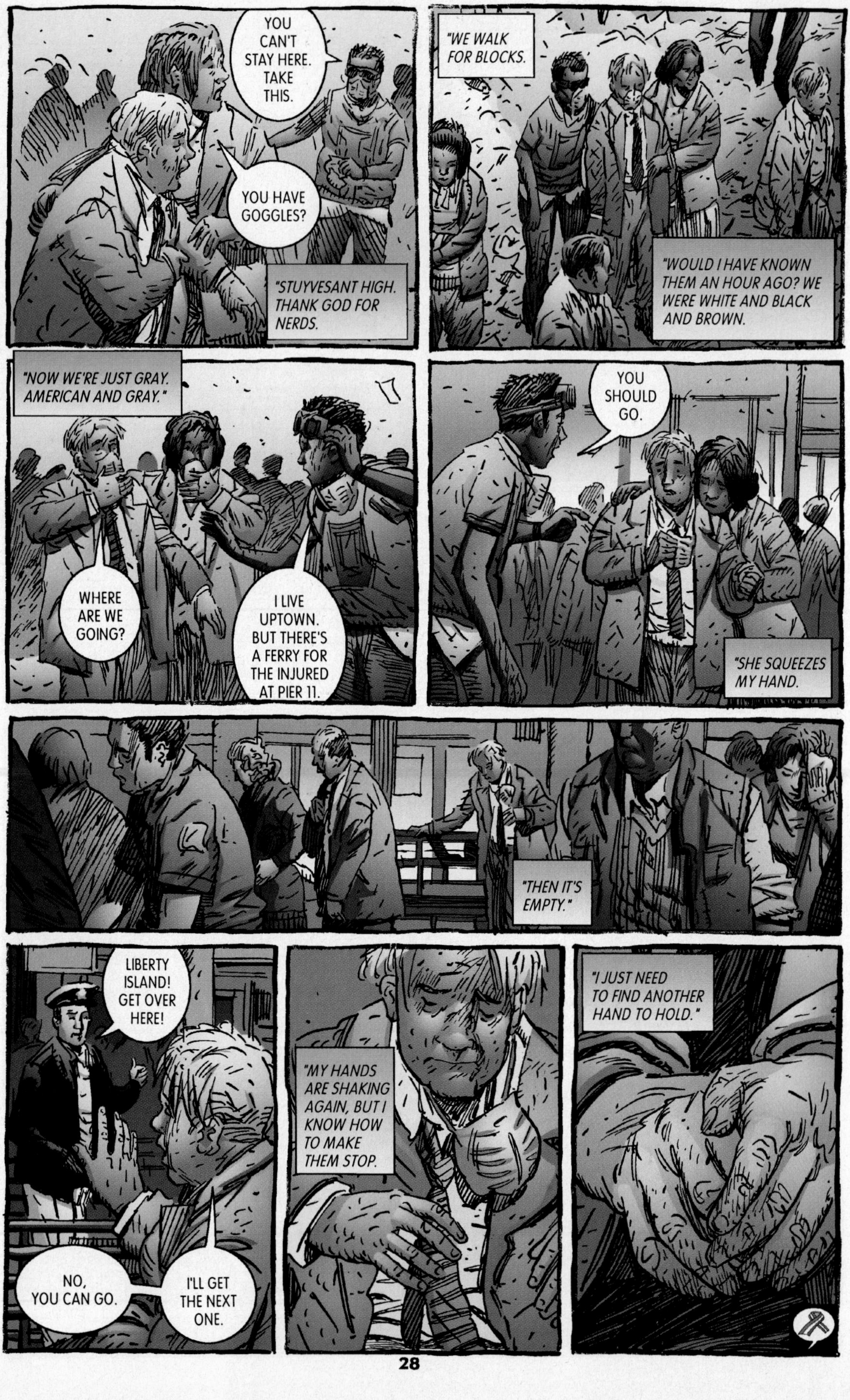
YOU CAN'T STAY HERE. TAKE THIS.
YOU HAVE GOGGLES?
"STUYVESANT HIGH. THANK GOD FOR NERDS.
"WE WALK FOR BLOCKS.
"WOULD I HAVE KNOWN THEM AN HOUR AGO? WE WERE WHITE AND BLACK AND BROWN.
"NOW WE'RE JUST GRAY. AMERICAN AND GRAY."
WHERE ARE WE GOING?
I LIVE UPTOWN. BUT THERE'S A FERRY FOR THE INJURED AT PIER 11.
YOU SHOULD GO.
"SHE SQUEEZES MY HAND.
"THEN IT'S EMPTY."
LIBERTY ISLAND! GET OVER HERE!
NO, YOU CAN GO.
I'LL GET THE NEXT ONE.
"MY HANDS ARE SHAKING AGAIN, BUT I KNOW HOW TO MAKE THEM STOP.
"I JUST NEED TO FIND ANOTHER HAND TO HOLD."

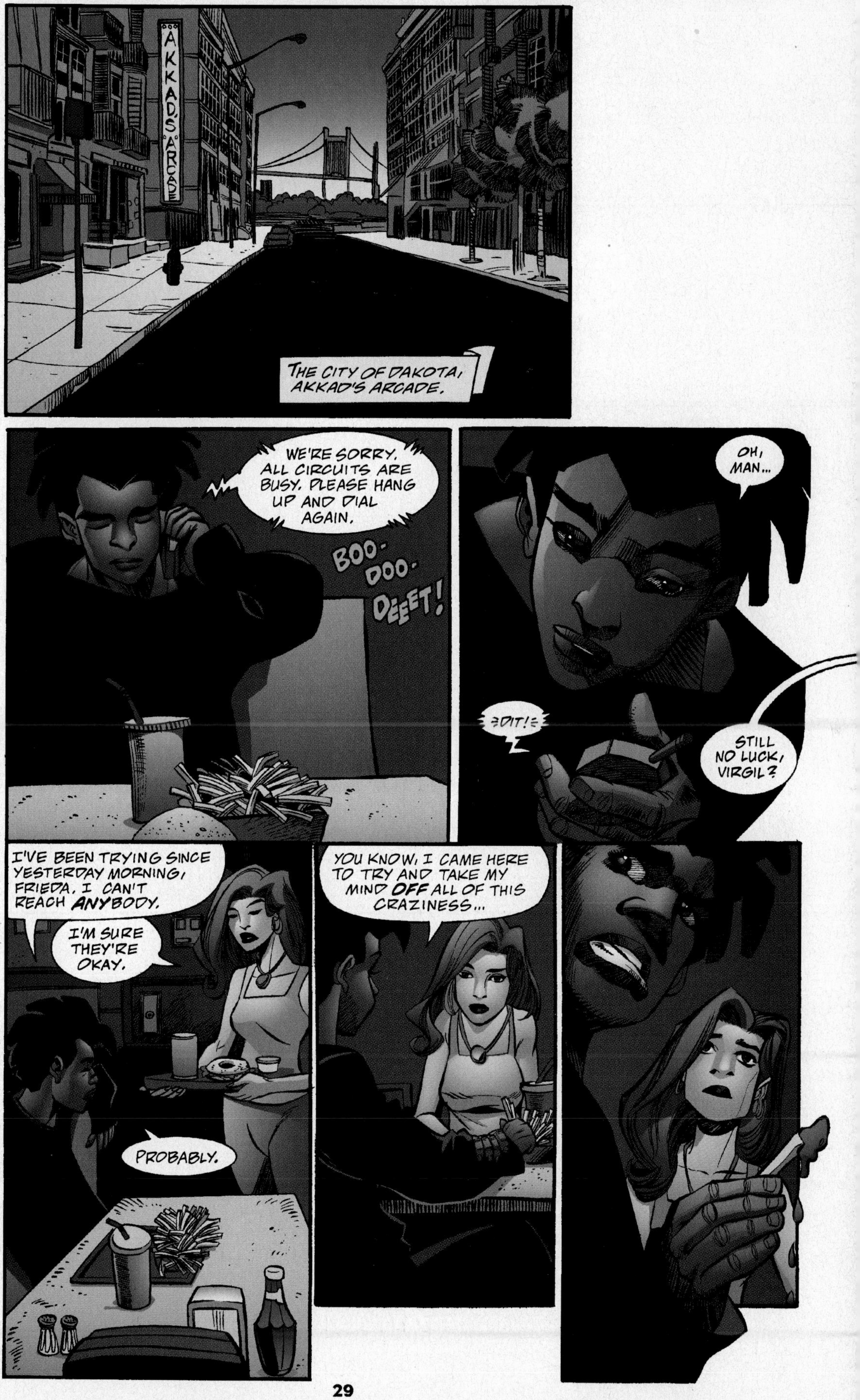
AKKAD'S ARCADE
THE CITY OF DAKOTA, AKKAD'S ARCADE.
WE'RE SORRY. ALL CIRCUITS ARE BUSY. PLEASE HANG UP AND DIAL AGAIN.
BOO-DOO-DEEET!
OH, MAN...
DIT!
STILL NO LUCK, VIRGIL?
I'VE BEEN TRYING SINCE YESTERDAY MORNING, FRIEDA. I CAN'T REACH ANYBODY.
I'M SURE THEY'RE OKAY.
PROBABLY.
YOU KNOW, I CAME HERE TO TRY AND TAKE MY MIND OFF ALL OF THIS CRAZINESS...

STORY DWAYNE McDUFFIE
ART DENYS COWAN AND PRENTIS ROLLINS
LETTERS PHIL FELIX
COLOR WILDSTORM

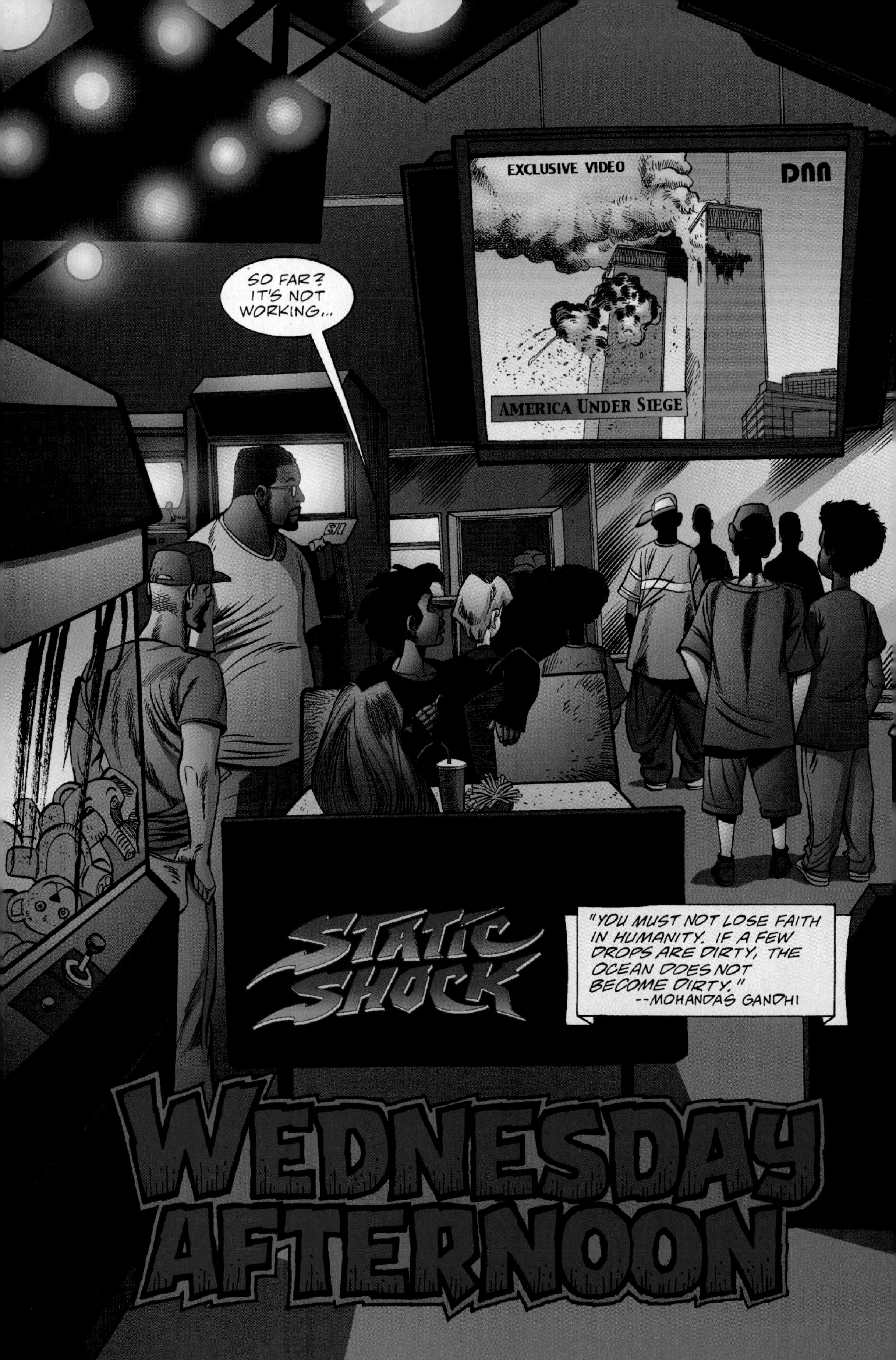
EXCLUSIVE VIDEO
DNN
AMERICA UNDER SIEGE
SO FAR? IT'S NOT WORKING...
STATIC SHOCK
"YOU MUST NOT LOSE FAITH IN HUMANITY. IF A FEW DROPS ARE DIRTY, THE OCEAN DOES NOT BECOME DIRTY."
--MOHANDAS GANDHI
WEDNESDAY AFTERNOON

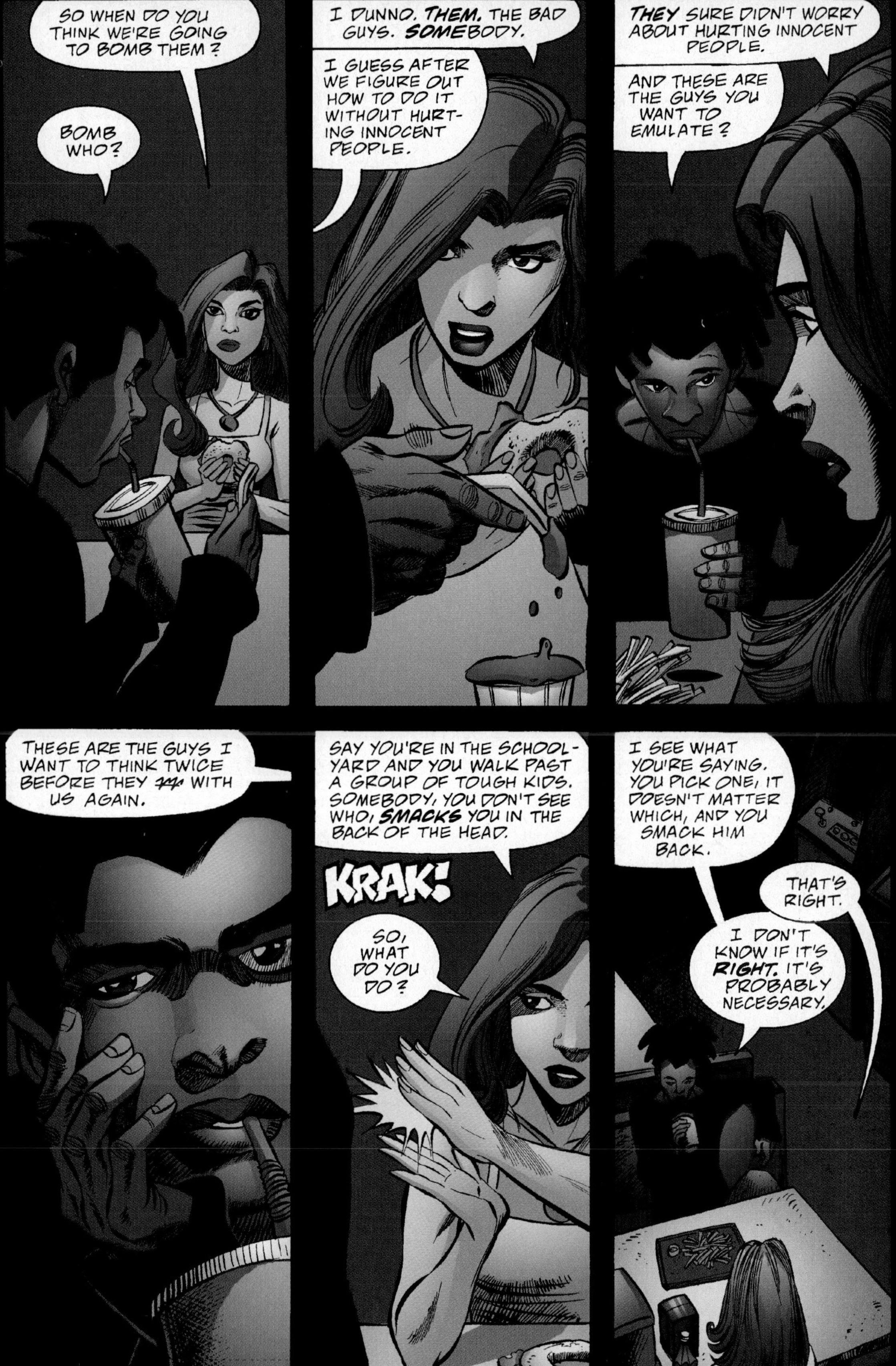
SO WHEN DO YOU THINK WE'RE GOING TO BOMB THEM?
BOMB WHO?
I DUNNO. THEM. THE BAD GUYS. SOMEBODY.
I GUESS AFTER WE FIGURE OUT HOW TO DO IT WITHOUT HURTING INNOCENT PEOPLE.
THEY SURE DIDN'T WORRY ABOUT HURTING INNOCENT PEOPLE.
AND THESE ARE THE GUYS YOU WANT TO EMULATE?
THESE ARE THE GUYS I WANT TO THINK TWICE BEFORE THEY WITH US AGAIN.
SAY YOU'RE IN THE SCHOOLYARD AND YOU WALK PAST A GROUP OF TOUGH KIDS. SOMEBODY, YOU DON'T SEE WHO, SMACKS YOU IN THE BACK OF THE HEAD.
KRAK!
SO, WHAT DO YOU DO?
I SEE WHAT YOU'RE SAYING. YOU PICK ONE, IT DOESN'T MATTER WHICH, AND YOU SMACK HIM BACK.
THAT'S RIGHT.
I DON'T KNOW IF IT'S RIGHT. IT'S PROBABLY NECESSARY.

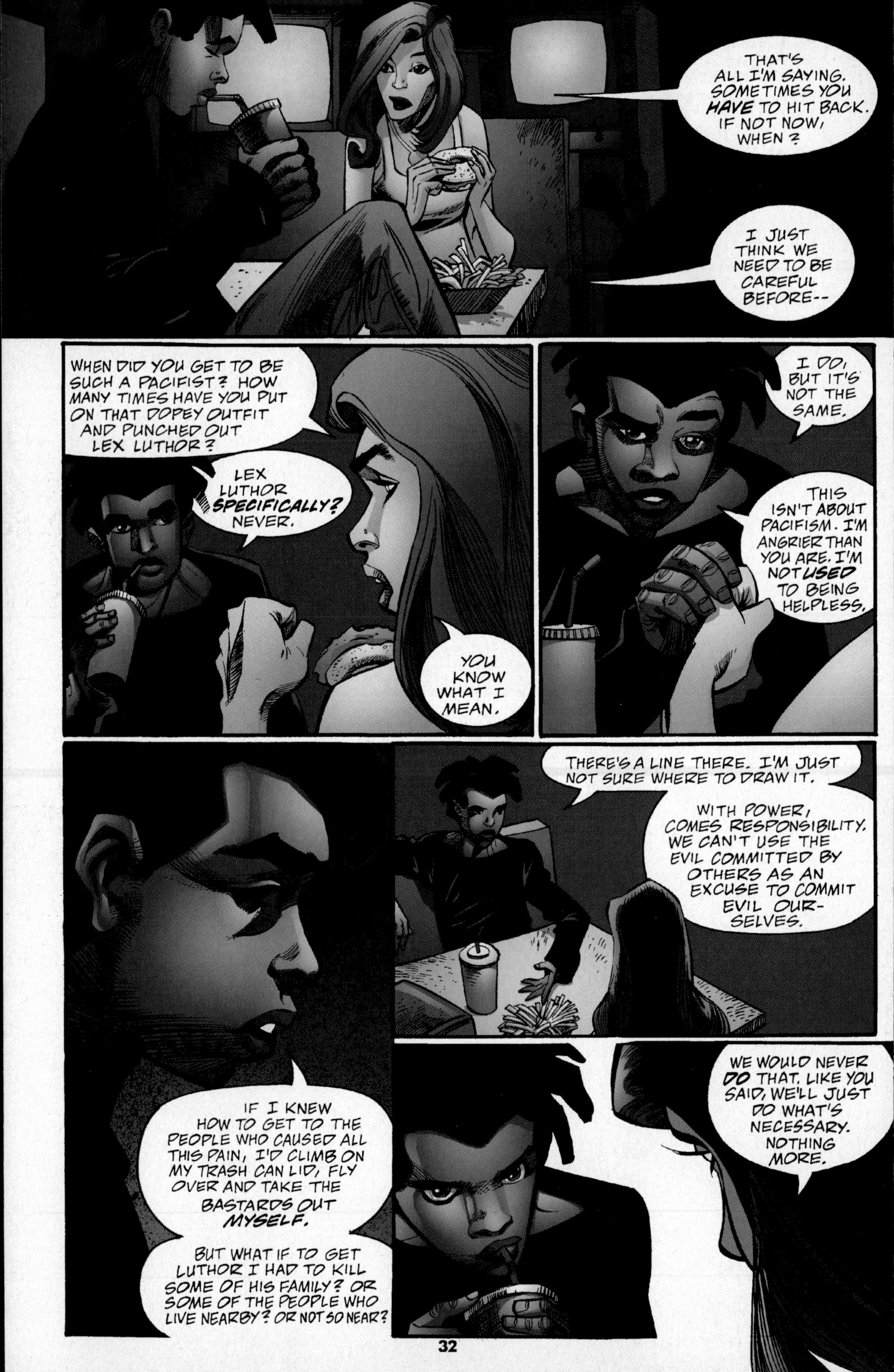

THAT'S ALL I'M SAYING. SOMETIMES YOU HAVE TO HIT BACK. IF NOT NOW, WHEN?
I JUST THINK WE NEED TO BE CAREFUL BEFORE--
WHEN DID YOU GET TO BE SUCH A PACIFIST? HOW MANY TIMES HAVE YOU PUT ON THAT DOPEY OUTFIT AND PUNCHED OUT LEX LUTHOR?
LEX LUTHOR SPECIFICALLY? NEVER.
YOU KNOW WHAT I MEAN.
I DO, BUT IT'S NOT THE SAME.
THIS ISN'T ABOUT PACIFISM. I'M ANGRIER THAN YOU ARE. I'M NOT USED TO BEING HELPLESS.
IF I KNEW HOW TO GET TO THE PEOPLE WHO CAUSED ALL THIS PAIN, I'D CLIMB ON MY TRASH CAN LID, FLY OVER AND TAKE THE BASTARDS OUT MYSELF.
BUT WHAT IF TO GET LUTHOR I HAD TO KILL SOME OF HIS FAMILY? OR SOME OF THE PEOPLE WHO LIVE NEARBY? OR NOT SO NEAR?
THERE'S A LINE THERE. I'M JUST NOT SURE WHERE TO DRAW IT.
WITH POWER, COMES RESPONSIBILITY. WE CAN'T USE THE EVIL COMMITTED BY OTHERS AS AN EXCUSE TO COMMIT EVIL OUR-SELVES.
WE WOULD NEVER DO THAT. LIKE YOU SAID, WE'LL JUST DO WHAT'S NECESSARY. NOTHING MORE.

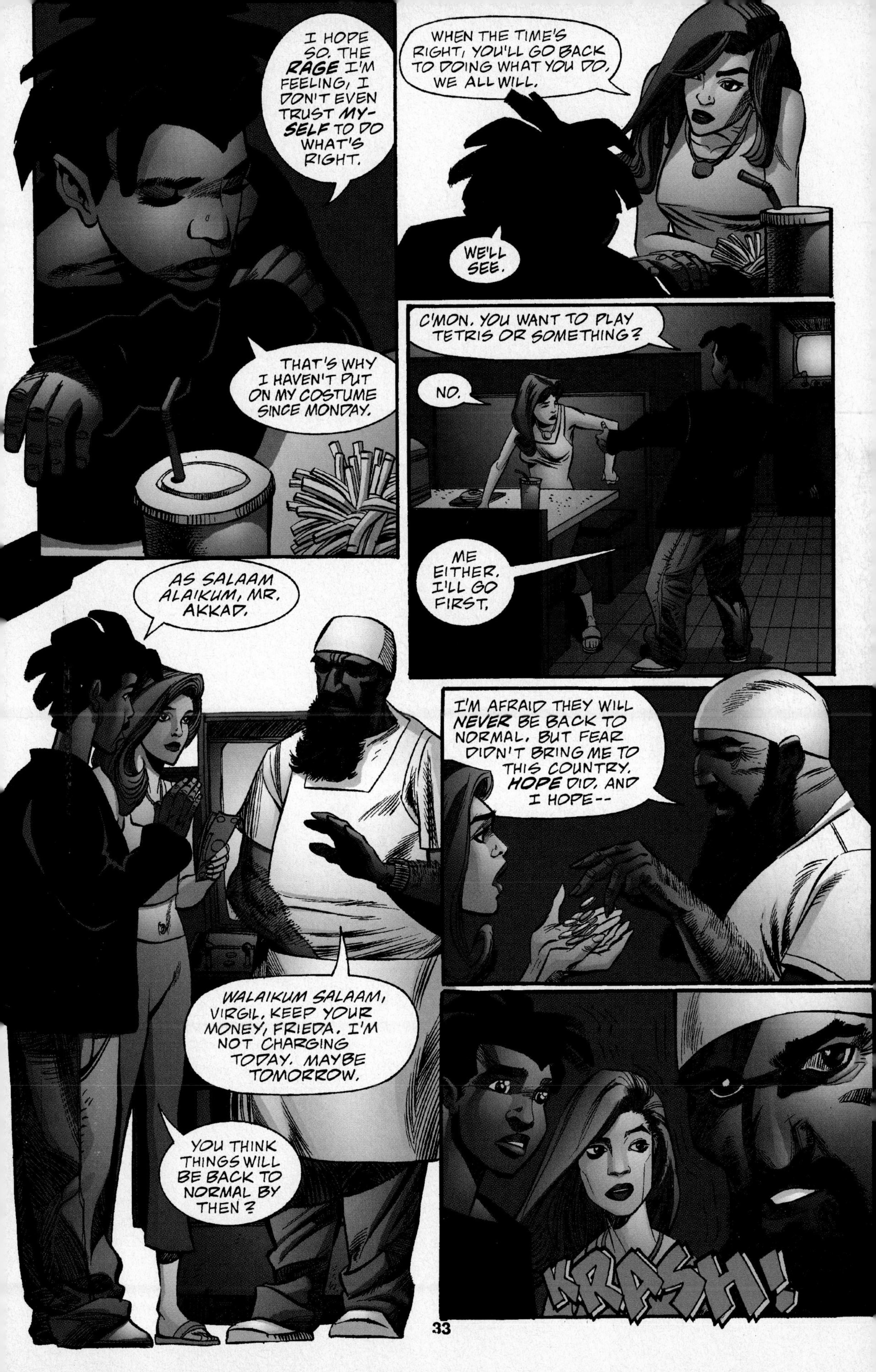
I HOPE SO. THE RAGE I'M FEELING, I DON'T EVEN TRUST MYSELF TO DO WHAT'S RIGHT.
THAT'S WHY I HAVEN'T PUT ON MY COSTUME SINCE MONDAY.
WHEN THE TIME'S RIGHT, YOU'LL GO BACK TO DOING WHAT YOU DO. WE ALL WILL.
WE'LL SEE.
C'MON. YOU WANT TO PLAY TETRIS OR SOMETHING?
NO.
ME EITHER. I'LL GO FIRST.
AS SALAAM ALAIKUM, MR. AKKAD.
WALAIKUM SALAAM, VIRGIL. KEEP YOUR MONEY, FRIEDA. I'M NOT CHARGING TODAY. MAYBE TOMORROW.
YOU THINK THINGS WILL BE BACK TO NORMAL BY THEN?
I'M AFRAID THEY WILL NEVER BE BACK TO NORMAL. BUT FEAR DIDN'T BRING ME TO THIS COUNTRY. HOPE DID. AND I HOPE--
KRASH!

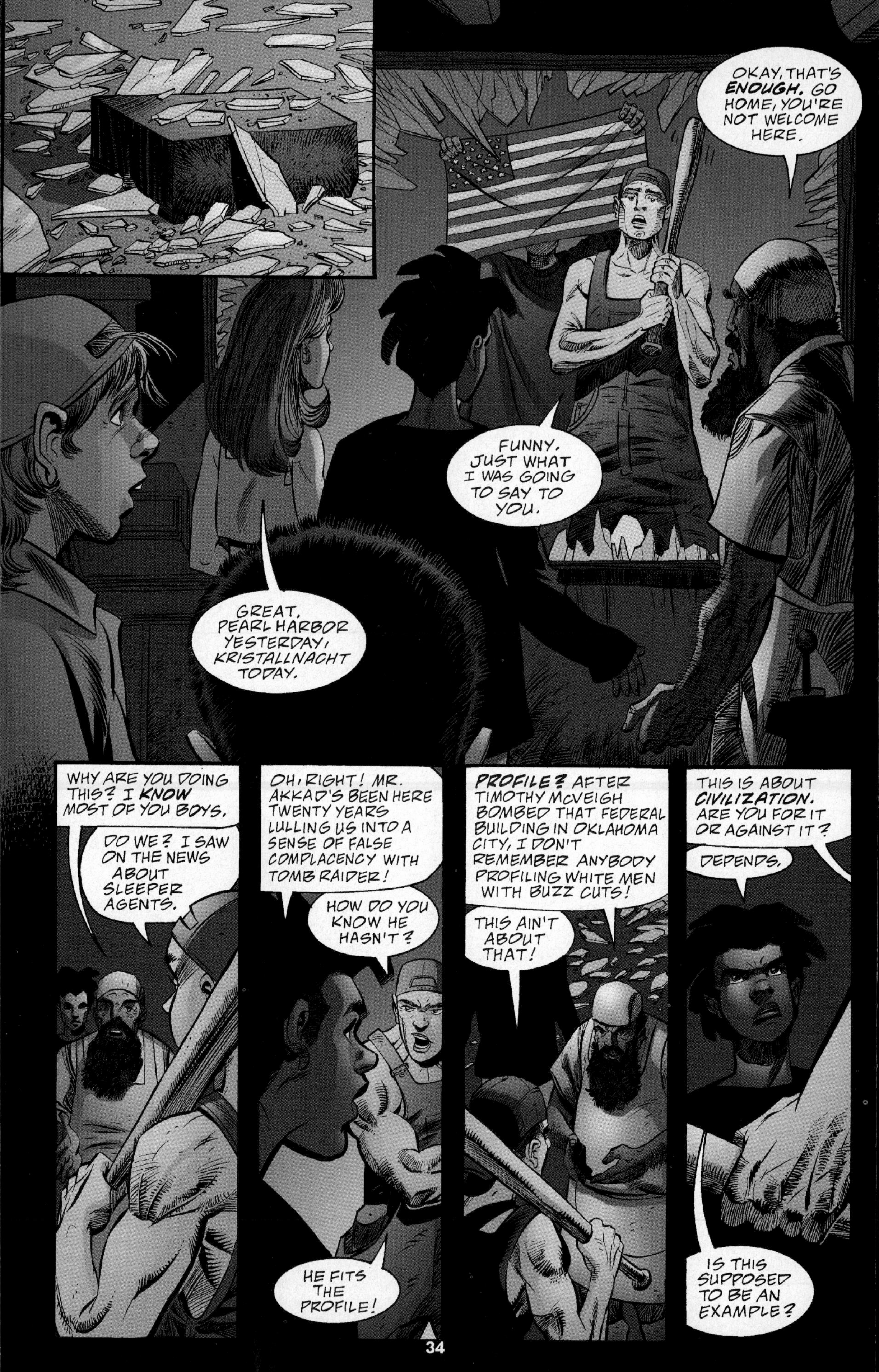
OKAY, THAT'S ENOUGH. GO HOME, YOU'RE NOT WELCOME HERE.
FUNNY. JUST WHAT I WAS GOING TO SAY TO YOU.
GREAT. PEARL HARBOR YESTERDAY, KRISTALLNACHT TODAY.
WHY ARE YOU DOING THIS? I KNOW MOST OF YOU BOYS.
DO WE? I SAW ON THE NEWS ABOUT SLEEPER AGENTS.
OH, RIGHT! MR. AKKAD'S BEEN HERE TWENTY YEARS LULLING US INTO A SENSE OF FALSE COMPLACENCY WITH TOMB RAIDER!
HOW DO YOU KNOW HE HASN'T?
HE FITS THE PROFILE!
PROFILE? AFTER TIMOTHY McVEIGH BOMBED THAT FEDERAL BUILDING IN OKLAHOMA CITY, I DON'T REMEMBER ANYBODY PROFILING WHITE MEN WITH BUZZ CUTS!
THIS AIN'T ABOUT THAT!
THIS IS ABOUT CIVILIZATION. ARE YOU FOR IT OR AGAINST IT?
DEPENDS.
IS THIS SUPPOSED TO BE AN EXAMPLE?

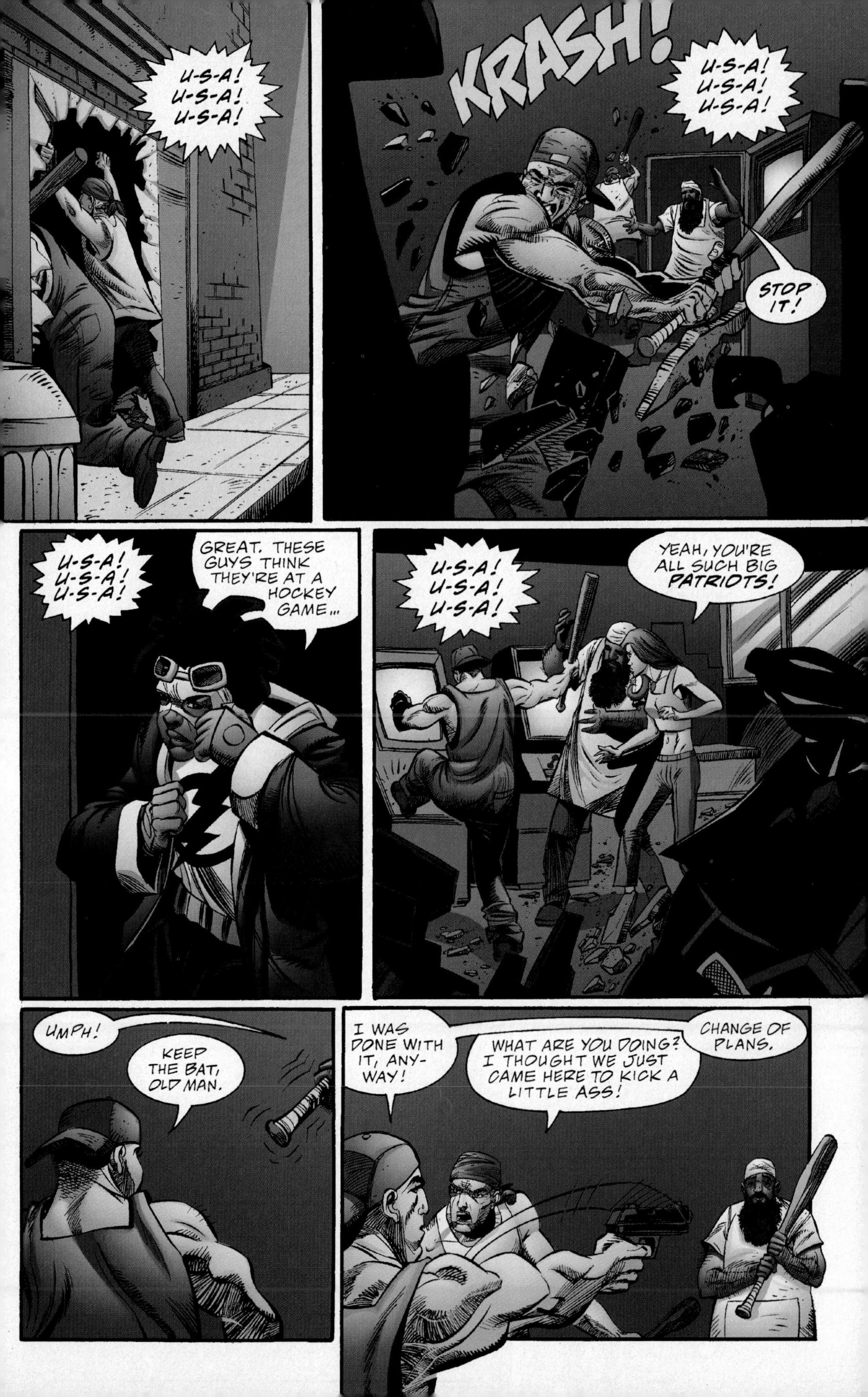
U-S-A!
U-S-A!
U-S-A!
KRASH!
U-S-A!
U-S-A!
U-S-A!
STOP IT!
U-S-A!
U-S-A!
U-S-A!
GREAT. THESE GUYS THINK THEY'RE AT A HOCKEY GAME...
U-S-A!
U-S-A!
U-S-A!
YEAH, YOU'RE ALL SUCH BIG PATRIOTS!
UMPH!
KEEP THE BAT, OLD MAN.
I WAS DONE WITH IT, ANY-WAY!
WHAT ARE YOU DOING? I THOUGHT WE JUST CAME HERE TO KICK A LITTLE ASS!
CHANGE OF PLANS.

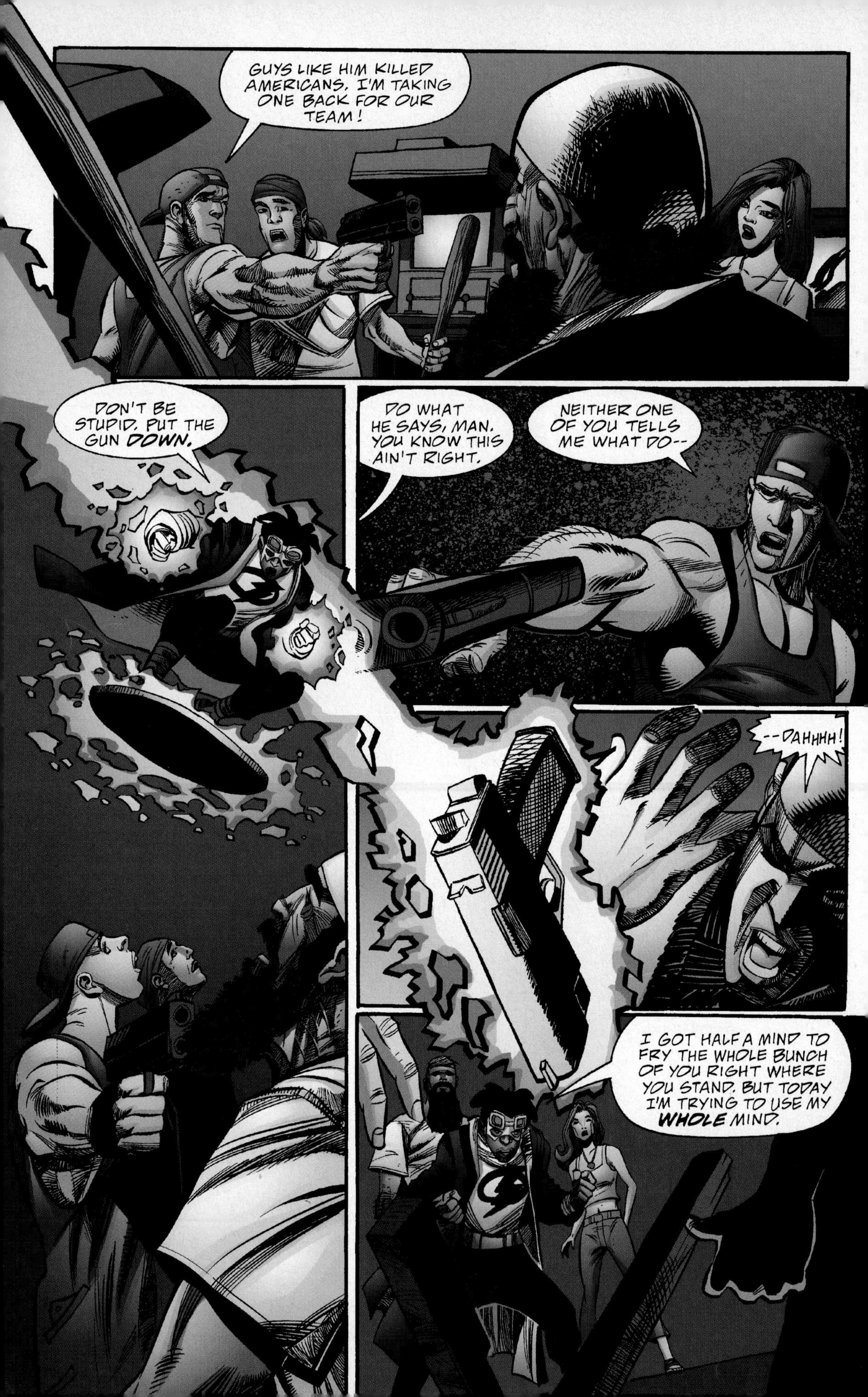
GUYS LIKE HIM KILLED AMERICANS. I'M TAKING ONE BACK FOR OUR TEAM!
DON'T BE STUPID. PUT THE GUN DOWN.
DO WHAT HE SAYS, MAN. YOU KNOW THIS AIN'T RIGHT.
NEITHER ONE OF YOU TELLS ME WHAT DO--
--DAHHHH!
I GOT HALF A MIND TO FRY THE WHOLE BUNCH OF YOU RIGHT WHERE YOU STAND. BUT TODAY I'M TRYING TO USE MY WHOLE MIND.

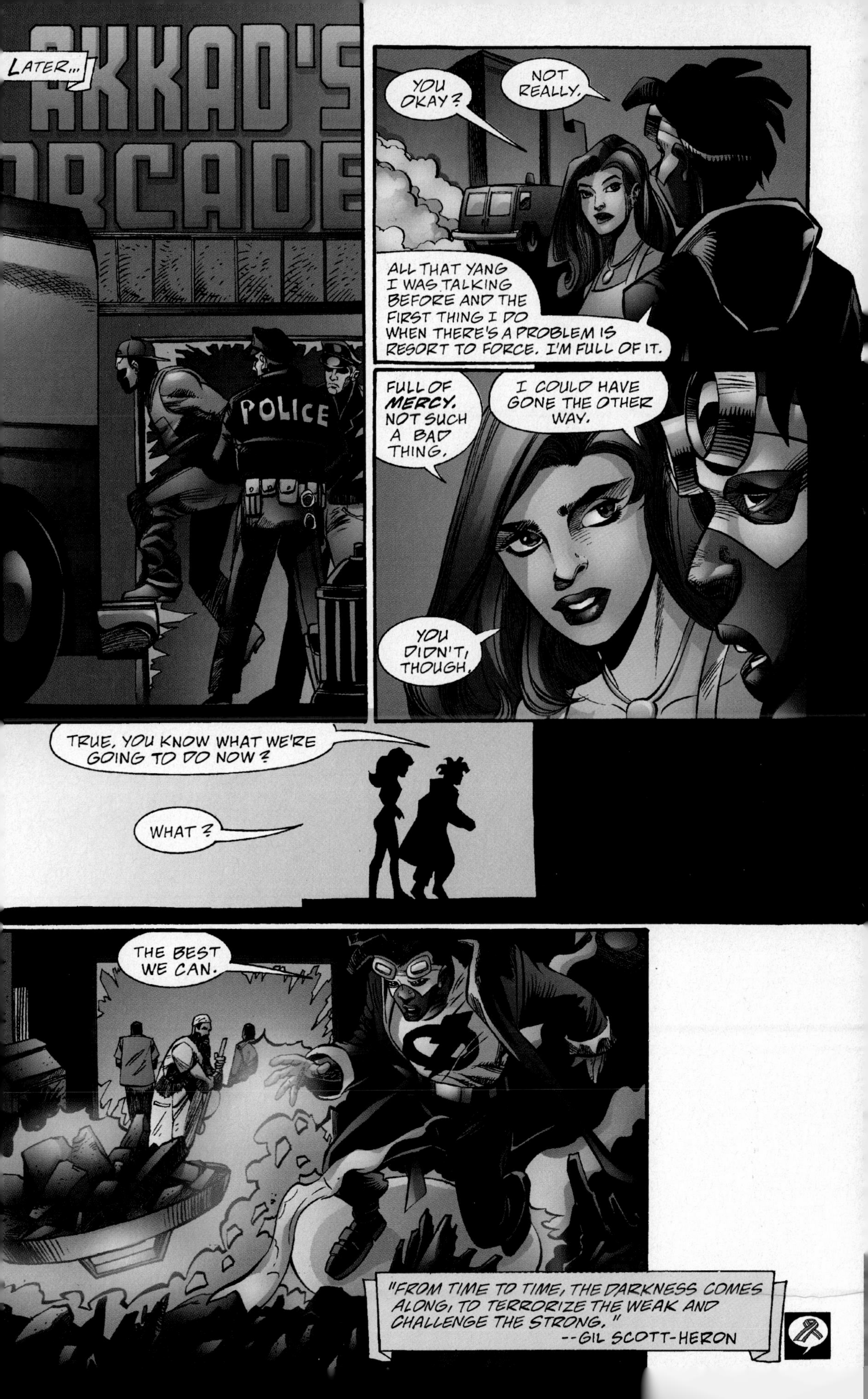
LATER...
AKKAD'S ARCADE
POLICE
YOU OKAY?
NOT REALLY.
ALL THAT YANG I WAS TALKING BEFORE AND THE FIRST THING I DO WHEN THERE'S A PROBLEM IS RESORT TO FORCE. I'M FULL OF IT.
FULL OF MERCY. NOT SUCH A BAD THING.
I COULD HAVE GONE THE OTHER WAY.
YOU DIDN'T, THOUGH.
TRUE. YOU KNOW WHAT WE'RE GOING TO DO NOW?
WHAT?
THE BEST WE CAN.
"FROM TIME TO TIME, THE DARKNESS COMES ALONG, TO TERRORIZE THE WEAK AND CHALLENGE THE STRONG."
--GIL SCOTT-HERON

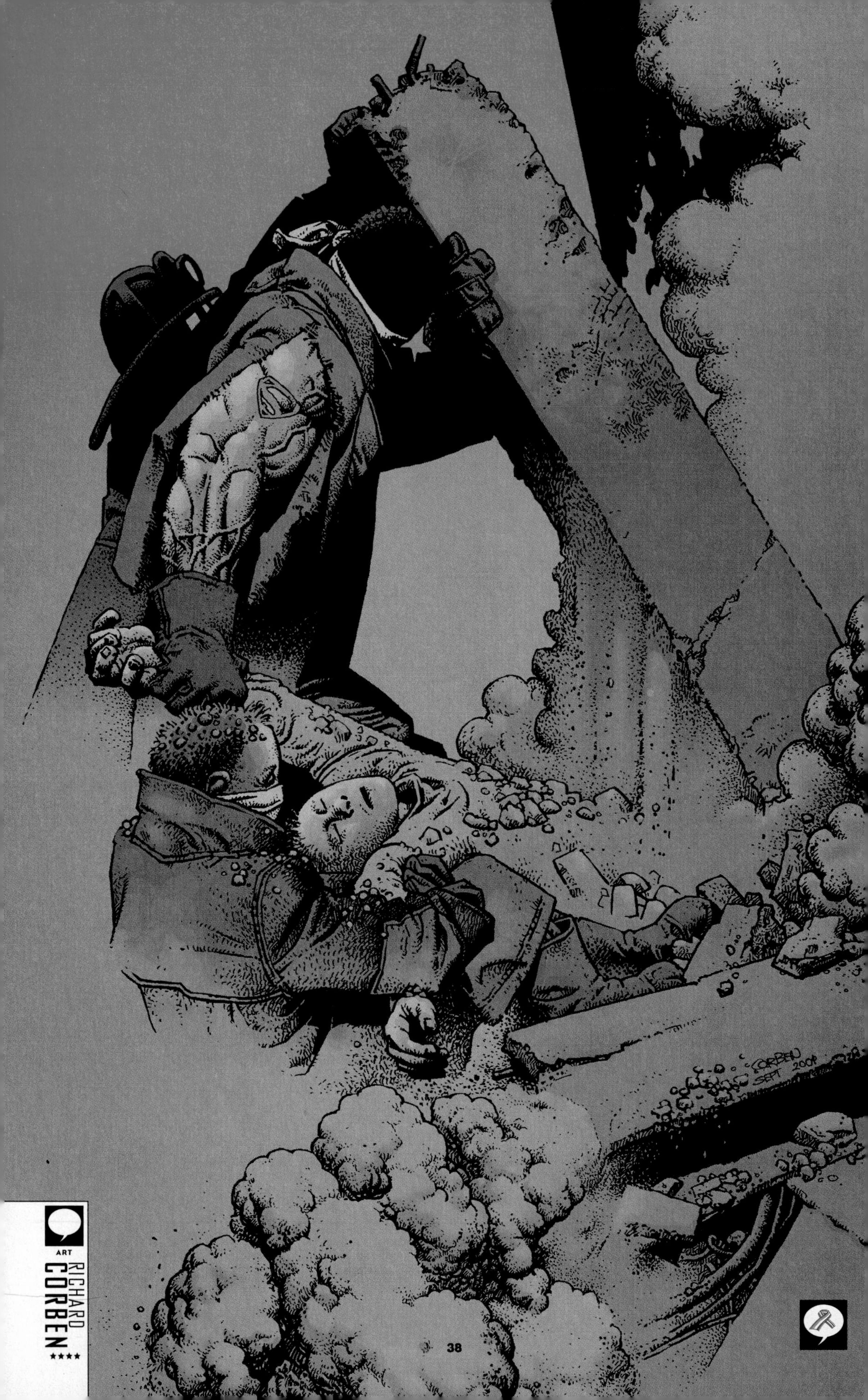
CORBEN
SEPT 2001

ART
RICHARD
CORBEN

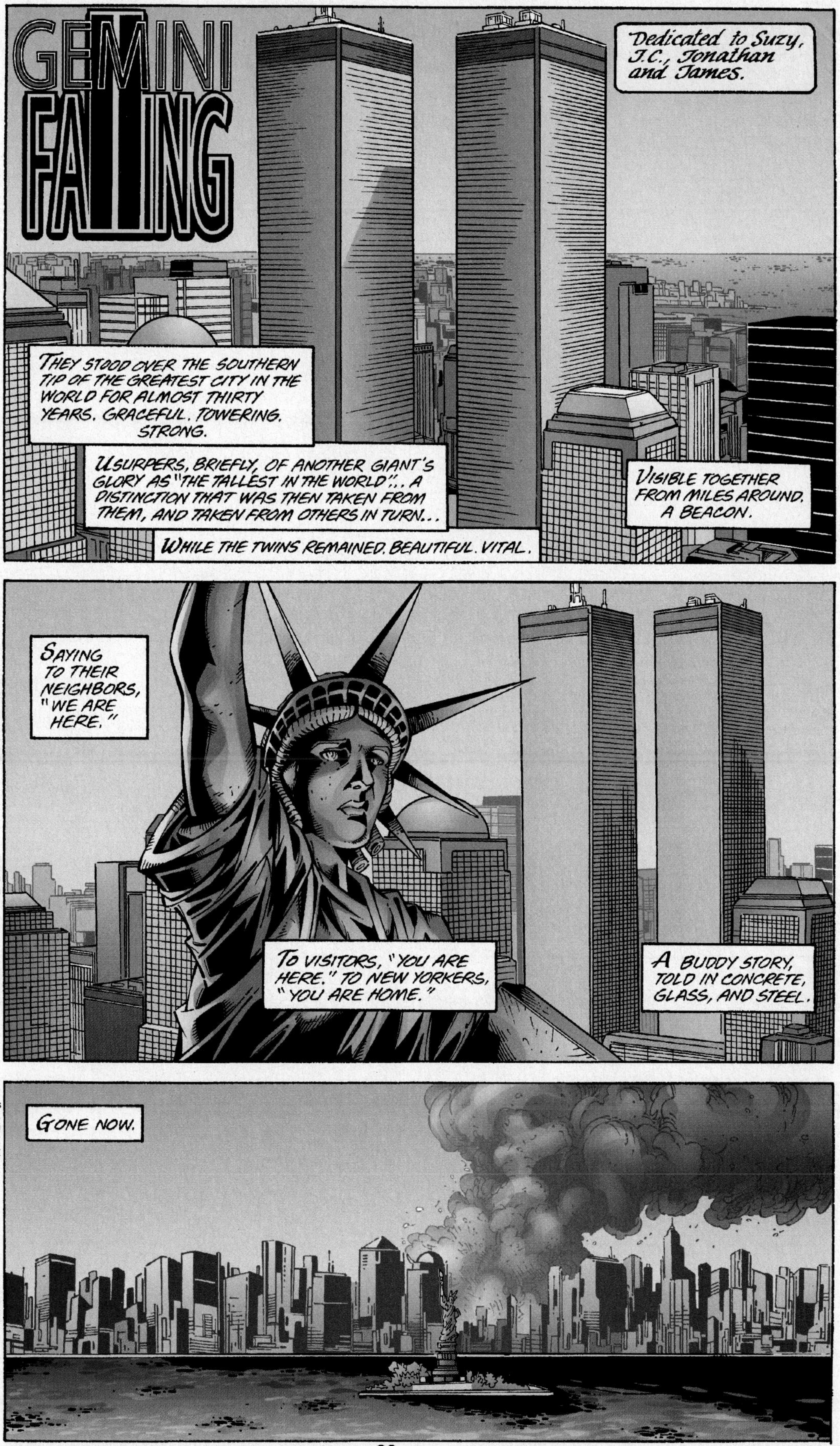
GEMINI FALLING
Dedicated to Suzy, J.C., Jonathan and James.
THEY STOOD OVER THE SOUTHERN TIP OF THE GREATEST CITY IN THE WORLD FOR ALMOST THIRTY YEARS. GRACEFUL. TOWERING. STRONG.
USURPERS, BRIEFLY, OF ANOTHER GIANT'S GLORY AS "THE TALLEST IN THE WORLD"... A DISTINCTION THAT WAS THEN TAKEN FROM THEM, AND TAKEN FROM OTHERS IN TURN...
VISIBLE TOGETHER FROM MILES AROUND. A BEACON.
WHILE THE TWINS REMAINED. BEAUTIFUL. VITAL.
SAYING TO THEIR NEIGHBORS, "WE ARE HERE."
TO VISITORS, "YOU ARE HERE." TO NEW YORKERS, "YOU ARE HOME."
A BUDDY STORY, TOLD IN CONCRETE, GLASS, AND STEEL.
GONE NOW.

STORY JO DUFFY
ART TODD NAUCK AND JAIME MENDOZA
LETTERS JOHN COSTANZA
COLOR DIGITAL CHAMELEON

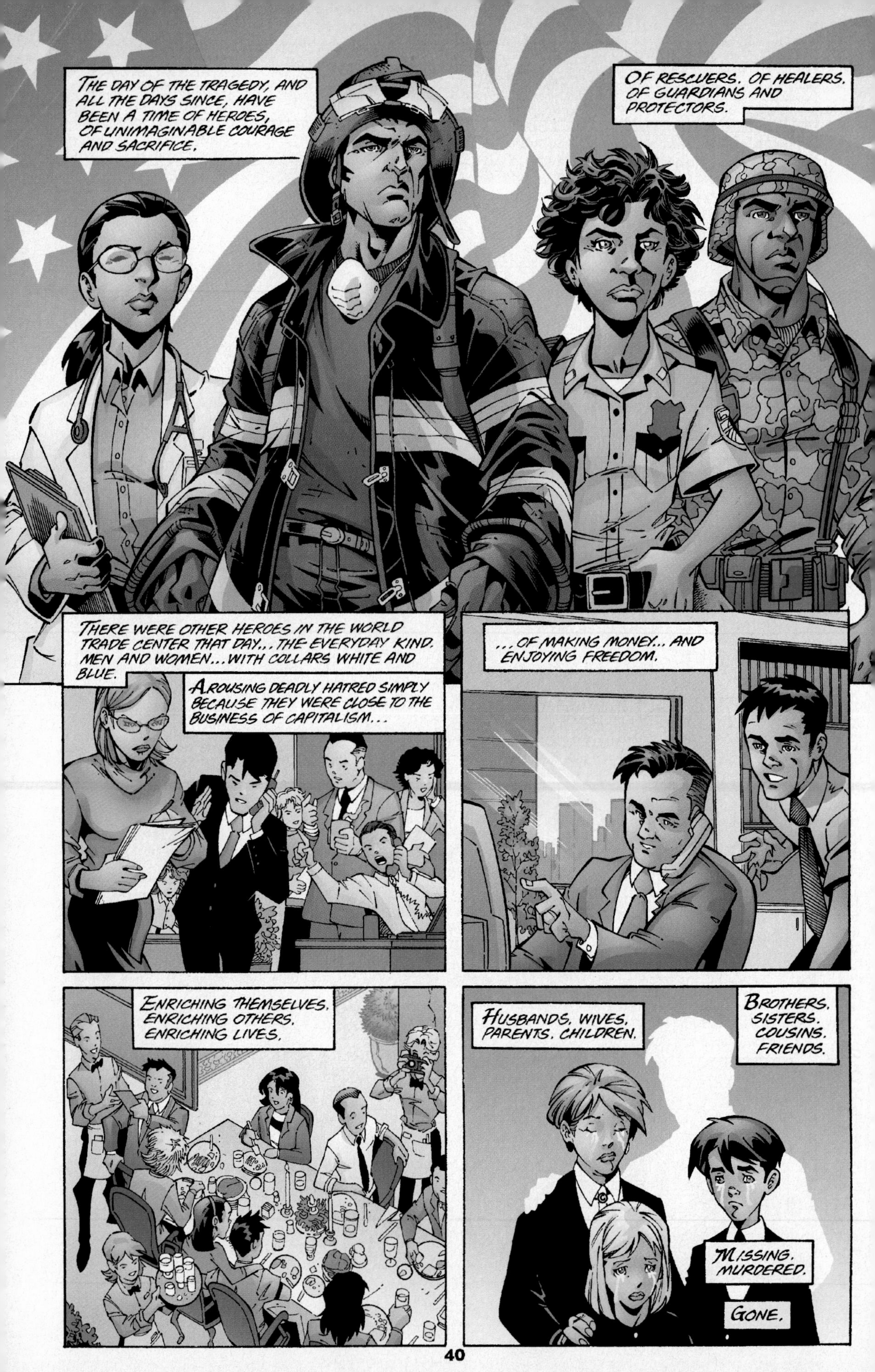
THE DAY OF THE TRAGEDY, AND ALL THE DAYS SINCE, HAVE BEEN A TIME OF HEROES, OF UNIMAGINABLE COURAGE AND SACRIFICE.
OF RESCUERS. OF HEALERS. OF GUARDIANS AND PROTECTORS.
THERE WERE OTHER HEROES IN THE WORLD TRADE CENTER THAT DAY... THE EVERYDAY KIND. MEN AND WOMEN... WITH COLLARS WHITE AND BLUE.
AROUSING DEADLY HATRED SIMPLY BECAUSE THEY WERE CLOSE TO THE BUSINESS OF CAPITALISM...
...OF MAKING MONEY... AND ENJOYING FREEDOM.
ENRICHING THEMSELVES. ENRICHING OTHERS. ENRICHING LIVES.
HUSBANDS, WIVES, PARENTS, CHILDREN.
BROTHERS. SISTERS. COUSINS. FRIENDS.
MISSING. MURDERED.
GONE.

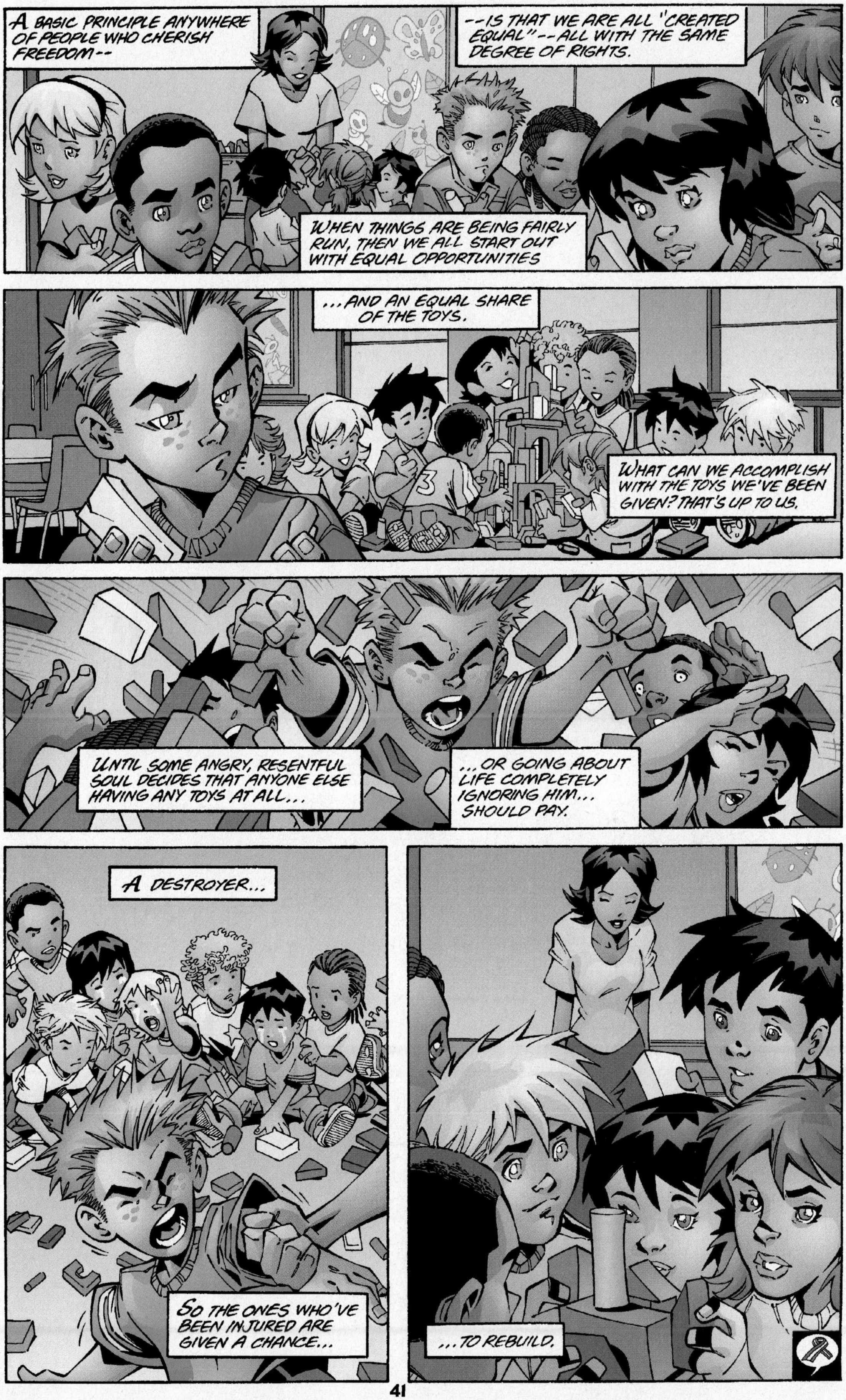
A BASIC PRINCIPLE ANYWHERE OF PEOPLE WHO CHERISH FREEDOM--
--IS THAT WE ARE ALL "CREATED EQUAL"--ALL WITH THE SAME DEGREE OF RIGHTS.
WHEN THINGS ARE BEING FAIRLY RUN, THEN WE ALL START OUT WITH EQUAL OPPORTUNITIES
...AND AN EQUAL SHARE OF THE TOYS.
WHAT CAN WE ACCOMPLISH WITH THE TOYS WE'VE BEEN GIVEN? THAT'S UP TO US.
UNTIL SOME ANGRY, RESENTFUL SOUL DECIDES THAT ANYONE ELSE HAVING ANY TOYS AT ALL...
...OR GOING ABOUT LIFE COMPLETELY IGNORING HIM... SHOULD PAY.
A DESTROYER...
SO THE ONES WHO'VE BEEN INJURED ARE GIVEN A CHANCE...
...TO REBUILD.

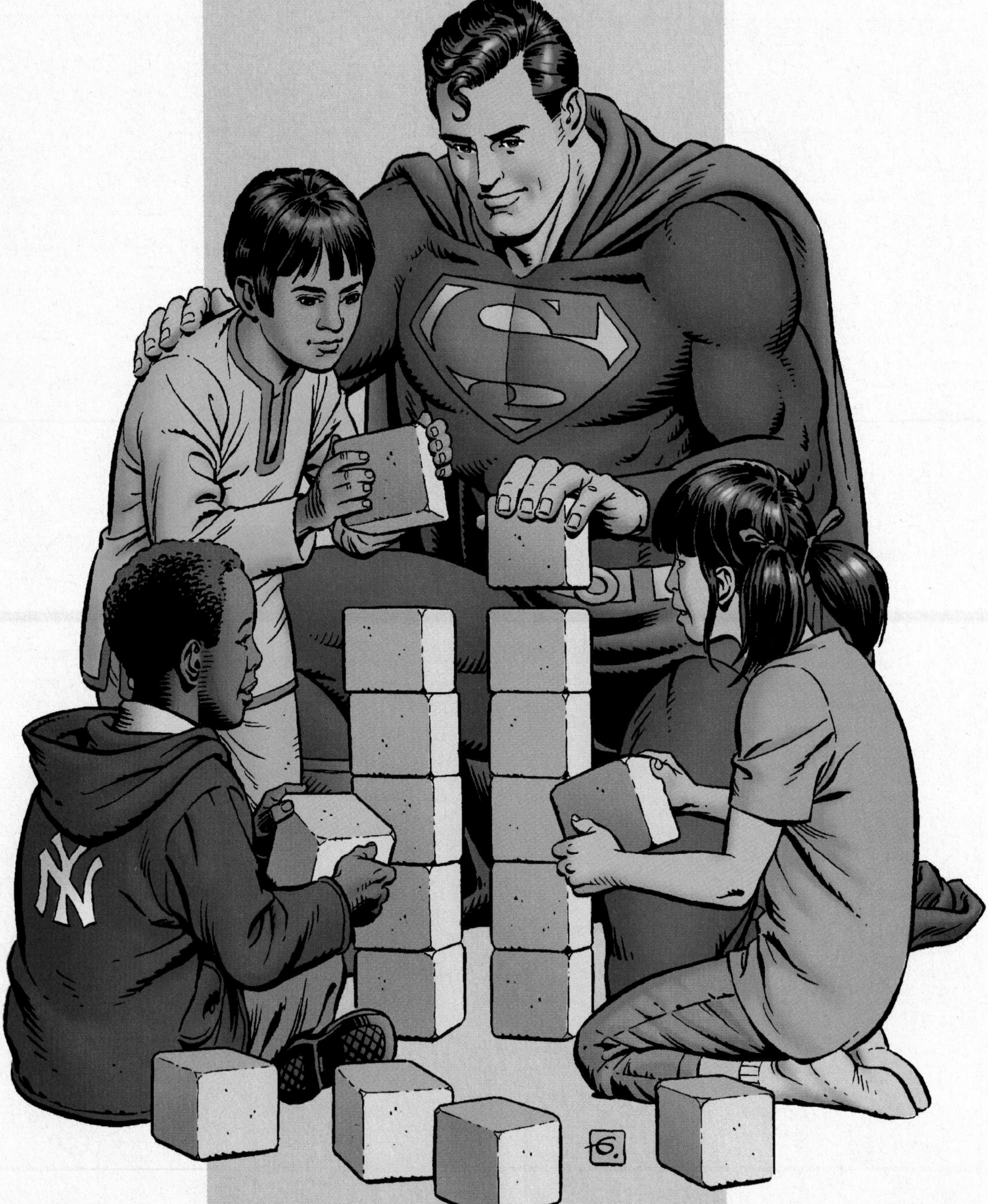

ART
DAVE GIBBONS
★★★★
COLOR
PATRICIA MULVIHILL
★★★★

"HAVE YOU SEEN...?"

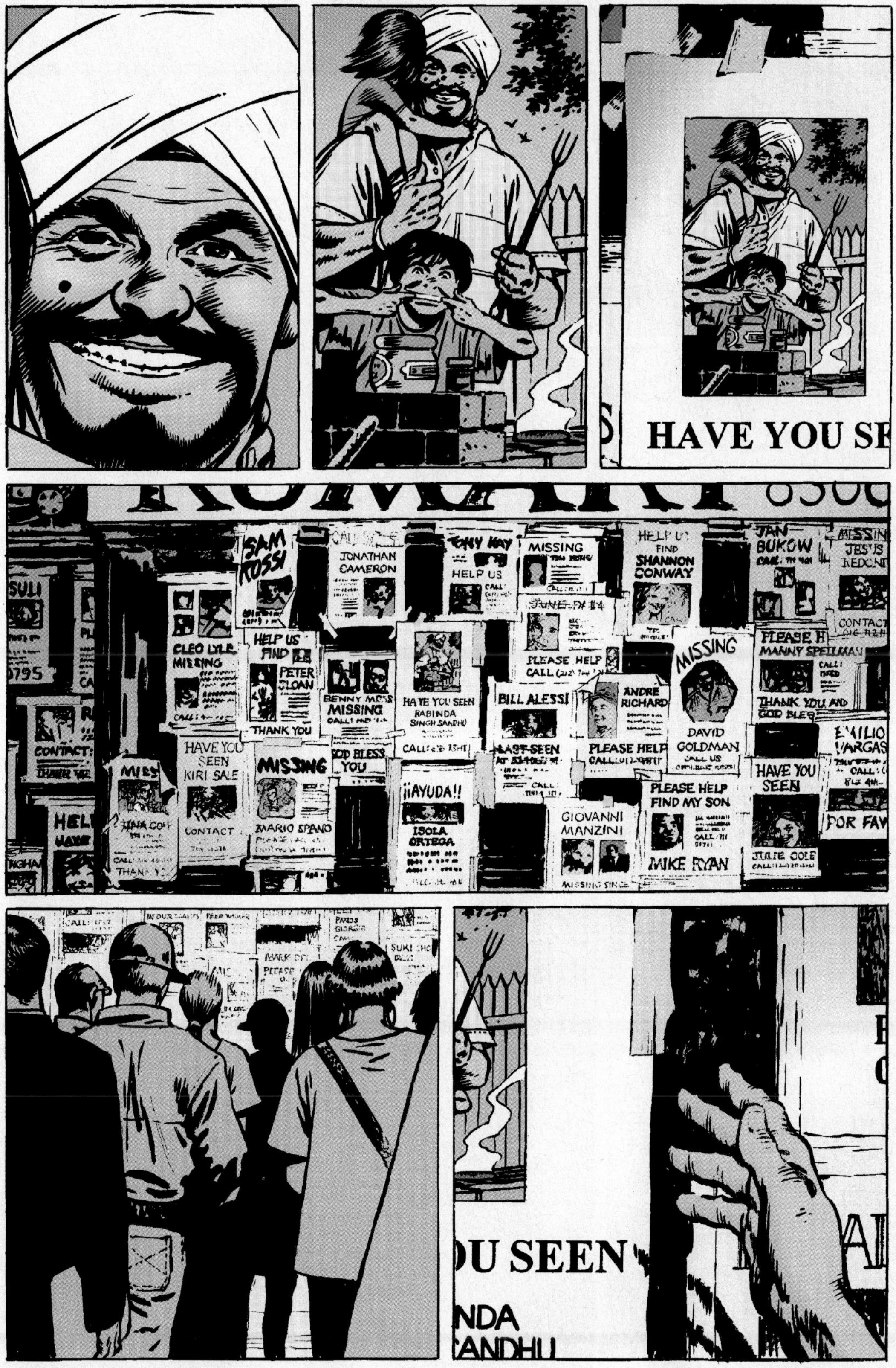
HAVE YOU SE
SAM ROSSI
JONATHAN CAMERON
TONY KAY HELP US
MISSING
HELP US FIND SHANNON CONWAY
JAN BUKOW
CLEO LYLE MISSING
HELP US FIND PETER SLOAN
THANK YOU
BENNY MOSS MISSING
HAVE YOU SEEN RABINDA SINGH SANDHU
PLEASE HELP
BILL ALESSI
LAST SEEN
ANDRE RICHARD
PLEASE HELP
MISSING DAVID GOLDMAN
PLEASE H MANNY SPELLMAN
THANK YOU, AND GOD BLESS
EMILIO VARGAS
HAVE YOU SEEN KIRI SALE
CONTACT
MISSING MARIO SPANO
GOD BLESS YOU
¡¡AYUDA!! ISOLA ORTEGA
GIOVANNI MANZINI
PLEASE HELP FIND MY SON MIKE RYAN
HAVE YOU SEEN JULIE COLE
POR FAV
OU SEEN
NDA
ANDHU

TORY DAN
AND ANDY
RT & TTERS COLOR DAVID

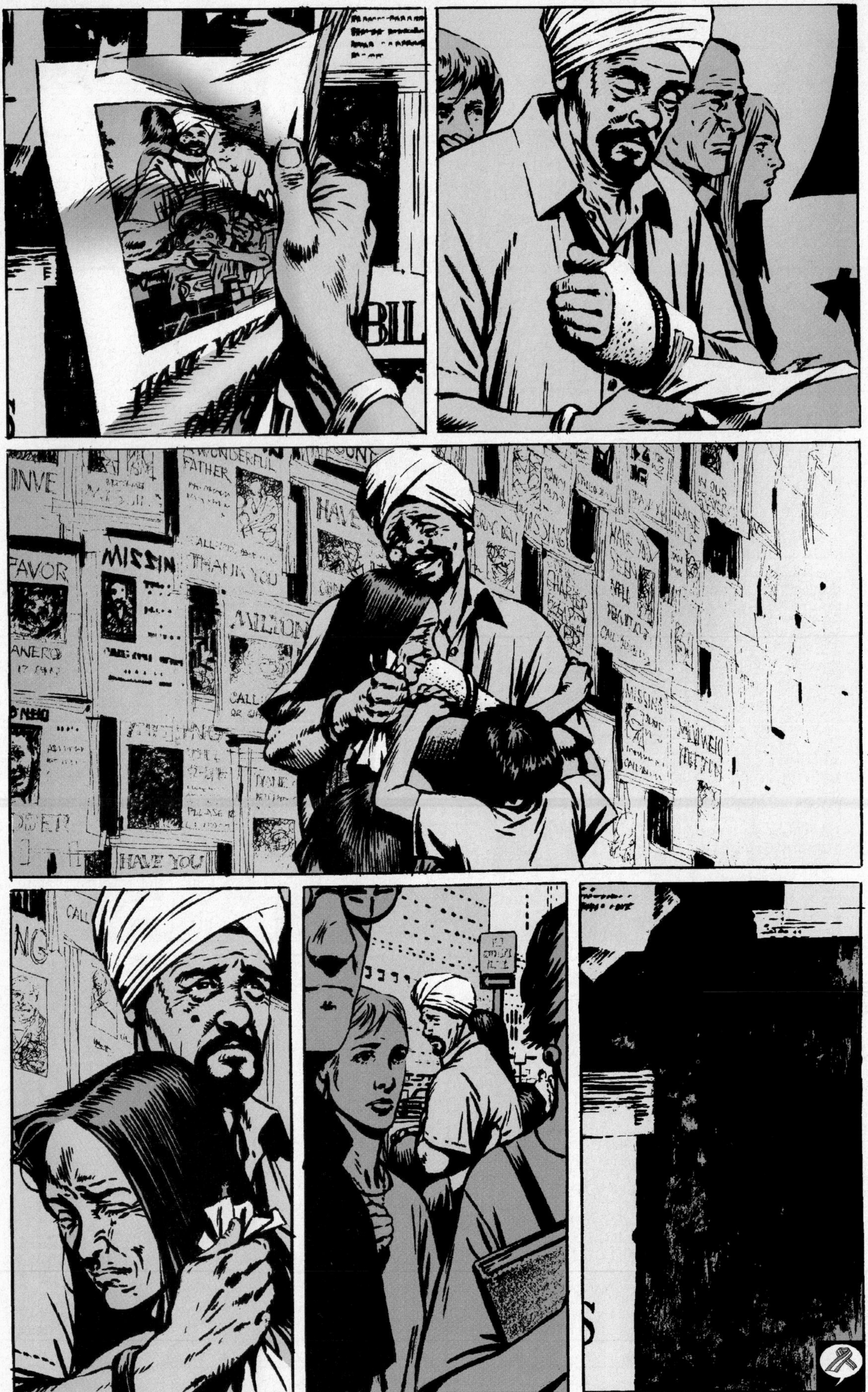
WONDERFUL
FATHER
FAVOR
THANK YOU
HAVE YOU SEEN
MISSING
HAVE YOU

TRADITION

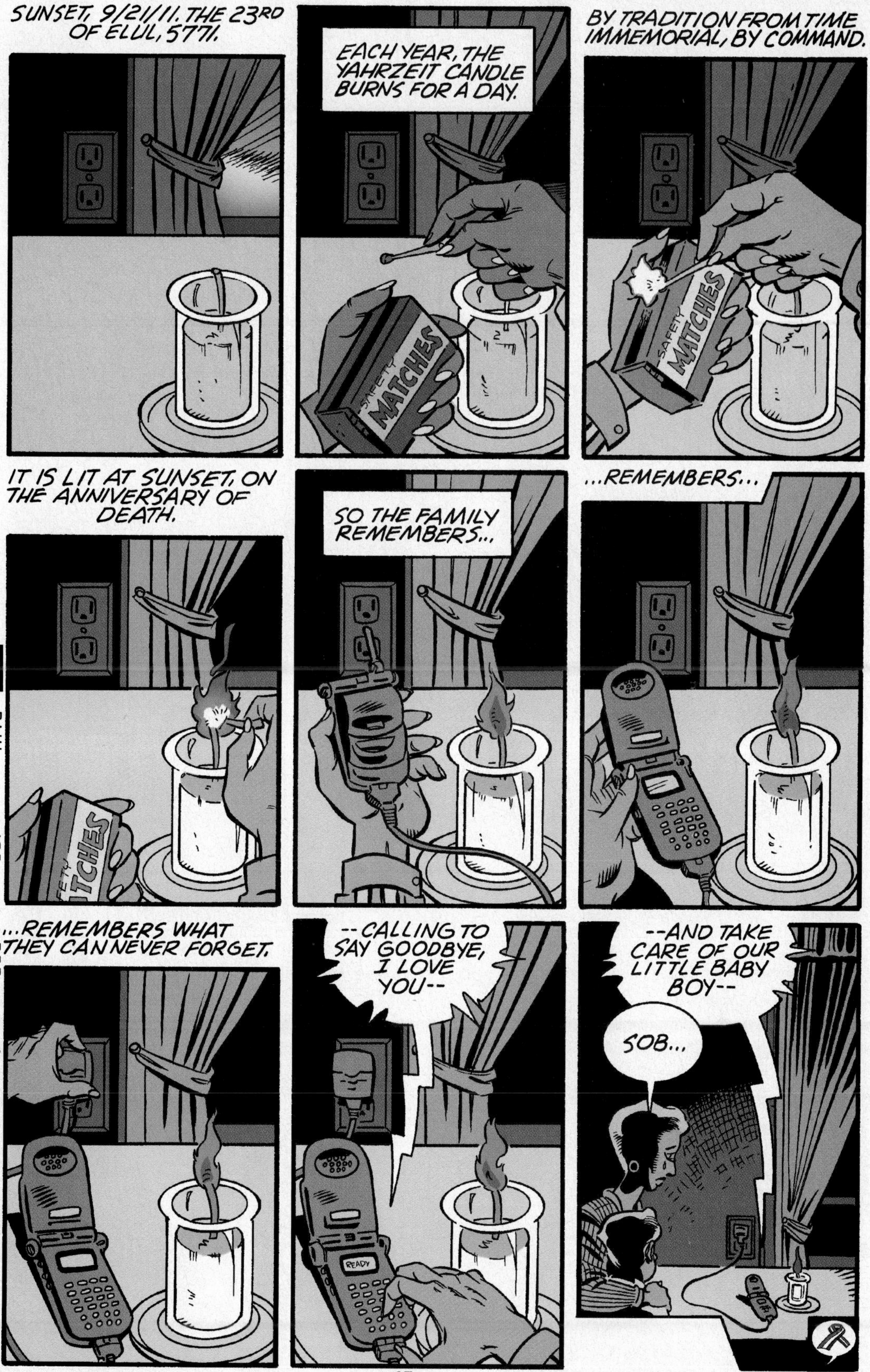

SUNSET, 9/21/11. THE 23RD OF ELUL, 5771.
EACH YEAR, THE YAHRZEIT CANDLE BURNS FOR A DAY.
SAFETY MATCHES
BY TRADITION FROM TIME IMMEMORIAL, BY COMMAND.
SAFETY MATCHES
IT IS LIT AT SUNSET, ON THE ANNIVERSARY OF DEATH.
SO THE FAMILY REMEMBERS...
...REMEMBERS...
...REMEMBERS WHAT THEY CAN NEVER FORGET.
--CALLING TO SAY GOODBYE, I LOVE YOU--
READY
--AND TAKE CARE OF OUR LITTLE BABY BOY--
SOB...

STORY PAUL LEVITZ
ART JOE STATON AND BOB SMITH
LETTERS JOHN WORKMAN
COLOR NOELLE GIDDINGS

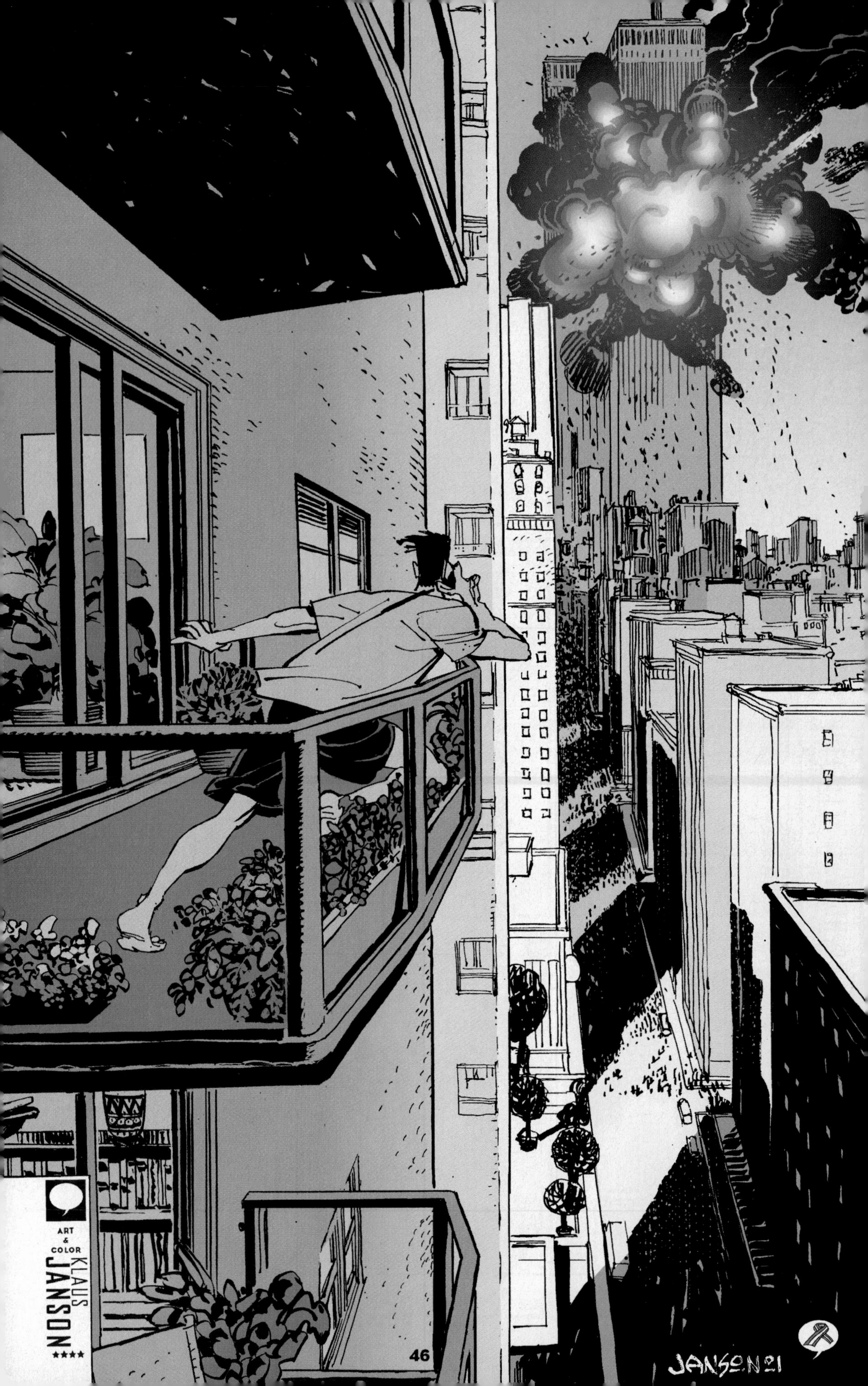
ART & COLOR
KLAUS JANSON

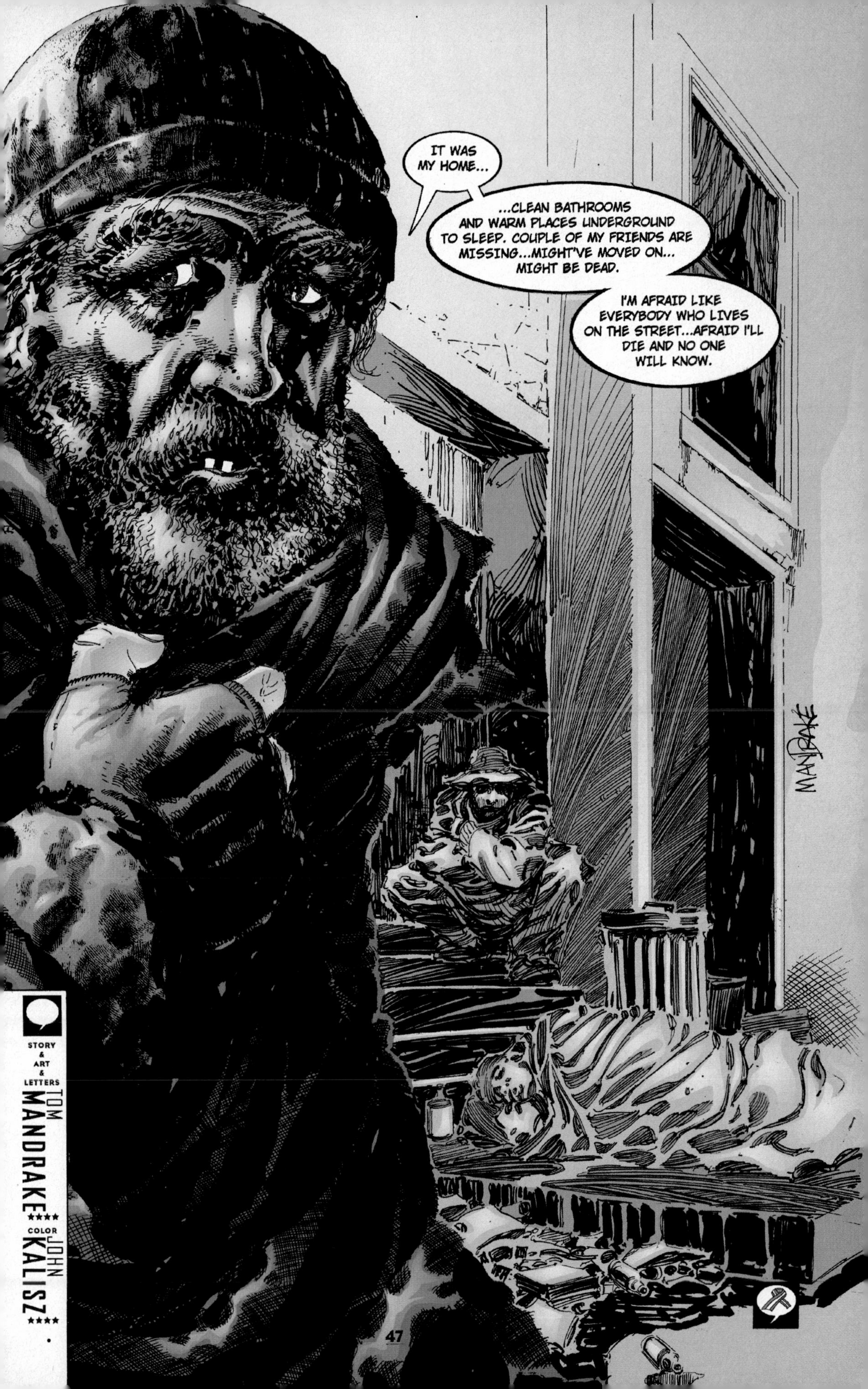
IT WAS MY HOME...
...CLEAN BATHROOMS AND WARM PLACES UNDERGROUND TO SLEEP. COUPLE OF MY FRIENDS ARE MISSING...MIGHT'VE MOVED ON... MIGHT BE DEAD.
I'M AFRAID LIKE EVERYBODY WHO LIVES ON THE STREET...AFRAID I'LL DIE AND NO ONE WILL KNOW.
MANDRAKE

STORY & ART & LETTERS TOM MANDRAKE

COLOR JOHN KALISZ

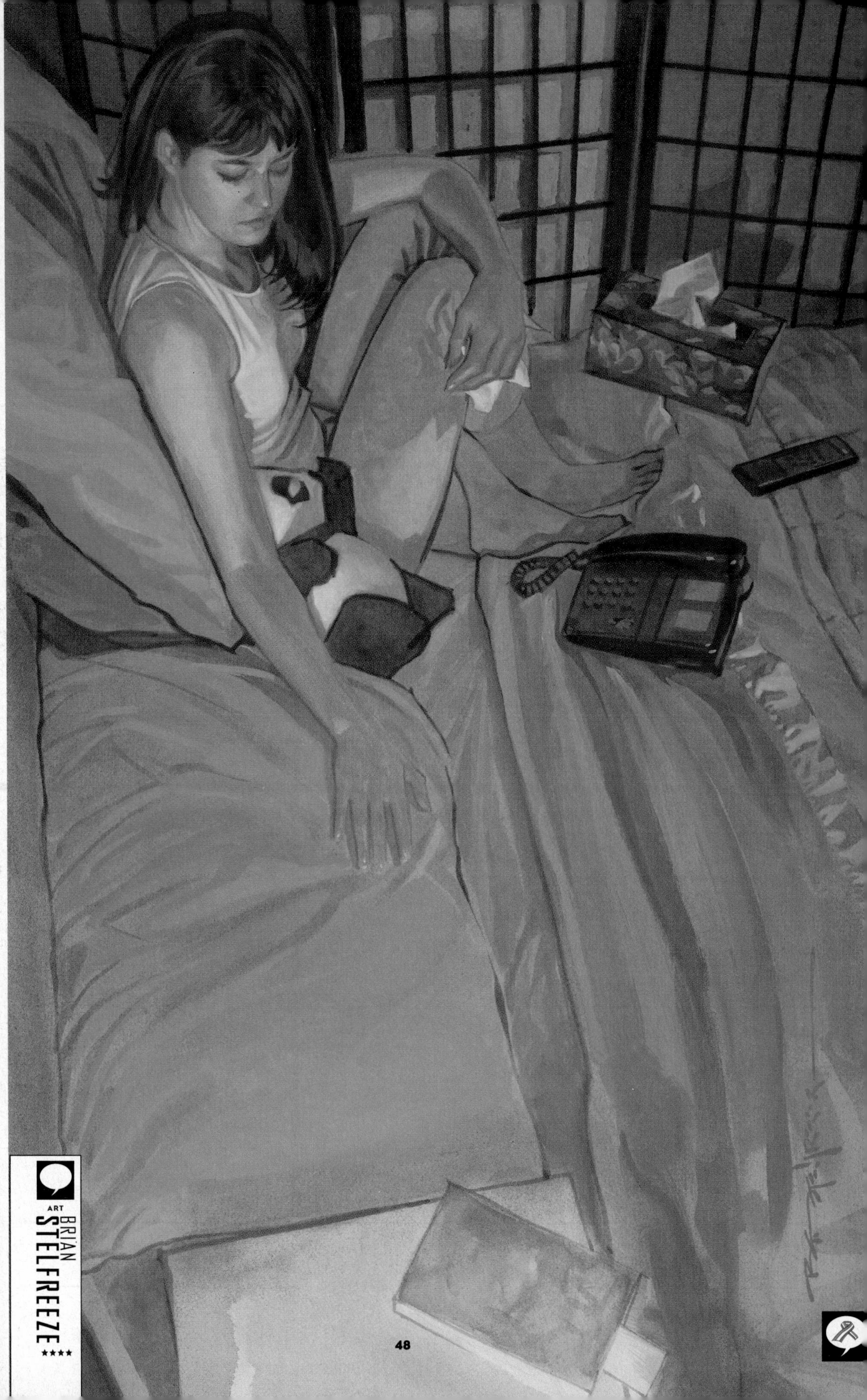

ART
BRIAN
STELFREEZE

HEROES

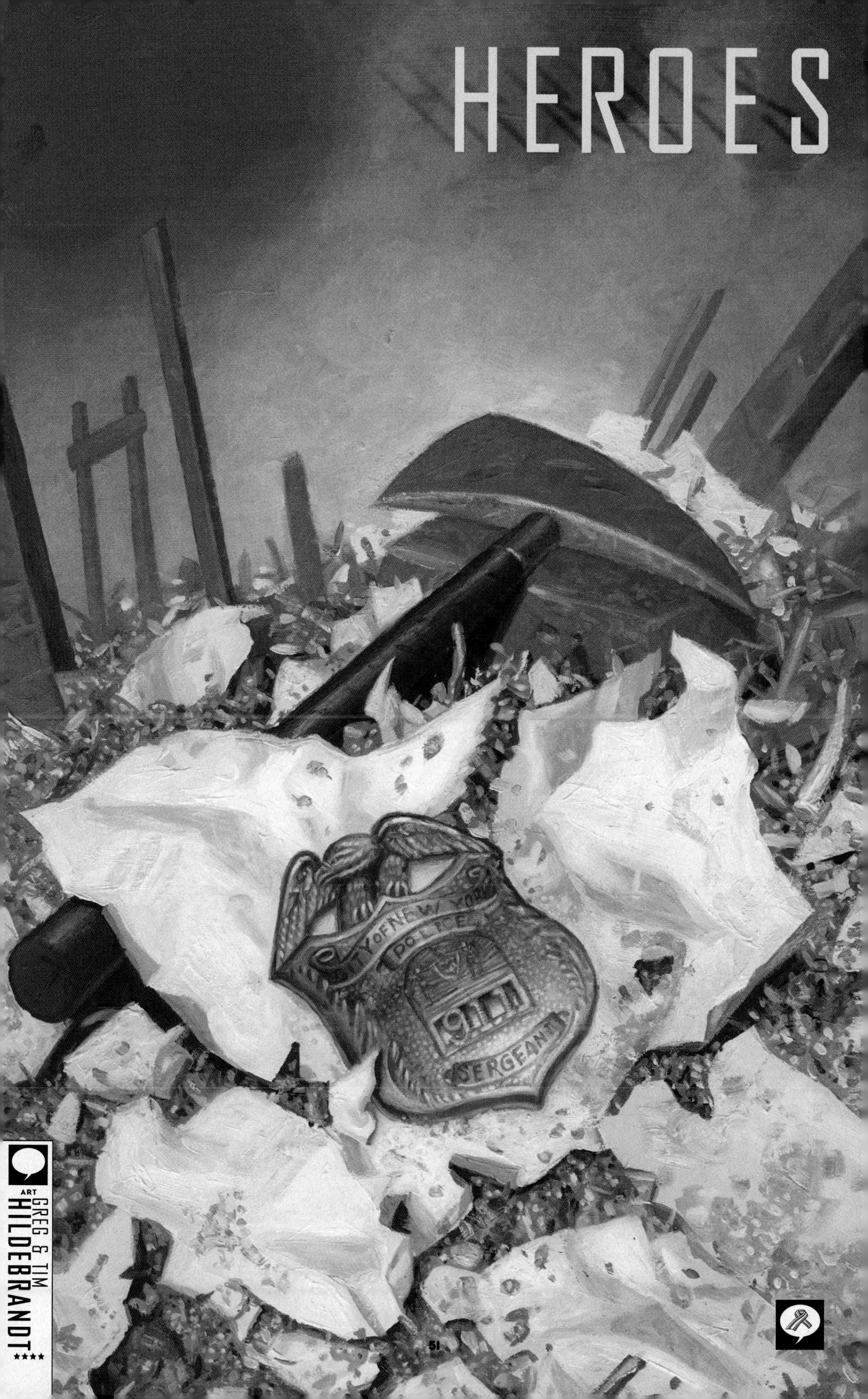

CITY of NEW YORK
POLICE
9111
SERGEANT

ART GREG & TIM HILDEBRANDT

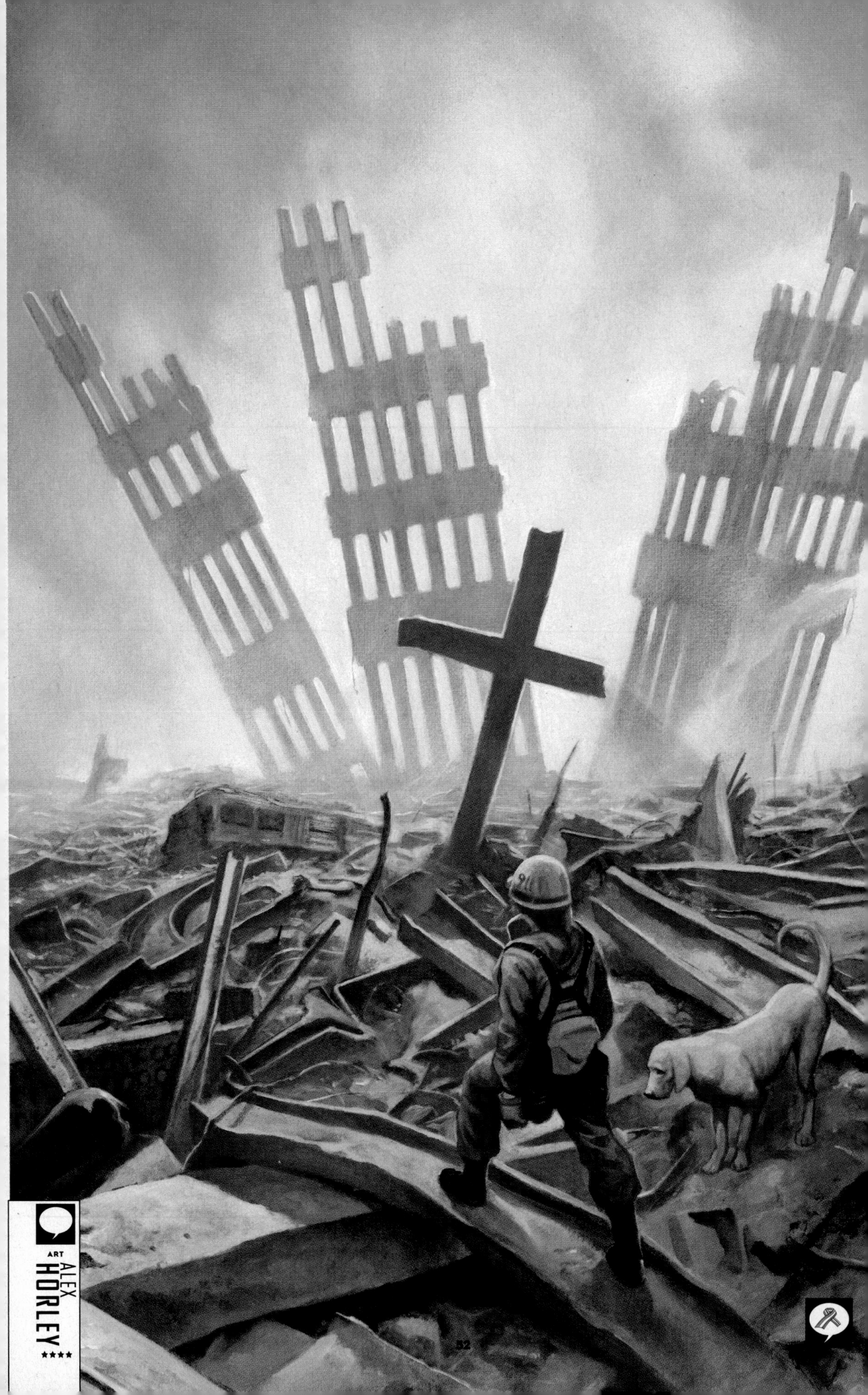
ART
ALEX HORLEY

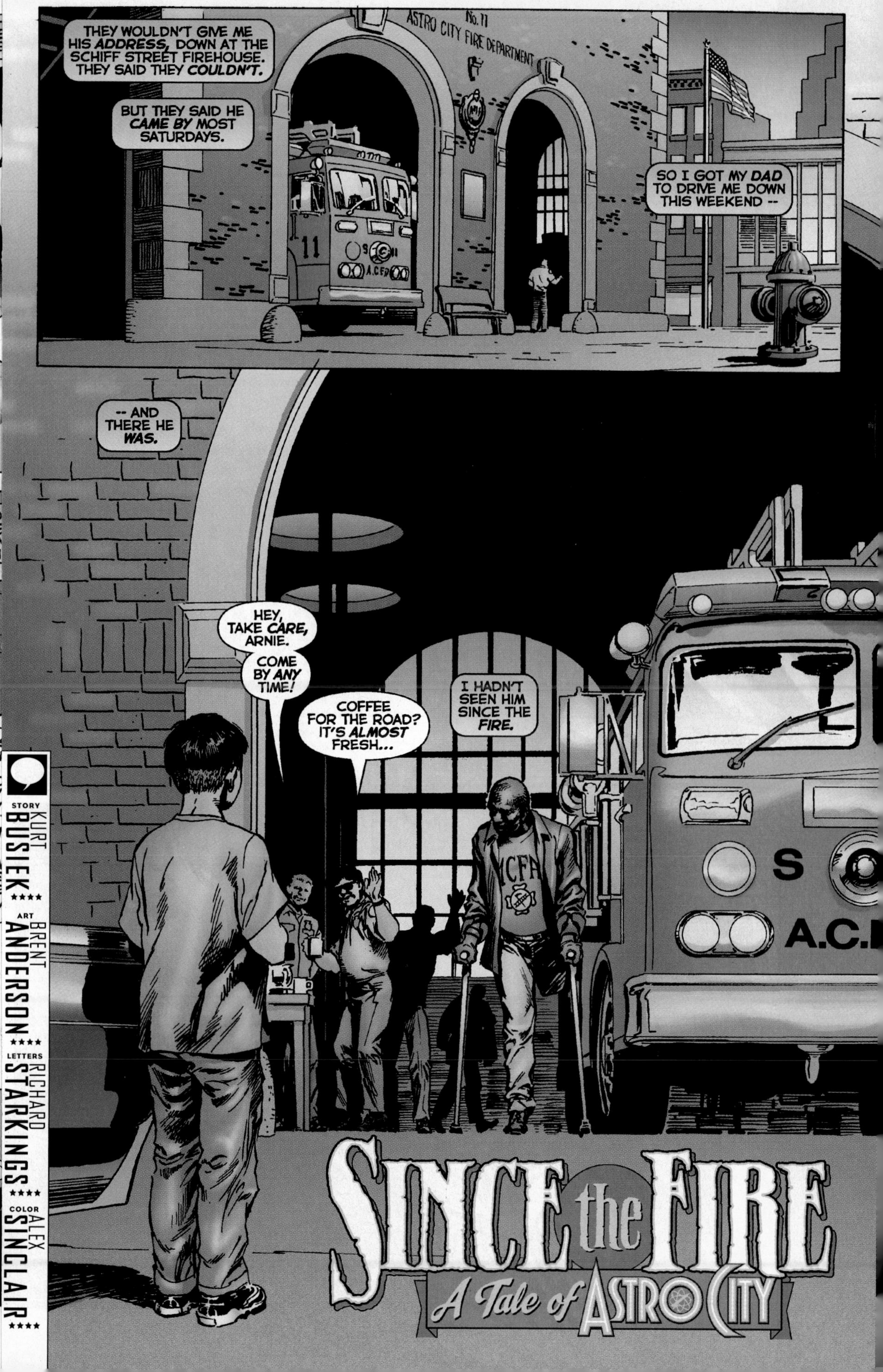
No. 11
ASTRO CITY FIRE DEPARTMENT
THEY WOULDN'T GIVE ME HIS ADDRESS, DOWN AT THE SCHIFF STREET FIREHOUSE. THEY SAID THEY COULDN'T.
BUT THEY SAID HE CAME BY MOST SATURDAYS.
SO I GOT MY DAD TO DRIVE ME DOWN THIS WEEKEND --
-- AND THERE HE WAS.
HEY, TAKE CARE, ARNIE.
COME BY ANY TIME!
COFFEE FOR THE ROAD? IT'S ALMOST FRESH...
I HADN'T SEEN HIM SINCE THE FIRE.
STORY KURT BUSIEK
ART BRENT ANDERSON
LETTERS RICHARD STARKINGS
COLOR ALEX SINCLAIR
SINCE the FIRE
A Tale of ASTRO CITY

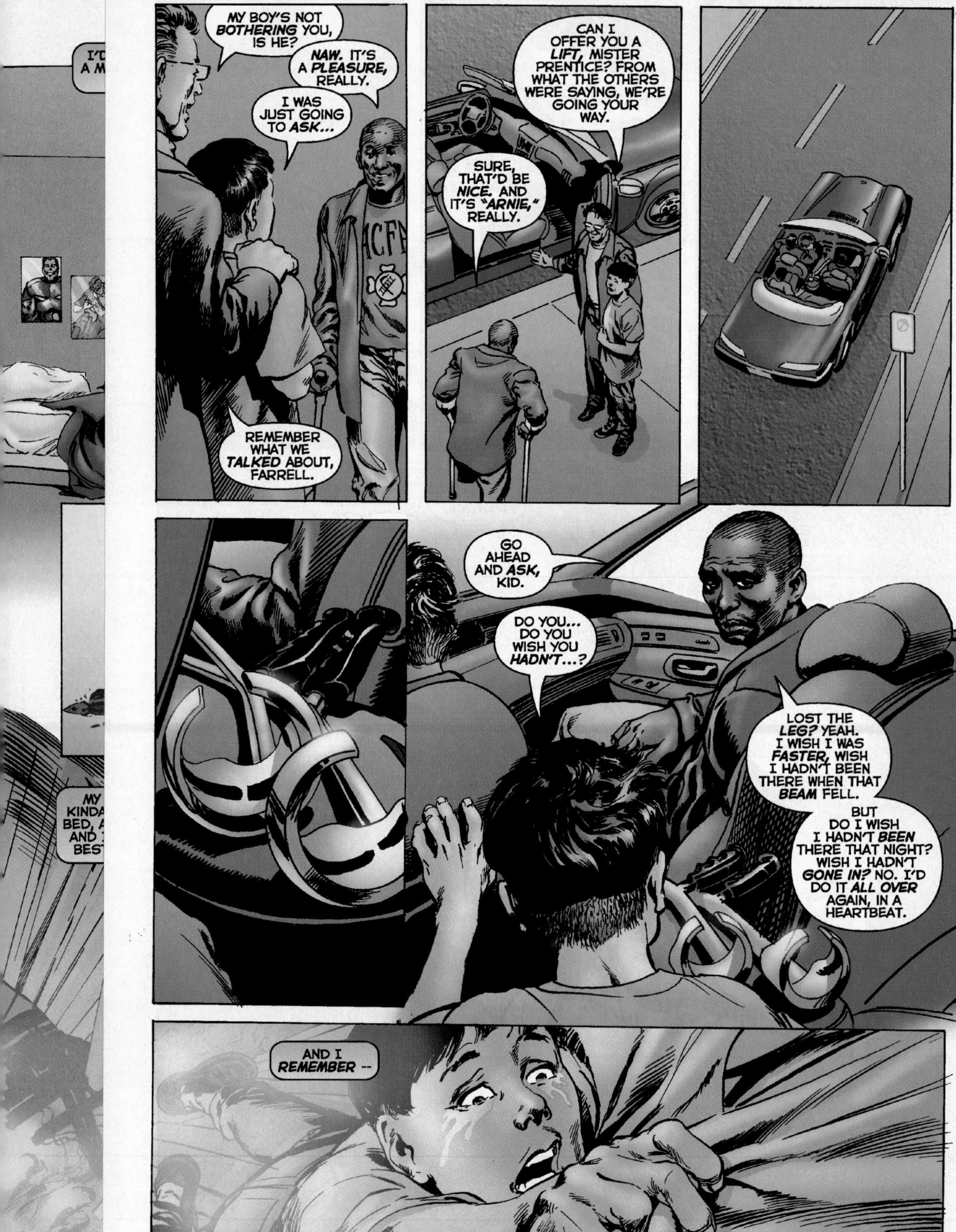

MY BOY'S NOT BOTHERING YOU, IS HE?
NAW. IT'S A PLEASURE, REALLY.
I WAS JUST GOING TO ASK...
REMEMBER WHAT WE TALKED ABOUT, FARRELL.
CAN I OFFER YOU A LIFT, MISTER PRENTICE? FROM WHAT THE OTHERS WERE SAYING, WE'RE GOING YOUR WAY.
SURE, THAT'D BE NICE. AND IT'S "ARNIE," REALLY.
GO AHEAD AND ASK, KID.
DO YOU... DO YOU WISH YOU HADN'T...?
LOST THE LEG? YEAH. I WISH I WAS FASTER, WISH I HADN'T BEEN THERE WHEN THAT BEAM FELL.
BUT DO I WISH I HADN'T BEEN THERE THAT NIGHT? WISH I HADN'T GONE IN? NO. I'D DO IT ALL OVER AGAIN, IN A HEARTBEAT.
AND I REMEMBER --

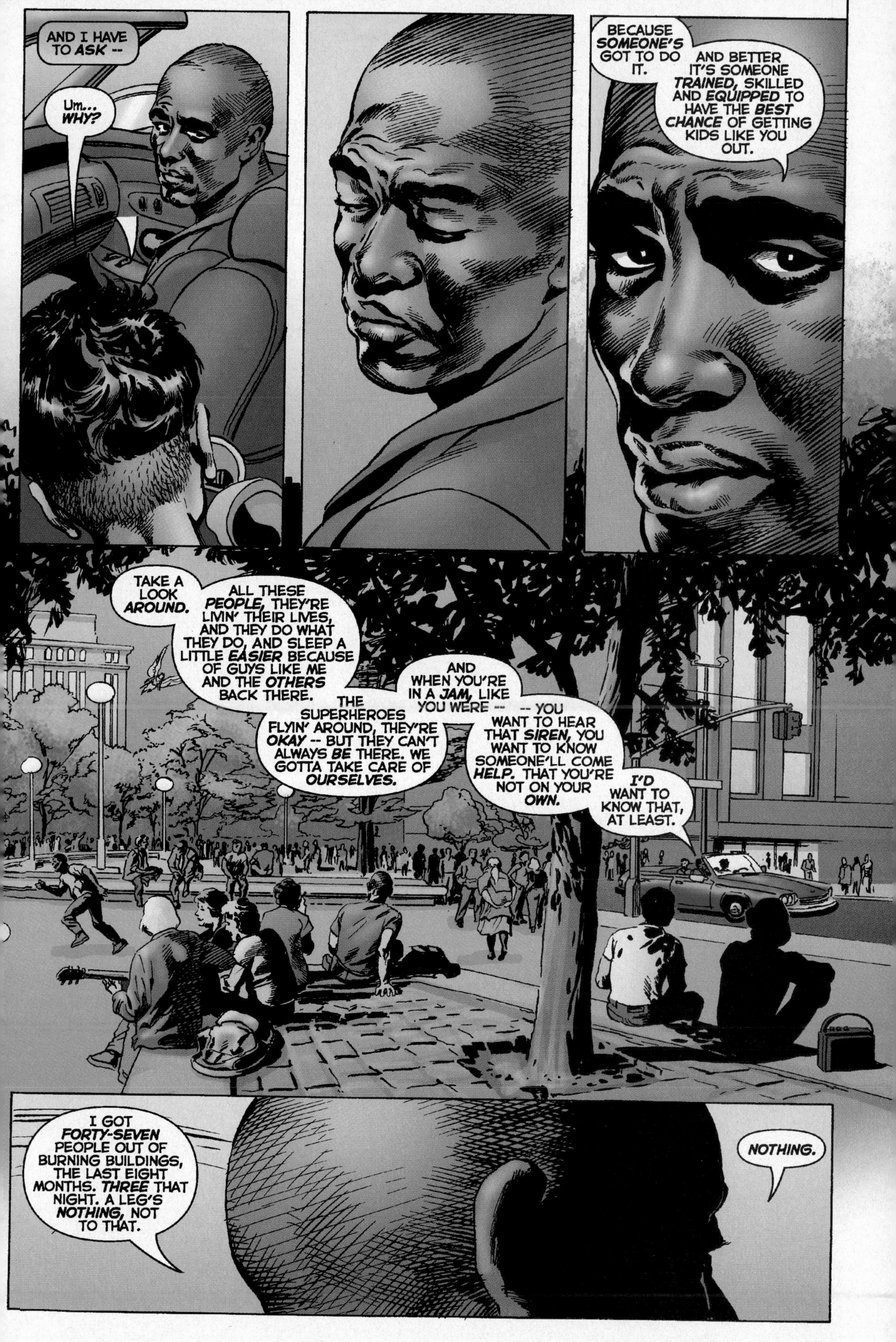
AND I HAVE TO ASK --
Um... WHY?
BECAUSE SOMEONE'S GOT TO DO IT.
AND BETTER IT'S SOMEONE TRAINED, SKILLED AND EQUIPPED TO HAVE THE BEST CHANCE OF GETTING KIDS LIKE YOU OUT.
TAKE A LOOK AROUND.
ALL THESE PEOPLE, THEY'RE LIVIN' THEIR LIVES, AND THEY DO WHAT THEY DO, AND SLEEP A LITTLE EASIER BECAUSE OF GUYS LIKE ME AND THE OTHERS BACK THERE.
THE SUPERHEROES FLYIN' AROUND, THEY'RE OKAY -- BUT THEY CAN'T ALWAYS BE THERE. WE GOTTA TAKE CARE OF OURSELVES.
AND WHEN YOU'RE IN A JAM, LIKE YOU WERE --
-- YOU WANT TO HEAR THAT SIREN, YOU WANT TO KNOW SOMEONE'LL COME HELP. THAT YOU'RE NOT ON YOUR OWN.
I'D WANT TO KNOW THAT, AT LEAST.
I GOT FORTY-SEVEN PEOPLE OUT OF BURNING BUILDINGS, THE LAST EIGHT MONTHS. THREE THAT NIGHT. A LEG'S NOTHING, NOT TO THAT.
NOTHING.

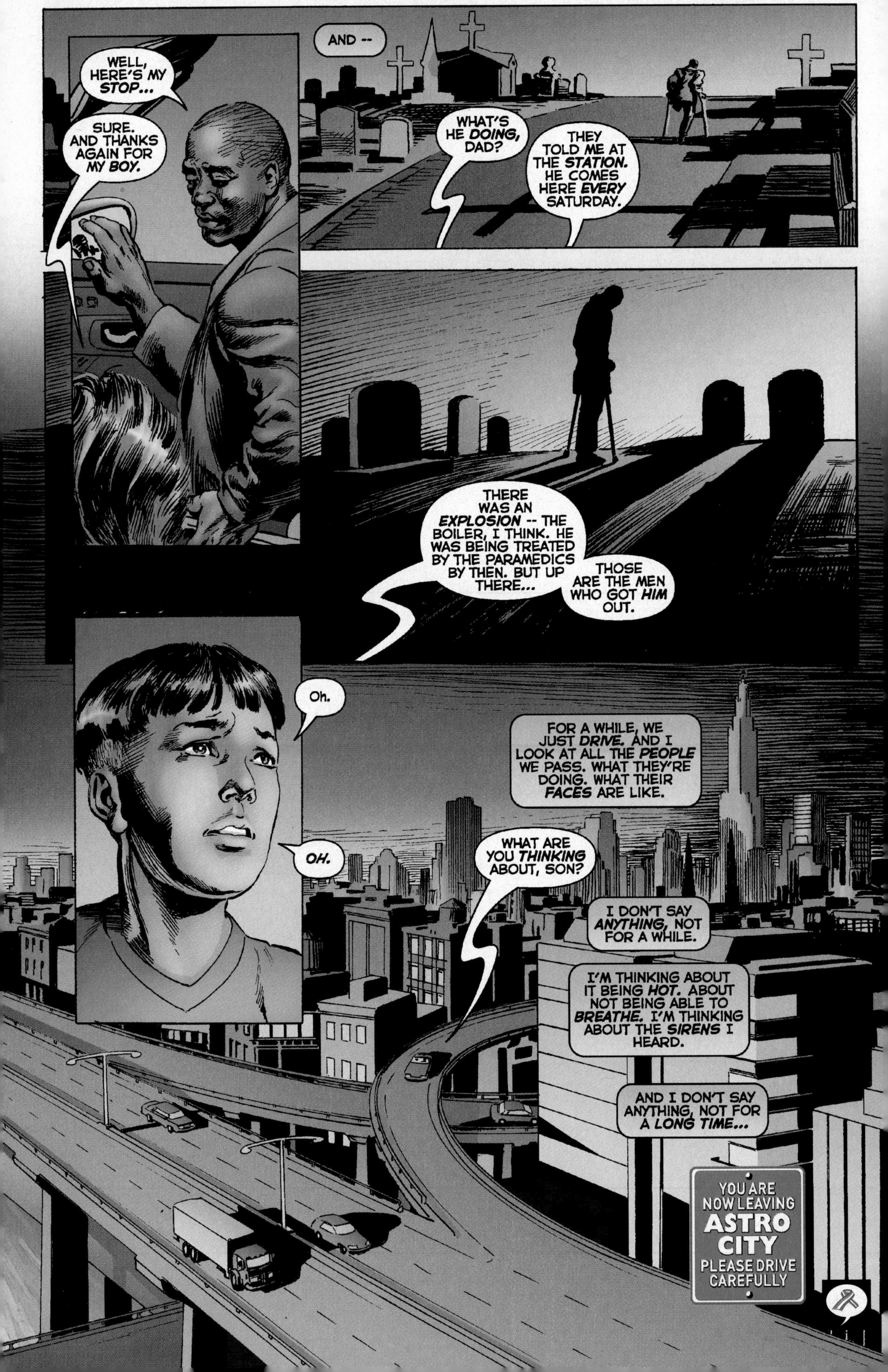
WELL, HERE'S MY STOP...
SURE. AND THANKS AGAIN FOR MY BOY.
AND --
WHAT'S HE DOING, DAD?
THEY TOLD ME AT THE STATION. HE COMES HERE EVERY SATURDAY.
THERE WAS AN EXPLOSION -- THE BOILER, I THINK. HE WAS BEING TREATED BY THE PARAMEDICS BY THEN. BUT UP THERE...
THOSE ARE THE MEN WHO GOT HIM OUT.
Oh.
OH.
FOR A WHILE, WE JUST DRIVE. AND I LOOK AT ALL THE PEOPLE WE PASS. WHAT THEY'RE DOING. WHAT THEIR FACES ARE LIKE.
WHAT ARE YOU THINKING ABOUT, SON?
I DON'T SAY ANYTHING, NOT FOR A WHILE.
I'M THINKING ABOUT IT BEING HOT. ABOUT NOT BEING ABLE TO BREATHE. I'M THINKING ABOUT THE SIRENS I HEARD.
AND I DON'T SAY ANYTHING, NOT FOR A LONG TIME...
YOU ARE NOW LEAVING ASTRO CITY PLEASE DRIVE CAREFULLY

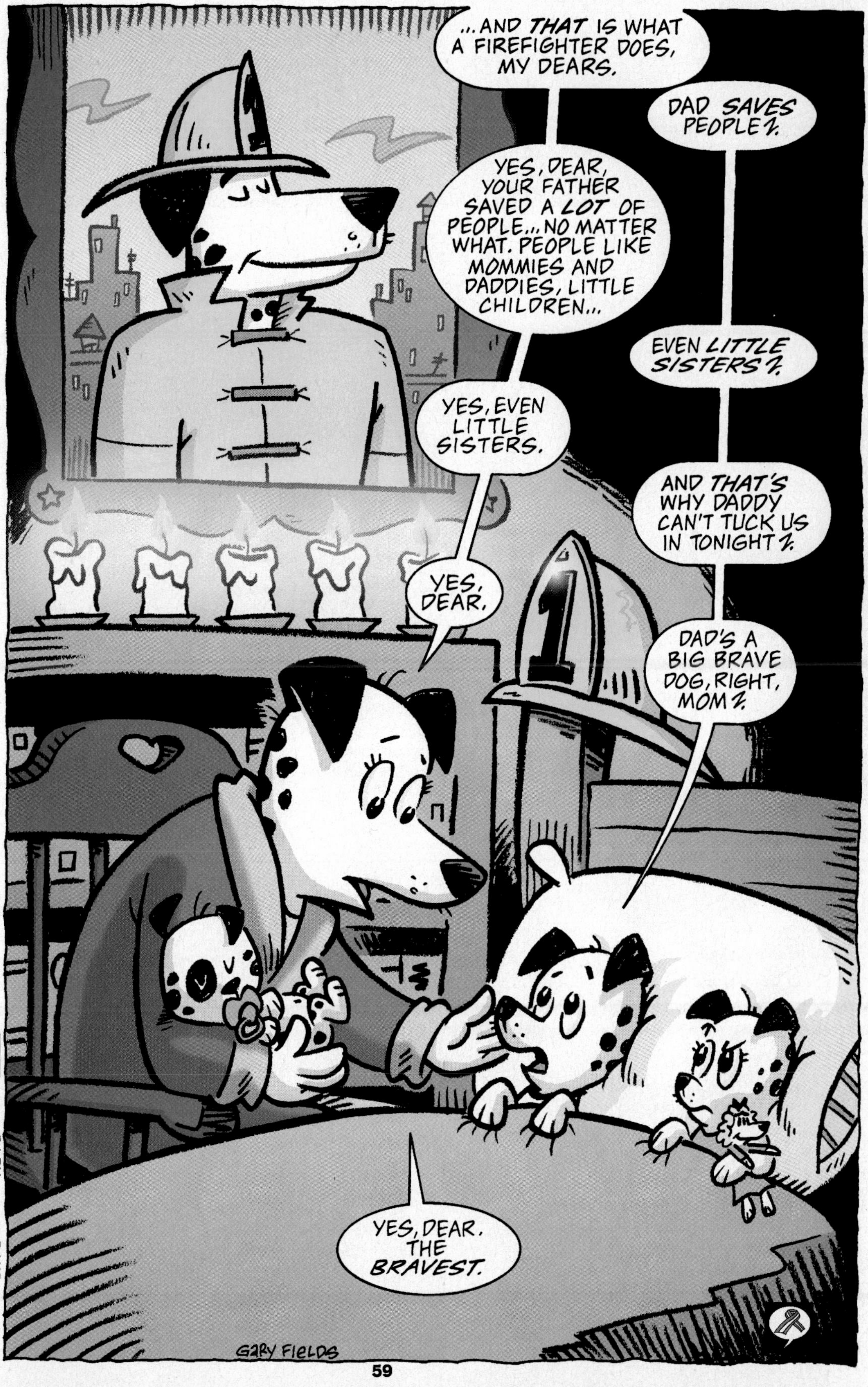

...AND THAT IS WHAT A FIREFIGHTER DOES, MY DEARS.
DAD SAVES PEOPLE?
YES, DEAR, YOUR FATHER SAVED A LOT OF PEOPLE... NO MATTER WHAT. PEOPLE LIKE MOMMIES AND DADDIES, LITTLE CHILDREN...
EVEN LITTLE SISTERS?
YES, EVEN LITTLE SISTERS.
AND THAT'S WHY DADDY CAN'T TUCK US IN TONIGHT?
YES, DEAR.
DAD'S A BIG BRAVE DOG, RIGHT, MOM?
YES, DEAR. THE BRAVEST.
GARY FIELDS

STORY & ART & LETTERS GARY

COLOR DAVE

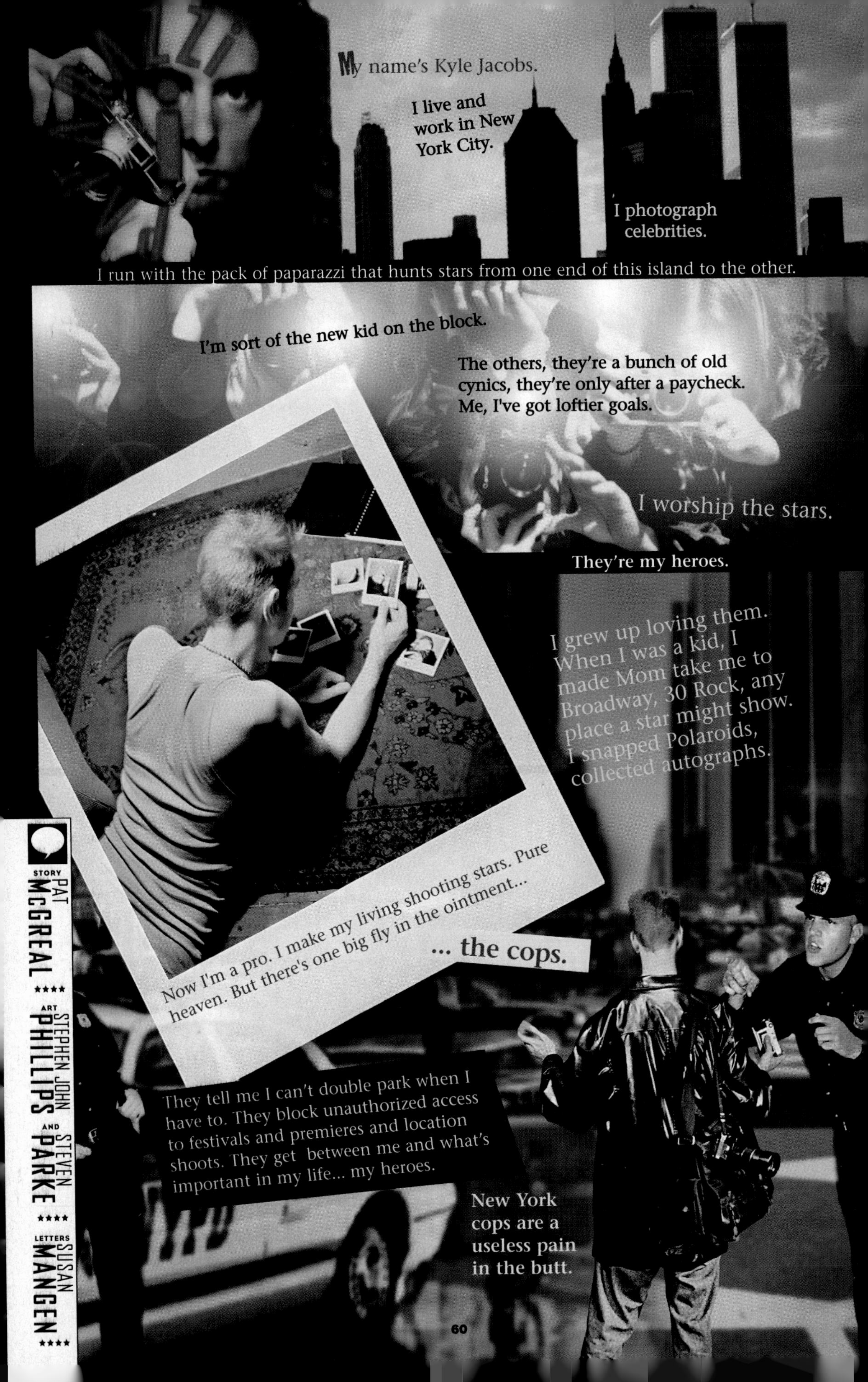
My name's Kyle Jacobs.
I live and work in New York City.
I photograph celebrities.
I run with the pack of paparazzi that hunts stars from one end of this island to the other.
I'm sort of the new kid on the block.
The others, they're a bunch of old cynics, they're only after a paycheck. Me, I've got loftier goals.
I worship the stars.
They're my heroes.
I grew up loving them. When I was a kid, I made Mom take me to Broadway, 30 Rock, any place a star might show. I snapped Polaroids, collected autographs.
Now I'm a pro. I make my living shooting stars. Pure heaven. But there's one big fly in the ointment...
... the cops.
They tell me I can't double park when I have to. They block unauthorized access to festivals and premieres and location shoots. They get between me and what's important in my life... my heroes.
New York cops are a useless pain in the butt.
STORY PAT McGREAL
ART STEPHEN JOHN PHILLIPS AND STEVEN PARKE
LETTERS SUSAN MANGEN

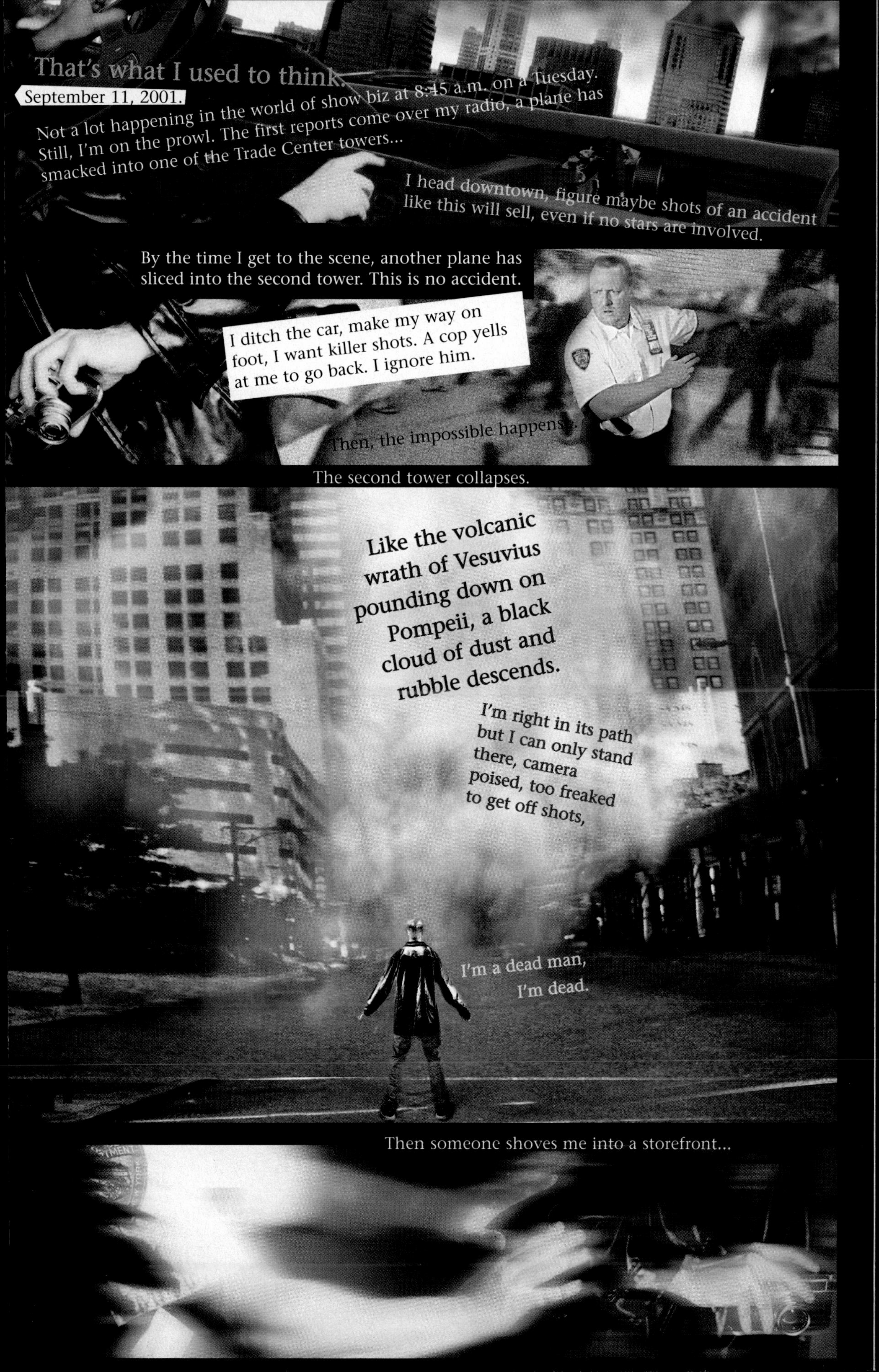
That's what I used to think.
September 11, 2001.
Not a lot happening in the world of show biz at 8:45 a.m. on a Tuesday. Still, I'm on the prowl. The first reports come over my radio, a plane has smacked into one of the Trade Center towers...
I head downtown, figure maybe shots of an accident like this will sell, even if no stars are involved.
By the time I get to the scene, another plane has sliced into the second tower. This is no accident.
I ditch the car, make my way on foot, I want killer shots. A cop yells at me to go back. I ignore him.
Then, the impossible happens.
The second tower collapses.
Like the volcanic wrath of Vesuvius pounding down on Pompeii, a black cloud of dust and rubble descends.
I'm right in its path but I can only stand there, camera poised, too freaked to get off shots,
I'm a dead man, I'm dead.
Then someone shoves me into a storefront...

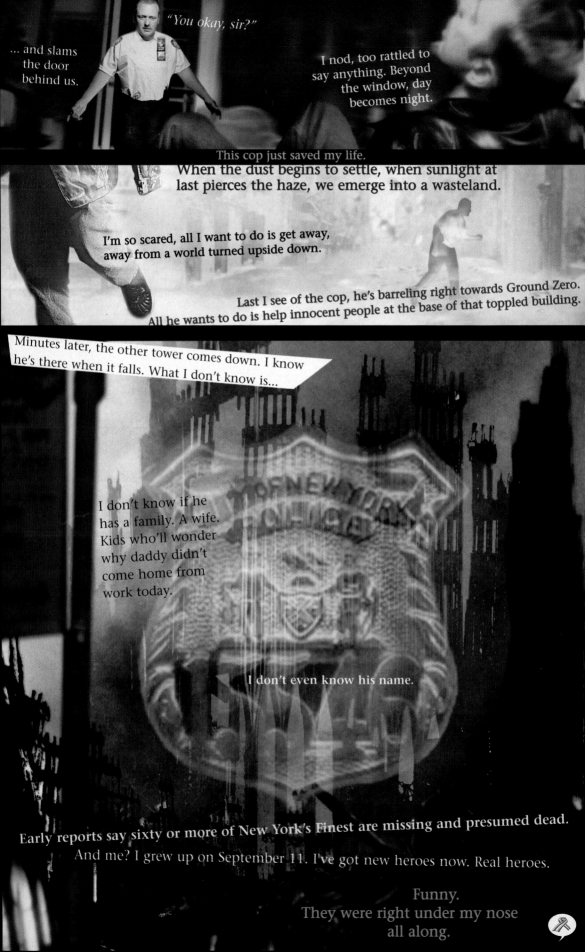

"You okay, sir?"

... and slams the door behind us.

I nod, too rattled to say anything. Beyond the window, day becomes night.

This cop just saved my life.

When the dust begins to settle, when sunlight at last pierces the haze, we emerge into a wasteland.

I'm so scared, all I want to do is get away, away from a world turned upside down.

Last I see of the cop, he's barreling right towards Ground Zero. All he wants to do is help innocent people at the base of that toppled building.

Minutes later, the other tower comes down. I know he's there when it falls. What I don't know is...

I don't know if he has a family. A wife. Kids who'll wonder why daddy didn't come home from work today.

I don't even know his name.

Early reports say sixty or more of New York's Finest are missing and presumed dead.

And me? I grew up on September 11. I've got new heroes now. Real heroes.

Funny.
They were right under my nose
all along.

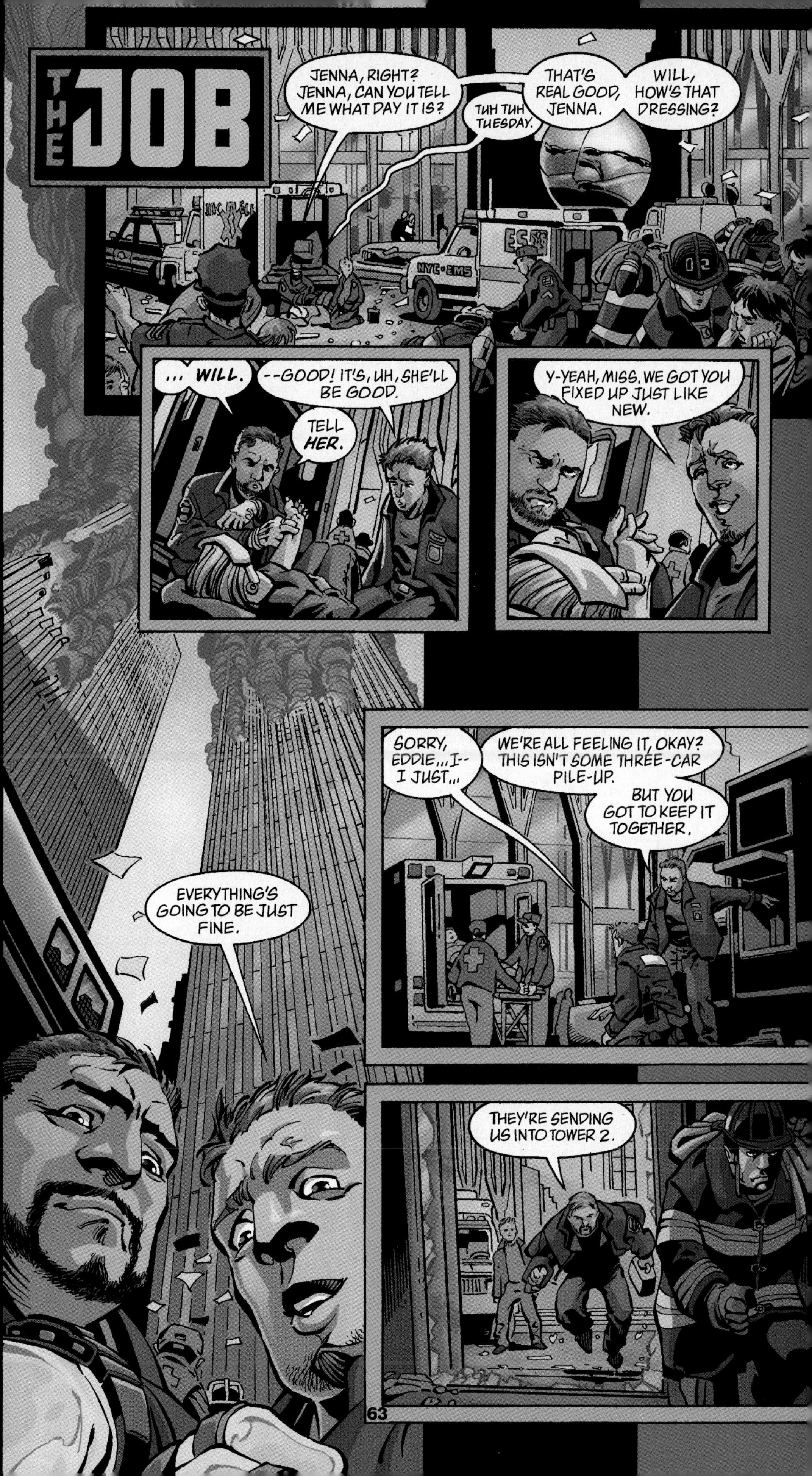
THE JOB
JENNA, RIGHT? JENNA, CAN YOU TELL ME WHAT DAY IT IS?
TUH TUH TUESDAY.
THAT'S REAL GOOD, JENNA.
WILL, HOW'S THAT DRESSING?
NYC EMS
... WILL.
--GOOD! IT'S, UH, SHE'LL BE GOOD.
TELL HER.
Y-YEAH, MISS. WE GOT YOU FIXED UP JUST LIKE NEW.
EVERYTHING'S GOING TO BE JUST FINE.
SORRY, EDDIE... I-- I JUST...
WE'RE ALL FEELING IT, OKAY? THIS ISN'T SOME THREE-CAR PILE-UP.
BUT YOU GOT TO KEEP IT TOGETHER.
THEY'RE SENDING US INTO TOWER 2.

STORY JOSH KRACH
ART SCOTT McDANIEL AND JAMES PASCOE
LETTERS TODD KLEIN
COLOR DAVE STEWART

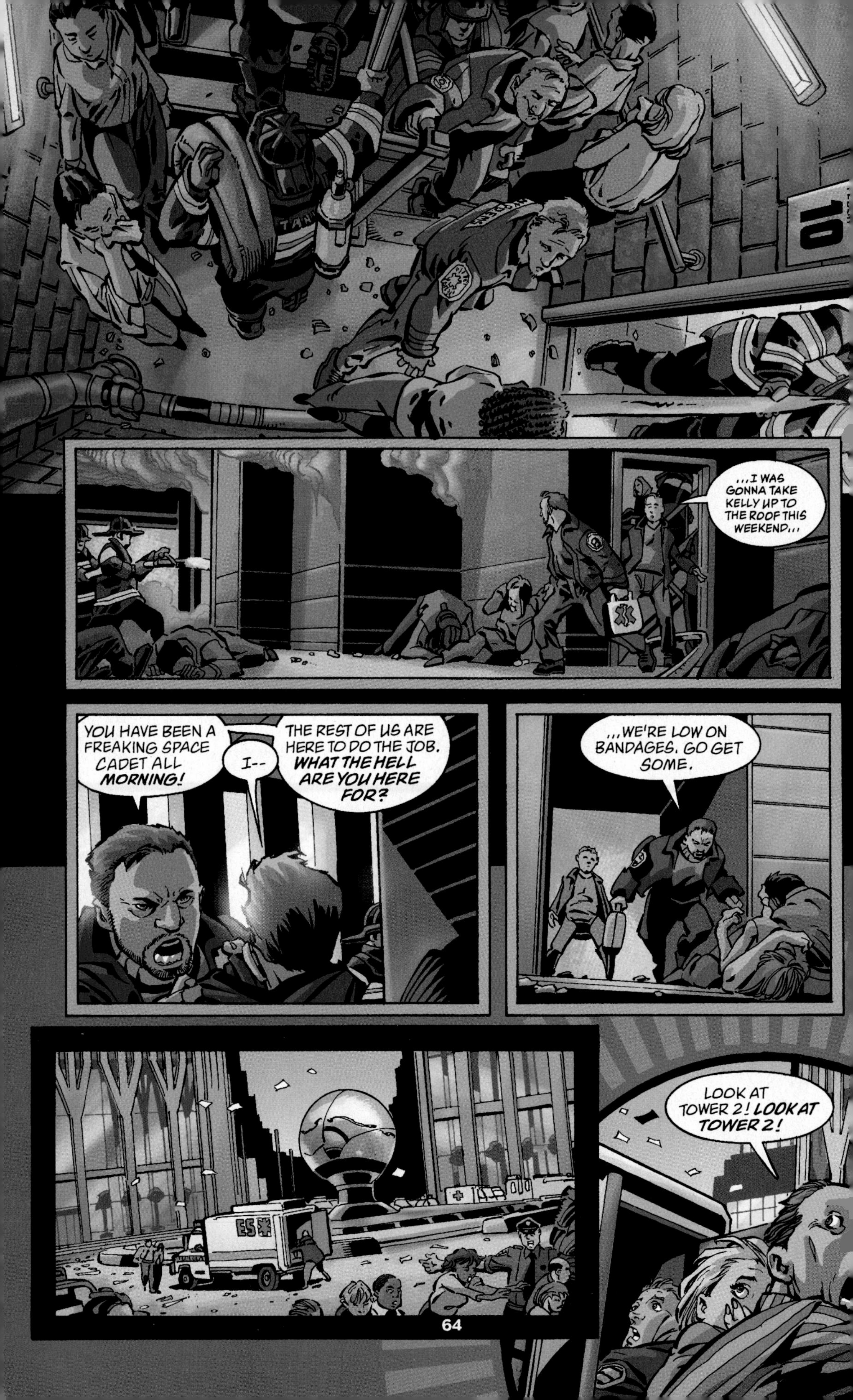
10
...I WAS GONNA TAKE KELLY UP TO THE ROOF THIS WEEKEND...
YOU HAVE BEEN A FREAKING SPACE CADET ALL MORNING!
I--
THE REST OF US ARE HERE TO DO THE JOB. WHAT THE HELL ARE YOU HERE FOR?
...WE'RE LOW ON BANDAGES. GO GET SOME.
LOOK AT TOWER 2! LOOK AT TOWER 2!

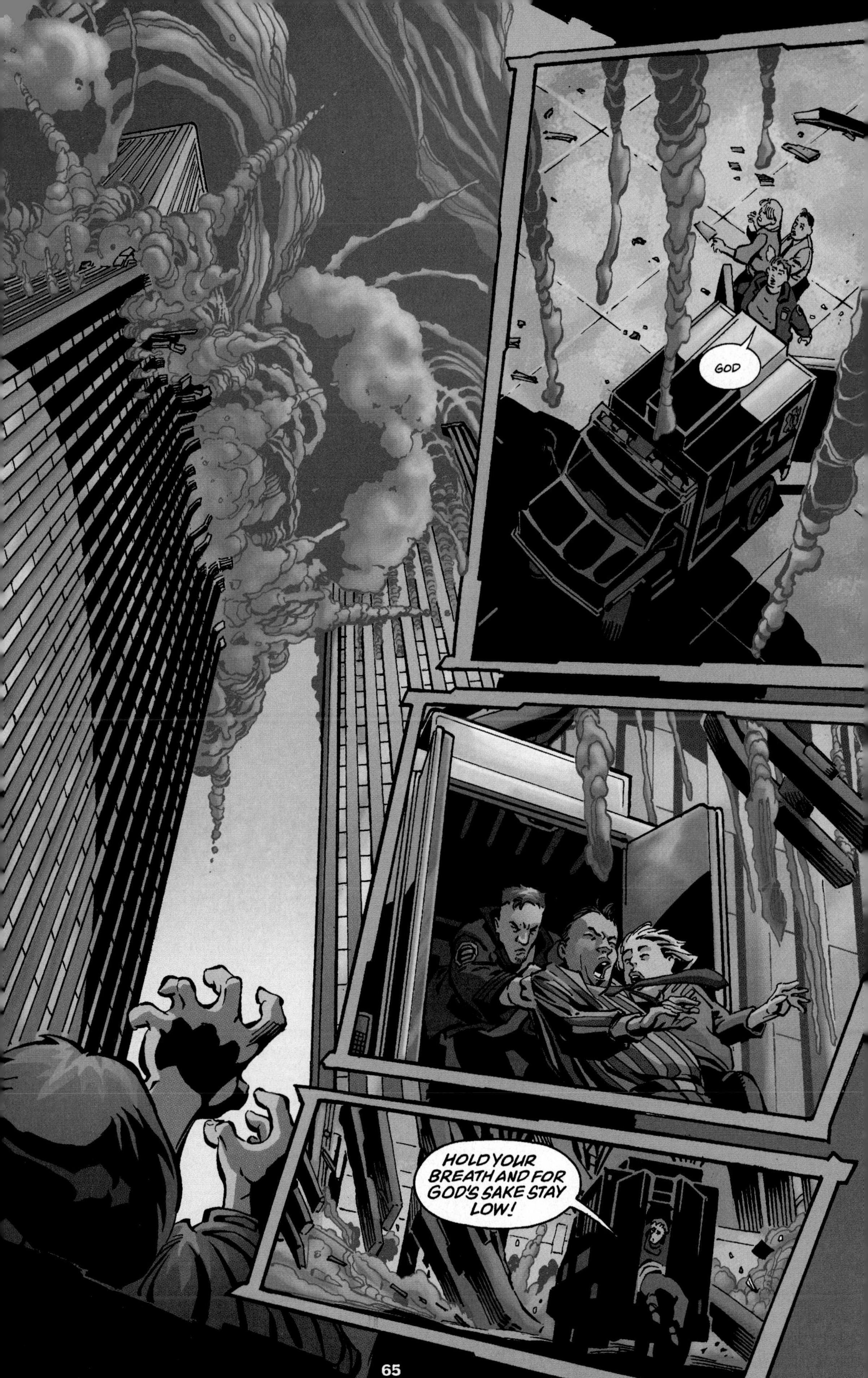
GOD
HOLD YOUR BREATH AND FOR GOD'S SAKE STAY LOW!

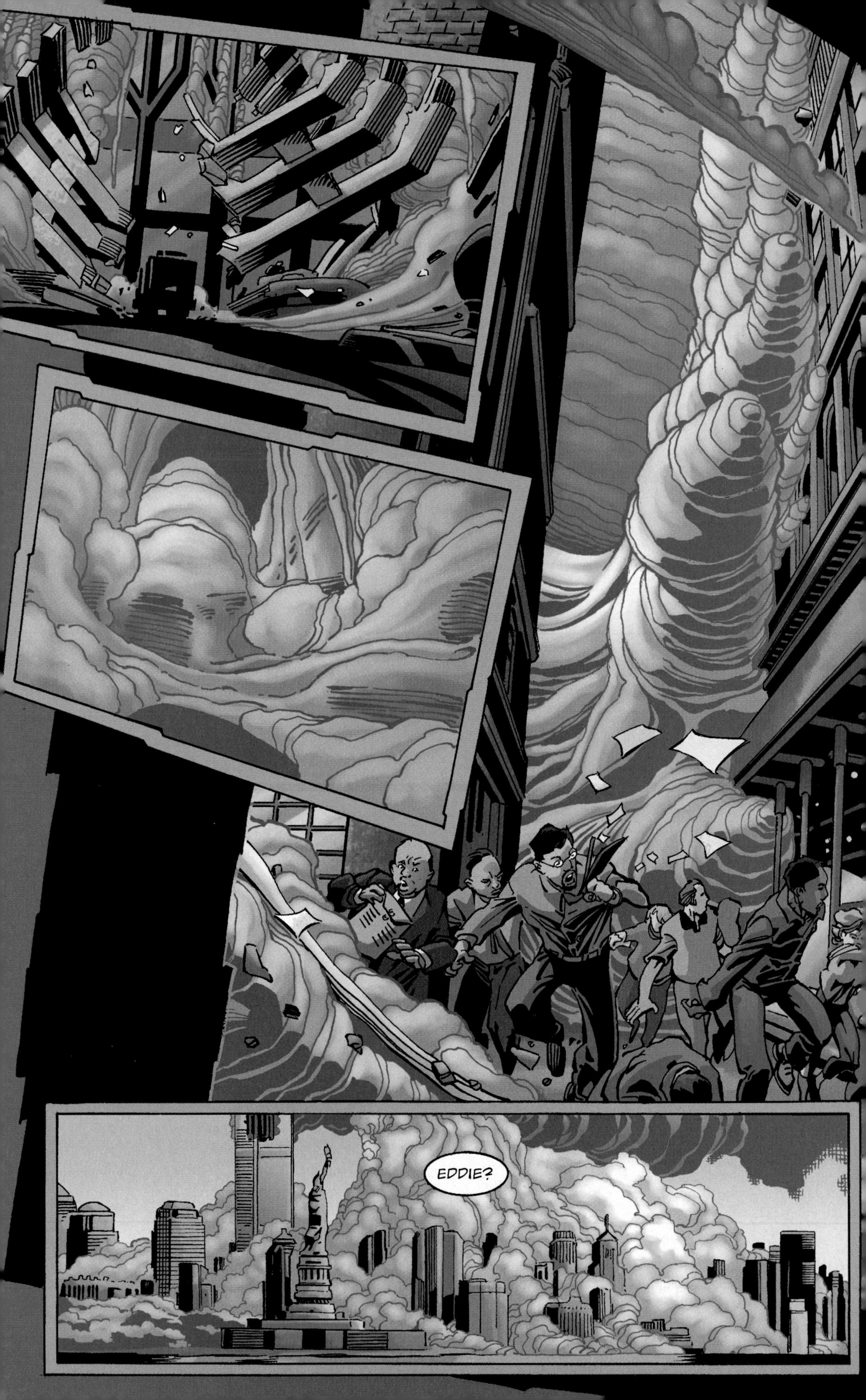
EDDIE?

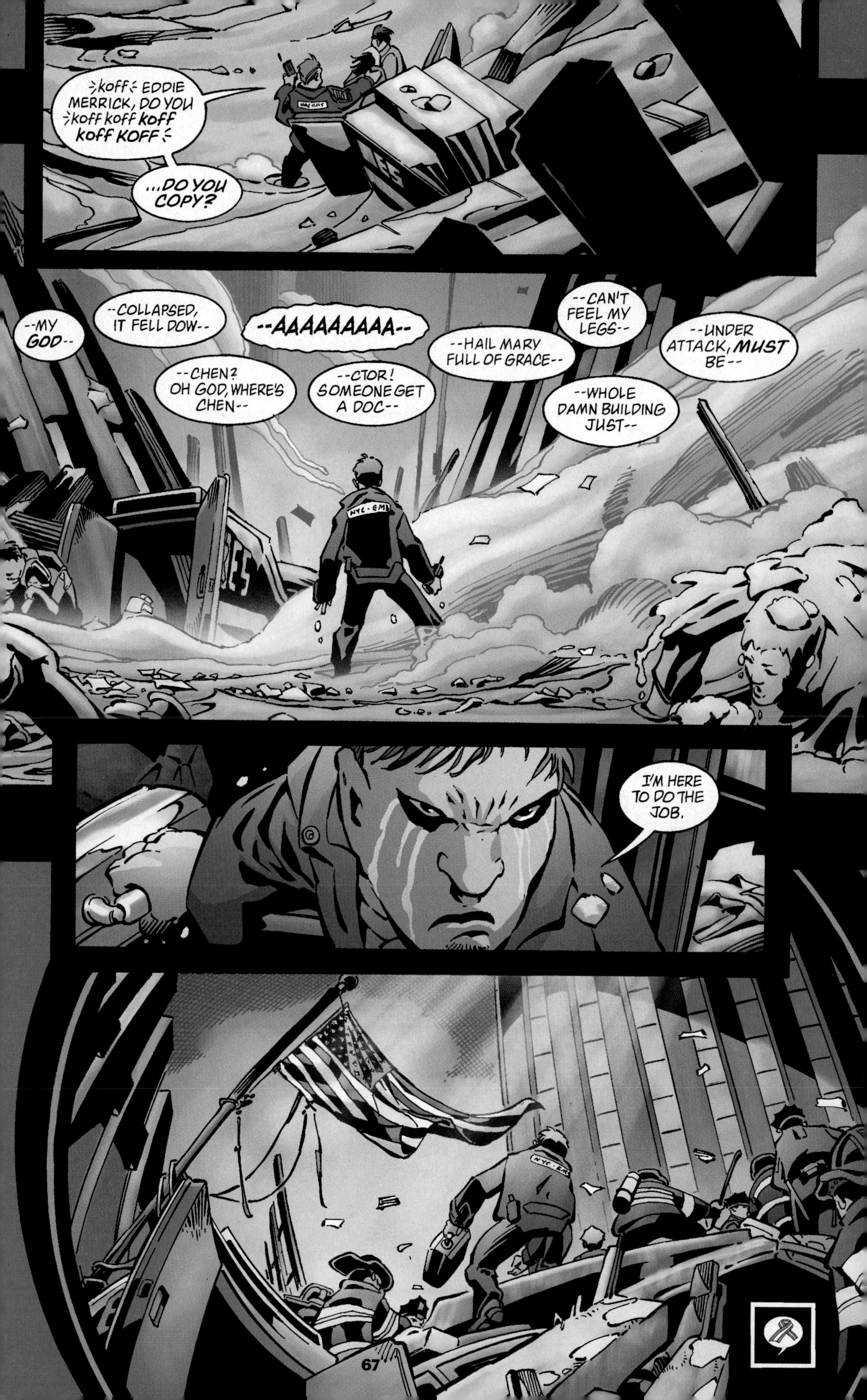

>koff< EDDIE MERRICK, DO YOU >koff koff koff koff KOFF<
...DO YOU COPY?
--MY GOD--
--COLLAPSED, IT FELL DOW--
--CHEN? OH GOD, WHERE'S CHEN--
--AAAAAAAAA--
--CTOR! SOMEONE GET A DOC--
--HAIL MARY FULL OF GRACE--
--CAN'T FEEL MY LEGS--
--WHOLE DAMN BUILDING JUST--
--UNDER ATTACK, MUST BE--
I'M HERE TO DO THE JOB.

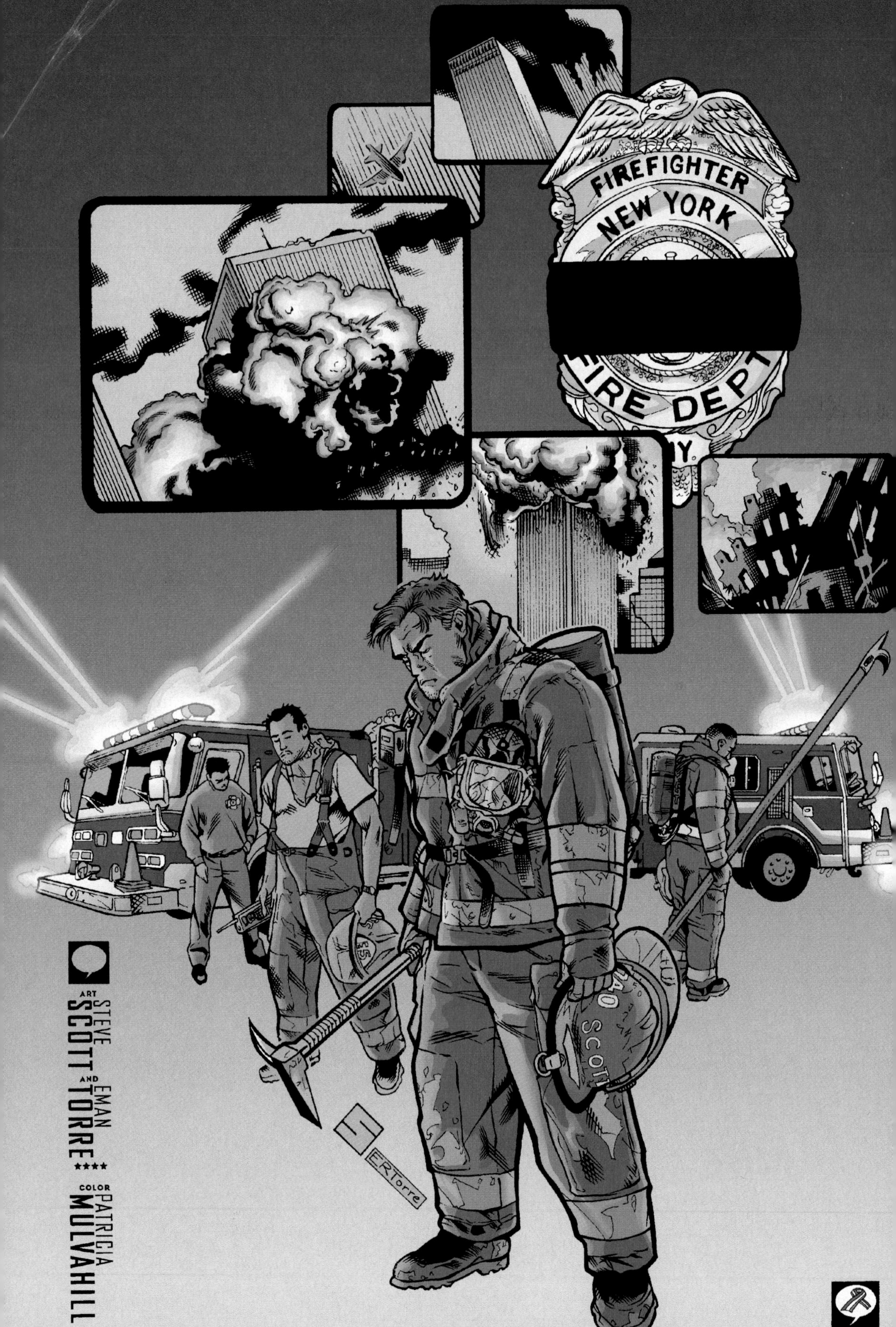
FIREFIGHTER
NEW YORK
FIRE DEPT
N.Y.
40 SCOTT
SERTorre

ART STEVE SCOTT AND EMAN TORRE

COLOR PATRICIA MULVAHILL

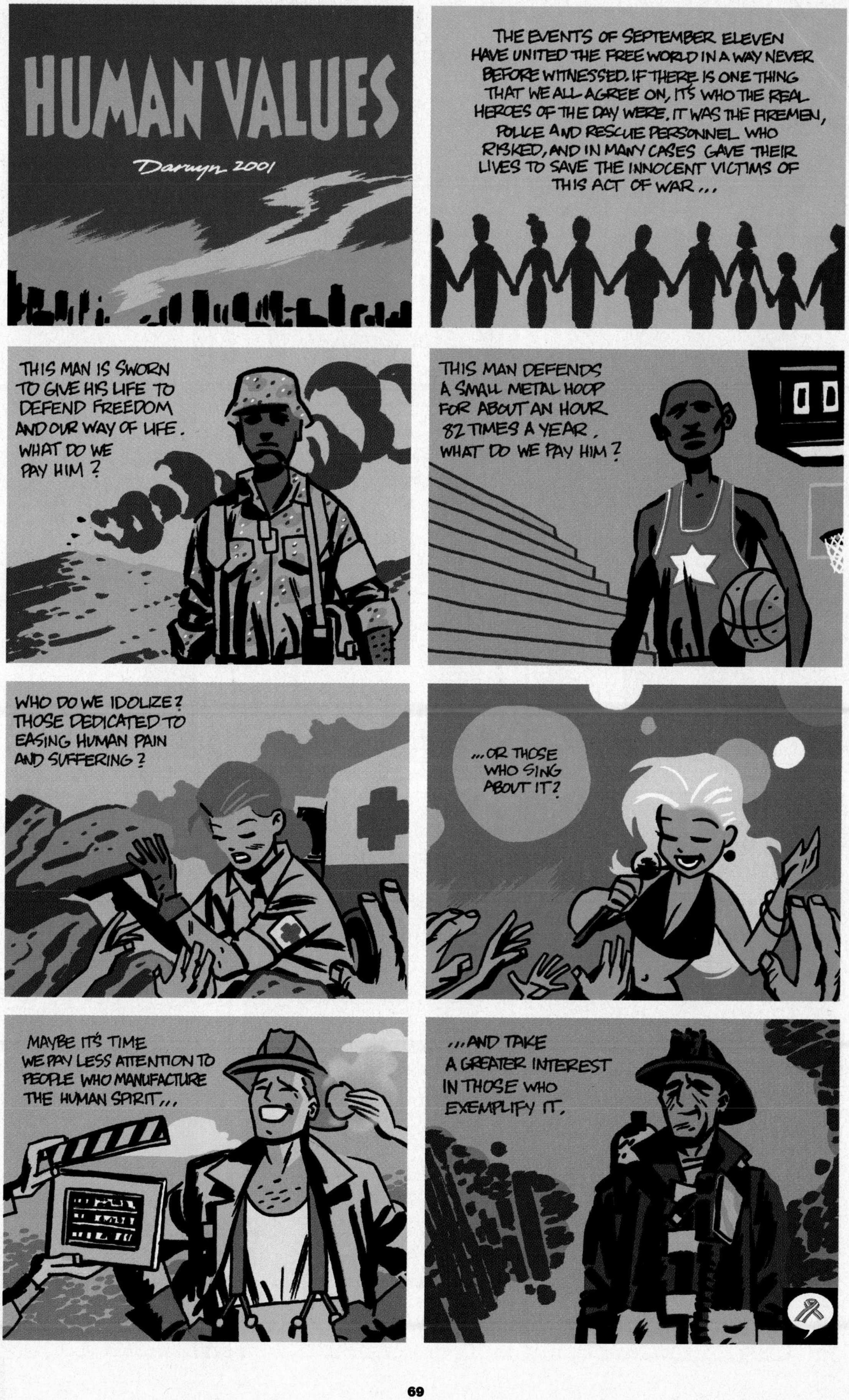
HUMAN VALUES
Darwyn 2001
THE EVENTS OF SEPTEMBER ELEVEN HAVE UNITED THE FREE WORLD IN A WAY NEVER BEFORE WITNESSED. IF THERE IS ONE THING THAT WE ALL AGREE ON, IT'S WHO THE REAL HEROES OF THE DAY WERE. IT WAS THE FIREMEN, POLICE AND RESCUE PERSONNEL WHO RISKED, AND IN MANY CASES GAVE THEIR LIVES TO SAVE THE INNOCENT VICTIMS OF THIS ACT OF WAR...
THIS MAN IS SWORN TO GIVE HIS LIFE TO DEFEND FREEDOM AND OUR WAY OF LIFE. WHAT DO WE PAY HIM?
THIS MAN DEFENDS A SMALL METAL HOOP FOR ABOUT AN HOUR 82 TIMES A YEAR. WHAT DO WE PAY HIM?
WHO DO WE IDOLIZE? THOSE DEDICATED TO EASING HUMAN PAIN AND SUFFERING?
...OR THOSE WHO SING ABOUT IT?
MAYBE IT'S TIME WE PAY LESS ATTENTION TO PEOPLE WHO MANUFACTURE THE HUMAN SPIRIT...
...AND TAKE A GREATER INTEREST IN THOSE WHO EXEMPLIFY IT.

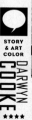

STORY & ART COLOR
DARWYN COOKE

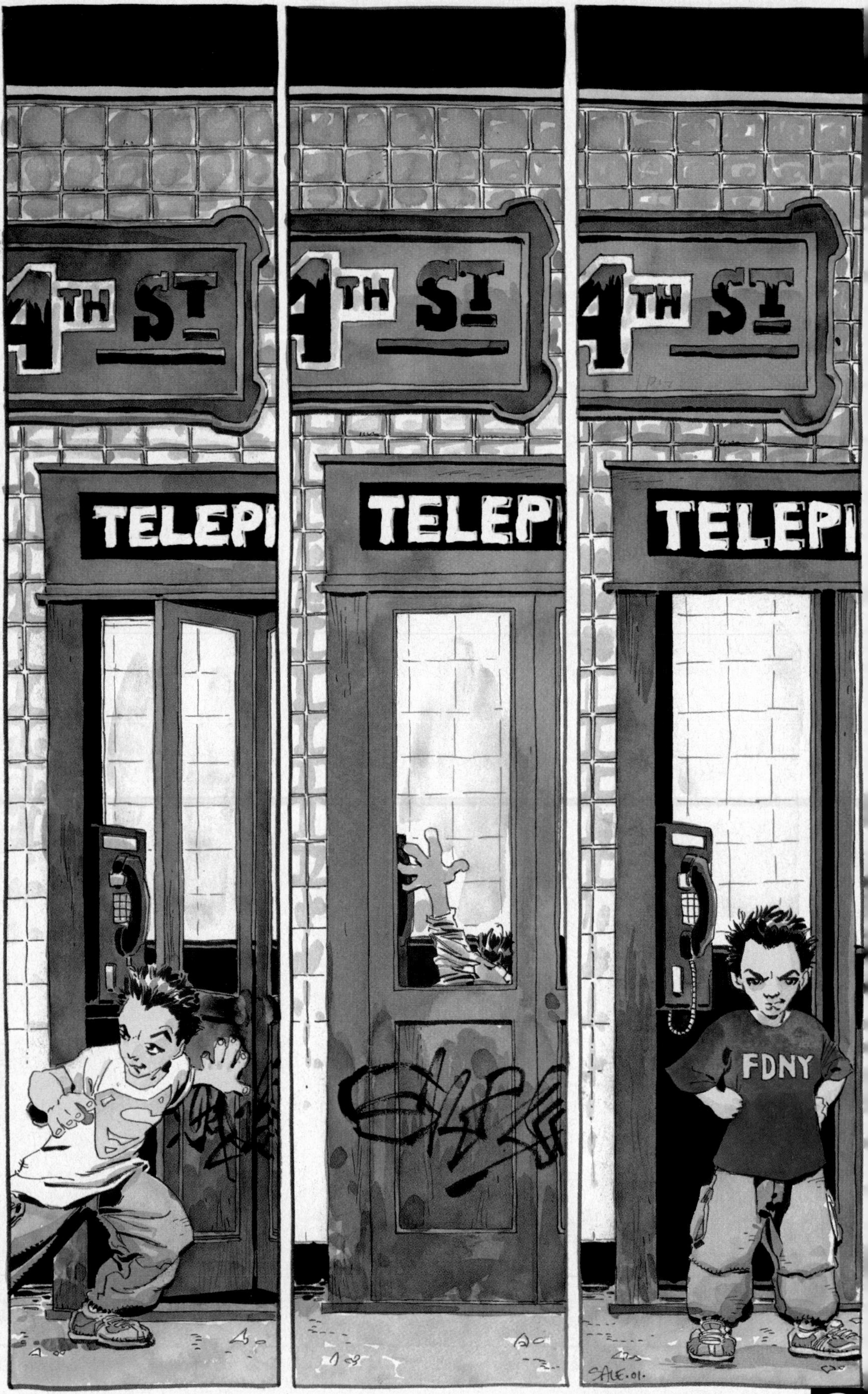
4TH ST
TELEP
4TH ST
TELEP
4TH ST
TELEP
FDNY
SALE.01.

ART TIM SALE
FROM AN IDEA BY CHUCK KIM
COLOR MARK CHIARELLO

A HARD DAY'S NIGHT

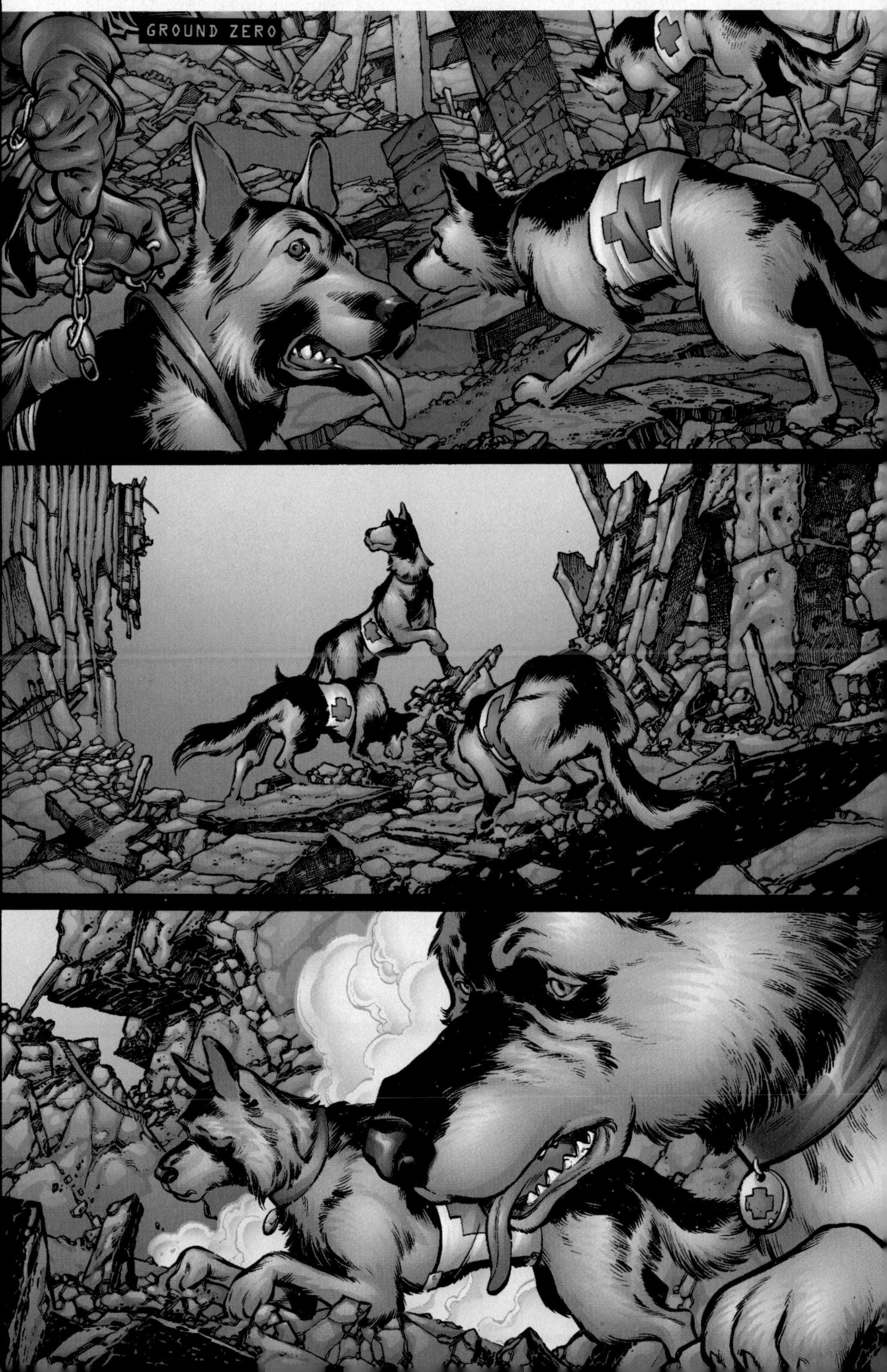
GROUND ZERO

STORY JEPH LOEB ★★★★ ART CARLOS PACHECO AND JESUS MERINO ★★★★ LETTERS COMICRAFT ★★★★ COLOR RICHARD & TANYA HORIE ★★★★

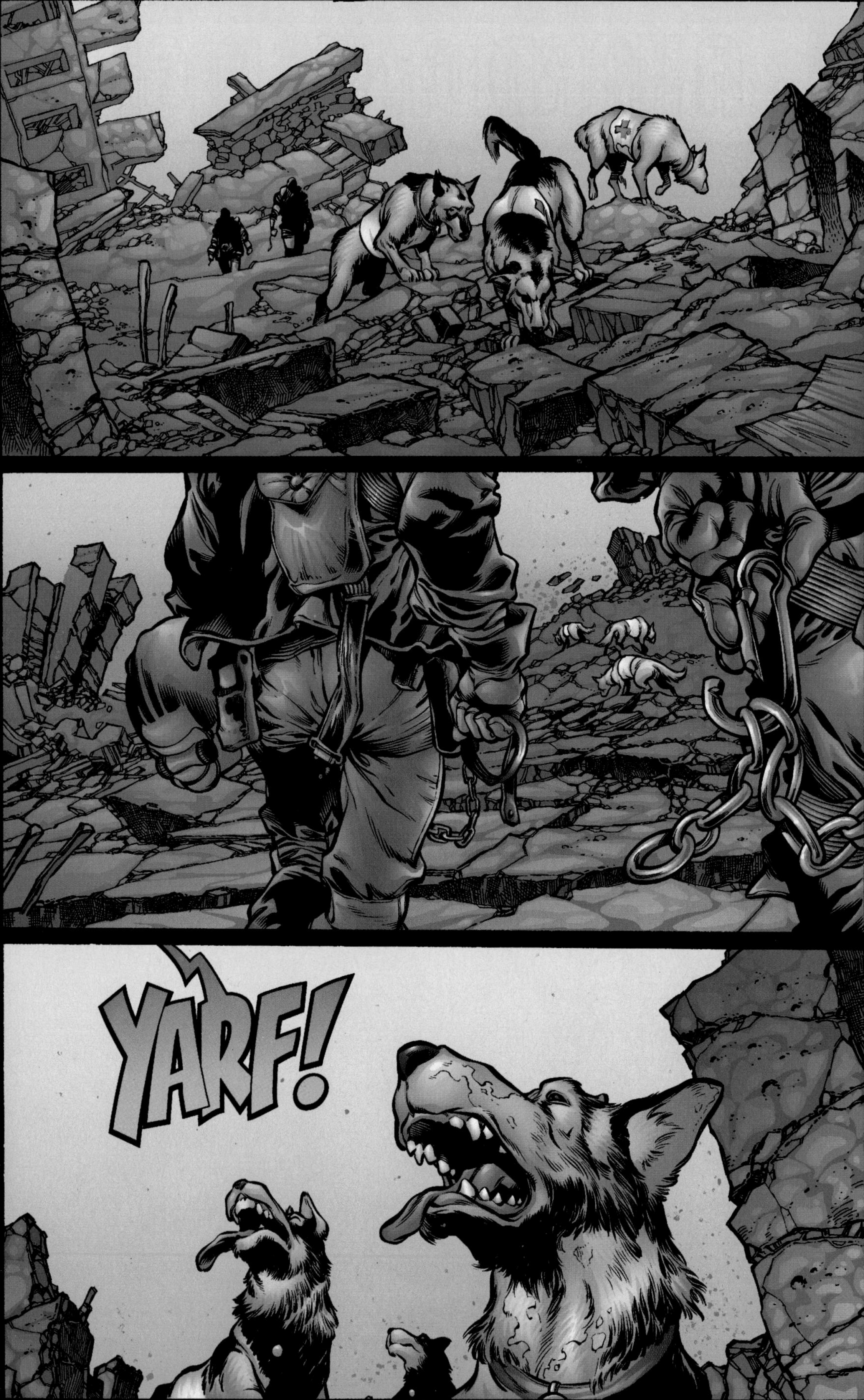
YARF!

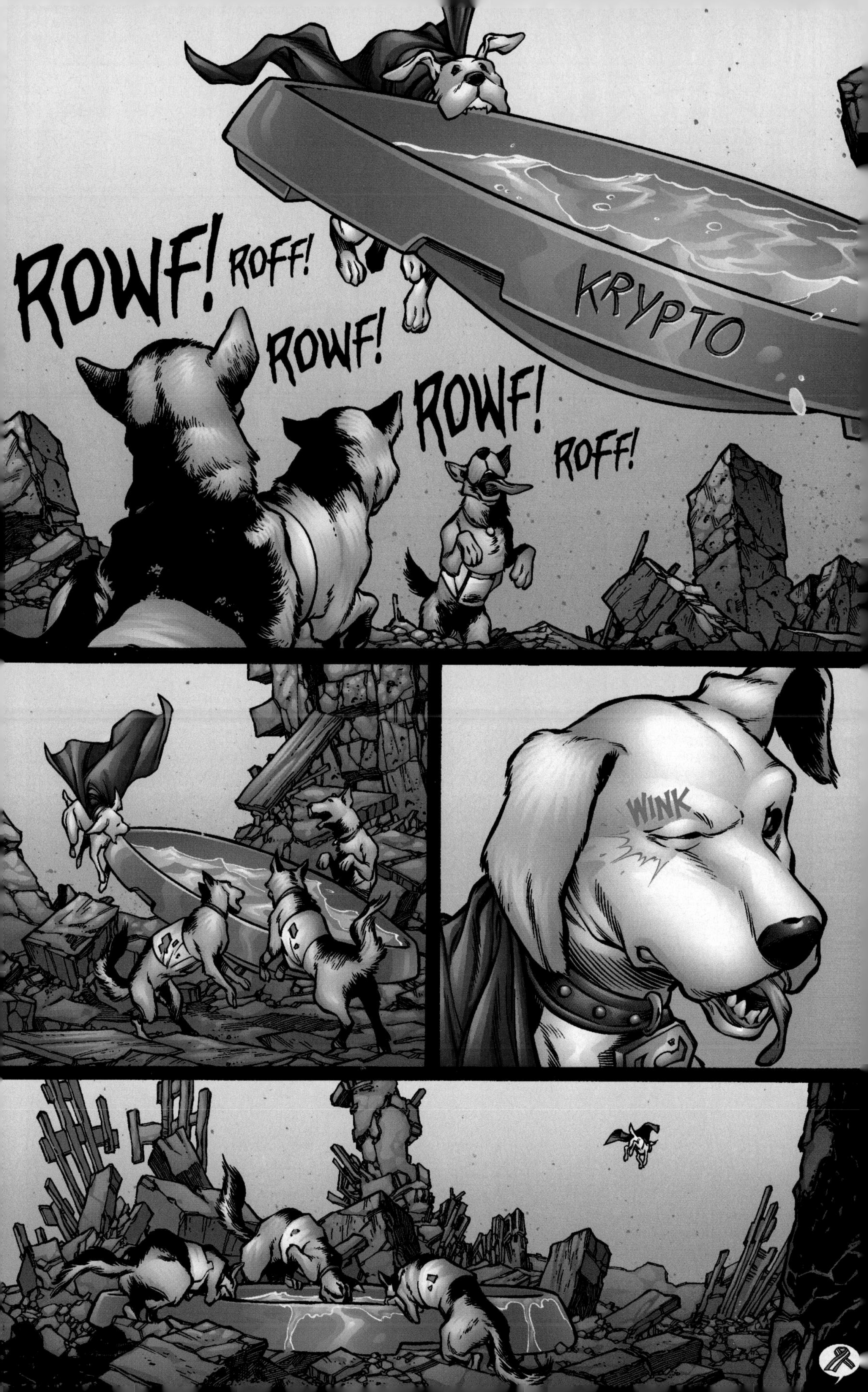
KRYPTO
ROWF! ROFF!
ROWF!
ROWF!
ROFF!
WINK

The FIRSTS DIVISION

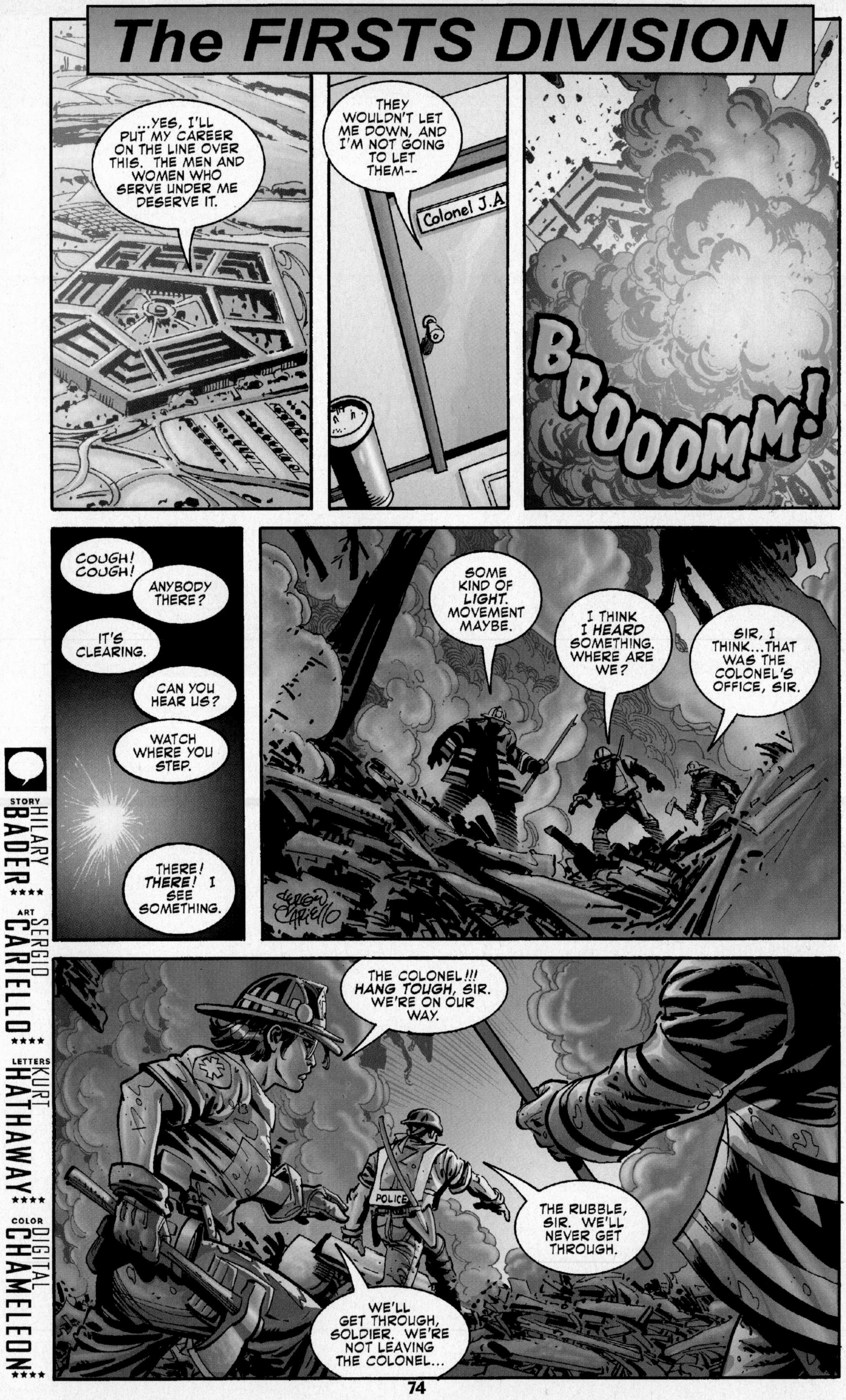

...YES, I'LL PUT MY CAREER ON THE LINE OVER THIS. THE MEN AND WOMEN WHO SERVE UNDER ME DESERVE IT.
THEY WOULDN'T LET ME DOWN, AND I'M NOT GOING TO LET THEM--
Colonel J.A
BROOOOMM!
COUGH! COUGH!
ANYBODY THERE?
IT'S CLEARING.
CAN YOU HEAR US?
WATCH WHERE YOU STEP.
THERE! THERE! I SEE SOMETHING.
SOME KIND OF LIGHT. MOVEMENT MAYBE.
I THINK I HEARD SOMETHING. WHERE ARE WE?
SIR, I THINK...THAT WAS THE COLONEL'S OFFICE, SIR.
THE COLONEL!!! HANG TOUGH, SIR. WE'RE ON OUR WAY.
POLICE
THE RUBBLE, SIR. WE'LL NEVER GET THROUGH.
WE'LL GET THROUGH, SOLDIER. WE'RE NOT LEAVING THE COLONEL...

STORY HILARY BADER
ART SERGIO CARIELLO
LETTERS KURT HATHAWAY
COLOR DIGITAL CHAMELEON

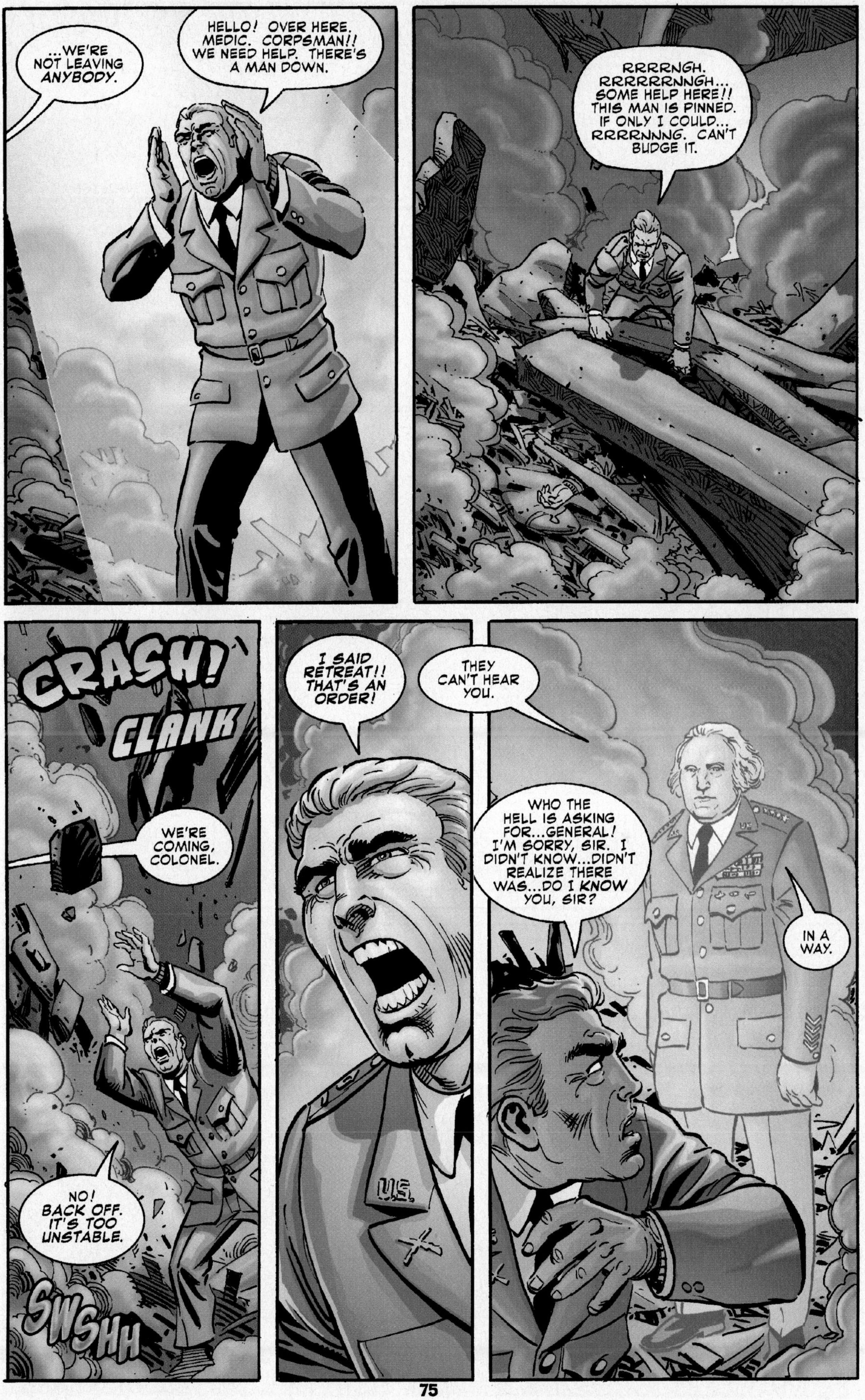
...WE'RE NOT LEAVING ANYBODY.
HELLO! OVER HERE. MEDIC. CORPSMAN!! WE NEED HELP. THERE'S A MAN DOWN.
RRRRNGH. RRRRRRNNGH... SOME HELP HERE!! THIS MAN IS PINNED. IF ONLY I COULD... RRRRNNNG. CAN'T BUDGE IT.
CRASH!
CLANK
WE'RE COMING, COLONEL.
NO! BACK OFF. IT'S TOO UNSTABLE.
SWSHH
I SAID RETREAT!! THAT'S AN ORDER!
THEY CAN'T HEAR YOU.
WHO THE HELL IS ASKING FOR...GENERAL! I'M SORRY, SIR. I DIDN'T KNOW...DIDN'T REALIZE THERE WAS...DO I KNOW YOU, SIR?
IN A WAY.

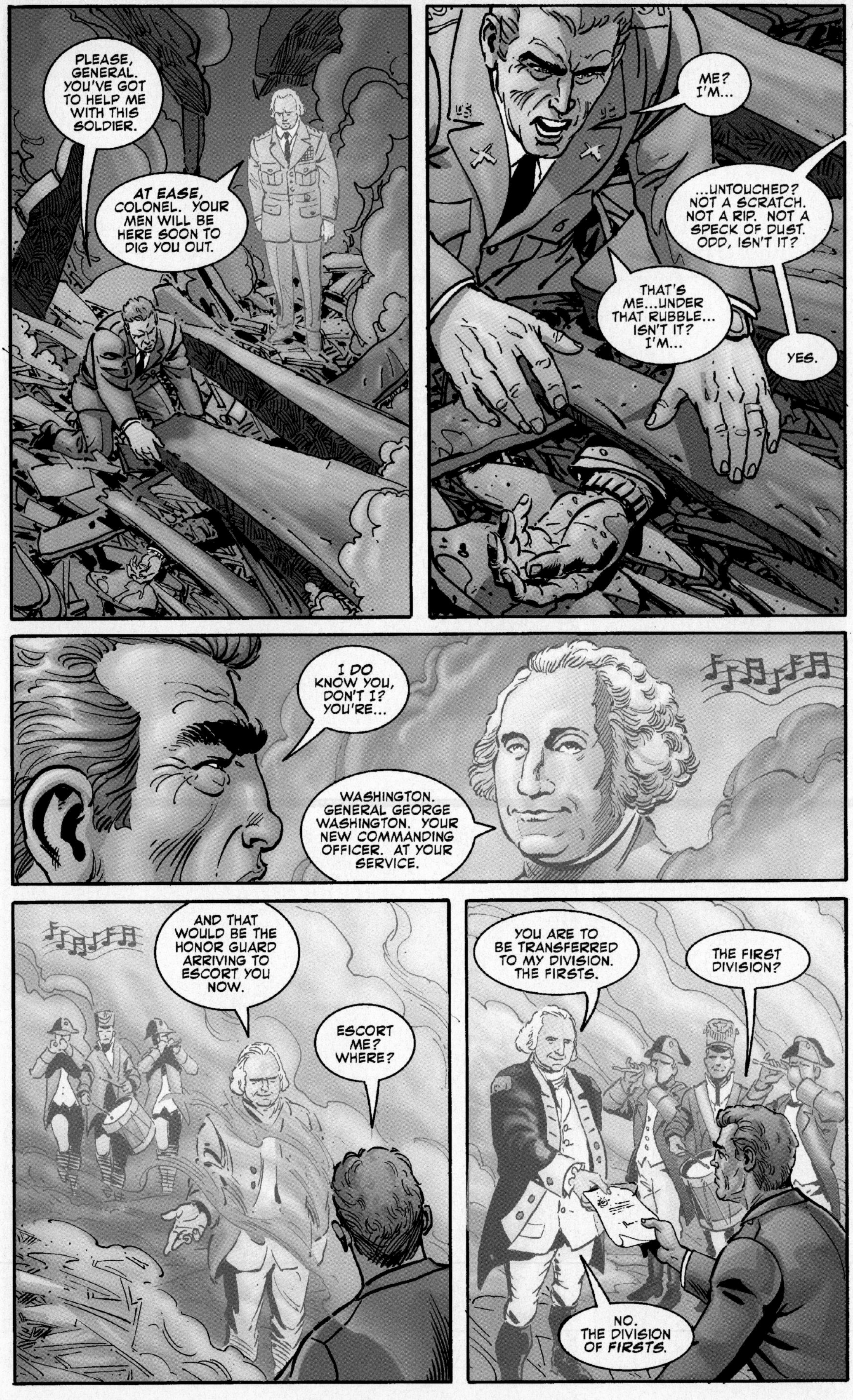
PLEASE, GENERAL. YOU'VE GOT TO HELP ME WITH THIS SOLDIER.
AT EASE, COLONEL. YOUR MEN WILL BE HERE SOON TO DIG YOU OUT.
ME? I'M...
...UNTOUCHED? NOT A SCRATCH. NOT A RIP. NOT A SPECK OF DUST. ODD, ISN'T IT?
THAT'S ME...UNDER THAT RUBBLE... ISN'T IT? I'M...
YES.
I DO KNOW YOU, DON'T I? YOU'RE...
WASHINGTON. GENERAL GEORGE WASHINGTON. YOUR NEW COMMANDING OFFICER. AT YOUR SERVICE.
AND THAT WOULD BE THE HONOR GUARD ARRIVING TO ESCORT YOU NOW.
ESCORT ME? WHERE?
YOU ARE TO BE TRANSFERRED TO MY DIVISION. THE FIRSTS.
THE FIRST DIVISION?
NO. THE DIVISION OF FIRSTS.

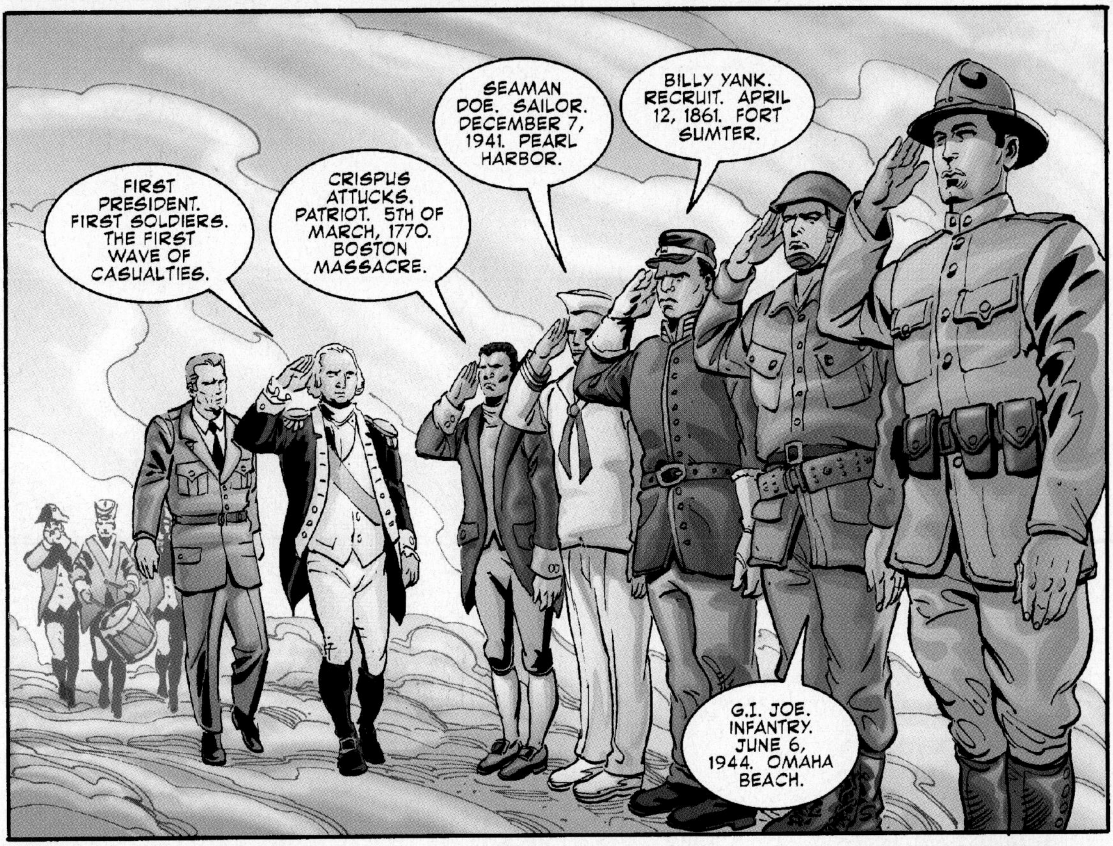
FIRST PRESIDENT. FIRST SOLDIERS. THE FIRST WAVE OF CASUALTIES.
CRISPUS ATTUCKS. PATRIOT. 5TH OF MARCH, 1770. BOSTON MASSACRE.
SEAMAN DOE. SAILOR. DECEMBER 7, 1941. PEARL HARBOR.
BILLY YANK. RECRUIT. APRIL 12, 1861. FORT SUMTER.
G.I. JOE. INFANTRY. JUNE 6, 1944. OMAHA BEACH.

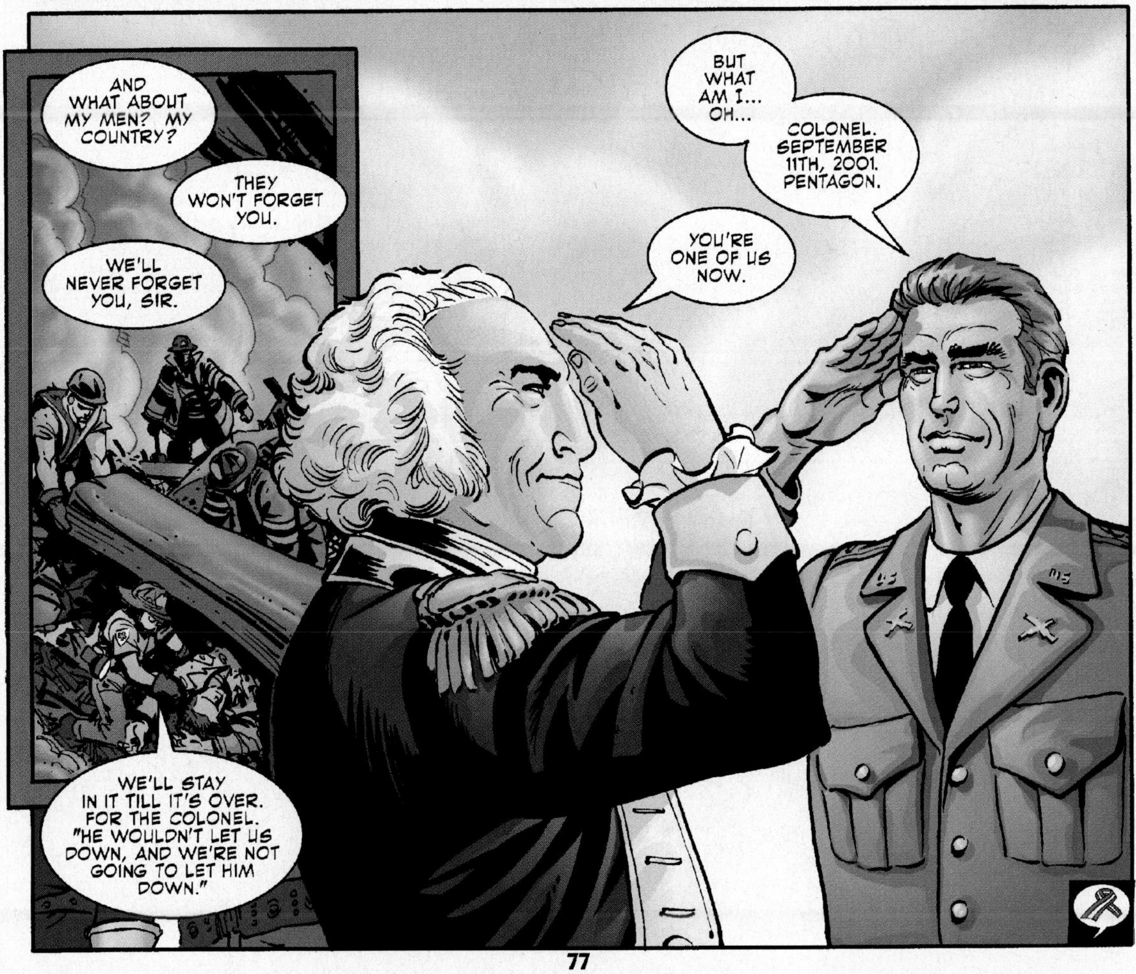
BUT WHAT AM I... OH...
COLONEL. SEPTEMBER 11TH, 2001. PENTAGON.
AND WHAT ABOUT MY MEN? MY COUNTRY?
THEY WON'T FORGET YOU.
WE'LL NEVER FORGET YOU, SIR.
YOU'RE ONE OF US NOW.
WE'LL STAY IN IT TILL IT'S OVER. FOR THE COLONEL. "HE WOULDN'T LET US DOWN, AND WE'RE NOT GOING TO LET HIM DOWN."

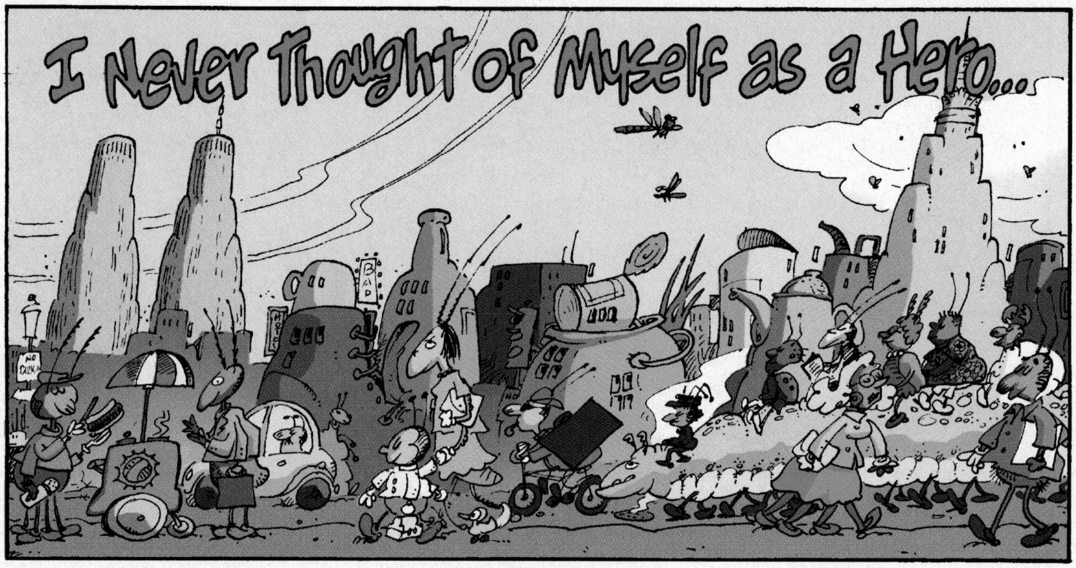
I Never Thought of Myself as a Hero...

I'm just another salarybug swarming into *ANTHATTAN* on his morning commute.

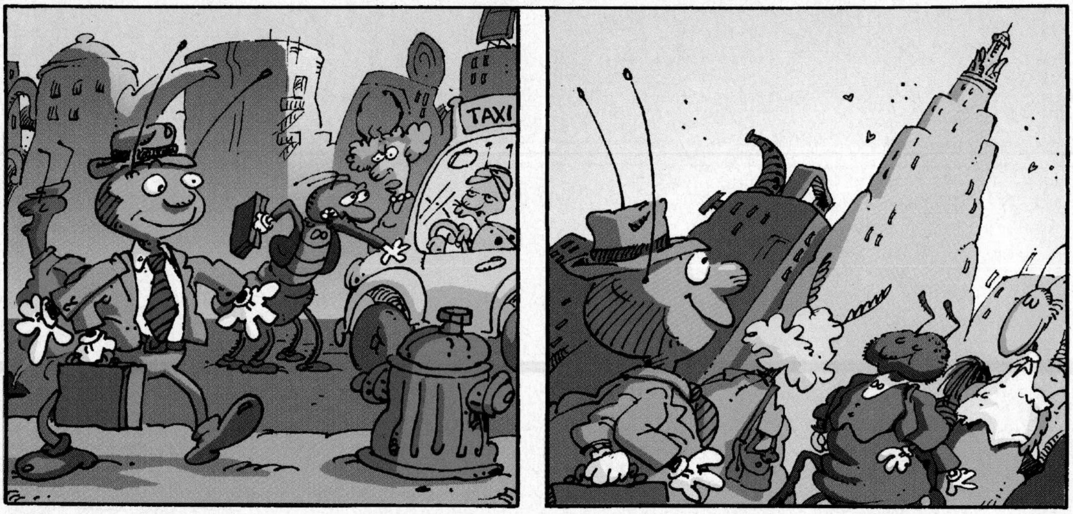
TAXI

Hustling into midtown and hopping the elevator to get into work on time never required much in the way of bravery.

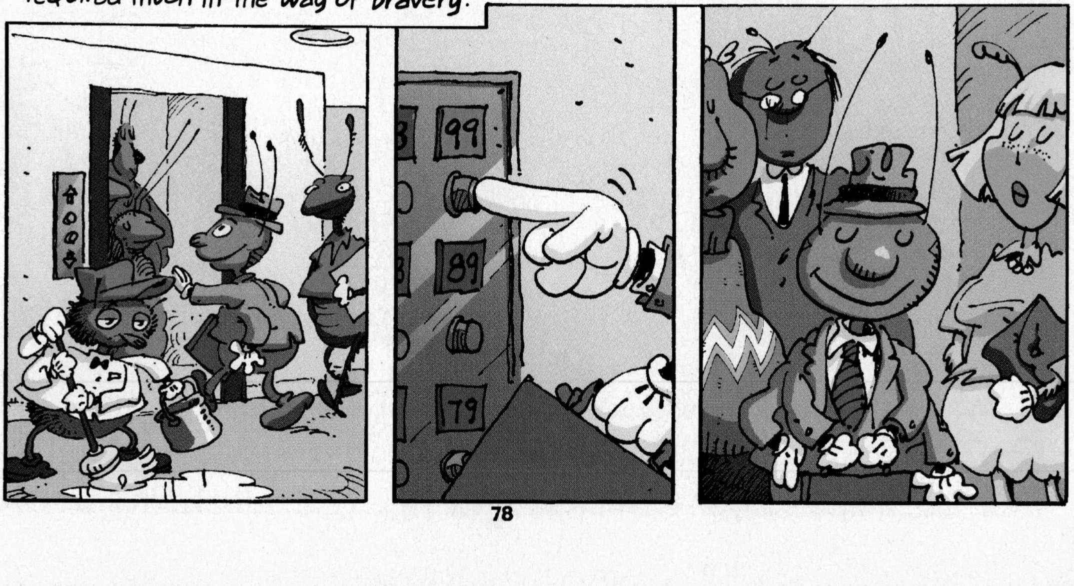
99
89
79

STORY RICK VEITCH
ART SERGIO ARAGONÉS
LETTERS JOHN COSTANZA
COLOR WILDSTORM

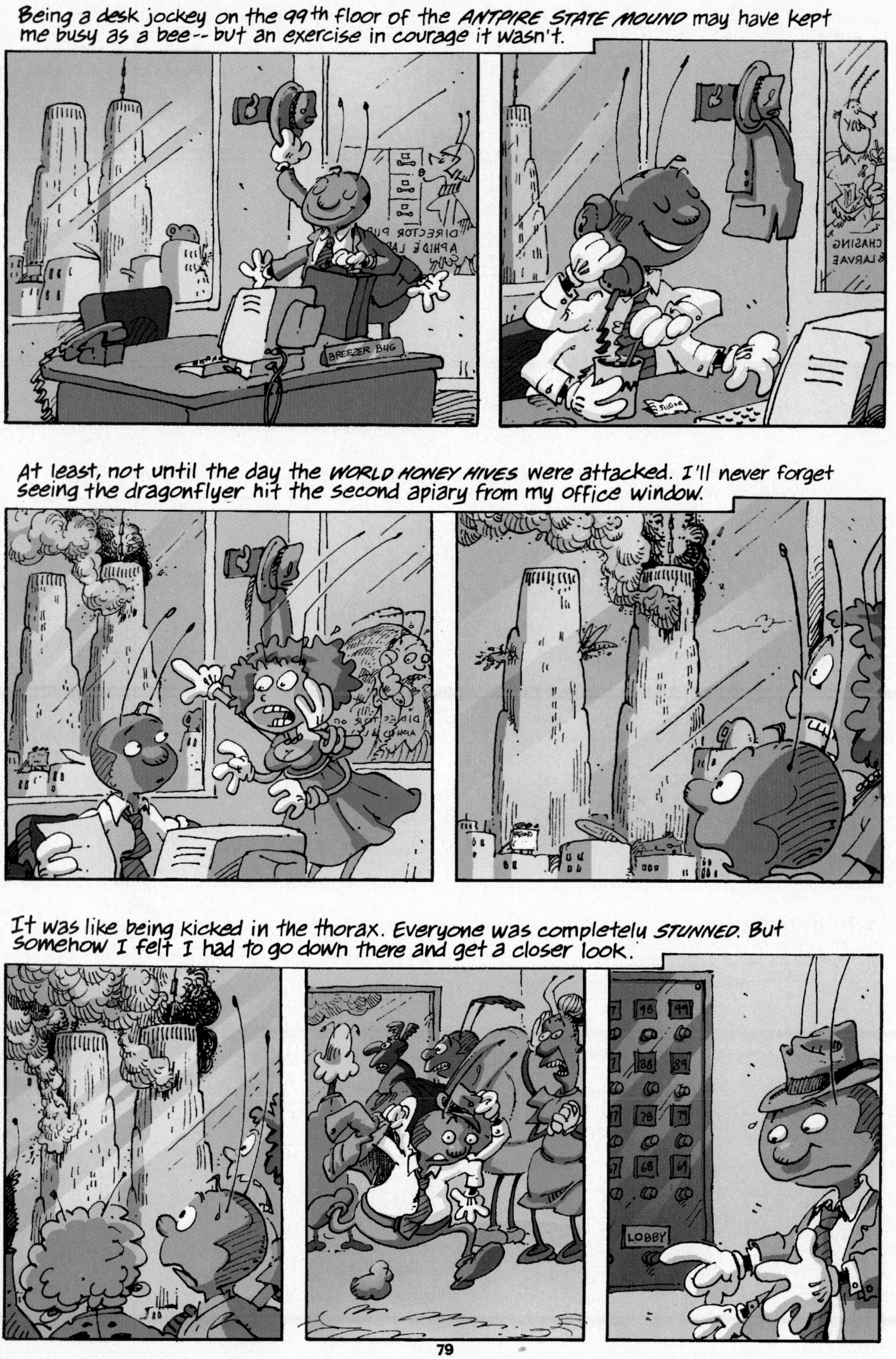
Being a desk jockey on the 99th floor of the ANTPIRE STATE MOUND may have kept me busy as a bee-- but an exercise in courage it wasn't.
BREEZER BUG
At least, not until the day the WORLD HONEY HIVES were attacked. I'll never forget seeing the dragonflyer hit the second apiary from my office window.
It was like being kicked in the thorax. Everyone was completelu STUNNED. But somehow I felt I had to go down there and get a closer look.
LOBBY

I wasn't alone. Hordes of workers were pouring from their offices and marching downtown, like colonies of moths attracted to a single dancing flame.

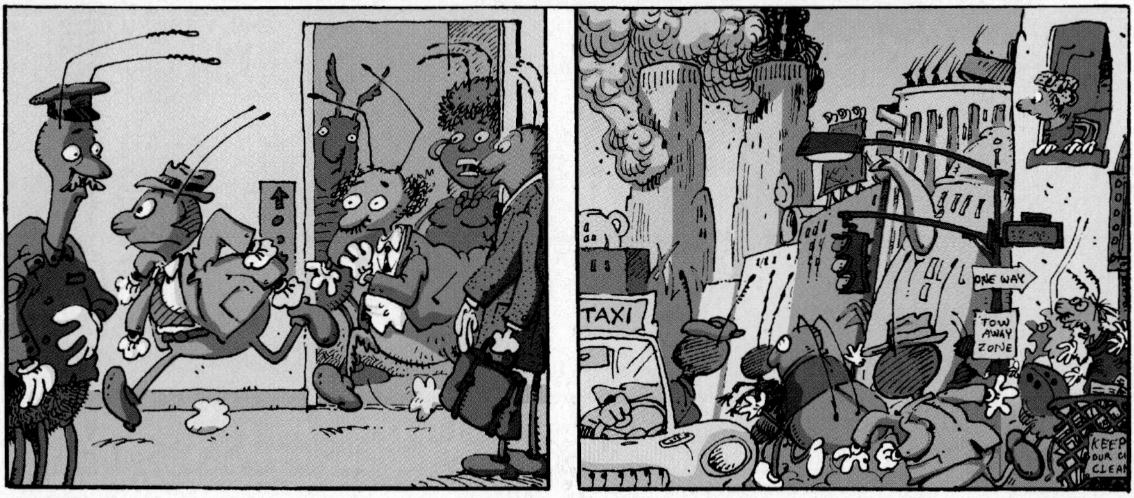
TAXI
ONE WAY
TOW AWAY ZONE

When I reached the scene, emergency teams were already on the job, running into the burning hives and leading swarms to safety.

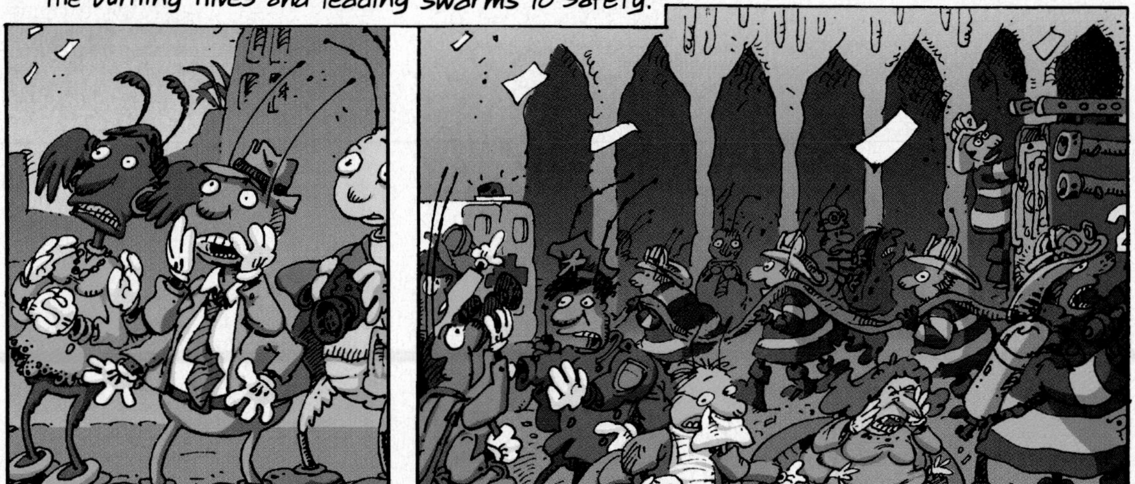

Those *FIREANTS* were the *REAL* heroes. But even they couldn't save everyone.

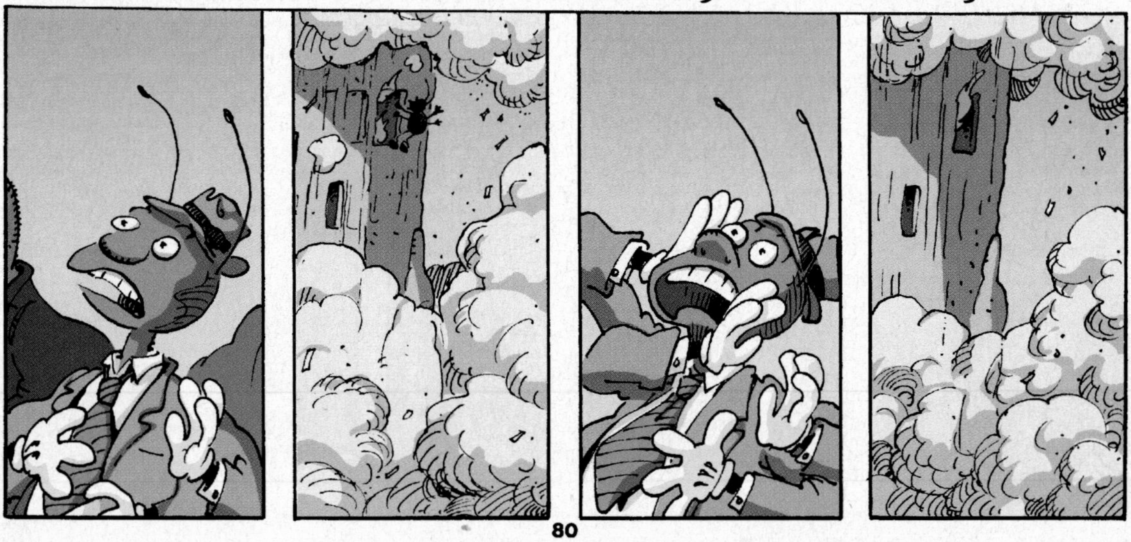

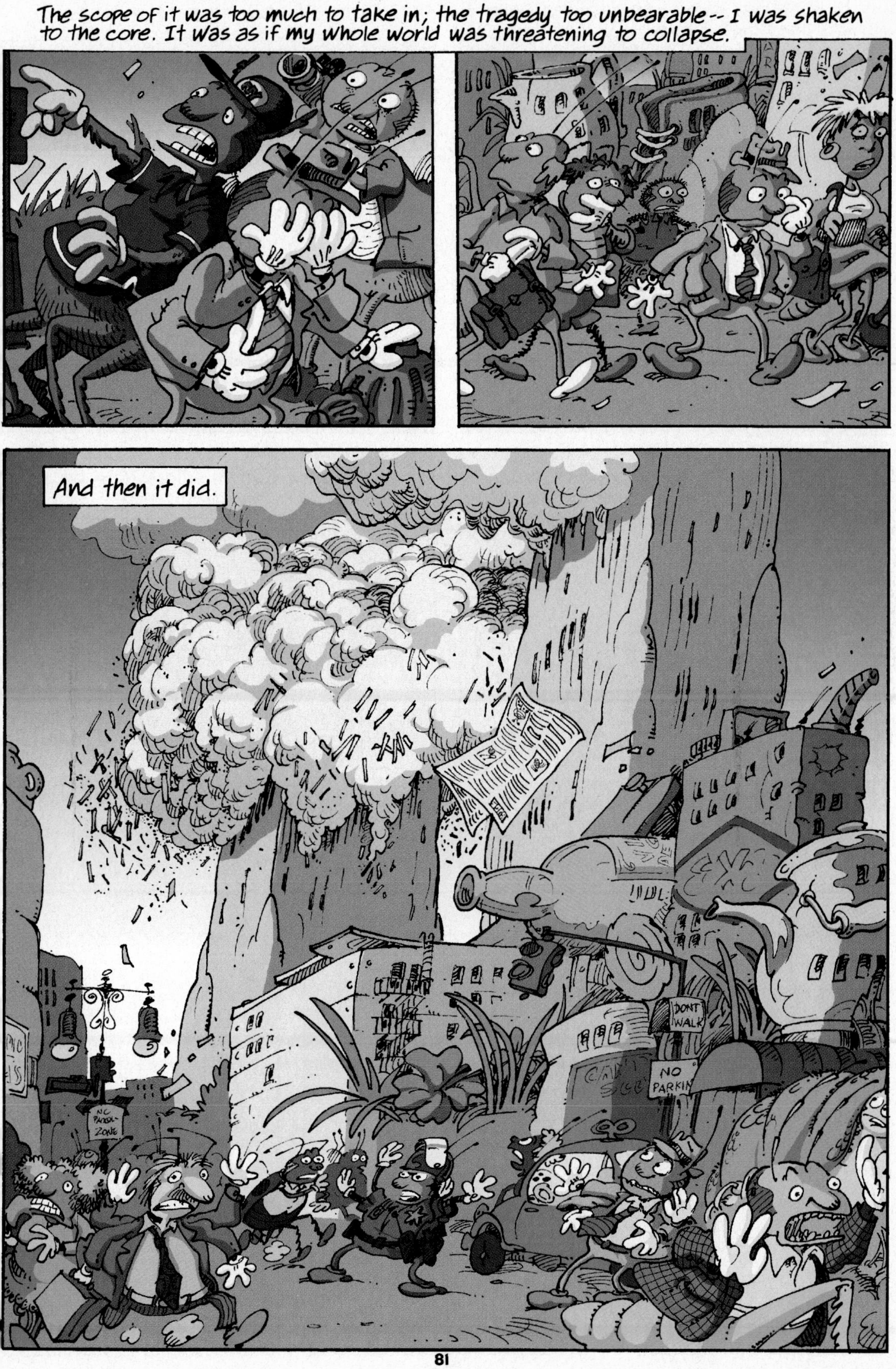
The scope of it was too much to take in; the tragedy too unbearable -- I was shaken to the core. It was as if my whole world was threatening to collapse.
And then it did.
DONT WALK
NO PARKIN

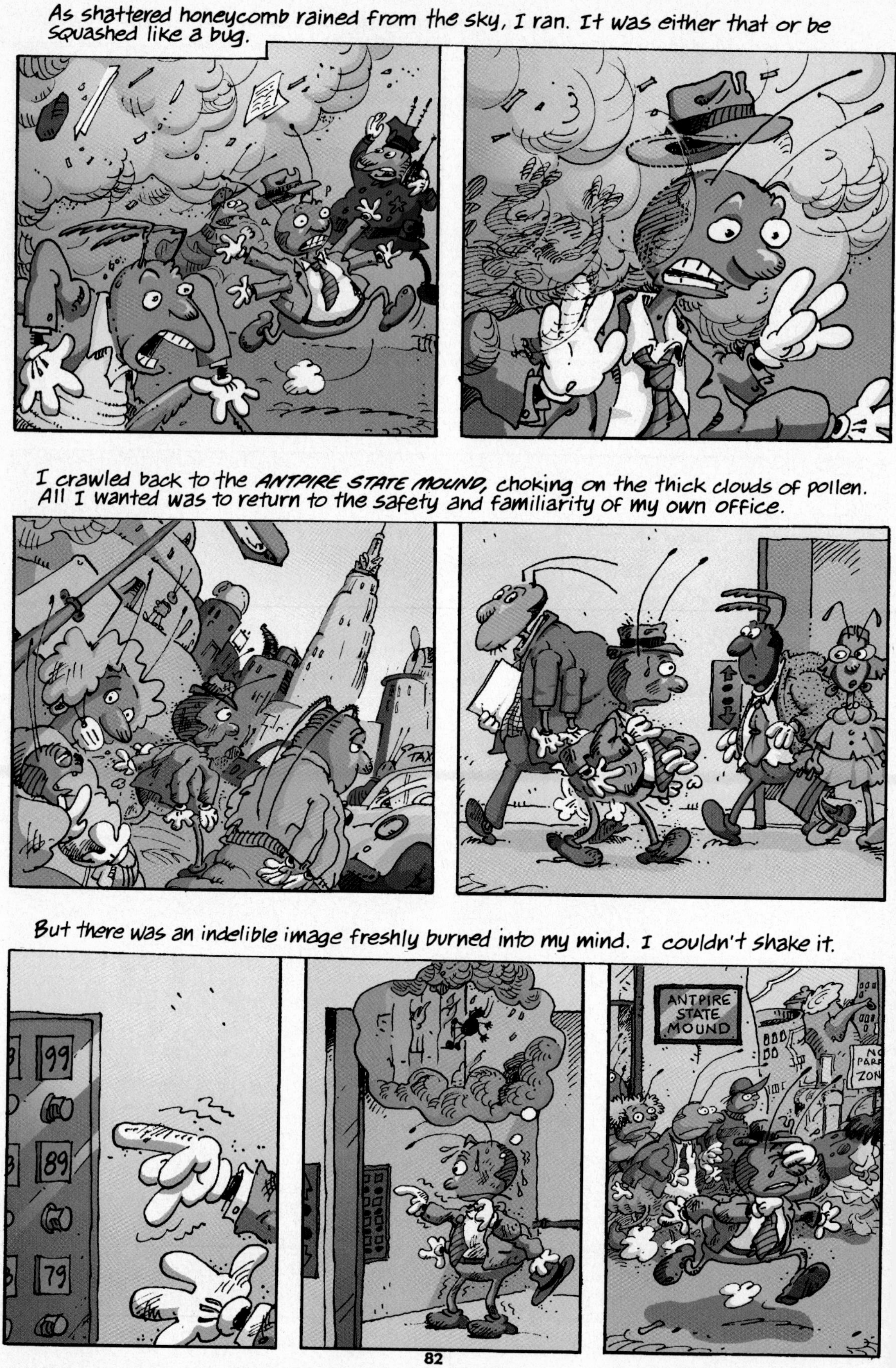
As shattered honeycomb rained from the sky, I ran. It was either that or be squashed like a bug.
I crawled back to the ANTPIRE STATE MOUND, choking on the thick clouds of pollen. All I wanted was to return to the safety and familiarity of my own office.
But there was an indelible image freshly burned into my mind. I couldn't shake it.
99
89
79
ANTPIRE STATE MOUND

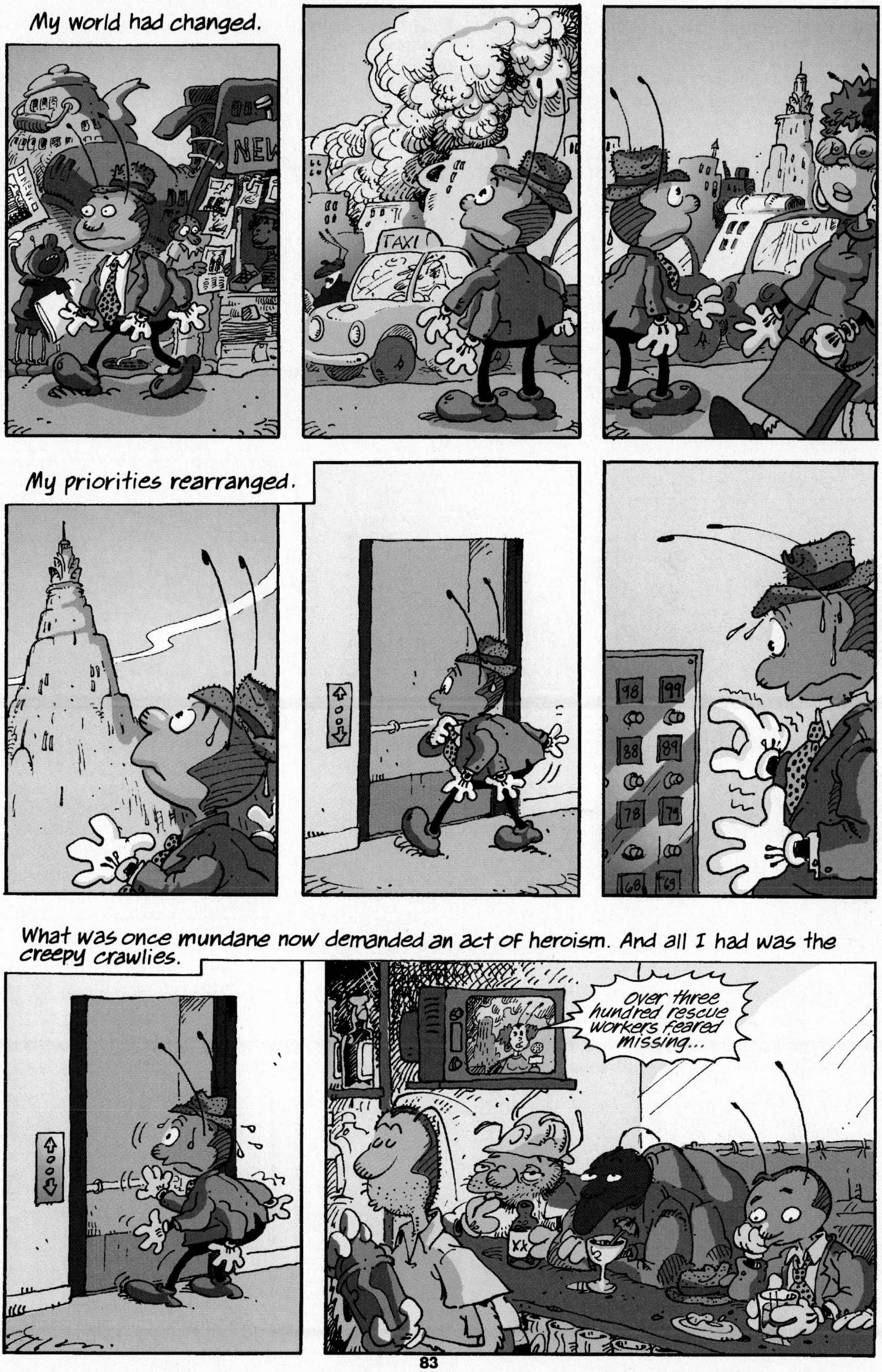
My world had changed.
NEW
TAXI
My priorities rearranged.
98 99
88 89
78 79
68 69
What was once mundane now demanded an act of heroism. And all I had was the creepy crawlies.
Over three hundred rescue workers feared missing...
XX

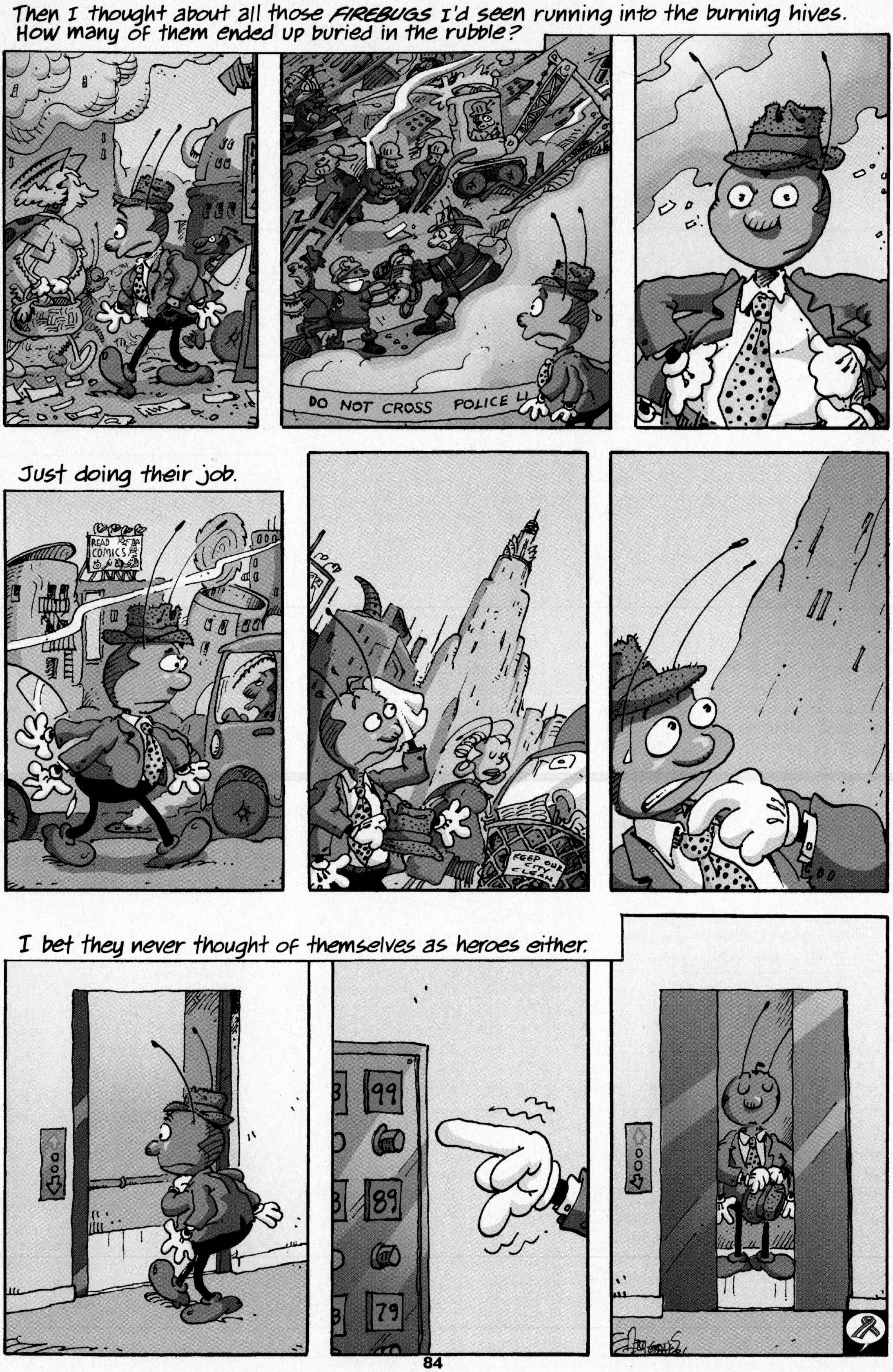
Then I thought about all those FIREBUGS I'd seen running into the burning hives. How many of them ended up buried in the rubble?
DO NOT CROSS POLICE LI
Just doing their job.
READ COMICS
KEEP OUR CITY CLEAN
I bet they never thought of themselves as heroes either.
99
89
79

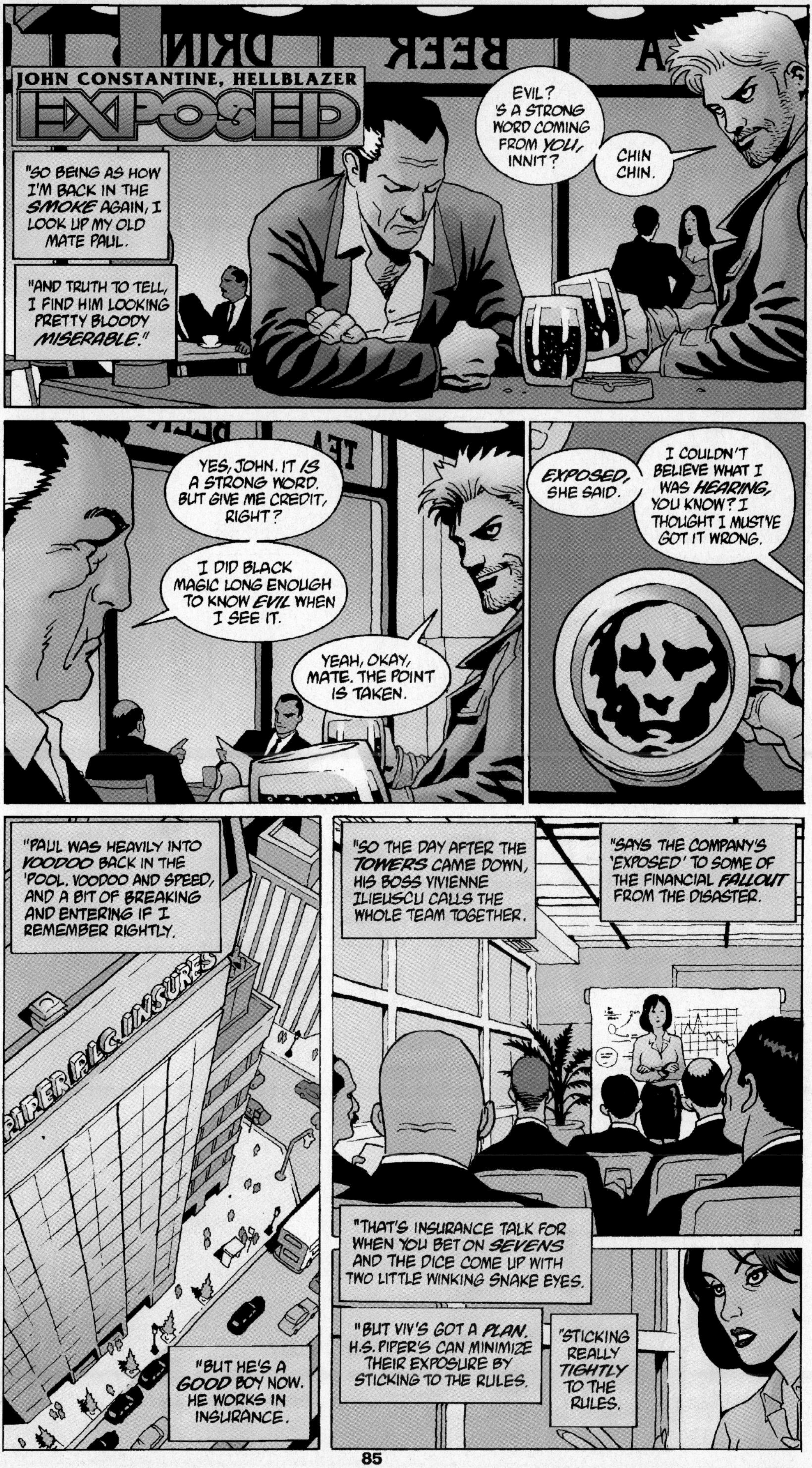
DRIN
BEER
A
JOHN CONSTANTINE, HELLBLAZER
EXPOSED
"SO BEING AS HOW I'M BACK IN THE SMOKE AGAIN, I LOOK UP MY OLD MATE PAUL.
"AND TRUTH TO TELL, I FIND HIM LOOKING PRETTY BLOODY MISERABLE."
EVIL? 'S A STRONG WORD COMING FROM YOU, INNIT?
CHIN CHIN.
TEA
YES, JOHN. IT IS A STRONG WORD. BUT GIVE ME CREDIT, RIGHT?
I DID BLACK MAGIC LONG ENOUGH TO KNOW EVIL WHEN I SEE IT.
YEAH, OKAY, MATE. THE POINT IS TAKEN.
EXPOSED, SHE SAID.
I COULDN'T BELIEVE WHAT I WAS HEARING, YOU KNOW? I THOUGHT I MUST'VE GOT IT WRONG.
"PAUL WAS HEAVILY INTO VOODOO BACK IN THE 'POOL. VOODOO AND SPEED, AND A BIT OF BREAKING AND ENTERING IF I REMEMBER RIGHTLY.
PIPER PLC INSURES
"BUT HE'S A GOOD BOY NOW. HE WORKS IN INSURANCE.
"SO THE DAY AFTER THE TOWERS CAME DOWN, HIS BOSS VIVIENNE ILIEUSCU CALLS THE WHOLE TEAM TOGETHER.
"SAYS THE COMPANY'S 'EXPOSED' TO SOME OF THE FINANCIAL FALLOUT FROM THE DISASTER.
"THAT'S INSURANCE TALK FOR WHEN YOU BET ON SEVENS AND THE DICE COME UP WITH TWO LITTLE WINKING SNAKE EYES.
"BUT VIV'S GOT A PLAN. H.S. PIPER'S CAN MINIMIZE THEIR EXPOSURE BY STICKING TO THE RULES.
"STICKING REALLY TIGHTLY TO THE RULES.

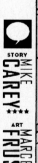

STORY MIKE CAREY
ART MARCELO FRUSIN
LETTERS CLEM ROBINS
COLOR PATRICIA MULVIHILL

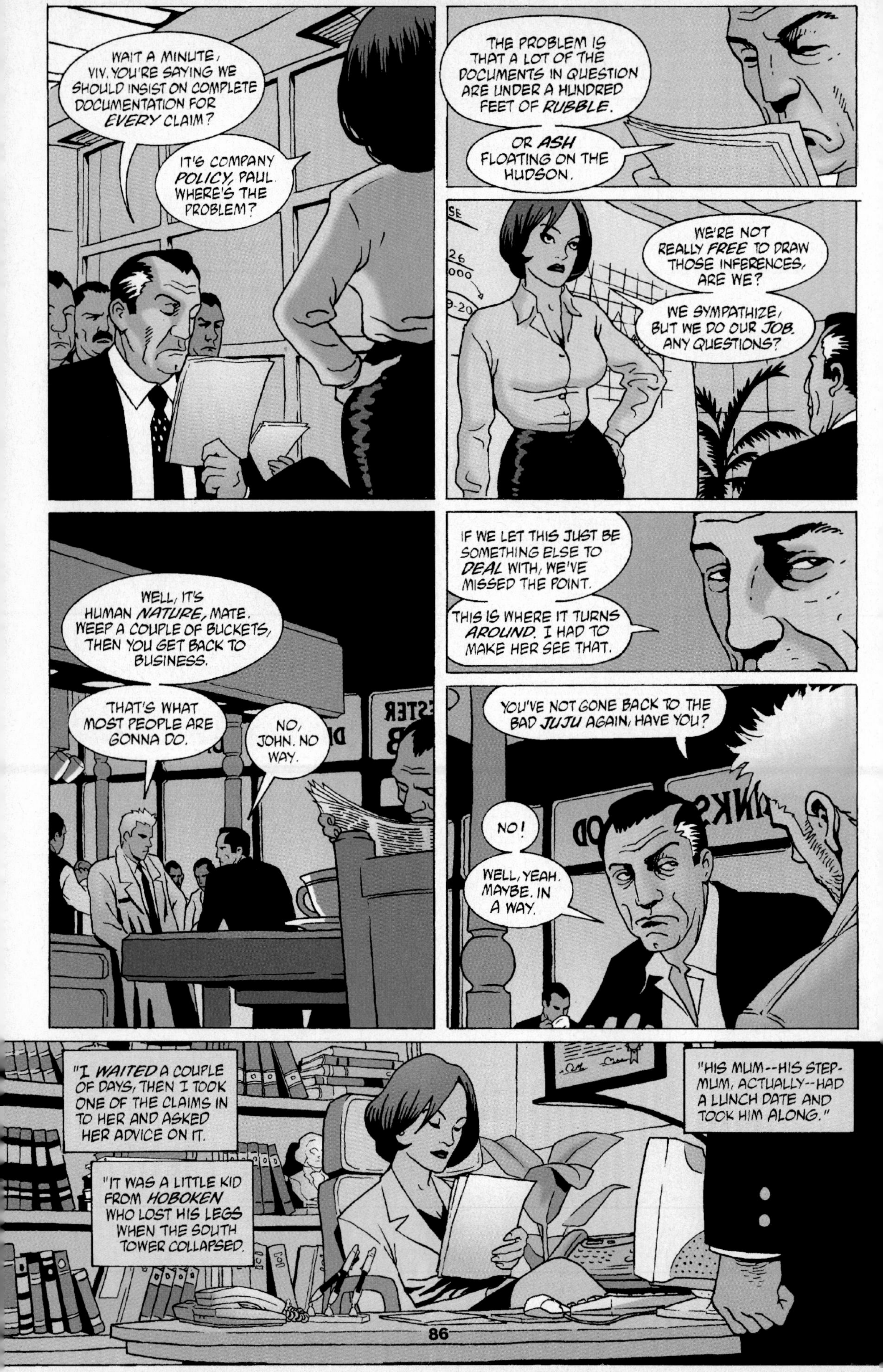
WAIT A MINUTE, VIV. YOU'RE SAYING WE SHOULD INSIST ON COMPLETE DOCUMENTATION FOR EVERY CLAIM?
IT'S COMPANY POLICY, PAUL. WHERE'S THE PROBLEM?
THE PROBLEM IS THAT A LOT OF THE DOCUMENTS IN QUESTION ARE UNDER A HUNDRED FEET OF RUBBLE.
OR ASH FLOATING ON THE HUDSON.
WE'RE NOT REALLY FREE TO DRAW THOSE INFERENCES, ARE WE?
WE SYMPATHIZE, BUT WE DO OUR JOB. ANY QUESTIONS?
WELL, IT'S HUMAN NATURE, MATE. WEEP A COUPLE OF BUCKETS, THEN YOU GET BACK TO BUSINESS.
THAT'S WHAT MOST PEOPLE ARE GONNA DO.
NO, JOHN. NO WAY.
IF WE LET THIS JUST BE SOMETHING ELSE TO DEAL WITH, WE'VE MISSED THE POINT.
THIS IS WHERE IT TURNS AROUND. I HAD TO MAKE HER SEE THAT.
YOU'VE NOT GONE BACK TO THE BAD JUJU AGAIN, HAVE YOU?
NO!
WELL, YEAH. MAYBE. IN A WAY.
"I WAITED A COUPLE OF DAYS, THEN I TOOK ONE OF THE CLAIMS IN TO HER AND ASKED HER ADVICE ON IT.
"IT WAS A LITTLE KID FROM HOBOKEN WHO LOST HIS LEGS WHEN THE SOUTH TOWER COLLAPSED.
"HIS MUM--HIS STEP-MUM, ACTUALLY--HAD A LUNCH DATE AND TOOK HIM ALONG."

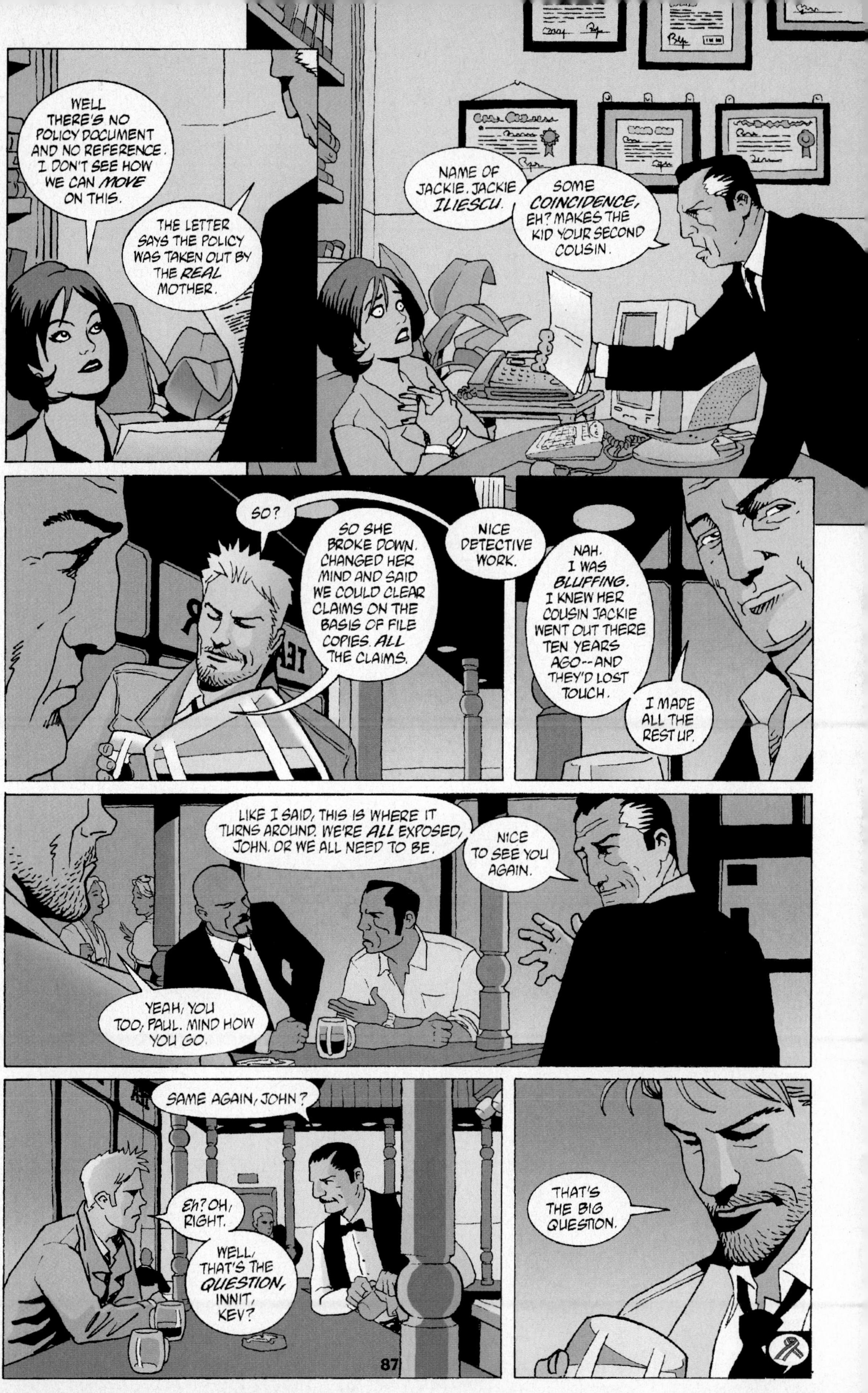
WELL THERE'S NO POLICY DOCUMENT AND NO REFERENCE. I DON'T SEE HOW WE CAN MOVE ON THIS.
THE LETTER SAYS THE POLICY WAS TAKEN OUT BY THE REAL MOTHER.
NAME OF JACKIE. JACKIE ILIESCU.
SOME COINCIDENCE, EH? MAKES THE KID YOUR SECOND COUSIN.
SO?
SO SHE BROKE DOWN. CHANGED HER MIND AND SAID WE COULD CLEAR CLAIMS ON THE BASIS OF FILE COPIES. ALL THE CLAIMS.
NICE DETECTIVE WORK.
NAH. I WAS BLUFFING. I KNEW HER COUSIN JACKIE WENT OUT THERE TEN YEARS AGO--AND THEY'D LOST TOUCH.
I MADE ALL THE REST UP.
LIKE I SAID, THIS IS WHERE IT TURNS AROUND. WE'RE ALL EXPOSED, JOHN. OR WE ALL NEED TO BE.
NICE TO SEE YOU AGAIN.
YEAH, YOU TOO, PAUL. MIND HOW YOU GO.
SAME AGAIN, JOHN?
Eh? OH, RIGHT.
WELL, THAT'S THE QUESTION, INNIT, KEV?
THAT'S THE BIG QUESTION.

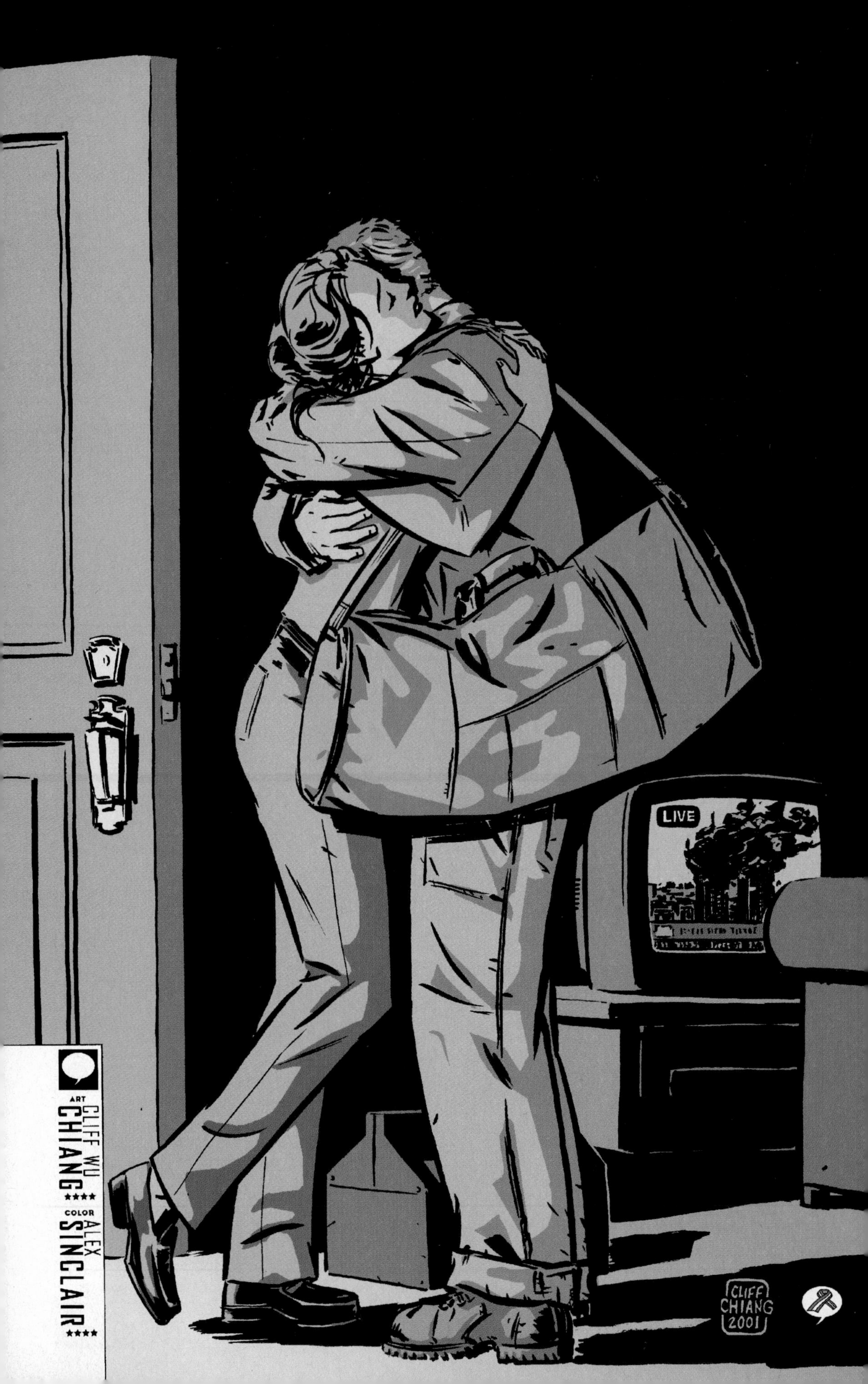
LIVE
CLIFF CHIANG 2001
ART CLIFF WU CHIANG ★★★★
COLOR ALEX SINCLAIR ★★★★

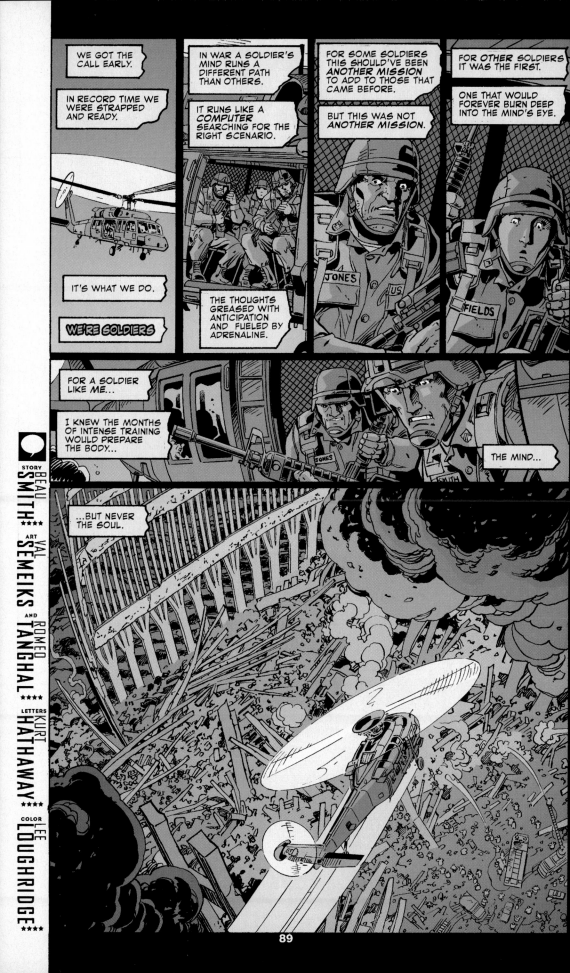

WE GOT THE CALL EARLY.

IN RECORD TIME WE WERE STRAPPED AND READY.

IN WAR A SOLDIER'S MIND RUNS A DIFFERENT PATH THAN OTHERS.

IT RUNS LIKE A *COMPUTER* SEARCHING FOR THE RIGHT SCENARIO.

FOR SOME SOLDIERS THIS SHOULD'VE BEEN *ANOTHER MISSION* TO ADD TO THOSE THAT CAME BEFORE.

BUT THIS WAS NOT *ANOTHER MISSION.*

FOR *OTHER* SOLDIERS IT WAS THE FIRST.

ONE THAT WOULD FOREVER BURN DEEP INTO THE MIND'S EYE.

IT'S WHAT WE DO.

WE'RE SOLDIERS

THE THOUGHTS GREASED WITH ANTICIPATION AND FUELED BY ADRENALINE.

FOR A SOLDIER LIKE ME...

I KNEW THE MONTHS OF INTENSE TRAINING WOULD PREPARE THE BODY...

THE MIND...

...BUT NEVER THE SOUL.

STORY
BEAU SMITH ****

ART
VAL SEMEIKS **** AND ROMEO TANGHAL ****

LETTERS
KURT HATHAWAY ****

COLOR
LEE LOUGHRIDGE ****

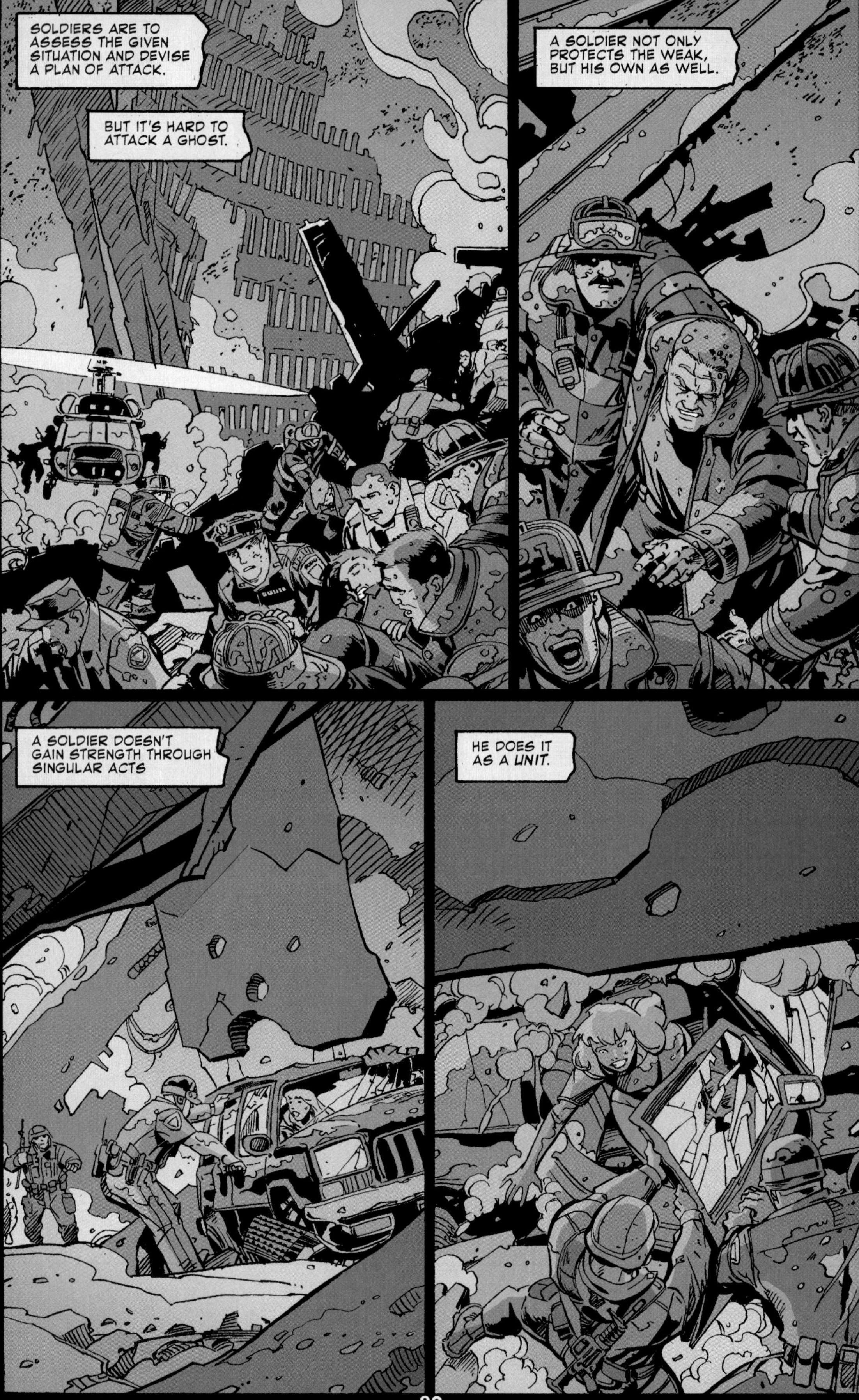
SOLDIERS ARE TO ASSESS THE GIVEN SITUATION AND DEVISE A PLAN OF ATTACK.
BUT IT'S HARD TO ATTACK A GHOST.
A SOLDIER NOT ONLY PROTECTS THE WEAK, BUT HIS OWN AS WELL.
A SOLDIER DOESN'T GAIN STRENGTH THROUGH SINGULAR ACTS
HE DOES IT AS A UNIT.

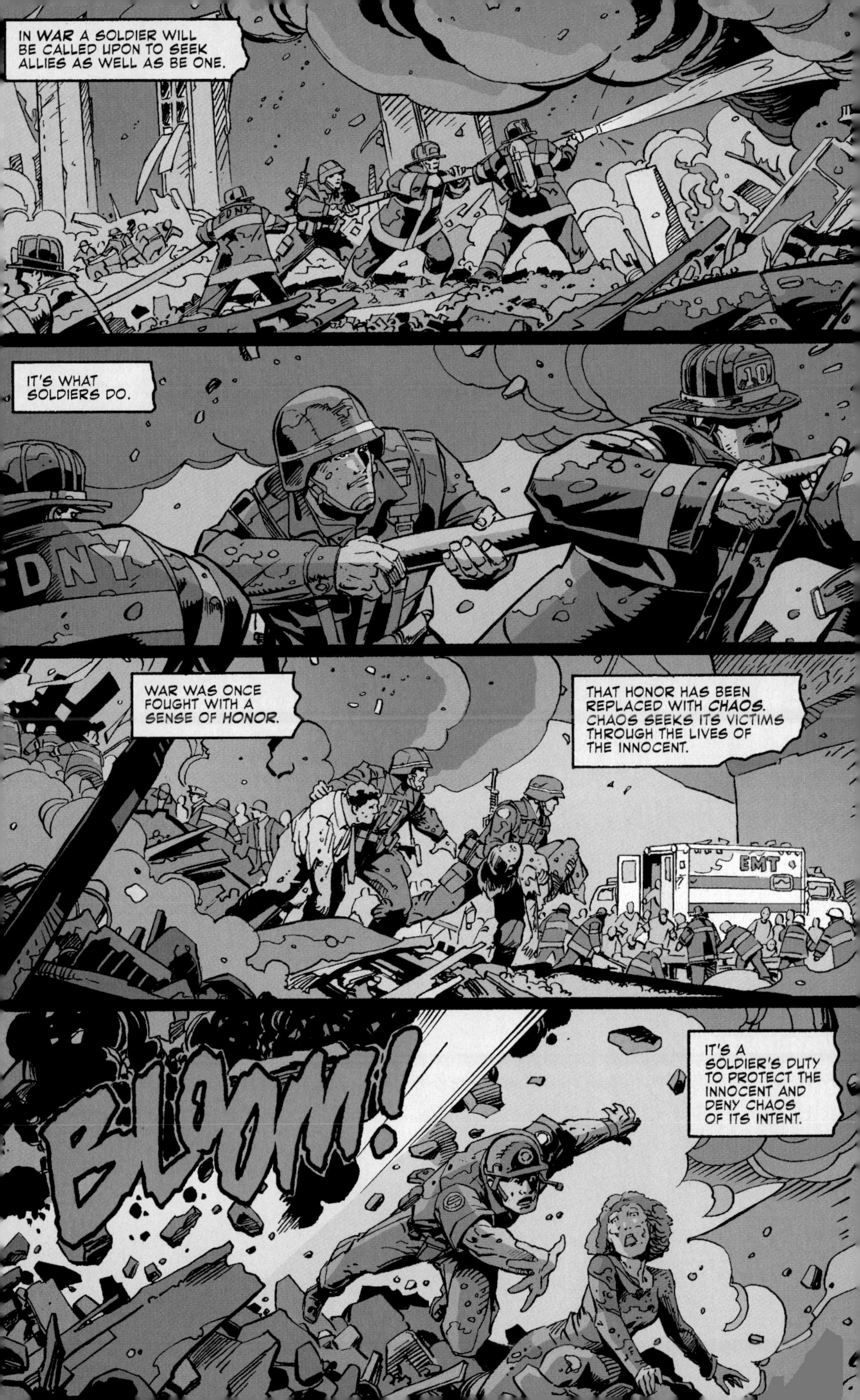
IN WAR A SOLDIER WILL BE CALLED UPON TO SEEK ALLIES AS WELL AS BE ONE.
IT'S WHAT SOLDIERS DO.
WAR WAS ONCE FOUGHT WITH A SENSE OF HONOR.
THAT HONOR HAS BEEN REPLACED WITH CHAOS. CHAOS SEEKS ITS VICTIMS THROUGH THE LIVES OF THE INNOCENT.
EMT
BLOOM!
IT'S A SOLDIER'S DUTY TO PROTECT THE INNOCENT AND DENY CHAOS OF ITS INTENT.

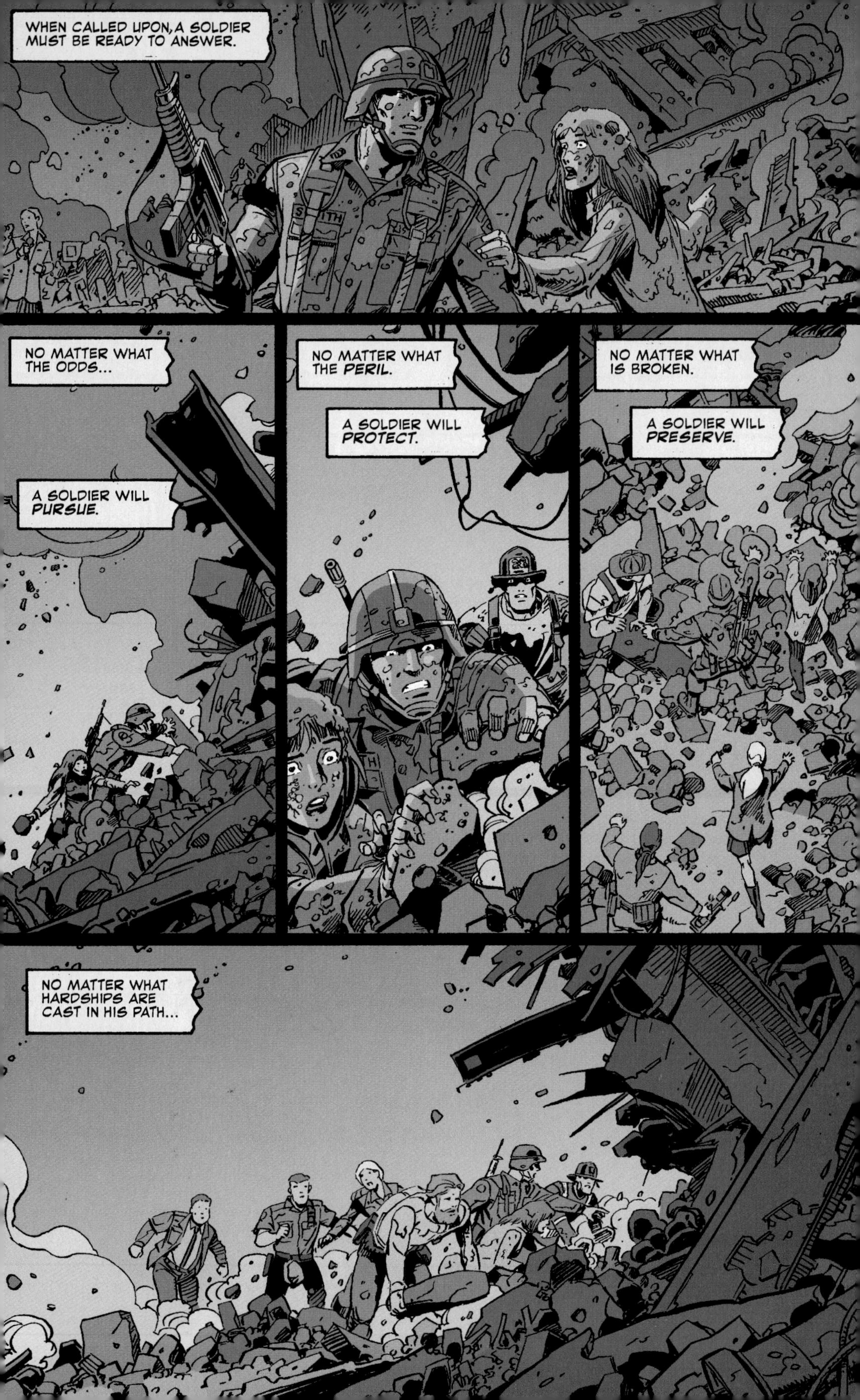
WHEN CALLED UPON, A SOLDIER MUST BE READY TO ANSWER.
NO MATTER WHAT THE ODDS...
A SOLDIER WILL PURSUE.
NO MATTER WHAT THE PERIL.
A SOLDIER WILL PROTECT.
NO MATTER WHAT IS BROKEN.
A SOLDIER WILL PRESERVE.
NO MATTER WHAT HARDSHIPS ARE CAST IN HIS PATH...

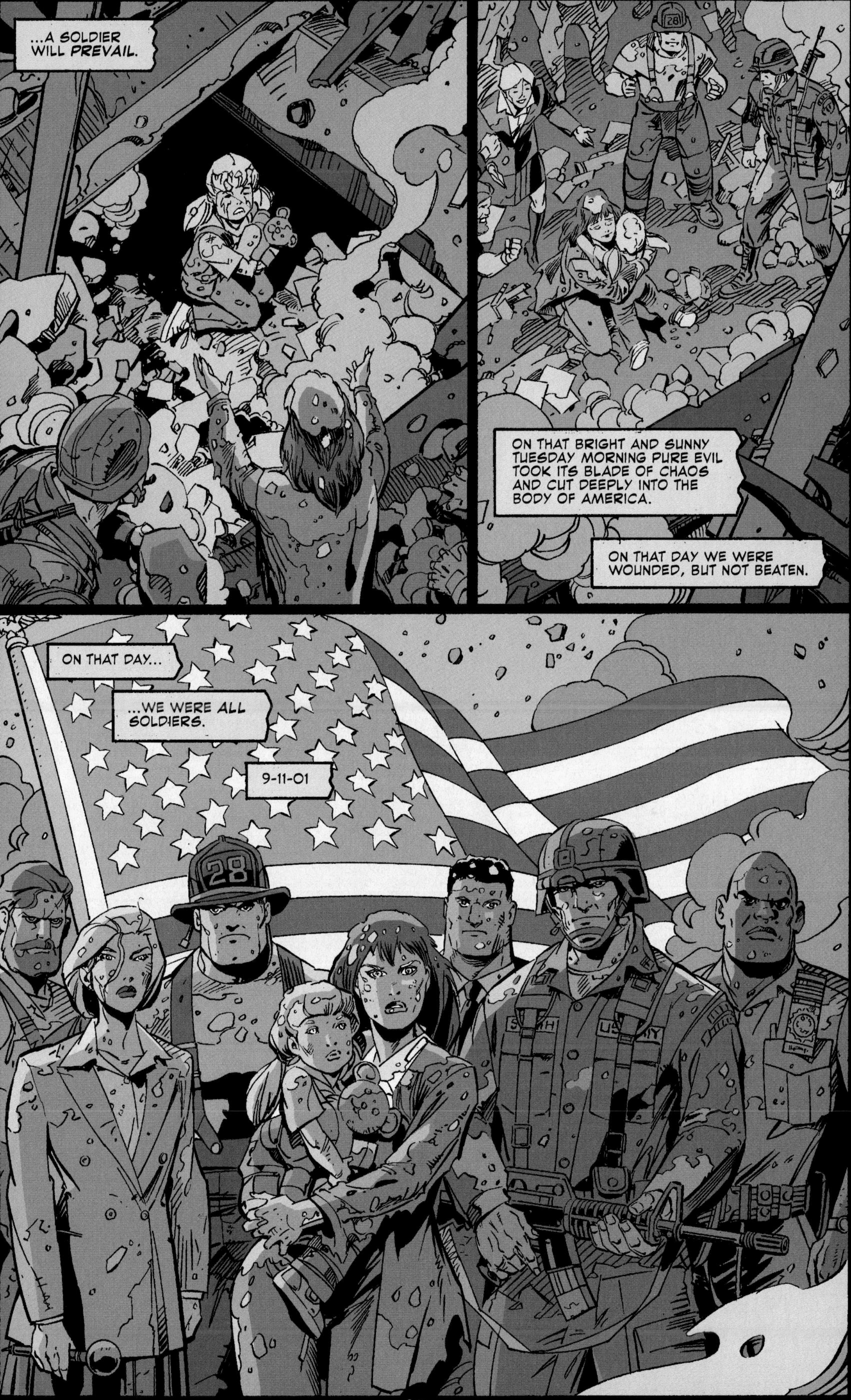

...A SOLDIER WILL PREVAIL.
ON THAT BRIGHT AND SUNNY TUESDAY MORNING PURE EVIL TOOK ITS BLADE OF CHAOS AND CUT DEEPLY INTO THE BODY OF AMERICA.
ON THAT DAY WE WERE WOUNDED, BUT NOT BEATEN.
ON THAT DAY...
...WE WERE ALL SOLDIERS.
9-11-01

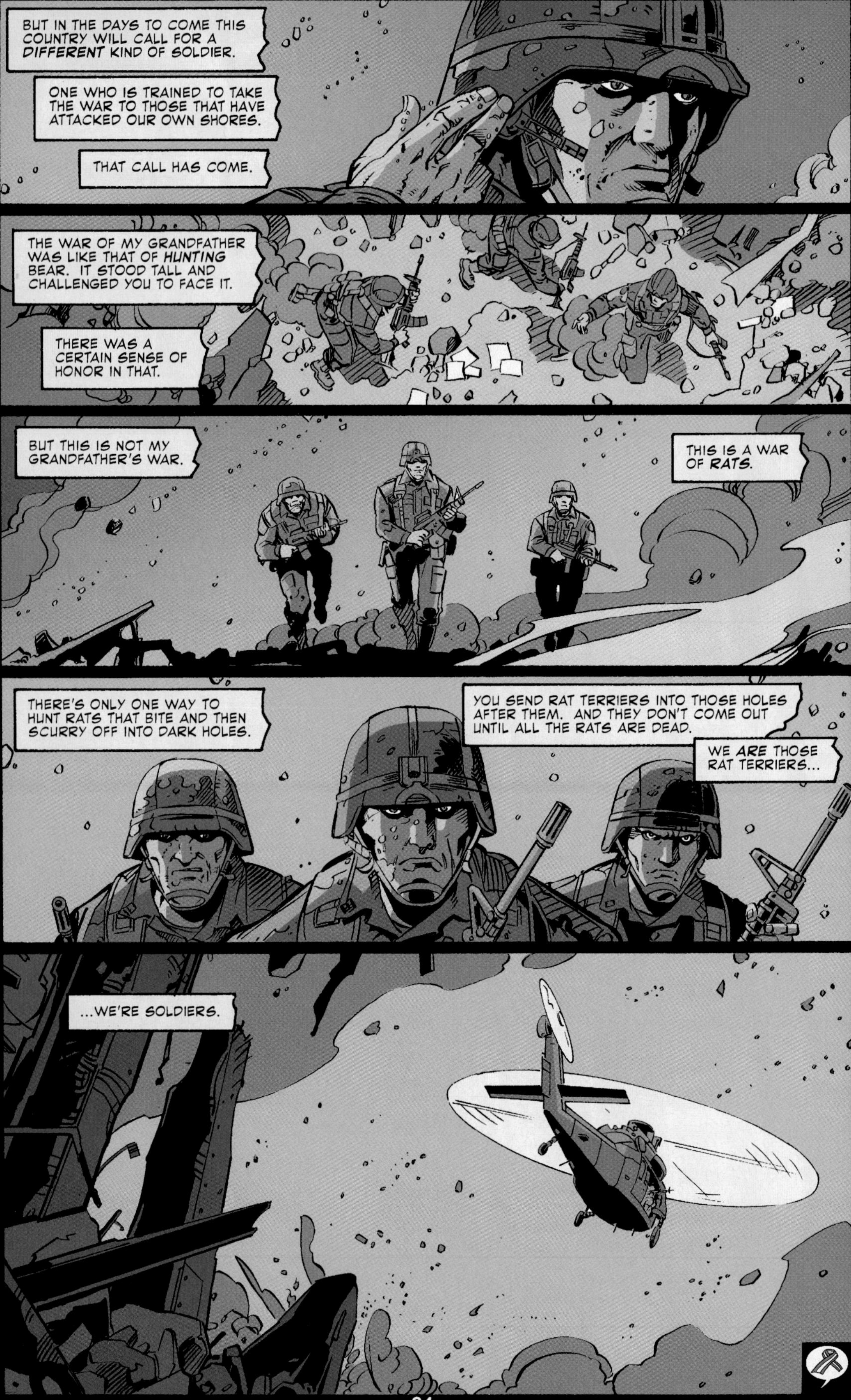
BUT IN THE DAYS TO COME THIS COUNTRY WILL CALL FOR A *DIFFERENT* KIND OF SOLDIER.
ONE WHO IS TRAINED TO TAKE THE WAR TO THOSE THAT HAVE ATTACKED OUR OWN SHORES.
THAT CALL HAS COME.
THE WAR OF MY GRANDFATHER WAS LIKE THAT OF *HUNTING* BEAR. IT STOOD TALL AND CHALLENGED YOU TO FACE IT.
THERE WAS A CERTAIN SENSE OF HONOR IN THAT.
BUT THIS IS NOT MY GRANDFATHER'S WAR.
THIS IS A WAR OF *RATS*.
THERE'S ONLY ONE WAY TO HUNT RATS THAT BITE AND THEN SCURRY OFF INTO DARK HOLES.
YOU SEND RAT TERRIERS INTO THOSE HOLES AFTER THEM. AND THEY DON'T COME OUT UNTIL ALL THE RATS ARE DEAD.
WE *ARE* THOSE RAT TERRIERS...
...WE'RE SOLDIERS.

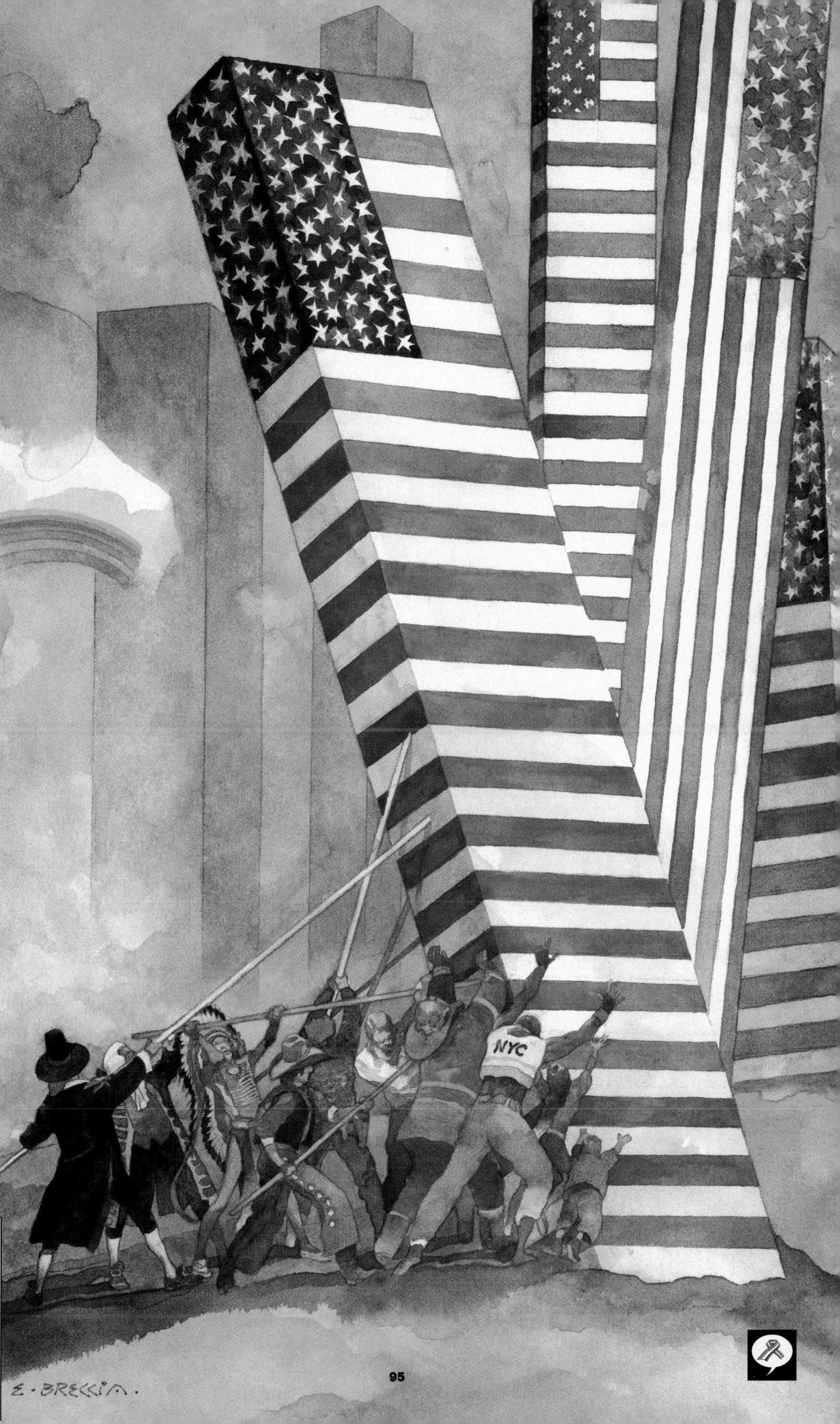
NYC
E. BRECCIA.

ART
ENRIQUE
BRECCIA
★★★★

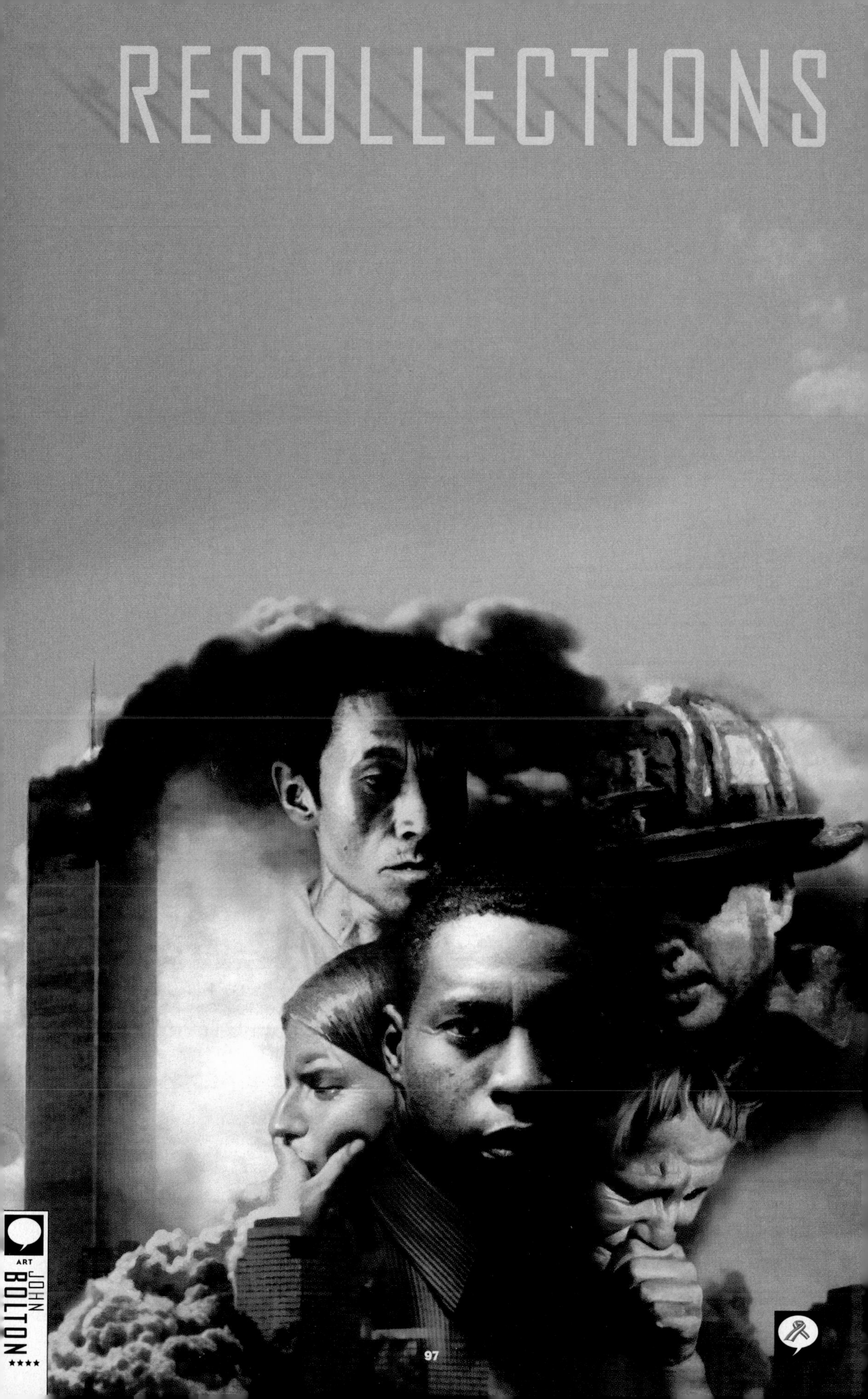
RECOLLECTIONS
ART
JOHN
BOLTON

PRIORITIES

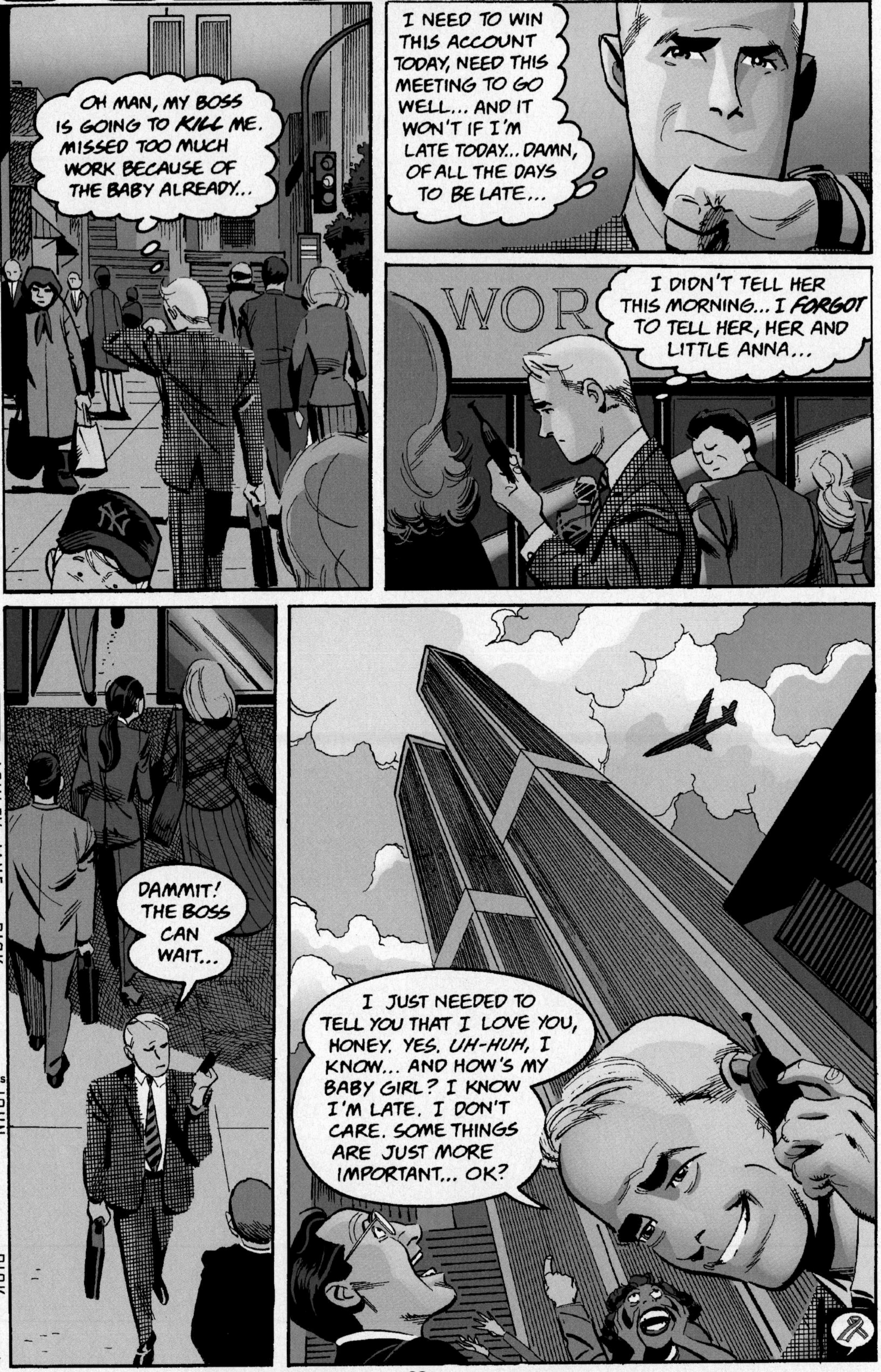

OH MAN, MY BOSS IS GOING TO KILL ME. MISSED TOO MUCH WORK BECAUSE OF THE BABY ALREADY...
I NEED TO WIN THIS ACCOUNT TODAY, NEED THIS MEETING TO GO WELL... AND IT WON'T IF I'M LATE TODAY... DAMN, OF ALL THE DAYS TO BE LATE...
WOR
I DIDN'T TELL HER THIS MORNING... I FORGOT TO TELL HER, HER AND LITTLE ANNA...
DAMMIT! THE BOSS CAN WAIT...
I JUST NEEDED TO TELL YOU THAT I LOVE YOU, HONEY. YES. UH-HUH, I KNOW... AND HOW'S MY BABY GIRL? I KNOW I'M LATE. I DON'T CARE. SOME THINGS ARE JUST MORE IMPORTANT... OK?

STORY ASHLEY-JANE NICOLAUS
ART RICK BURCHETT
LETTERS JOHN COSTANZA
COLOR RICK TAYLOR

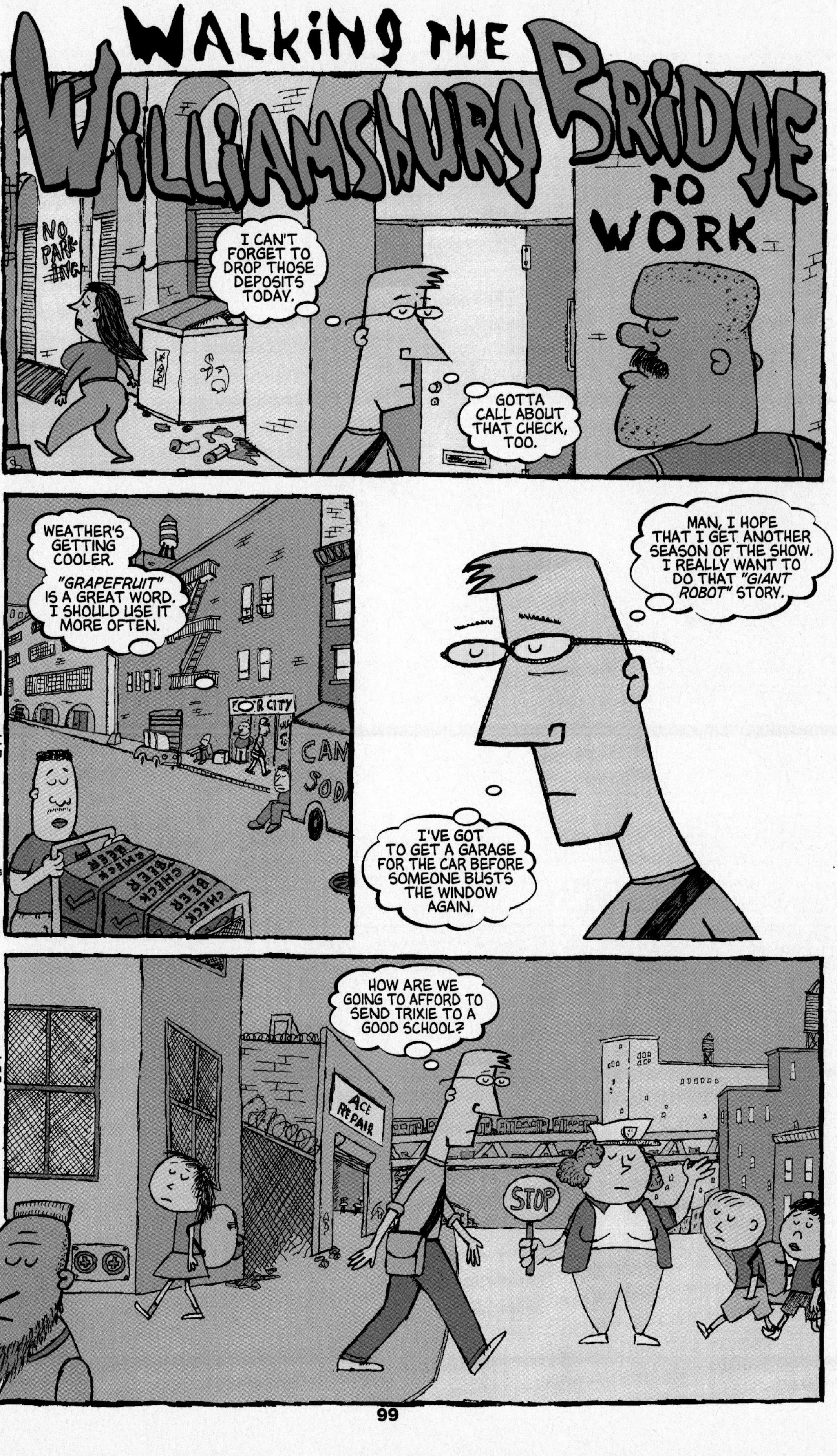
WALKING THE WILLIAMSBURG BRIDGE TO WORK
NO PARKING
I CAN'T FORGET TO DROP THOSE DEPOSITS TODAY.
GOTTA CALL ABOUT THAT CHECK, TOO.
WEATHER'S GETTING COOLER.
"GRAPEFRUIT" IS A GREAT WORD. I SHOULD USE IT MORE OFTEN.
MAN, I HOPE THAT I GET ANOTHER SEASON OF THE SHOW. I REALLY WANT TO DO THAT "GIANT ROBOT" STORY.
I'VE GOT TO GET A GARAGE FOR THE CAR BEFORE SOMEONE BUSTS THE WINDOW AGAIN.
CHECK BEER
HOW ARE WE GOING TO AFFORD TO SEND TRIXIE TO A GOOD SCHOOL?
ACE REPAIR
STOP

STORY & ART MO WILLEMS ****
LETTERS COMICRAFT ****
COLOR LEE LOUGHRIDGE ****

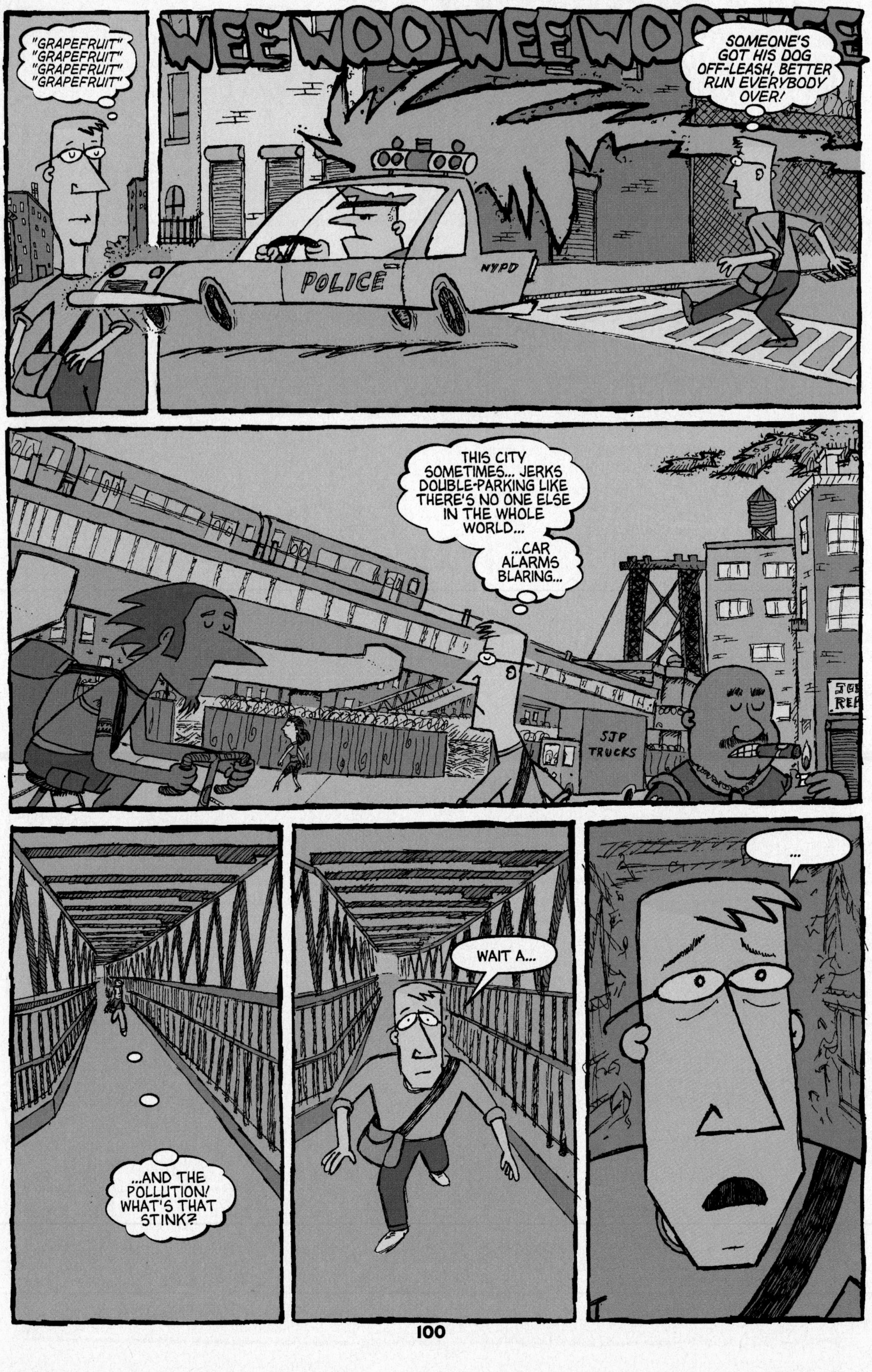
"GRAPEFRUIT"
"GRAPEFRUIT"
"GRAPEFRUIT"
"GRAPEFRUIT"
WEE WOO WEE WOO
SOMEONE'S GOT HIS DOG OFF-LEASH, BETTER RUN EVERYBODY OVER!
POLICE
NYPD
THIS CITY SOMETIMES... JERKS DOUBLE-PARKING LIKE THERE'S NO ONE ELSE IN THE WHOLE WORLD...
...CAR ALARMS BLARING...
SJP TRUCKS
...AND THE POLLUTION! WHAT'S THAT STINK?
WAIT A...
...

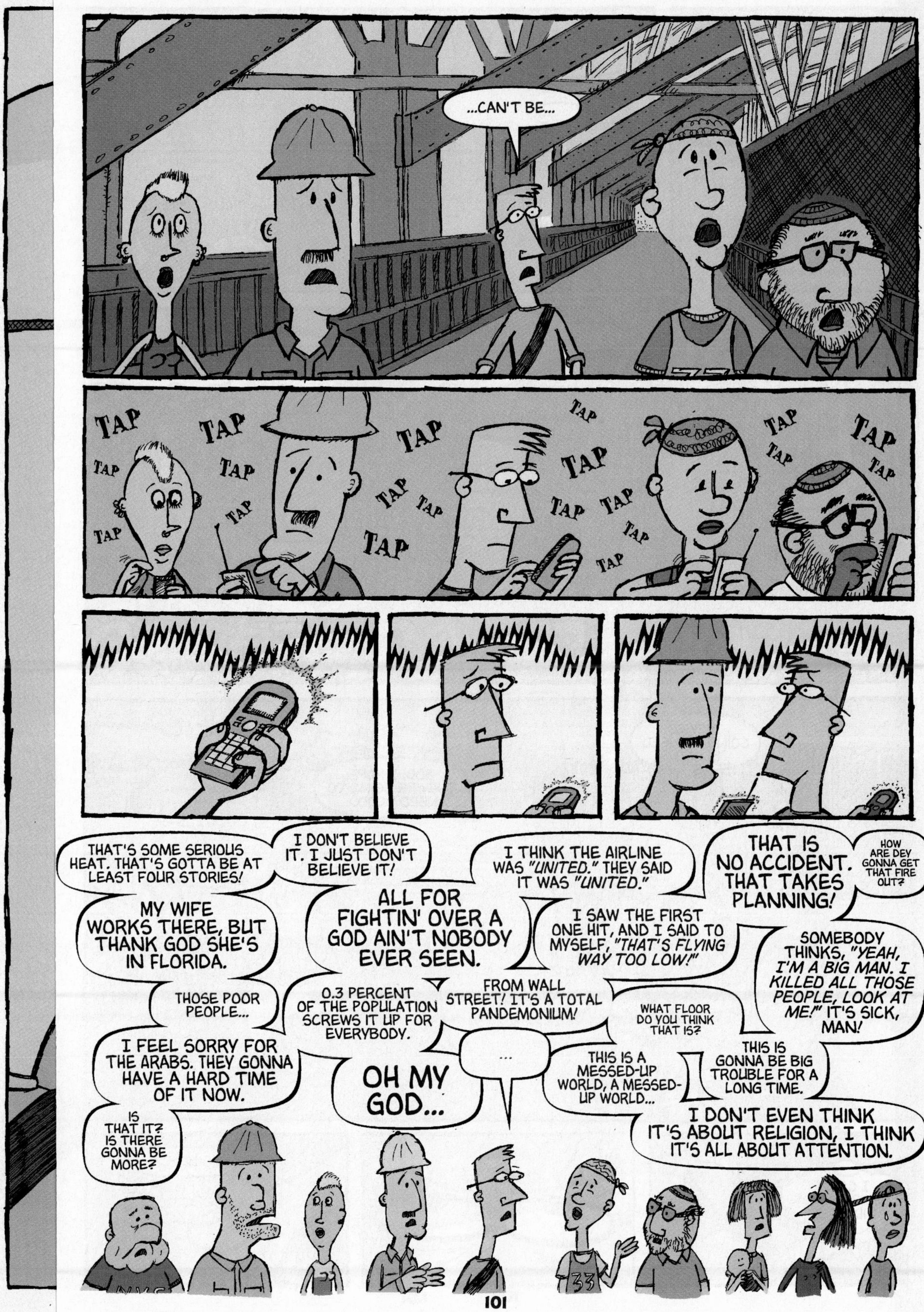
...CAN'T BE...
TAP TAP TAP TAP TAP TAP TAP TAP TAP TAP TAP TAP TAP TAP TAP TAP TAP TAP TAP
NNNNNNNNNNNNNNNNNN
THAT'S SOME SERIOUS HEAT. THAT'S GOTTA BE AT LEAST FOUR STORIES!
I DON'T BELIEVE IT. I JUST DON'T BELIEVE IT!
I THINK THE AIRLINE WAS "UNITED." THEY SAID IT WAS "UNITED."
THAT IS NO ACCIDENT. THAT TAKES PLANNING!
HOW ARE DEY GONNA GET THAT FIRE OUT?
MY WIFE WORKS THERE, BUT THANK GOD SHE'S IN FLORIDA.
ALL FOR FIGHTIN' OVER A GOD AIN'T NOBODY EVER SEEN.
I SAW THE FIRST ONE HIT, AND I SAID TO MYSELF, "THAT'S FLYING WAY TOO LOW!"
SOMEBODY THINKS, "YEAH, I'M A BIG MAN. I KILLED ALL THOSE PEOPLE, LOOK AT ME!" IT'S SICK, MAN!
THOSE POOR PEOPLE...
0.3 PERCENT OF THE POPULATION SCREWS IT UP FOR EVERYBODY.
FROM WALL STREET! IT'S A TOTAL PANDEMONIUM!
WHAT FLOOR DO YOU THINK THAT IS?
I FEEL SORRY FOR THE ARABS. THEY GONNA HAVE A HARD TIME OF IT NOW.
...
OH MY GOD...
THIS IS A MESSED-UP WORLD, A MESSED-UP WORLD...
THIS IS GONNA BE BIG TROUBLE FOR A LONG TIME.
IS THAT IT? IS THERE GONNA BE MORE?
I DON'T EVEN THINK IT'S ABOUT RELIGION, I THINK IT'S ALL ABOUT ATTENTION.

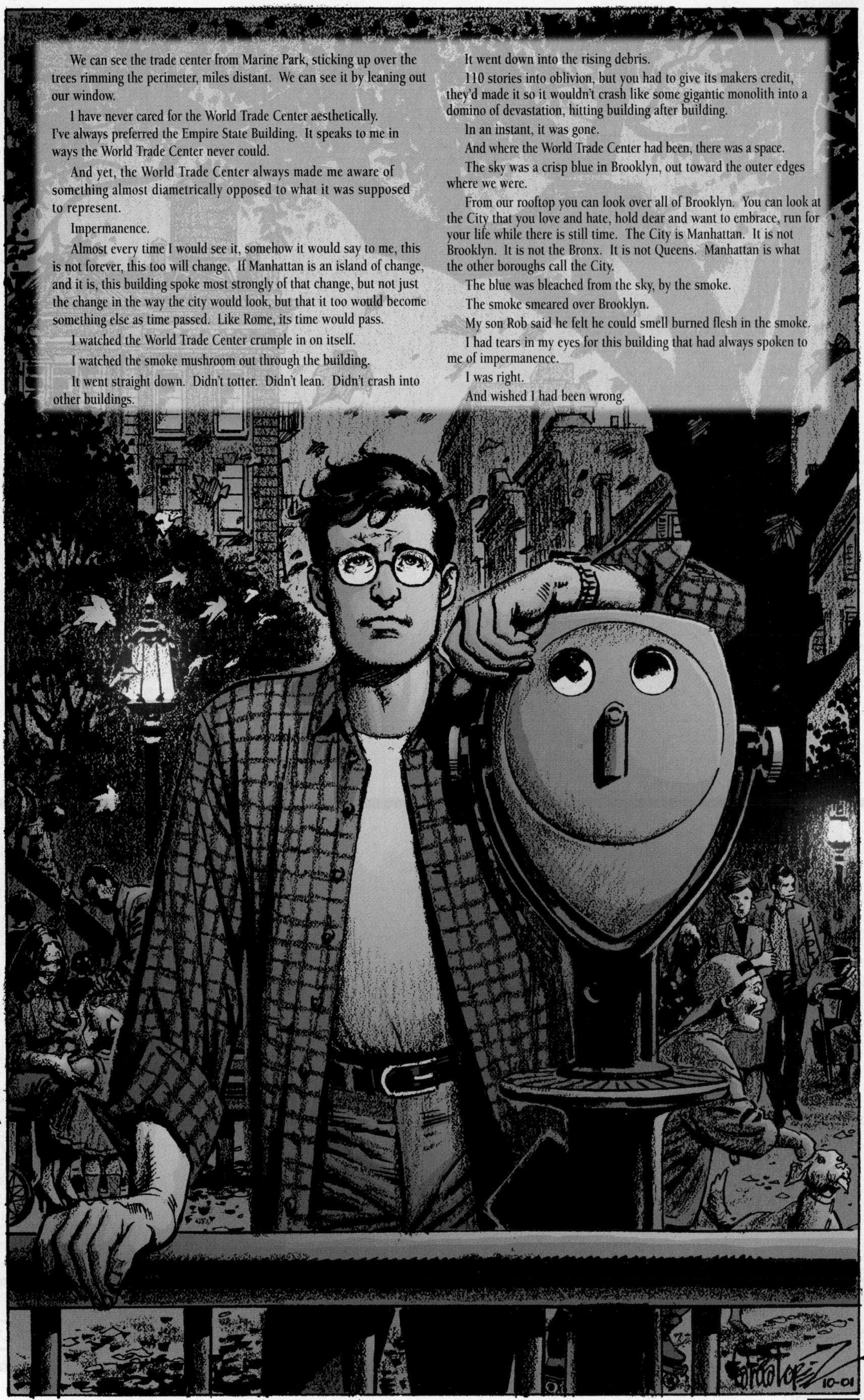
We can see the trade center from Marine Park, sticking up over the trees rimming the perimeter, miles distant. We can see it by leaning out our window.
I have never cared for the World Trade Center aesthetically. I've always preferred the Empire State Building. It speaks to me in ways the World Trade Center never could.
And yet, the World Trade Center always made me aware of something almost diametrically opposed to what it was supposed to represent.
Impermanence.
Almost every time I would see it, somehow it would say to me, this is not forever, this too will change. If Manhattan is an island of change, and it is, this building spoke most strongly of that change, but not just the change in the way the city would look, but that it too would become something else as time passed. Like Rome, its time would pass.
I watched the World Trade Center crumple in on itself.
I watched the smoke mushroom out through the building.
It went straight down. Didn't totter. Didn't lean. Didn't crash into other buildings.
It went down into the rising debris.
110 stories into oblivion, but you had to give its makers credit, they'd made it so it wouldn't crash like some gigantic monolith into a domino of devastation, hitting building after building.
In an instant, it was gone.
And where the World Trade Center had been, there was a space.
The sky was a crisp blue in Brooklyn, out toward the outer edges where we were.
From our rooftop you can look over all of Brooklyn. You can look at the City that you love and hate, hold dear and want to embrace, run for your life while there is still time. The City is Manhattan. It is not Brooklyn. It is not the Bronx. It is not Queens. Manhattan is what the other boroughs call the City.
The blue was bleached from the sky, by the smoke.
The smoke smeared over Brooklyn.
My son Rob said he felt he could smell burned flesh in the smoke.
I had tears in my eyes for this building that had always spoken to me of impermanence.
I was right.
And wished I had been wrong.

STORY DON McGREGOR ★★★★ ART JOSÉ LUIS GARCÍA-LÓPEZ ★★★★ COLOR JAMES SINCLAIR ★★★★

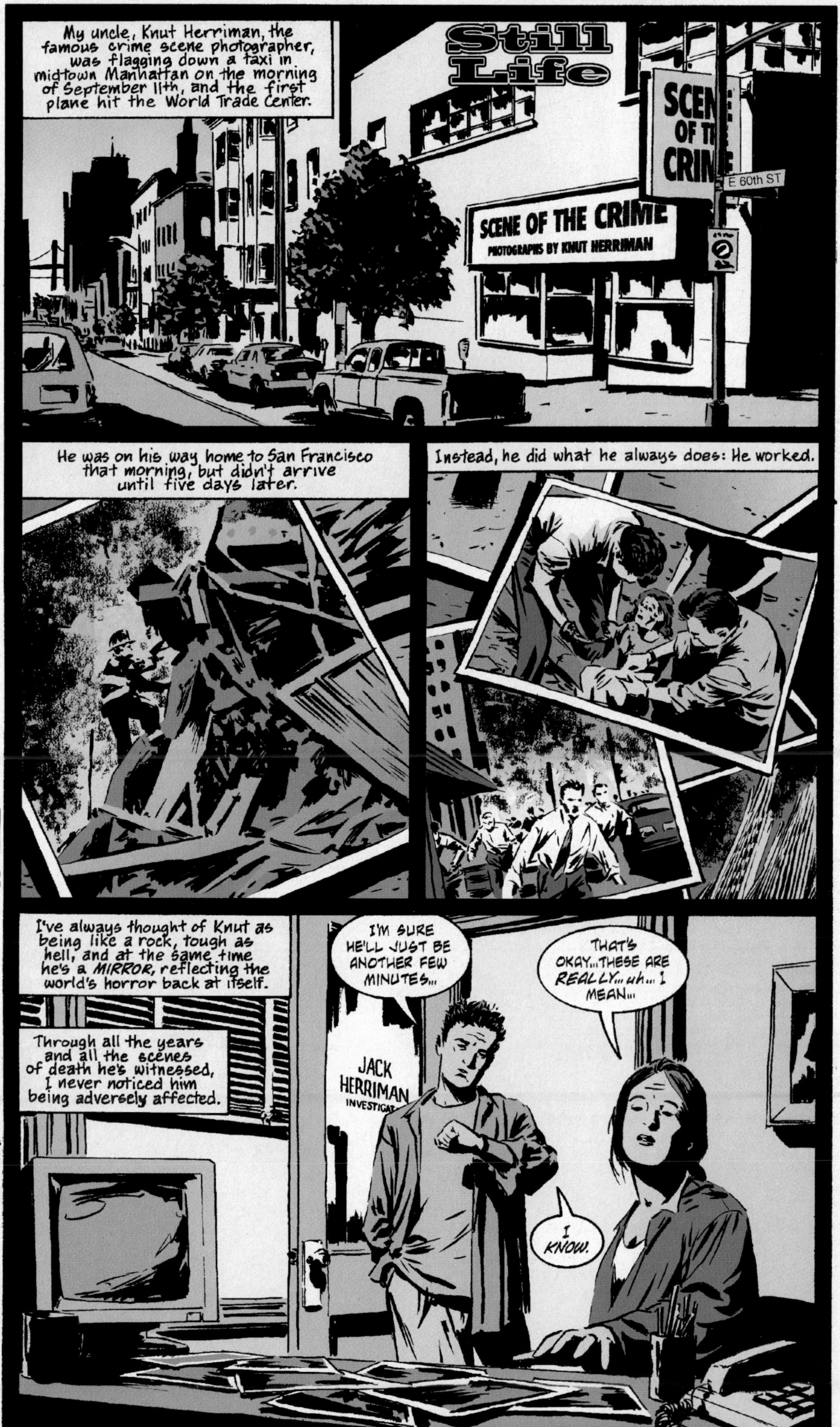
My uncle, Knut Herriman, the famous crime scene photographer, was flagging down a taxi in midtown Manhattan on the morning of September 11th, and the first plane hit the World Trade Center.
Still Life
SCENE OF THE CRIME
E 60th ST
SCENE OF THE CRIME
PHOTOGRAPHS BY KNUT HERRIMAN
He was on his way home to San Francisco that morning, but didn't arrive until five days later.
Instead, he did what he always does: He worked.
I've always thought of Knut as being like a rock, tough as hell, and at the same time he's a *MIRROR*, reflecting the world's horror back at itself.
Through all the years and all the scenes of death he's witnessed, I never noticed him being adversely affected.
I'M SURE HE'LL JUST BE ANOTHER FEW MINUTES...
THAT'S OKAY... THESE ARE *REALLY*... uh... I MEAN...
JACK HERRIMAN INVESTIGAT
I KNOW.

STORY ED BRUBAKER
ART MICHAEL LARK
LETTERS WILLIE SCHUBERT
COLOR NOELLE GIDDINGS

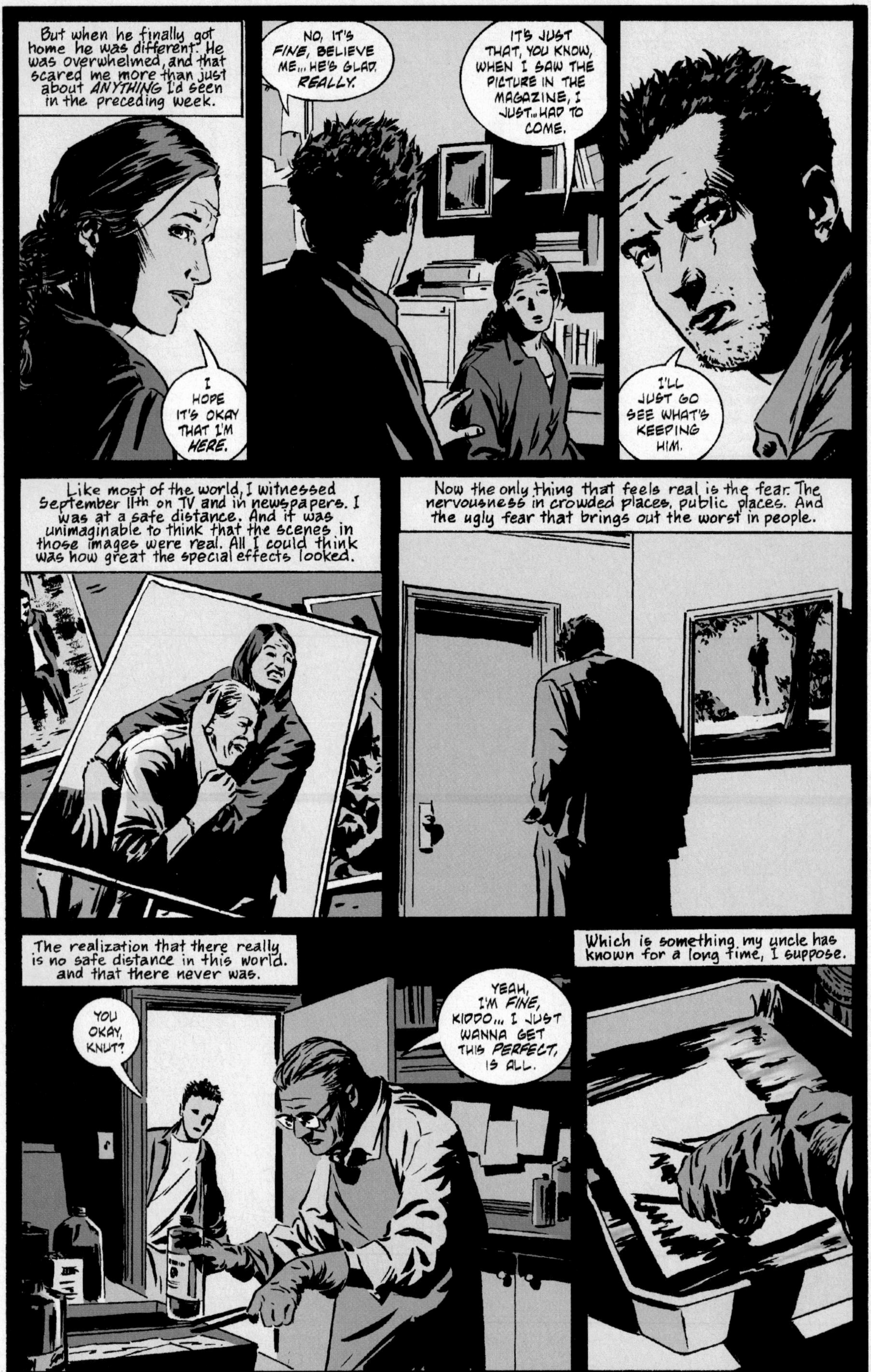
But when he finally got home he was different. He was overwhelmed, and that scared me more than just about ANYTHING I'd seen in the preceding week.
I HOPE IT'S OKAY THAT I'M HERE.
NO, IT'S FINE, BELIEVE ME... HE'S GLAD. REALLY.
IT'S JUST THAT, YOU KNOW, WHEN I SAW THE PICTURE IN THE MAGAZINE, I JUST... HAD TO COME.
I'LL JUST GO SEE WHAT'S KEEPING HIM.
Like most of the world, I witnessed September 11th on TV and in newspapers. I was at a safe distance. And it was unimaginable to think that the scenes in those images were real. All I could think was how great the special effects looked.
Now the only thing that feels real is the fear. The nervousness in crowded places, public places. And the ugly fear that brings out the worst in people.
The realization that there really is no safe distance in this world. and that there never was.
YOU OKAY, KNUT?
YEAH, I'M FINE, KIDDO... I JUST WANNA GET THIS PERFECT, IS ALL.
Which is something my uncle has known for a long time, I suppose.

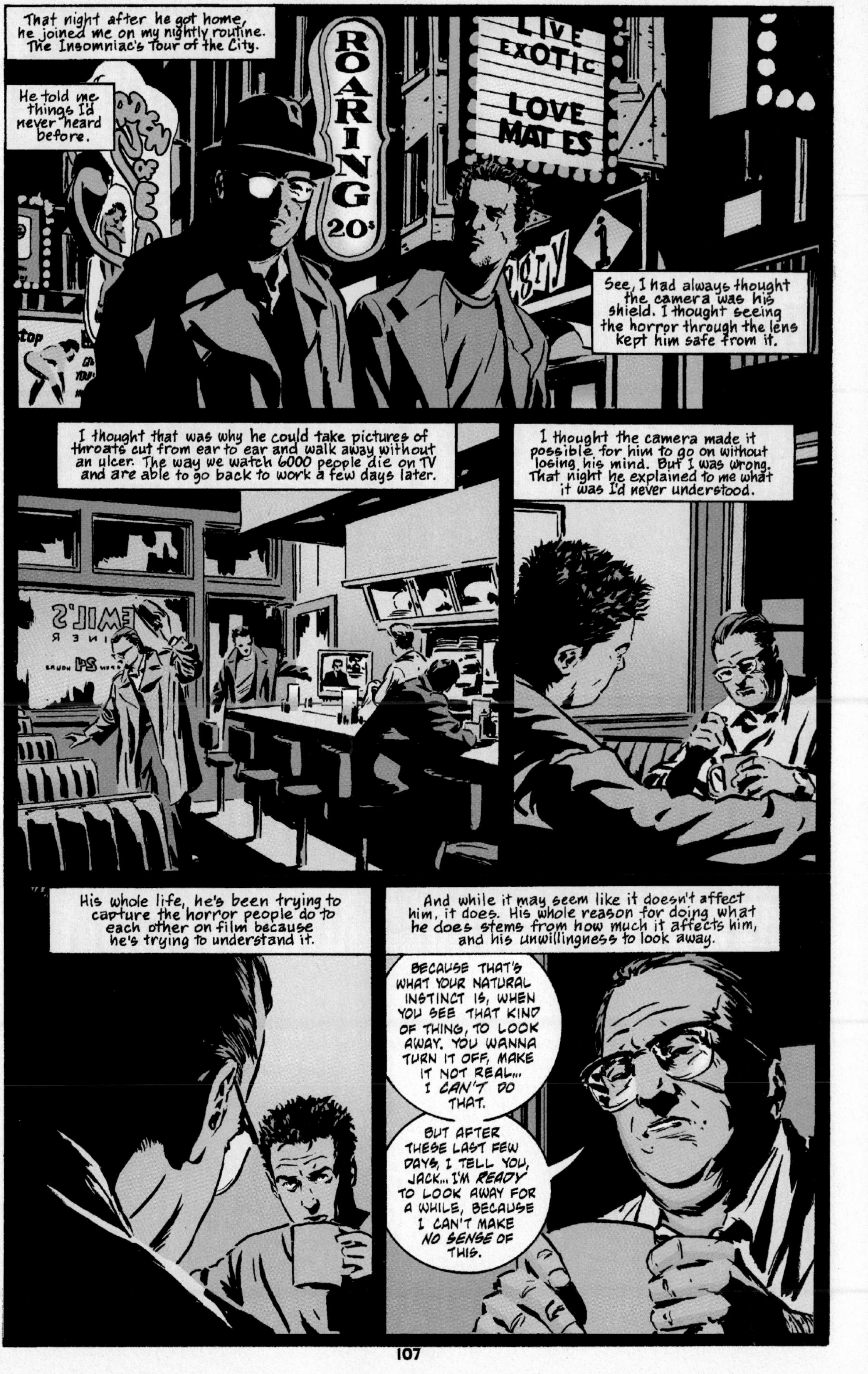

That night after he got home, he joined me on my nightly routine. The Insomniac's Tour of the City.
He told me things I'd never heard before.
ROARING 20s
LIVE EXOTIC LOVE MAT ES
See, I had always thought the camera was his shield. I thought seeing the horror through the lens kept him safe from it.
I thought that was why he could take pictures of throats cut from ear to ear and walk away without an ulcer. The way we watch 6000 people die on TV and are able to go back to work a few days later.
EMIL'S
I thought the camera made it possible for him to go on without losing his mind. But I was wrong. That night he explained to me what it was I'd never understood.
His whole life, he's been trying to capture the horror people do to each other on film because he's trying to understand it.
And while it may seem like it doesn't affect him, it does. His whole reason for doing what he does stems from how much it affects him, and his unwillingness to look away.
BECAUSE THAT'S WHAT YOUR NATURAL INSTINCT IS, WHEN YOU SEE THAT KIND OF THING, TO LOOK AWAY. YOU WANNA TURN IT OFF, MAKE IT NOT REAL... I CAN'T DO THAT.
BUT AFTER THESE LAST FEW DAYS, I TELL YOU, JACK... I'M READY TO LOOK AWAY FOR A WHILE, BECAUSE I CAN'T MAKE NO SENSE OF THIS.

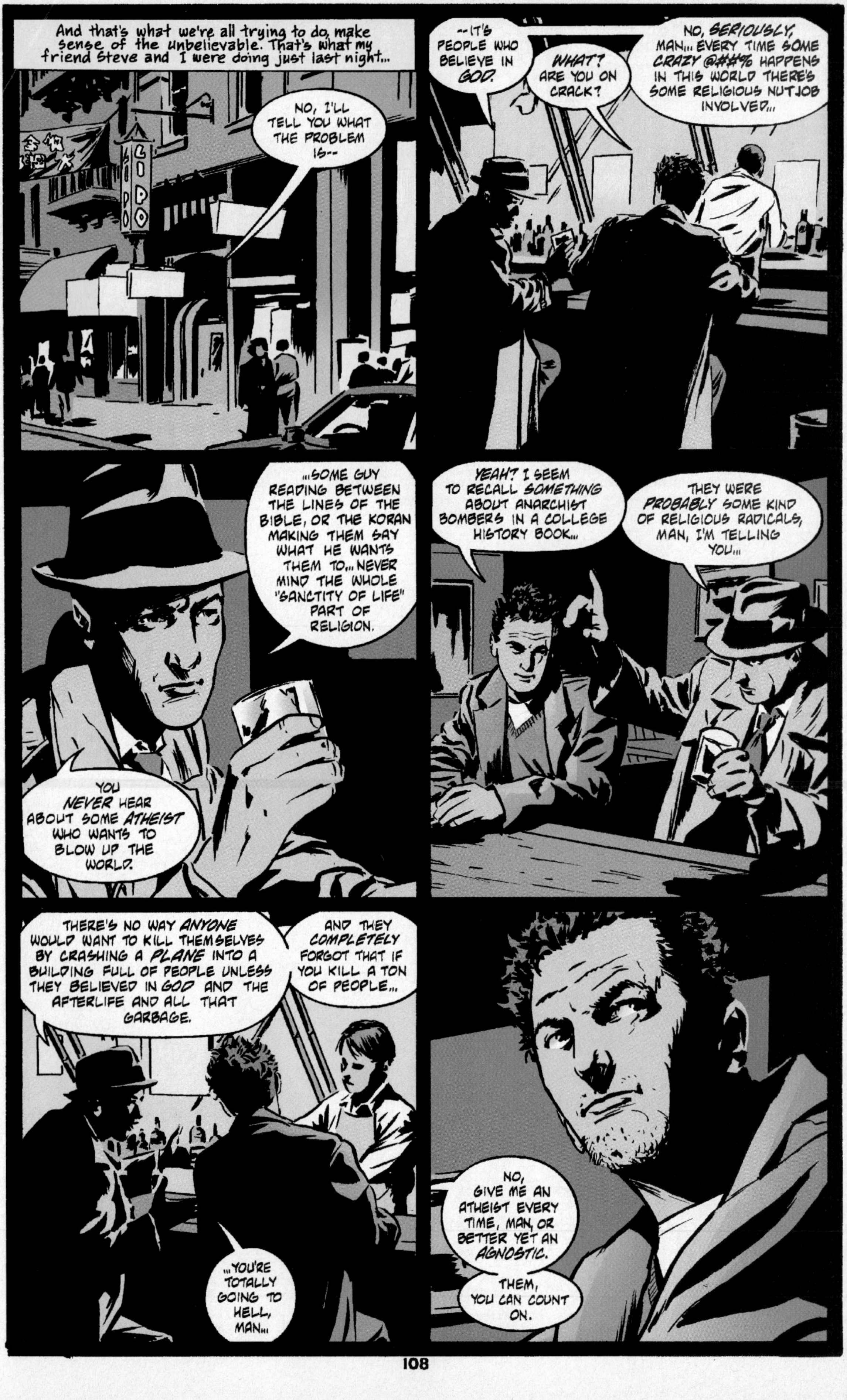
And that's what we're all trying to do, make sense of the unbelievable. That's what my friend Steve and I were doing just last night...
NO, I'LL TELL YOU WHAT THE PROBLEM IS--
LIDO
--IT'S PEOPLE WHO BELIEVE IN GOD.
WHAT? ARE YOU ON CRACK?
NO, SERIOUSLY, MAN... EVERY TIME SOME CRAZY @#*% HAPPENS IN THIS WORLD THERE'S SOME RELIGIOUS NUTJOB INVOLVED...
...SOME GUY READING BETWEEN THE LINES OF THE BIBLE, OR THE KORAN MAKING THEM SAY WHAT HE WANTS THEM TO... NEVER MIND THE WHOLE "SANCTITY OF LIFE" PART OF RELIGION.
YOU NEVER HEAR ABOUT SOME ATHEIST WHO WANTS TO BLOW UP THE WORLD.
YEAH? I SEEM TO RECALL SOMETHING ABOUT ANARCHIST BOMBERS IN A COLLEGE HISTORY BOOK...
THEY WERE PROBABLY SOME KIND OF RELIGIOUS RADICALS, MAN, I'M TELLING YOU...
THERE'S NO WAY ANYONE WOULD WANT TO KILL THEMSELVES BY CRASHING A PLANE INTO A BUILDING FULL OF PEOPLE UNLESS THEY BELIEVED IN GOD AND THE AFTERLIFE AND ALL THAT GARBAGE.
AND THEY COMPLETELY FORGOT THAT IF YOU KILL A TON OF PEOPLE...
...YOU'RE TOTALLY GOING TO HELL, MAN...
NO, GIVE ME AN ATHEIST EVERY TIME, MAN, OR BETTER YET AN AGNOSTIC.
THEM, YOU CAN COUNT ON.

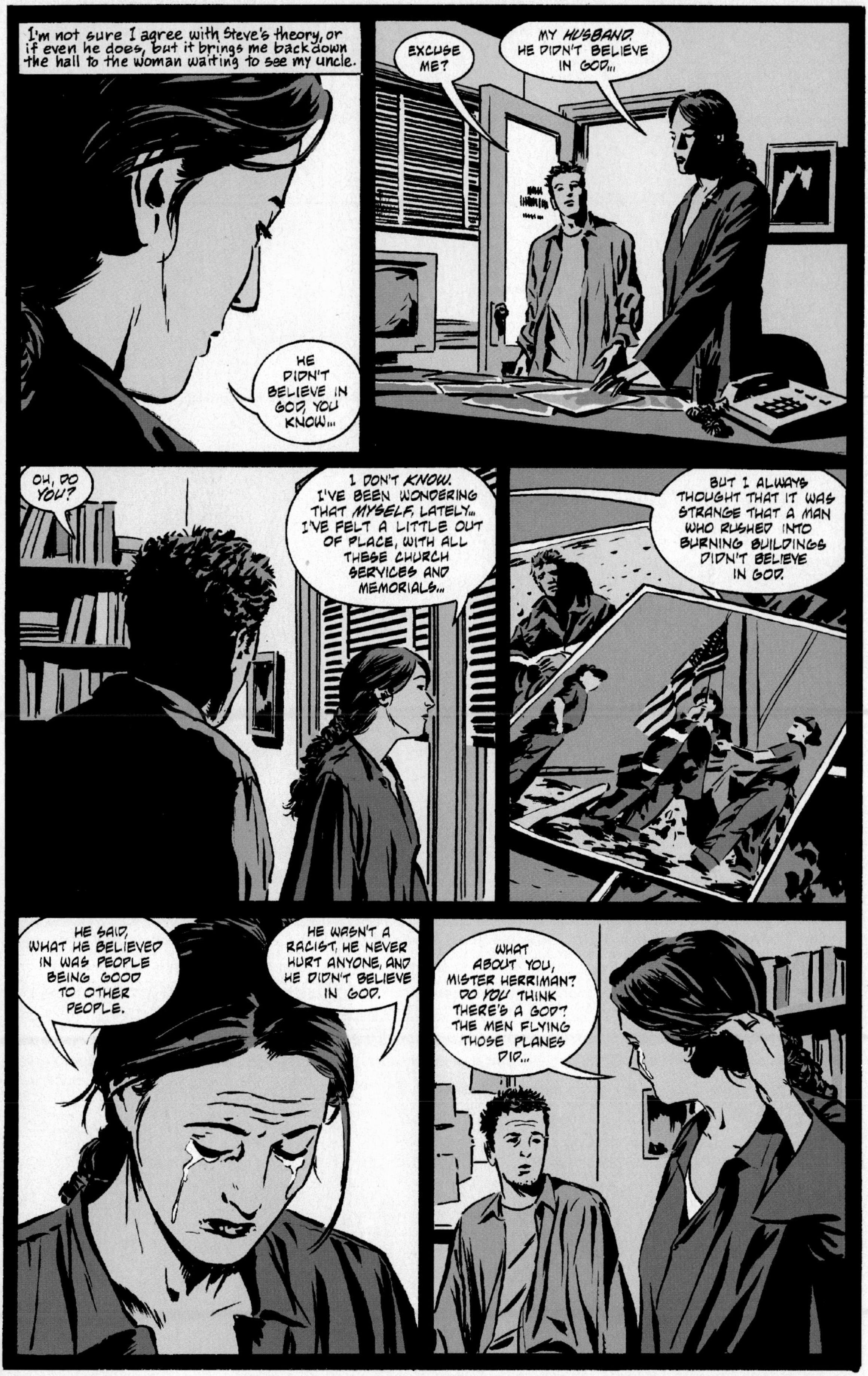
I'm not sure I agree with Steve's theory, or if even he does, but it brings me back down the hall to the woman waiting to see my uncle.
HE DIDN'T BELIEVE IN GOD, YOU KNOW...
EXCUSE ME?
MY HUSBAND. HE DIDN'T BELIEVE IN GOD...
OH, DO YOU?
I DON'T KNOW. I'VE BEEN WONDERING THAT MYSELF, LATELY... I'VE FELT A LITTLE OUT OF PLACE, WITH ALL THESE CHURCH SERVICES AND MEMORIALS...
BUT I ALWAYS THOUGHT THAT IT WAS STRANGE THAT A MAN WHO RUSHED INTO BURNING BUILDINGS DIDN'T BELIEVE IN GOD.
HE SAID, WHAT HE BELIEVED IN WAS PEOPLE BEING GOOD TO OTHER PEOPLE.
HE WASN'T A RACIST, HE NEVER HURT ANYONE, AND HE DIDN'T BELIEVE IN GOD.
WHAT ABOUT YOU, MISTER HERRIMAN? DO YOU THINK THERE'S A GOD? THE MEN FLYING THOSE PLANES DID...

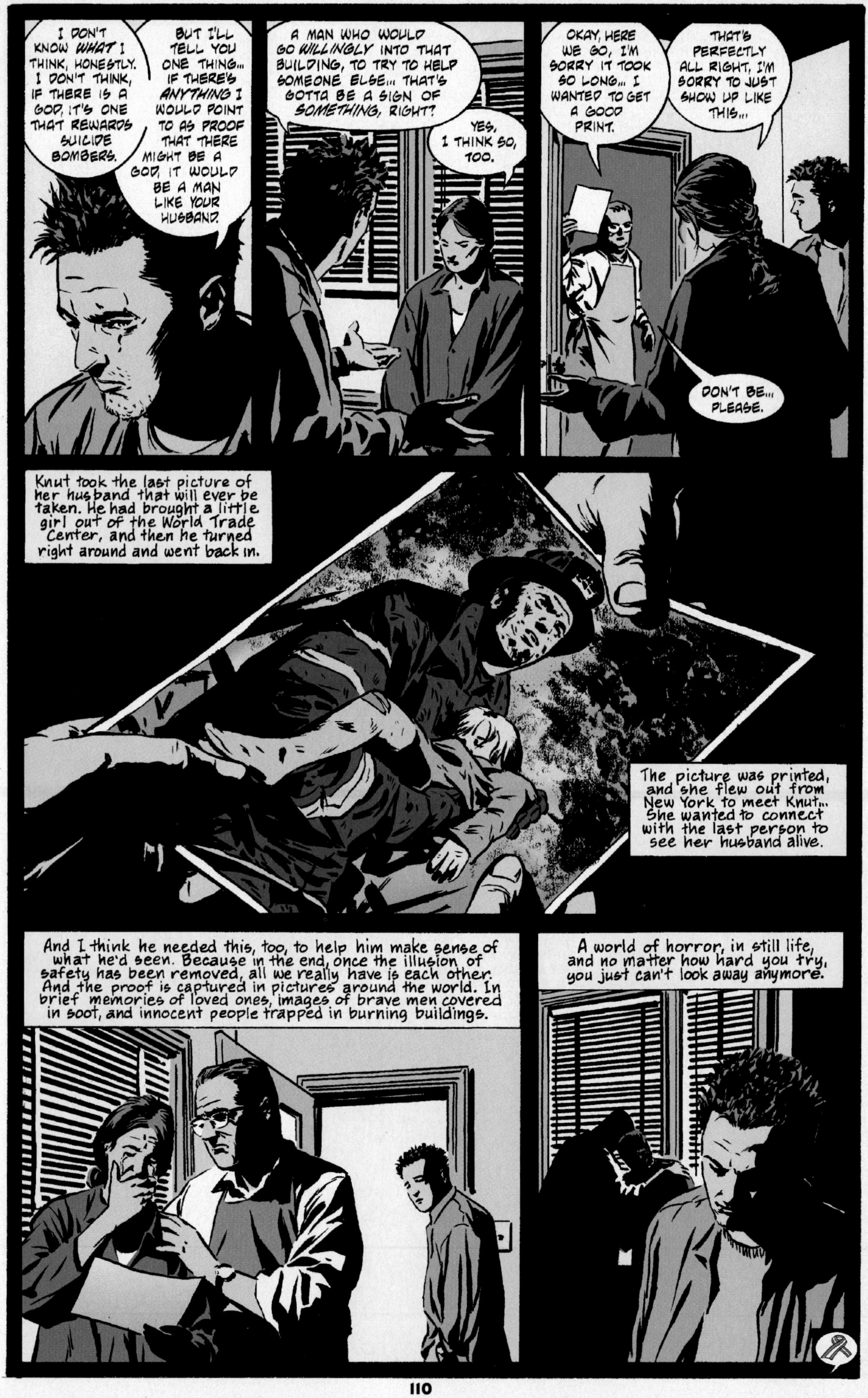
I DON'T KNOW *WHAT* I THINK, HONESTLY. I DON'T THINK, IF THERE IS A GOD, IT'S ONE THAT REWARDS SUICIDE BOMBERS.
BUT I'LL TELL YOU ONE THING... IF THERE'S *ANYTHING* I WOULD POINT TO AS PROOF THAT THERE MIGHT BE A GOD, IT WOULD BE A MAN LIKE YOUR HUSBAND.
A MAN WHO WOULD GO *WILLINGLY* INTO THAT BUILDING, TO TRY TO HELP SOMEONE ELSE... THAT'S GOTTA BE A SIGN OF *SOMETHING*, RIGHT?
YES, I THINK SO, TOO.
OKAY, HERE WE GO, I'M SORRY IT TOOK SO LONG... I WANTED TO GET A GOOD PRINT.
THAT'S PERFECTLY ALL RIGHT, I'M SORRY TO JUST SHOW UP LIKE THIS...
DON'T BE... PLEASE.
Knut took the last picture of her husband that will ever be taken. He had brought a little girl out of the World Trade Center, and then he turned right around and went back in.
The picture was printed, and she flew out from New York to meet Knut... She wanted to connect with the last person to see her husband alive.
And I think he needed this, too, to help him make sense of what he'd seen. Because in the end, once the illusion of safety has been removed, all we really have is each other. And the proof is captured in pictures around the world. In brief memories of loved ones, images of brave men covered in soot, and innocent people trapped in burning buildings.
A world of horror, in still life, and no matter how hard you try, you just can't look away anymore.

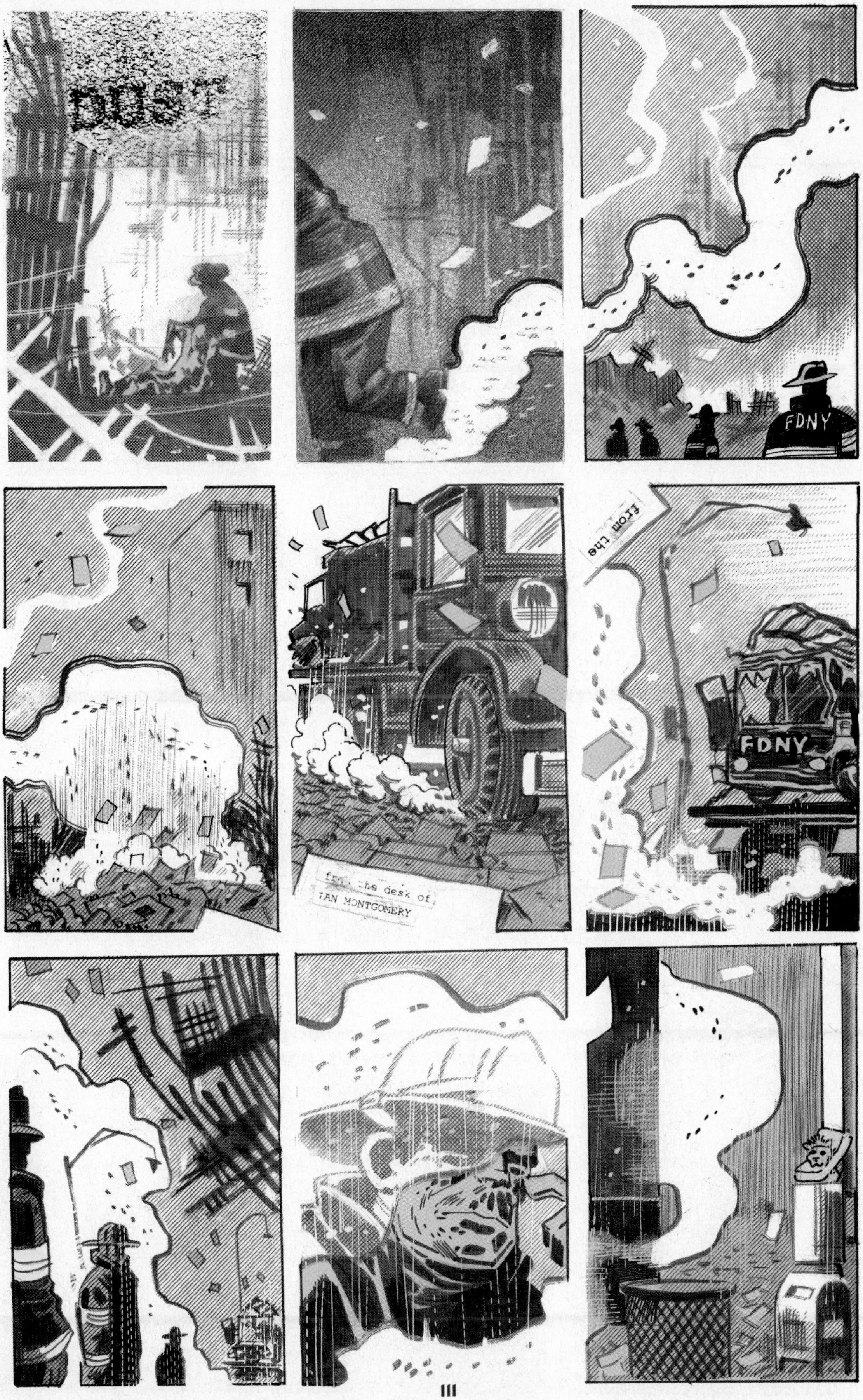
DUST
FDNY
the desk of
IAN MONTGOMERY
from the
FDNY

STORY KEITH GIFFEN
ART & COLOR WILLIAM WRAY

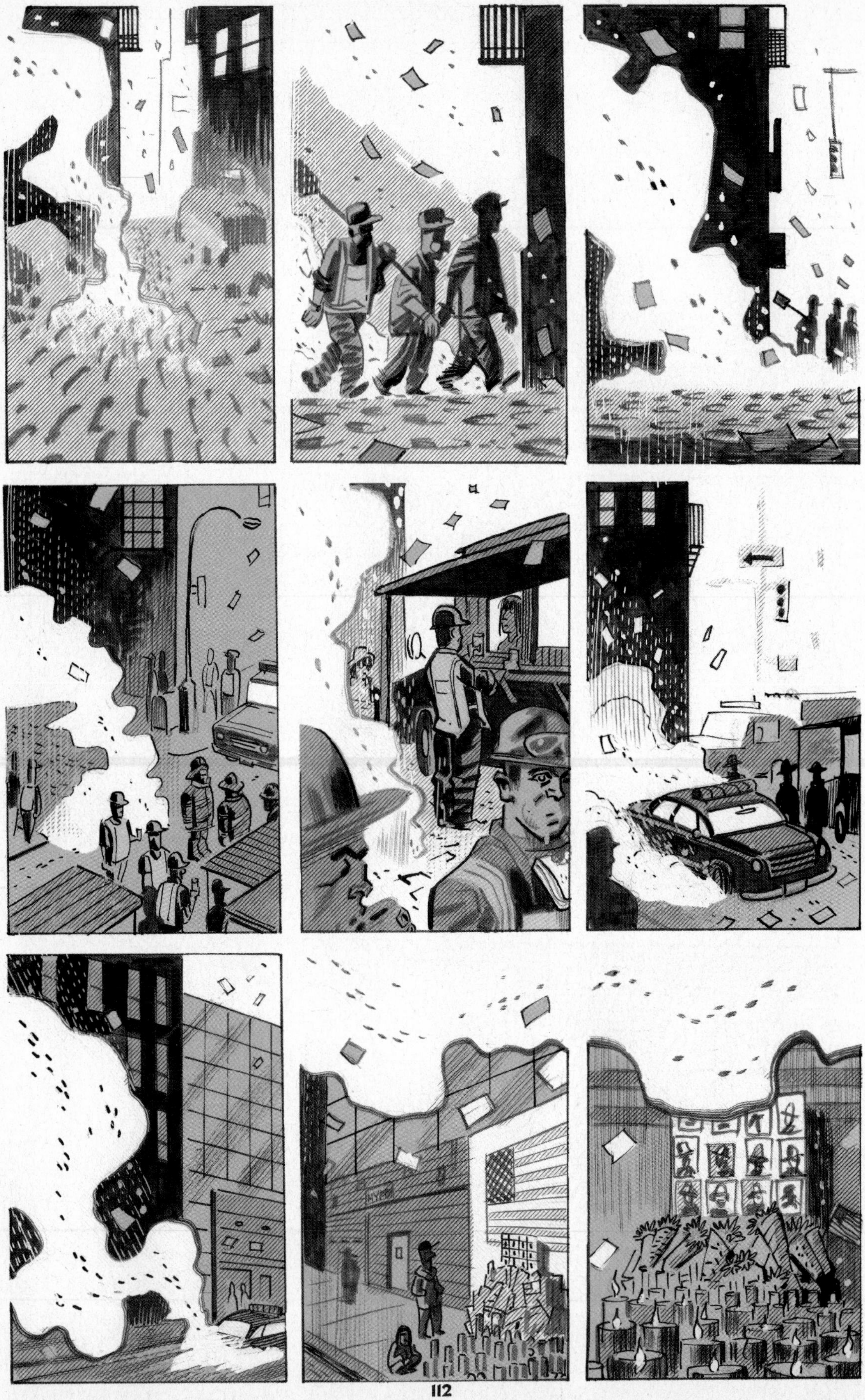

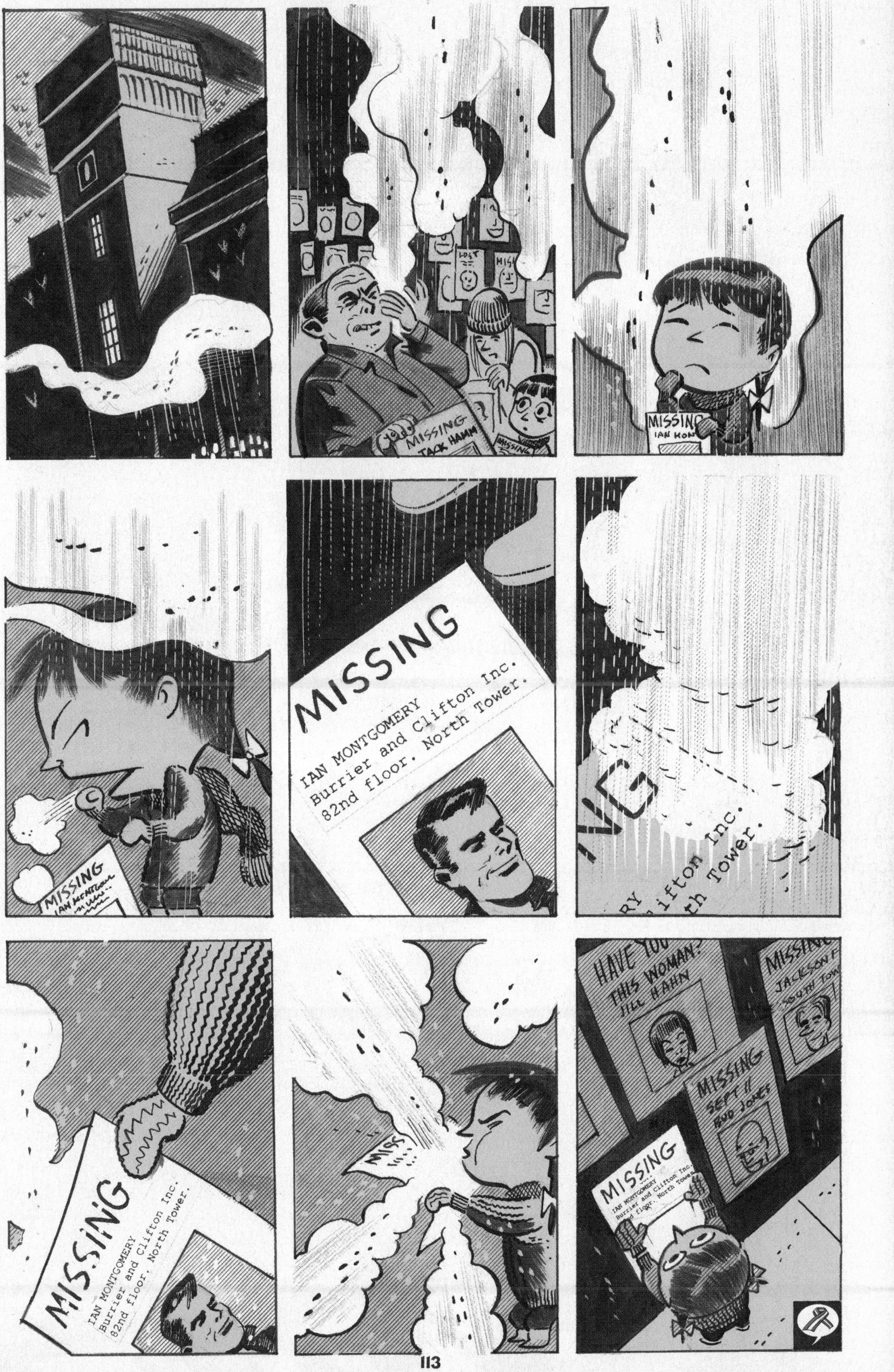
LOST
MISSING
JACK HAMM
MISSING
MISSING
IAN MONT
MISSING
MISSING
IAN MONTGOMERY
Burrier and Clifton Inc.
82nd floor. North Tower.
MISSING
IAN MONTGOMERY
Burrier and Clifton Inc.
82nd floor, North Tower.
THIS WOMAN?
JILL HAHN
MISSING
JACKSON
MISSING
SEPT 11
BUD JONES
MISSING
IAN MONTGOMERY
Burrier and Clifton Inc.

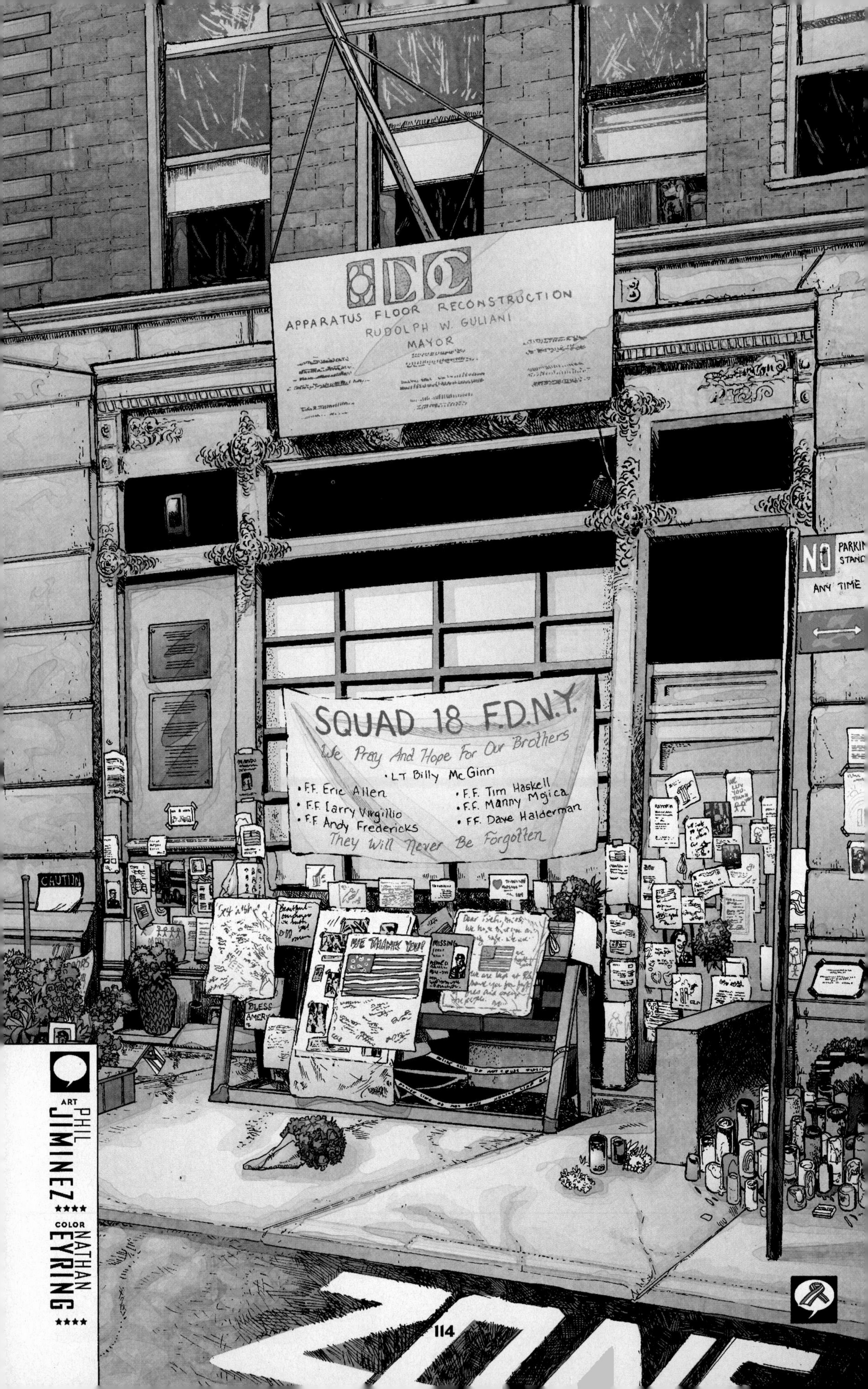
APPARATUS FLOOR RECONSTRUCTION
RUDOLPH W. GULIANI
MAYOR
NO
ANY TIME
SQUAD 18 F.D.N.Y.
We Pray And Hope For Our Brothers
• LT Billy McGinn
• F.F. Eric Allen
• F.F. Larry Virgillio
• F.F. Andy Fredericks
• F.F. Tim Haskell
• F.F. Manny Mojica
• F.F. Dave Halderman
They Will Never Be Forgotten
CAUTION
WE THANK YOU!
MISSING

ART PHIL JIMINEZ
COLOR NATHAN EYRING

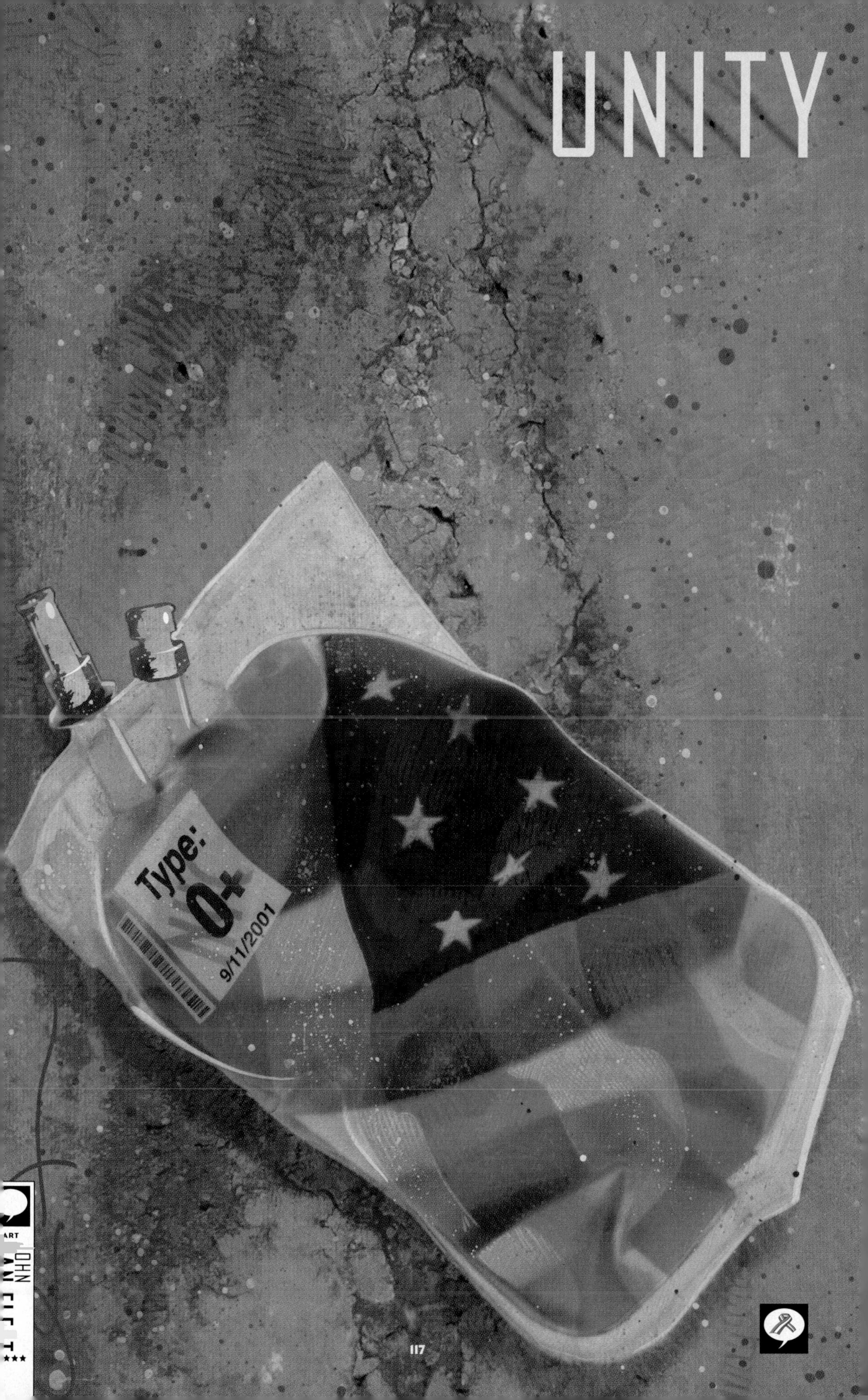
UNITY
Type:
O+
9/11/2001
ART

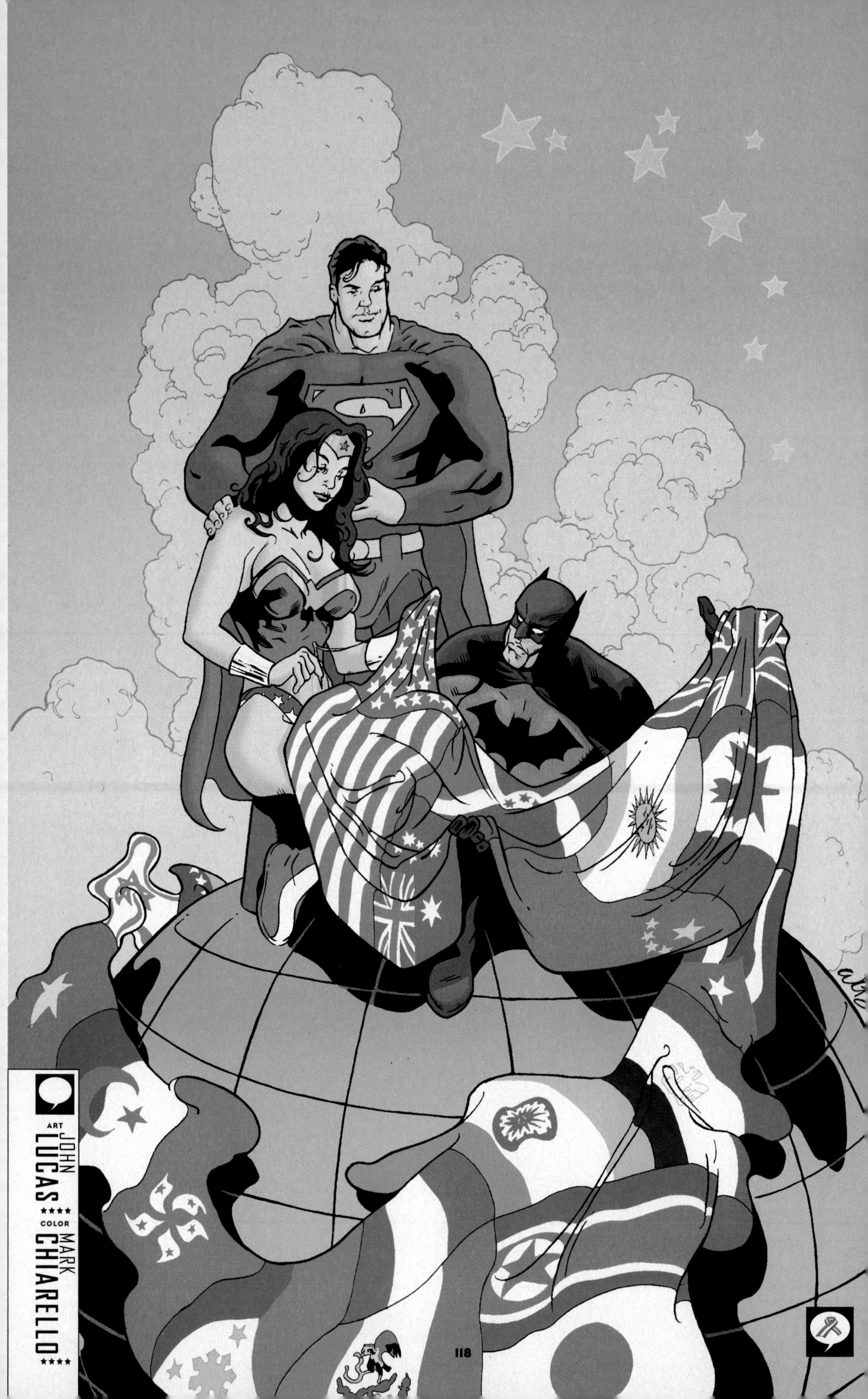

ART JOHN LUCAS
COLOR MARK CHIARELLO

9 A.M. EST

STORY
DAN ABNETT AND ANDY LANNING

ART
YANICK PAQUETTE AND JIM ROYAL

LETTERS
KURT HATHAWAY

COLOR
CHRIS CHUCKRY

NEW YORK: 9:00 A.M. EST

LONDON: 2:00 P.M. LOCAL TIME

ROME: 3:00 P.M. LOCAL TIME

JERUSALEM: 4:00 P.M. LOCAL TIME

CAPE TOWN: 4:00 P.M. LOCAL TIME.

MOSCOW: 5:00 P.M. LOCAL TIME

CALCUTTA: 7:30 P.M. LOCAL TIME

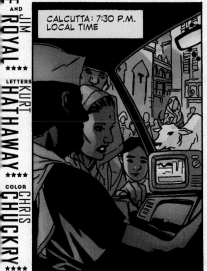

BEIJING: 10:00 P.M. LOCAL TIME

KABUL: 6:30 P.M. LOCAL TIME

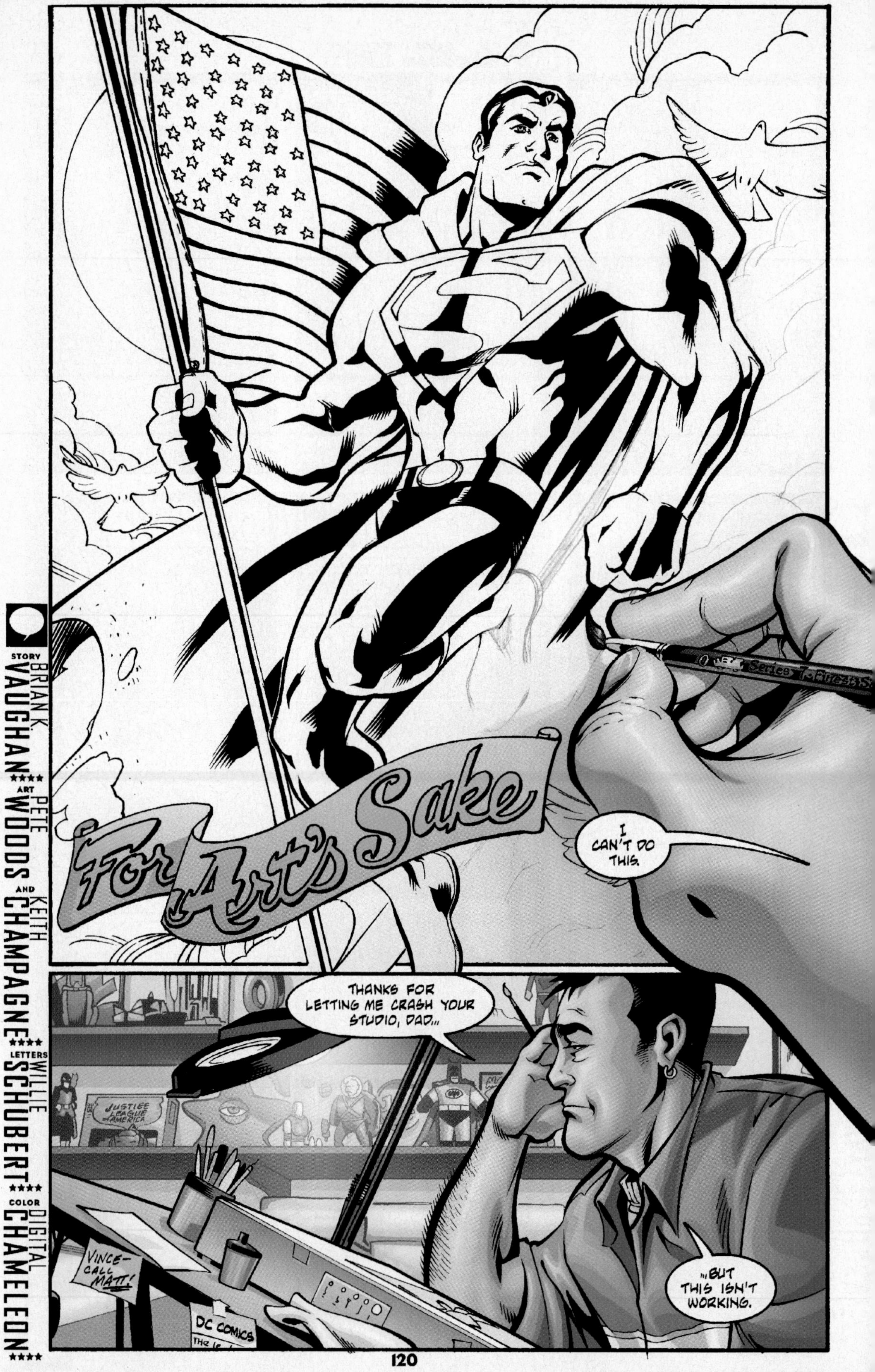
For Art's Sake
I CAN'T DO THIS.
THANKS FOR LETTING ME CRASH YOUR STUDIO, DAD...
JUSTICE LEAGUE of AMERICA
VINCE- CALL MATT!
DC COMICS
...BUT THIS ISN'T WORKING.

STORY BRIAN K. VAUGHAN ART PETE WOODS AND KEITH CHAMPAGNE LETTERS WILLIE SCHUBERT COLOR DIGITAL CHAMELEON

YOU NEED A HAND WITH LAYOUTS, VINCE?

NO, IT'S NOT THAT. I JUST...

I FEEL *STUPID* WORKING ON THIS STUFF AFTER... AFTER WHAT HAPPENED.

I WATCHED THE TRADE CENTER FALL FROM MY *ROOF,* DAD.

HOW AM I SUPPOSED TO GO BACK TO DRAWING COMICS AFTER THAT!

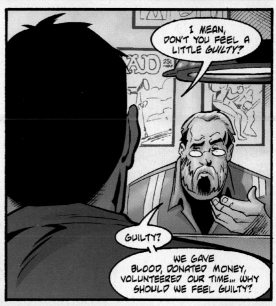

I MEAN, DON'T YOU FEEL A LITTLE *GUILTY?*

GUILTY?

WE GAVE BLOOD, DONATED MONEY, VOLUNTEERED OUR TIME... WHY SHOULD WE FEEL GUILTY?

BECAUSE WE'RE SITTING HERE TELLING MEANINGLESS STORIES ABOUT IMAGINARY HEROES...

...WHILE OUT THERE, HUNDREDS OF *REAL* HEROES ARE *DEAD.*

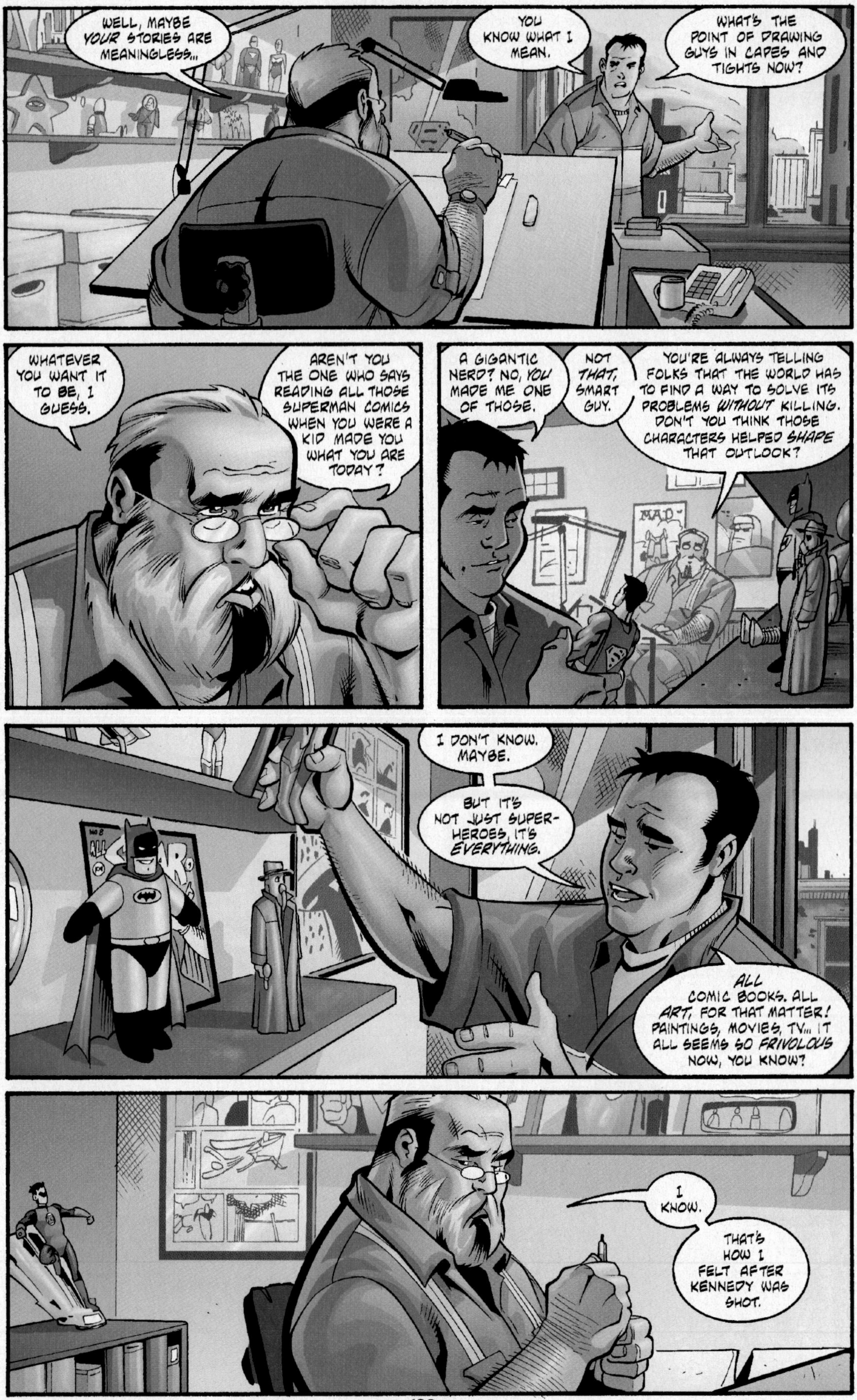
WELL, MAYBE YOUR STORIES ARE MEANINGLESS...
YOU KNOW WHAT I MEAN.
WHAT'S THE POINT OF DRAWING GUYS IN CAPES AND TIGHTS NOW?
WHATEVER YOU WANT IT TO BE, I GUESS.
AREN'T YOU THE ONE WHO SAYS READING ALL THOSE SUPERMAN COMICS WHEN YOU WERE A KID MADE YOU WHAT YOU ARE TODAY?
A GIGANTIC NERD? NO, YOU MADE ME ONE OF THOSE.
NOT THAT, SMART GUY.
YOU'RE ALWAYS TELLING FOLKS THAT THE WORLD HAS TO FIND A WAY TO SOLVE ITS PROBLEMS WITHOUT KILLING. DON'T YOU THINK THOSE CHARACTERS HELPED SHAPE THAT OUTLOOK?
MAD
I DON'T KNOW. MAYBE.
BUT IT'S NOT JUST SUPER-HEROES, IT'S EVERYTHING.
ALL COMIC BOOKS. ALL ART, FOR THAT MATTER! PAINTINGS, MOVIES, TV... IT ALL SEEMS SO FRIVOLOUS NOW, YOU KNOW?
I KNOW.
THAT'S HOW I FELT AFTER KENNEDY WAS SHOT.

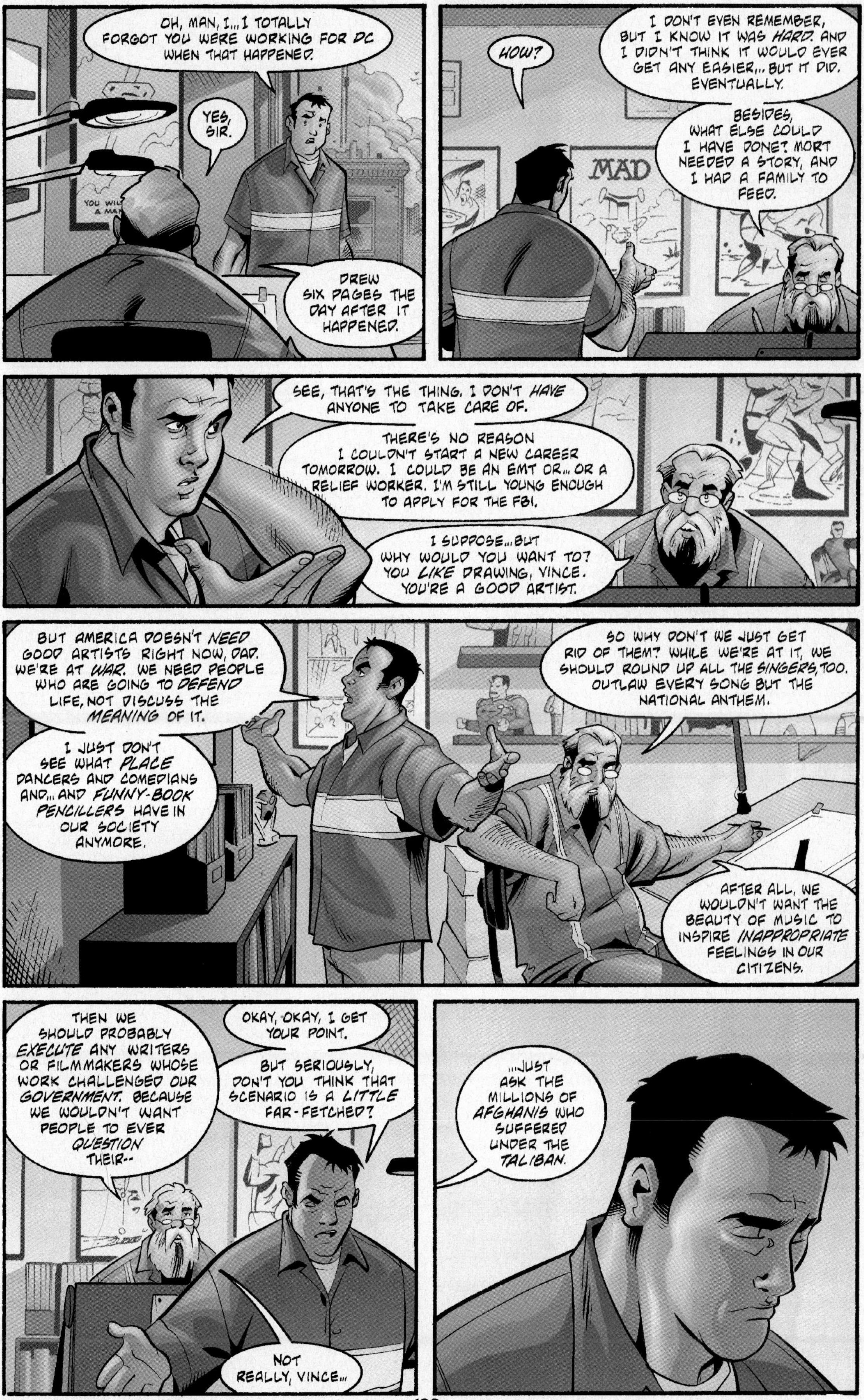
OH, MAN, I... I TOTALLY FORGOT YOU WERE WORKING FOR DC WHEN THAT HAPPENED.
YES, SIR.
DREW SIX PAGES THE DAY AFTER IT HAPPENED.
HOW?
I DON'T EVEN REMEMBER, BUT I KNOW IT WAS HARD. AND I DIDN'T THINK IT WOULD EVER GET ANY EASIER... BUT IT DID. EVENTUALLY.
BESIDES, WHAT ELSE COULD I HAVE DONE? MORT NEEDED A STORY, AND I HAD A FAMILY TO FEED.
MAD
SEE, THAT'S THE THING. I DON'T HAVE ANYONE TO TAKE CARE OF.
THERE'S NO REASON I COULDN'T START A NEW CAREER TOMORROW. I COULD BE AN EMT OR... OR A RELIEF WORKER. I'M STILL YOUNG ENOUGH TO APPLY FOR THE FBI.
I SUPPOSE... BUT WHY WOULD YOU WANT TO? YOU LIKE DRAWING, VINCE. YOU'RE A GOOD ARTIST.
BUT AMERICA DOESN'T NEED GOOD ARTISTS RIGHT NOW, DAD. WE'RE AT WAR. WE NEED PEOPLE WHO ARE GOING TO DEFEND LIFE, NOT DISCUSS THE MEANING OF IT.
I JUST DON'T SEE WHAT PLACE DANCERS AND COMEDIANS AND... AND FUNNY-BOOK PENCILLERS HAVE IN OUR SOCIETY ANYMORE.
SO WHY DON'T WE JUST GET RID OF THEM? WHILE WE'RE AT IT, WE SHOULD ROUND UP ALL THE SINGERS, TOO. OUTLAW EVERY SONG BUT THE NATIONAL ANTHEM.
AFTER ALL, WE WOULDN'T WANT THE BEAUTY OF MUSIC TO INSPIRE INAPPROPRIATE FEELINGS IN OUR CITIZENS.
THEN WE SHOULD PROBABLY EXECUTE ANY WRITERS OR FILMMAKERS WHOSE WORK CHALLENGED OUR GOVERNMENT. BECAUSE WE WOULDN'T WANT PEOPLE TO EVER QUESTION THEIR--
OKAY, OKAY, I GET YOUR POINT.
BUT SERIOUSLY, DON'T YOU THINK THAT SCENARIO IS A LITTLE FAR-FETCHED?
NOT REALLY, VINCE...
...JUST ASK THE MILLIONS OF AFGHANIS WHO SUFFERED UNDER THE TALIBAN.

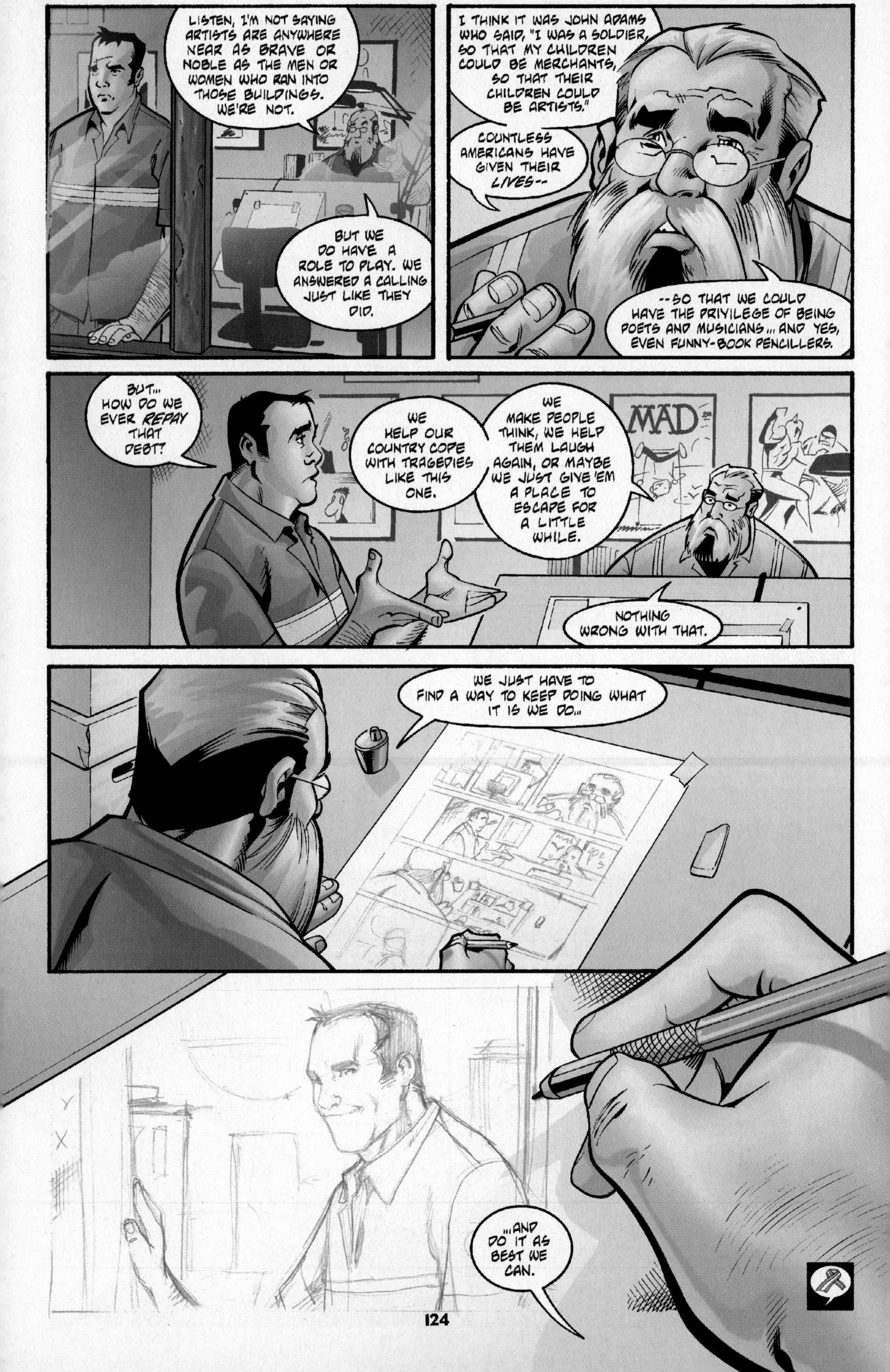
LISTEN, I'M NOT SAYING ARTISTS ARE ANYWHERE NEAR AS BRAVE OR NOBLE AS THE MEN OR WOMEN WHO RAN INTO THOSE BUILDINGS. WE'RE NOT.
BUT WE DO HAVE A ROLE TO PLAY. WE ANSWERED A CALLING JUST LIKE THEY DID.
I THINK IT WAS JOHN ADAMS WHO SAID, "I WAS A SOLDIER, SO THAT MY CHILDREN COULD BE MERCHANTS, SO THAT THEIR CHILDREN COULD BE ARTISTS."
COUNTLESS AMERICANS HAVE GIVEN THEIR *LIVES*--
--SO THAT WE COULD HAVE THE PRIVILEGE OF BEING POETS AND MUSICIANS... AND YES, EVEN FUNNY-BOOK PENCILLERS.
BUT... HOW DO WE EVER *REPAY* THAT DEBT?
WE HELP OUR COUNTRY COPE WITH TRAGEDIES LIKE THIS ONE.
WE MAKE PEOPLE THINK, WE HELP THEM LAUGH AGAIN, OR MAYBE WE JUST GIVE 'EM A PLACE TO ESCAPE FOR A LITTLE WHILE.
MAD
NOTHING WRONG WITH THAT.
WE JUST HAVE TO FIND A WAY TO KEEP DOING WHAT IT IS WE DO...
...AND DO IT AS BEST WE CAN.

NO SALE

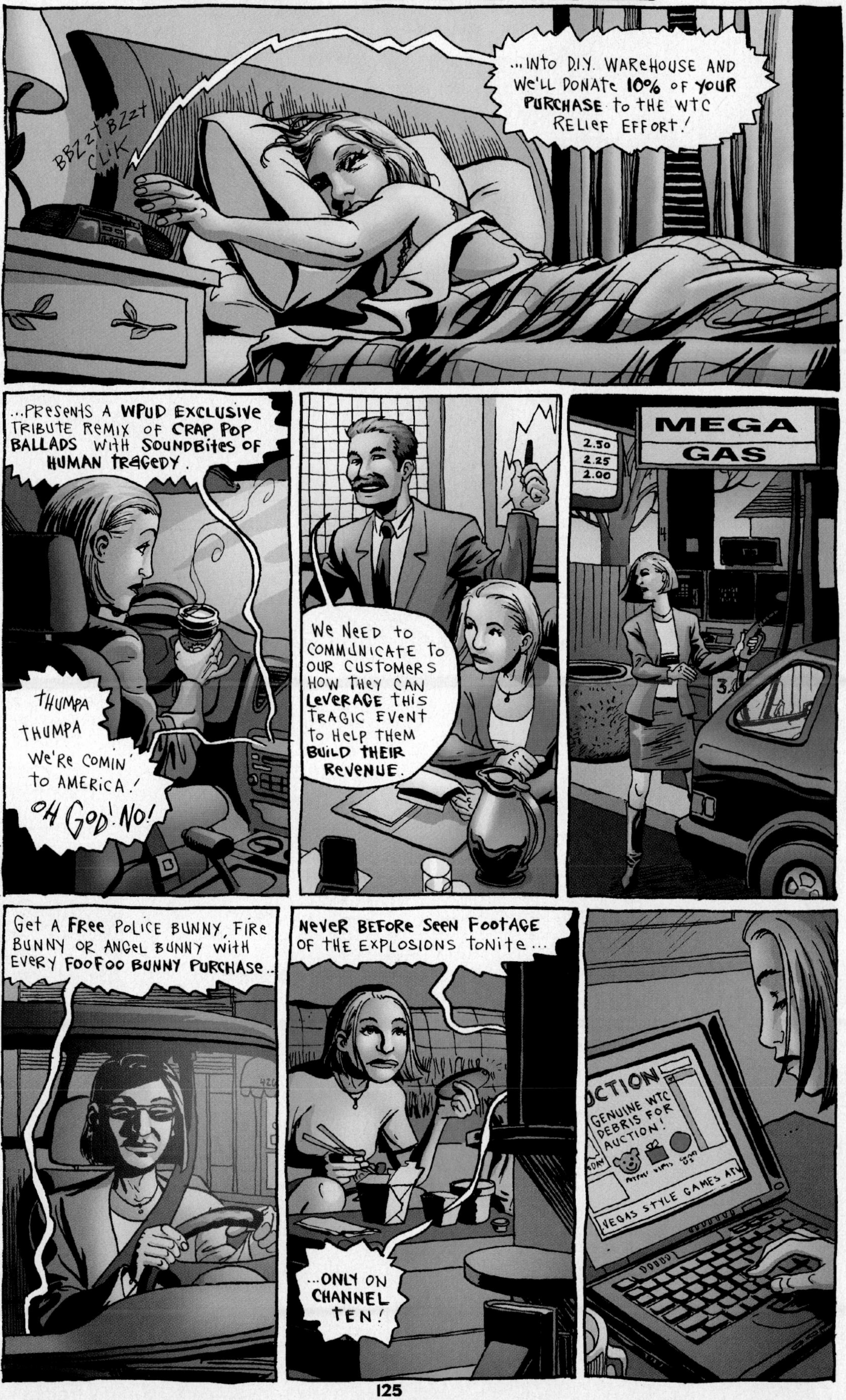

BBZzt BZzt CLiK
...INTO D.I.Y. WAREHOUSE AND WE'LL DONATE 10% OF YOUR PURCHASE TO THE WTC RELIEF EFFORT!
...PRESENTS A WPUD EXCLUSIVE TRIBUTE REMIX OF CRAP POP BALLADS WITH SOUNDBITES OF HUMAN TRAGEDY.
THUMPA THUMPA WE'RE COMIN' TO AMERICA! OH GOD! NO!
WE NEED TO COMMUNICATE TO OUR CUSTOMERS HOW THEY CAN LEVERAGE THIS TRAGIC EVENT TO HELP THEM BUILD THEIR REVENUE.
MEGA GAS
2.50
2.25
2.00
GET A FREE POLICE BUNNY, FIRE BUNNY OR ANGEL BUNNY WITH EVERY FOOFOO BUNNY PURCHASE...
NEVER BEFORE SEEN FOOTAGE OF THE EXPLOSIONS TONITE...
...ONLY ON CHANNEL TEN!
UCTION
GENUINE WTC DEBRIS FOR AUCTION!
VEGAS STYLE GAMES AT

STORY JENNIFER MOORE
ART & LETTERS JILL THOMPSON
COLOR WIL STOR

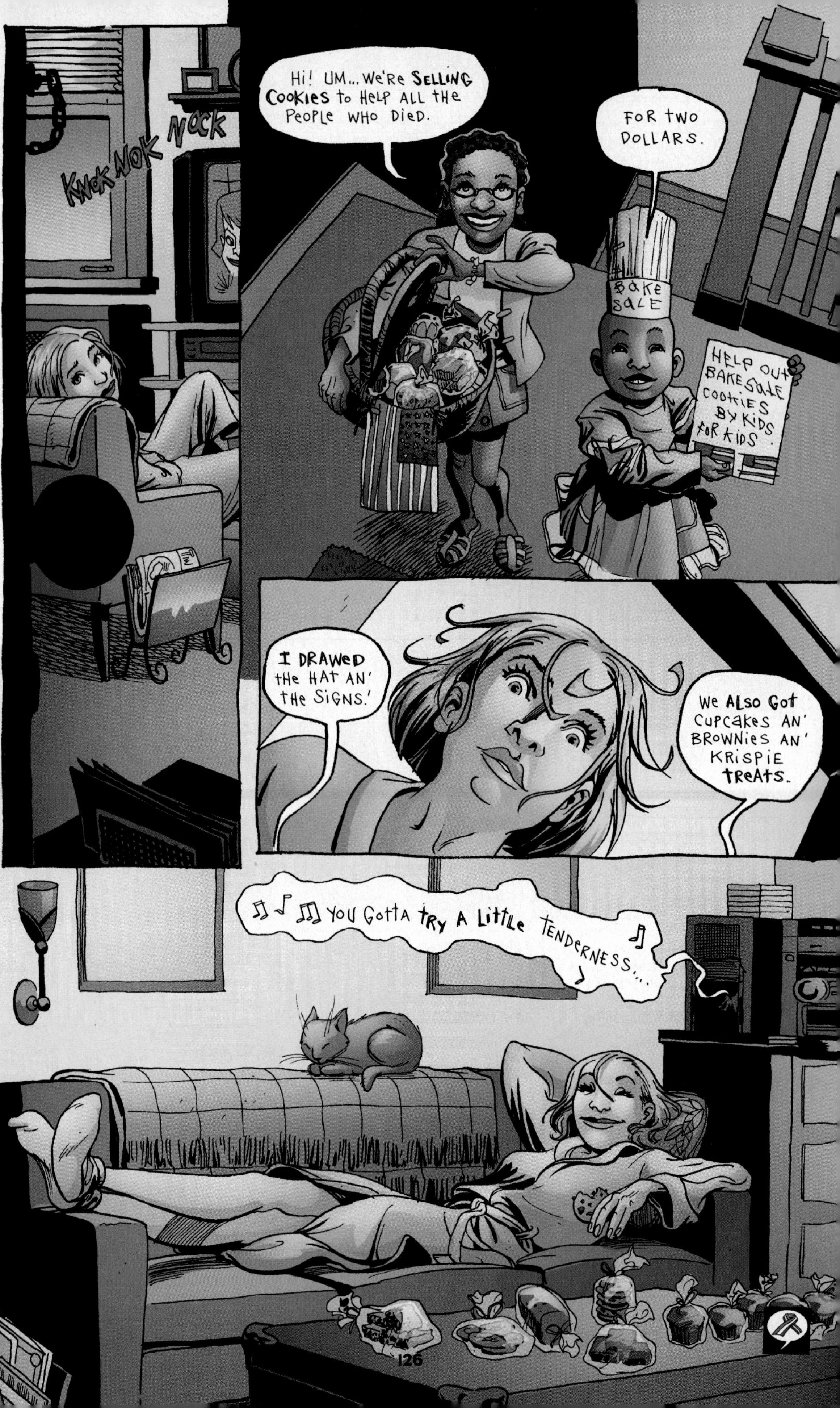
KNOCK NOK NOCK
Hi! UM... We're SELLING COOKIES to HELP ALL THE PEOPLE WHO DIED.
FOR TWO DOLLARS.
BAKE SALE
HELP OUT BAKE SALE COOKIES BY KIDS FOR KIDS.
I DRAWED THE HAT AN' THE SIGNS.
We ALSO GOT CUPCAKES AN' BROWNIES AN' KRISPIE TREATS.
YOU GOTTA TRY A LITTLE TENDERNESS...

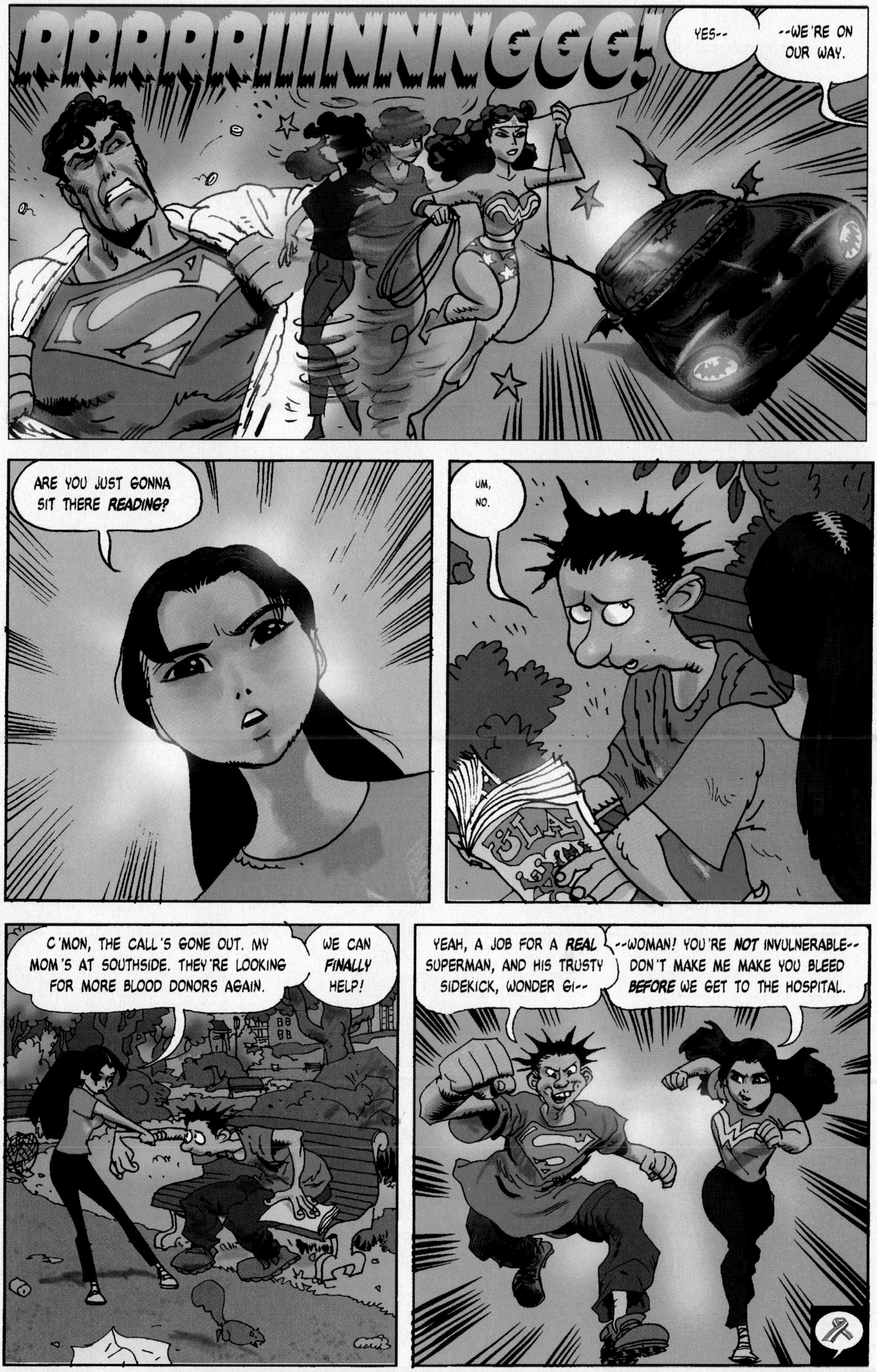
RRRRRIIIINNNNGGG!
YES--
--WE'RE ON OUR WAY.
ARE YOU JUST GONNA SIT THERE READING?
UM, NO.
C'MON, THE CALL'S GONE OUT. MY MOM'S AT SOUTHSIDE. THEY'RE LOOKING FOR MORE BLOOD DONORS AGAIN.
WE CAN FINALLY HELP!
YEAH, A JOB FOR A REAL SUPERMAN, AND HIS TRUSTY SIDEKICK, WONDER GI--
--WOMAN! YOU'RE NOT INVULNERABLE-- DON'T MAKE ME MAKE YOU BLEED BEFORE WE GET TO THE HOSPITAL.

THE CALL

STORY EDDIE BERGANZA

ART, COLOR & LETTERS KYLE BAKER

A Tale of Two Americans

STORY
BEN RAAB
★★★★
ART
ROGER ROBINSON
AND
DENNIS JANKE
★★★★
LETTERS
KURT HATHAWAY
★★★★
COLOR
WILDSTORM
★★★★

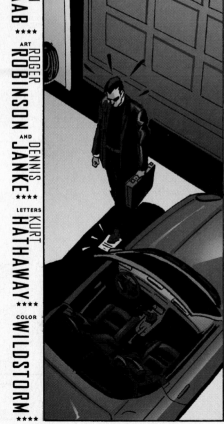

NEIGHBORHOOD CHARITY DRIVE & CANDLELIGHT VIGIL THIS FRIDAY NIGHT! COME ONE, COME ALL! DONATIONS WELCOME! HELP US HELP THE VIC- TIMS OF 9/11 ANY WAY YOU CAN!

HEY THERE, NEIGHBOR!

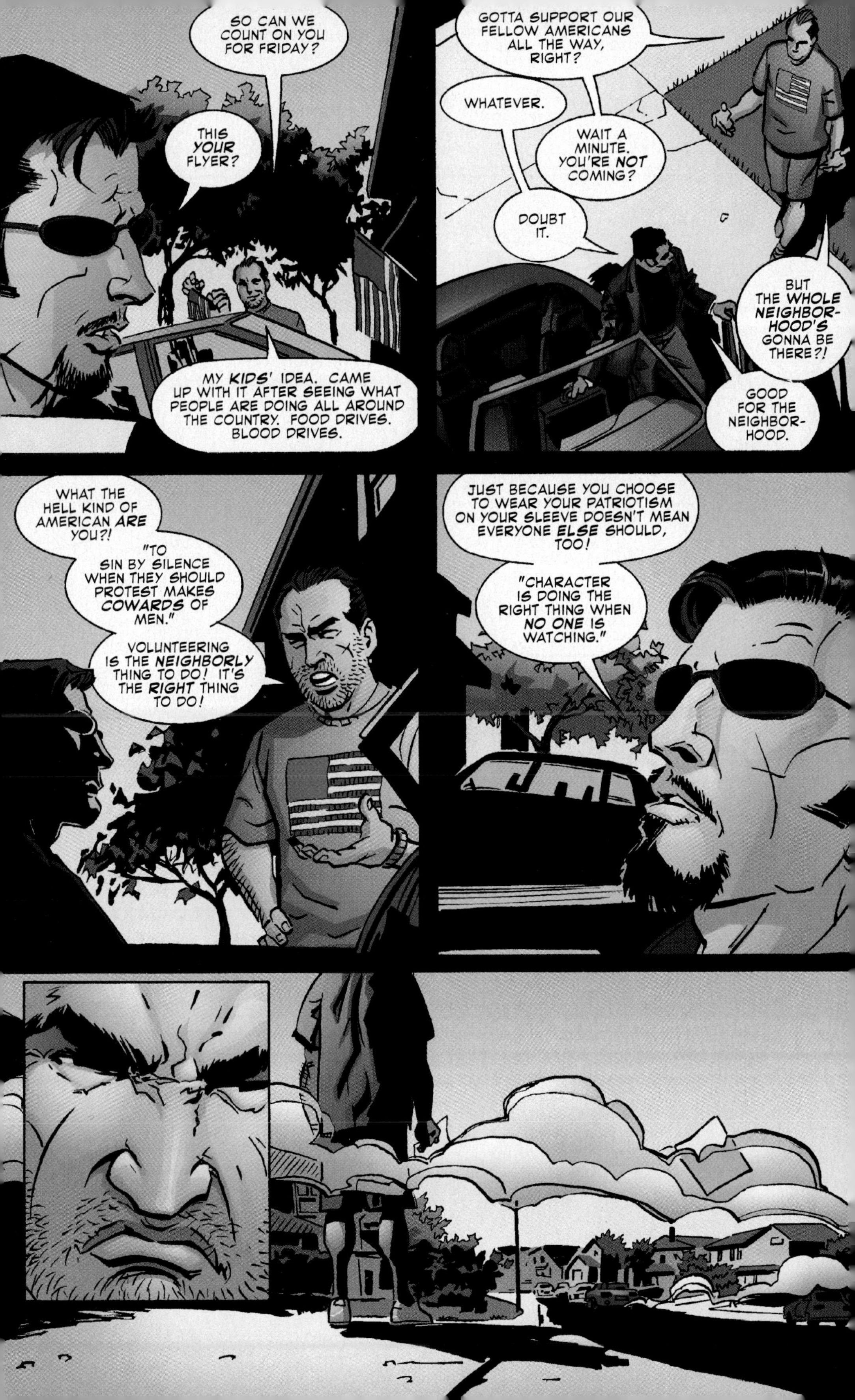
SO CAN WE COUNT ON YOU FOR FRIDAY?
THIS YOUR FLYER?
MY KIDS' IDEA. CAME UP WITH IT AFTER SEEING WHAT PEOPLE ARE DOING ALL AROUND THE COUNTRY. FOOD DRIVES. BLOOD DRIVES.
GOTTA SUPPORT OUR FELLOW AMERICANS ALL THE WAY, RIGHT?
WHATEVER.
WAIT A MINUTE. YOU'RE NOT COMING?
DOUBT IT.
BUT THE WHOLE NEIGHBOR-HOOD'S GONNA BE THERE?!
GOOD FOR THE NEIGHBOR-HOOD.
WHAT THE HELL KIND OF AMERICAN ARE YOU?!
"TO SIN BY SILENCE WHEN THEY SHOULD PROTEST MAKES COWARDS OF MEN."
VOLUNTEERING IS THE NEIGHBORLY THING TO DO! IT'S THE RIGHT THING TO DO!
JUST BECAUSE YOU CHOOSE TO WEAR YOUR PATRIOTISM ON YOUR SLEEVE DOESN'T MEAN EVERYONE ELSE SHOULD, TOO!
"CHARACTER IS DOING THE RIGHT THING WHEN NO ONE IS WATCHING."

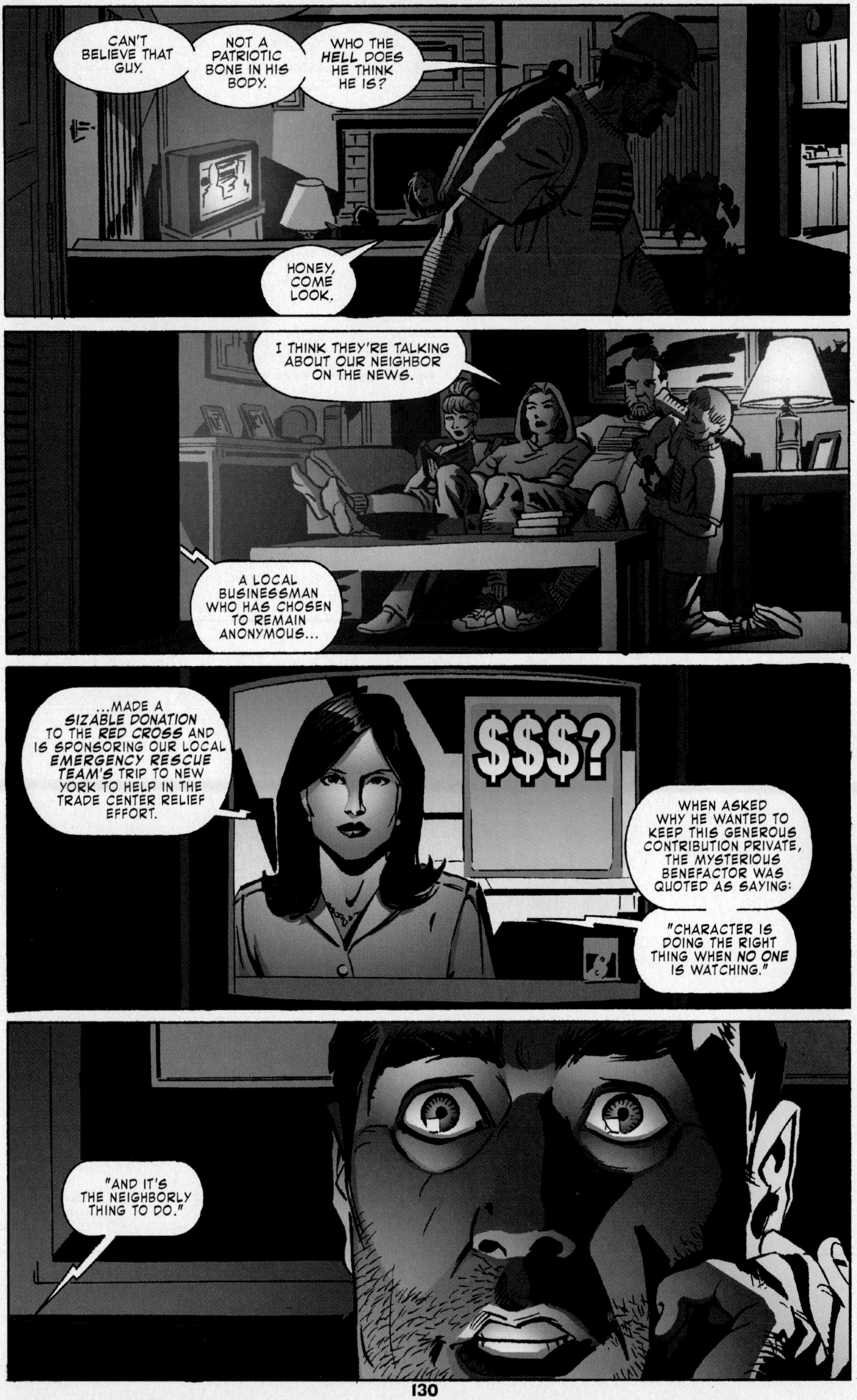
CAN'T BELIEVE THAT GUY.
NOT A PATRIOTIC BONE IN HIS BODY.
WHO THE HELL DOES HE THINK HE IS?
HONEY, COME LOOK.
I THINK THEY'RE TALKING ABOUT OUR NEIGHBOR ON THE NEWS.
A LOCAL BUSINESSMAN WHO HAS CHOSEN TO REMAIN ANONYMOUS...
...MADE A SIZABLE DONATION TO THE RED CROSS AND IS SPONSORING OUR LOCAL EMERGENCY RESCUE TEAM'S TRIP TO NEW YORK TO HELP IN THE TRADE CENTER RELIEF EFFORT.
$$$?
WHEN ASKED WHY HE WANTED TO KEEP THIS GENEROUS CONTRIBUTION PRIVATE, THE MYSTERIOUS BENEFACTOR WAS QUOTED AS SAYING:
"CHARACTER IS DOING THE RIGHT THING WHEN NO ONE IS WATCHING."
"AND IT'S THE NEIGHBORLY THING TO DO."

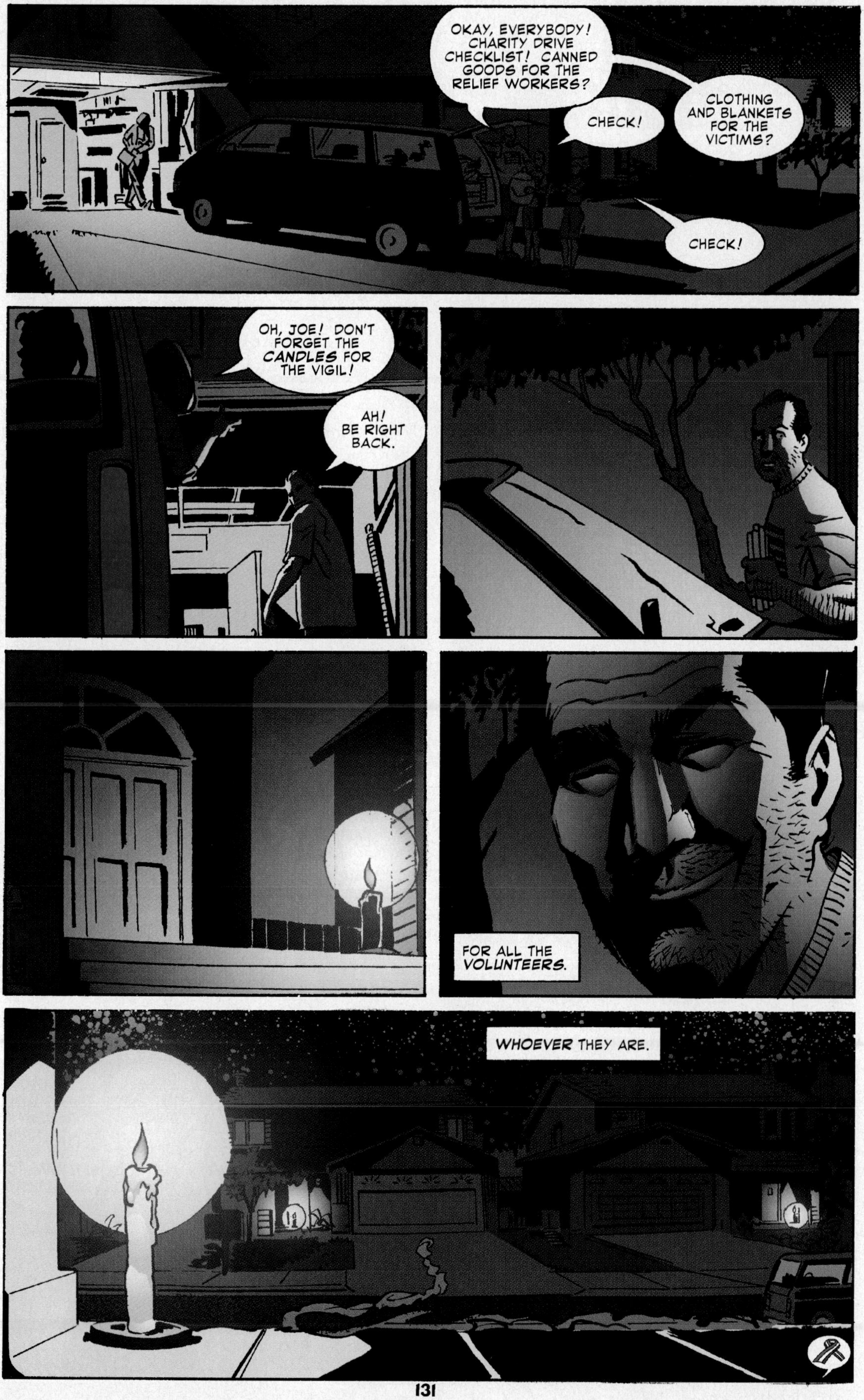
OKAY, EVERYBODY! CHARITY DRIVE CHECKLIST! CANNED GOODS FOR THE RELIEF WORKERS?
CHECK!
CLOTHING AND BLANKETS FOR THE VICTIMS?
CHECK!
OH, JOE! DON'T FORGET THE CANDLES FOR THE VIGIL!
AH! BE RIGHT BACK.
FOR ALL THE VOLUNTEERS.
WHOEVER THEY ARE.

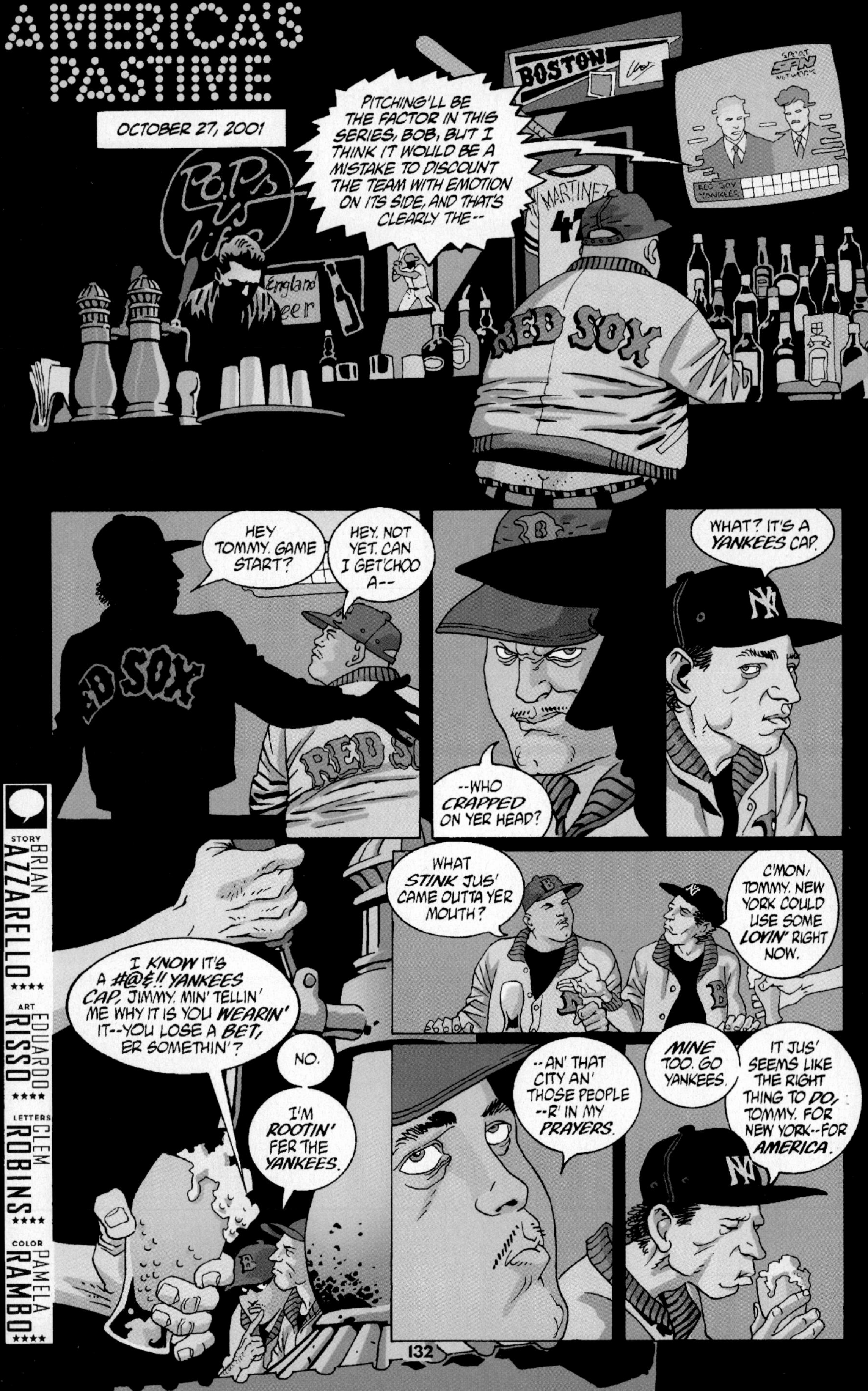
AMERICA'S PASTIME
OCTOBER 27, 2001
PITCHING'LL BE THE FACTOR IN THIS SERIES, BOB, BUT I THINK IT WOULD BE A MISTAKE TO DISCOUNT THE TEAM WITH EMOTION ON ITS SIDE, AND THAT'S CLEARLY THE--
BOSTON
RED SOX
HEY TOMMY. GAME START?
HEY. NOT YET. CAN I GET'CHOO A--
--WHO CRAPPED ON YER HEAD?
WHAT? IT'S A YANKEES CAP.
I KNOW IT'S A #@&!! YANKEES CAP, JIMMY. MIN' TELLIN' ME WHY IT IS YOU WEARIN' IT--YOU LOSE A BET, ER SOMETHIN'?
NO.
I'M ROOTIN' FER THE YANKEES.
WHAT STINK JUS' CAME OUTTA YER MOUTH?
C'MON, TOMMY. NEW YORK COULD USE SOME LOVIN' RIGHT NOW.
--AN' THAT CITY AN' THOSE PEOPLE --R' IN MY PRAYERS.
MINE TOO. GO YANKEES.
IT JUS' SEEMS LIKE THE RIGHT THING TO DO, TOMMY. FOR NEW YORK--FOR AMERICA.
STORY BRIAN AZZARELLO
ART EDUARDO RISSO
LETTERS CLEM ROBINS
COLOR PAMELA RAMBO

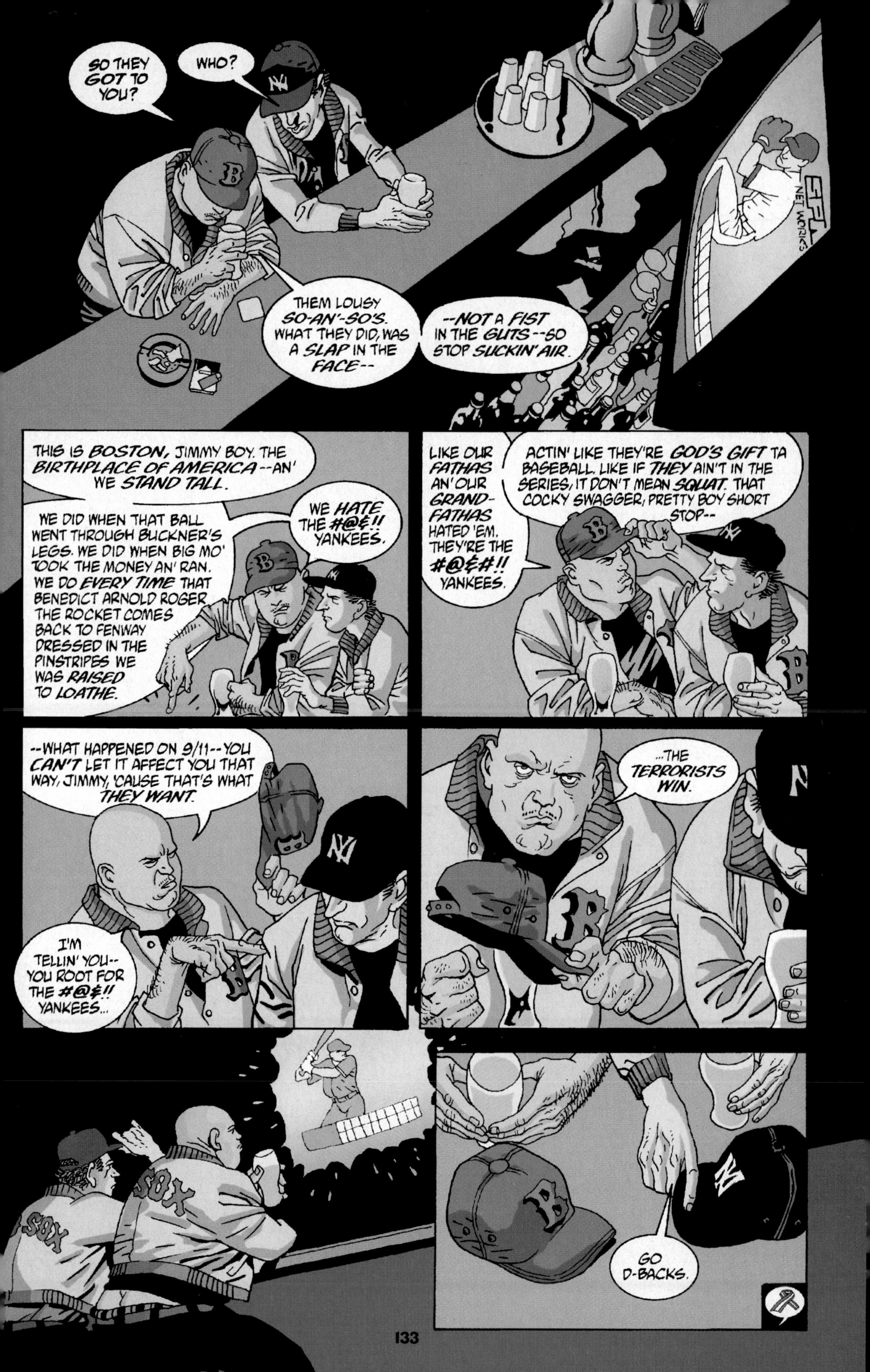
SO THEY GOT TO YOU?
WHO?
SPL NETWORKS
THEM LOUSY SO-AN'-SO'S. WHAT THEY DID, WAS A SLAP IN THE FACE--
--NOT A FIST IN THE GUTS--SO STOP SUCKIN' AIR.
THIS IS BOSTON, JIMMY BOY. THE BIRTHPLACE OF AMERICA--AN' WE STAND TALL.
WE DID WHEN THAT BALL WENT THROUGH BUCKNER'S LEGS. WE DID WHEN BIG MO' TOOK THE MONEY AN' RAN. WE DO EVERY TIME THAT BENEDICT ARNOLD ROGER THE ROCKET COMES BACK TO FENWAY DRESSED IN THE PINSTRIPES WE WAS RAISED TO LOATHE.
WE HATE THE #@₤!! YANKEES.
LIKE OUR FATHAS AN' OUR GRAND-FATHAS HATED 'EM. THEY'RE THE #@₤#!! YANKEES.
ACTIN' LIKE THEY'RE GOD'S GIFT TA BASEBALL. LIKE IF THEY AIN'T IN THE SERIES, IT DON'T MEAN SQUAT. THAT COCKY SWAGGER, PRETTY BOY SHORT STOP--
--WHAT HAPPENED ON 9/11--YOU CAN'T LET IT AFFECT YOU THAT WAY, JIMMY, 'CAUSE THAT'S WHAT THEY WANT.
I'M TELLIN' YOU--YOU ROOT FOR THE #@₤!! YANKEES...
...THE TERRORISTS WIN.
SOX
SOX
GO D-BACKS.

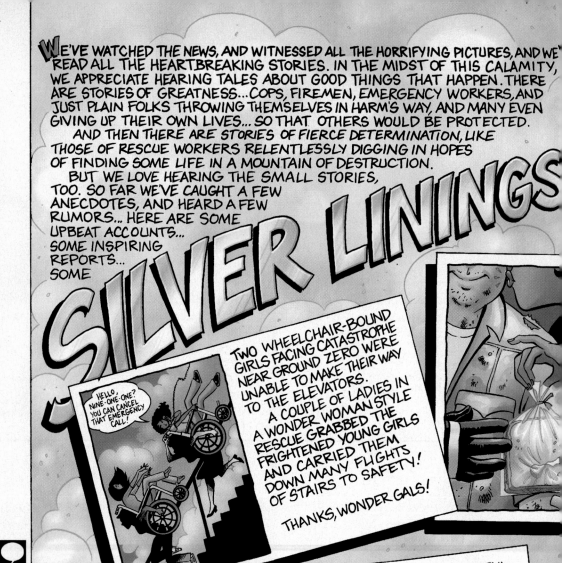

WE'VE WATCHED THE NEWS, AND WITNESSED ALL THE HORRIFYING PICTURES, AND WE READ ALL THE HEARTBREAKING STORIES. IN THE MIDST OF THIS CALAMITY, WE APPRECIATE HEARING TALES ABOUT GOOD THINGS THAT HAPPEN. THERE ARE STORIES OF GREATNESS...COPS, FIREMEN, EMERGENCY WORKERS, AND JUST PLAIN FOLKS THROWING THEMSELVES IN HARM'S WAY, AND MANY EVEN GIVING UP THEIR OWN LIVES... SO THAT OTHERS WOULD BE PROTECTED.

AND THEN THERE ARE STORIES OF FIERCE DETERMINATION, LIKE THOSE OF RESCUE WORKERS RELENTLESSLY DIGGING IN HOPES OF FINDING SOME LIFE IN A MOUNTAIN OF DESTRUCTION.

BUT WE LOVE HEARING THE SMALL STORIES, TOO. SO FAR WE'VE CAUGHT A FEW ANECDOTES, AND HEARD A FEW RUMORS... HERE ARE SOME UPBEAT ACCOUNTS... SOME INSPIRING REPORTS... SOME

SILVER LININGS

HELLO, NINE-ONE-ONE? YOU CAN CANCEL THAT EMERGENCY CALL!

TWO WHEELCHAIR-BOUND GIRLS FACING CATASTROPHE NEAR GROUND ZERO WERE UNABLE TO MAKE THEIR WAY TO THE ELEVATORS.

A COUPLE OF LADIES IN A WONDER WOMAN STYLE RESCUE GRABBED THE FRIGHTENED YOUNG GIRLS AND CARRIED THEM DOWN MANY FLIGHTS OF STAIRS TO SAFETY!

THANKS, WONDER GALS!

A COMPANY THAT MANUFACTURES PROTECTIVE FOOTWEAR TEMPORARILY HALTED PRODUCTION ON HUMAN FOOTWEAR ('CAUSE THERE WAS ALREADY PLENTY OF THAT), AND STARTED MAKING PROTECTIVE FOOTWEAR FOR ALL OF THE SNIFFER DOGS WORKING TIRELESSLY AT THE GLASS AND DEBRIS-LITTERED DISASTER SITE.

EXHAUSTED AND SORROWFUL RED CROSS VOLUNTEERS. WHO WERE FIELDING THOUSANDS OF MISSING PERSONS PHONE CALLS, TOOK AN UPLIFTING AND SORELY NEEDED BREAK TO HELP CELEBRATE THE WEDDING CEREMONY OF TWO FELLOW VOLUNTEERS IN AN OFFICE HALLWAY.

THE BRIDE WORE DAISIES FROM A LOCAL DELI AND A NEARBY CAFE SUPPLIED THE CAKE, ALL ON THE HOUSE!

STORY & ART
AMANDA CONNER AND JIMMY PALMIOTTI
★★★★
LETTERS AMANDA CONNOR
★★★★
COLOR PAUL MOUNTS
★★★★

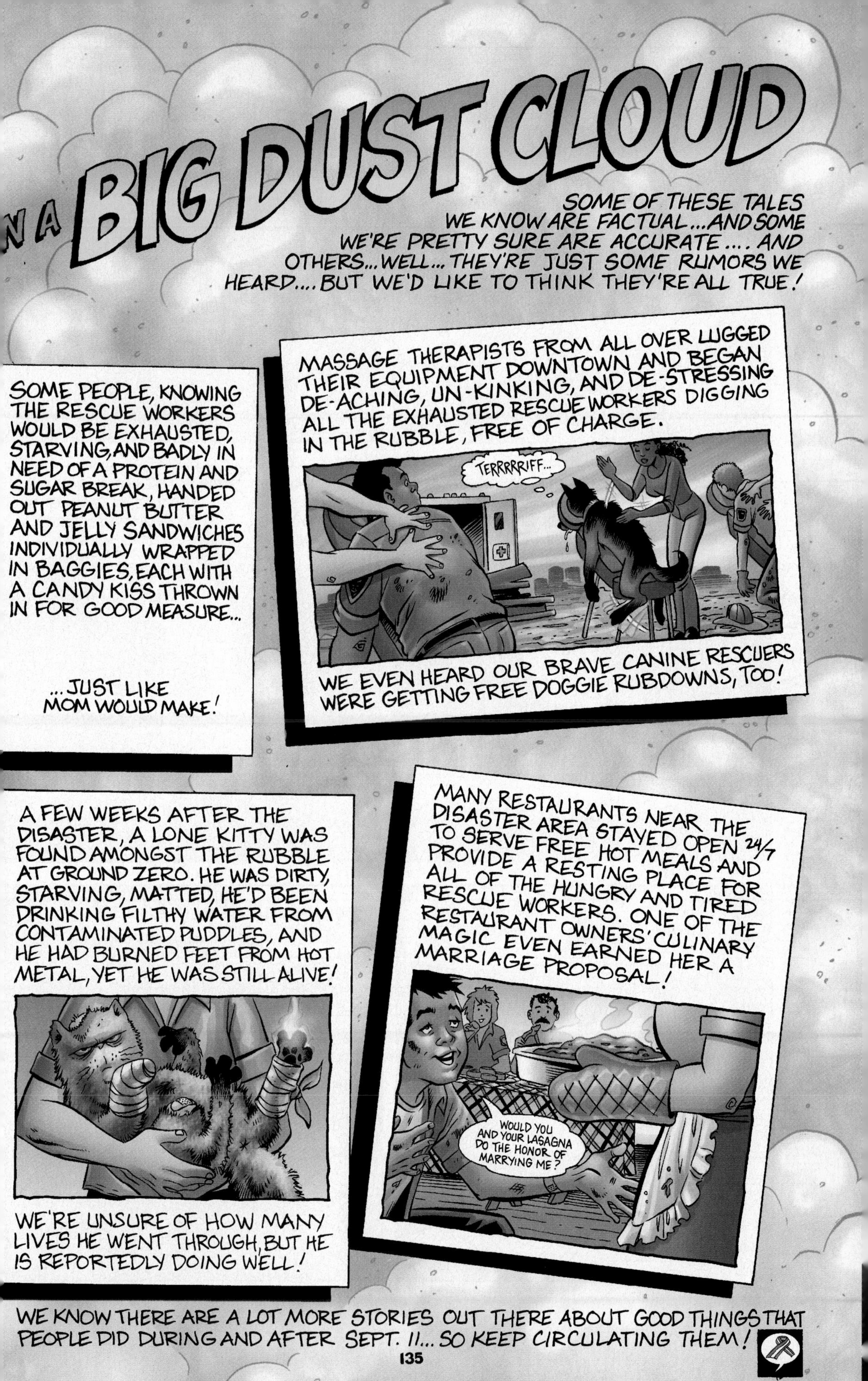
N A BIG DUST CLOUD
SOME OF THESE TALES WE KNOW ARE FACTUAL ... AND SOME WE'RE PRETTY SURE ARE ACCURATE .... AND OTHERS... WELL... THEY'RE JUST SOME RUMORS WE HEARD.... BUT WE'D LIKE TO THINK THEY'RE ALL TRUE!
SOME PEOPLE, KNOWING THE RESCUE WORKERS WOULD BE EXHAUSTED, STARVING, AND BADLY IN NEED OF A PROTEIN AND SUGAR BREAK, HANDED OUT PEANUT BUTTER AND JELLY SANDWICHES INDIVIDUALLY WRAPPED IN BAGGIES, EACH WITH A CANDY KISS THROWN IN FOR GOOD MEASURE...
...JUST LIKE MOM WOULD MAKE!
MASSAGE THERAPISTS FROM ALL OVER LUGGED THEIR EQUIPMENT DOWNTOWN AND BEGAN DE-ACHING, UN-KINKING, AND DE-STRESSING ALL THE EXHAUSTED RESCUE WORKERS DIGGING IN THE RUBBLE, FREE OF CHARGE.
TERRRRRIFF...
WE EVEN HEARD OUR BRAVE CANINE RESCUERS WERE GETTING FREE DOGGIE RUBDOWNS, TOO!
A FEW WEEKS AFTER THE DISASTER, A LONE KITTY WAS FOUND AMONGST THE RUBBLE AT GROUND ZERO. HE WAS DIRTY, STARVING, MATTED, HE'D BEEN DRINKING FILTHY WATER FROM CONTAMINATED PUDDLES, AND HE HAD BURNED FEET FROM HOT METAL, YET HE WAS STILL ALIVE!
WE'RE UNSURE OF HOW MANY LIVES HE WENT THROUGH, BUT HE IS REPORTEDLY DOING WELL!
MANY RESTAURANTS NEAR THE DISASTER AREA STAYED OPEN 24/7 TO SERVE FREE HOT MEALS AND PROVIDE A RESTING PLACE FOR ALL OF THE HUNGRY AND TIRED RESCUE WORKERS. ONE OF THE RESTAURANT OWNERS' CULINARY MAGIC EVEN EARNED HER A MARRIAGE PROPOSAL!
WOULD YOU AND YOUR LASAGNA DO THE HONOR OF MARRYING ME?
WE KNOW THERE ARE A LOT MORE STORIES OUT THERE ABOUT GOOD THINGS THAT PEOPLE DID DURING AND AFTER SEPT. 11... SO KEEP CIRCULATING THEM!

WHAT WE LEARNED TODAY

STORY **EDDIE BERGANZA**

ART, COLOR & LETTERS **KYLE BAKER**

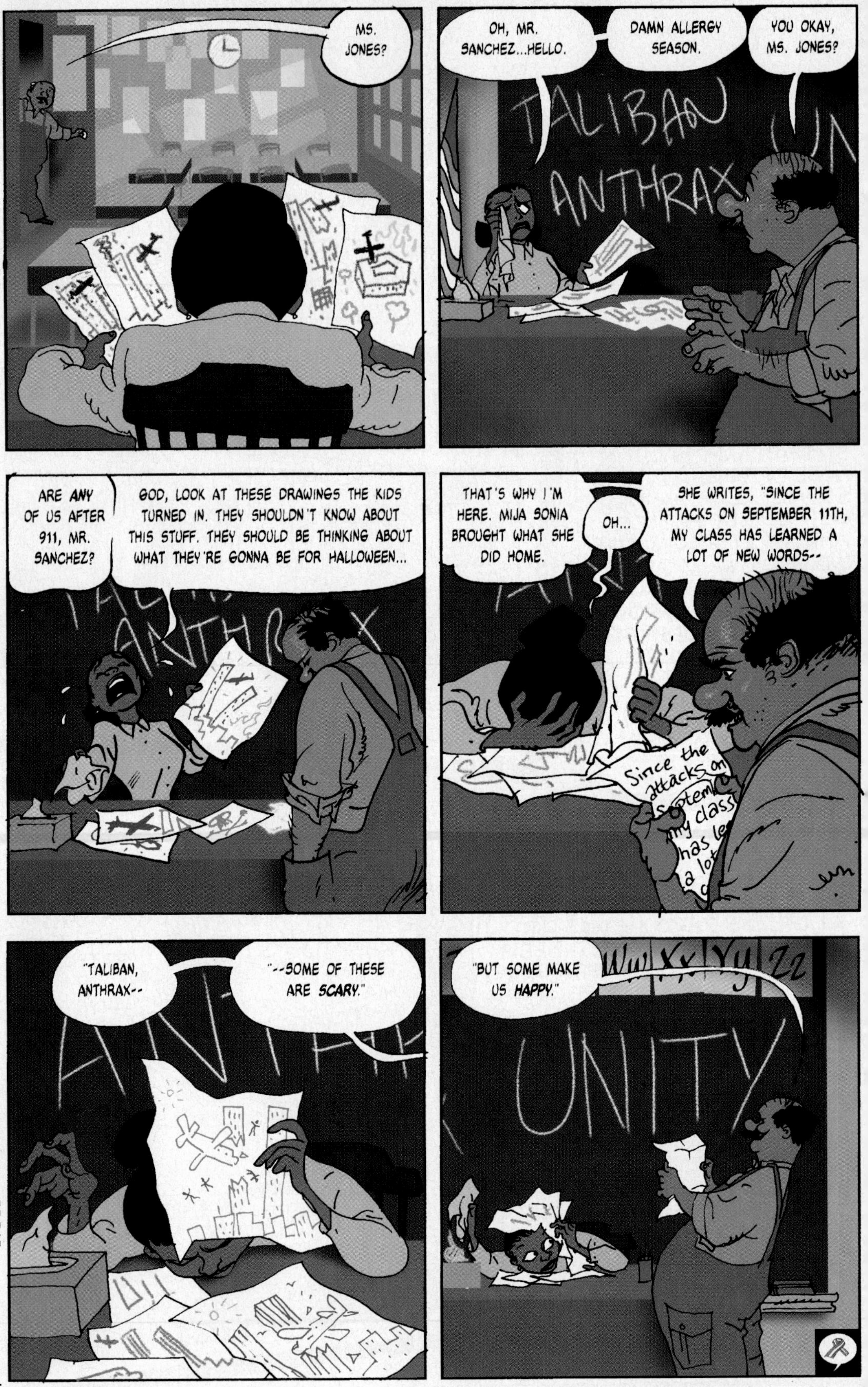
MS. JONES?
OH, MR. SANCHEZ...HELLO.
DAMN ALLERGY SEASON.
YOU OKAY, MS. JONES?
TALIBAN
ANTHRAX
ARE *ANY* OF US AFTER 911, MR. SANCHEZ?
GOD, LOOK AT THESE DRAWINGS THE KIDS TURNED IN. THEY SHOULDN'T KNOW ABOUT THIS STUFF. THEY SHOULD BE THINKING ABOUT WHAT THEY'RE GONNA BE FOR HALLOWEEN...
THAT'S WHY I'M HERE. MIJA SONIA BROUGHT WHAT SHE DID HOME.
OH...
SHE WRITES, "SINCE THE ATTACKS ON SEPTEMBER 11TH, MY CLASS HAS LEARNED A LOT OF NEW WORDS--
"TALIBAN, ANTHRAX--
"--SOME OF THESE ARE *SCARY*."
"BUT SOME MAKE US *HAPPY*."
UNITY

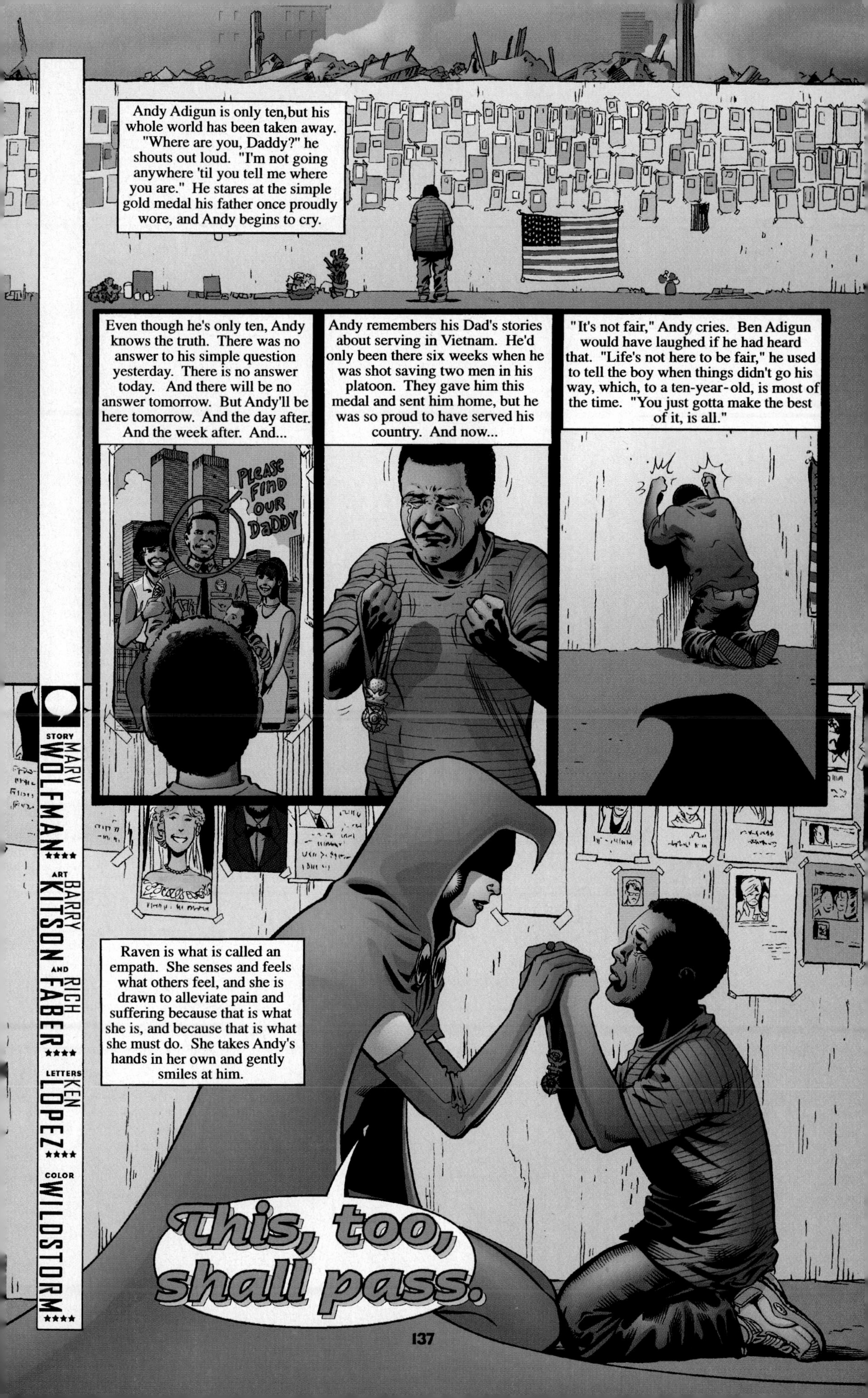

Andy Adigun is only ten, but his whole world has been taken away. "Where are you, Daddy?" he shouts out loud. "I'm not going anywhere 'til you tell me where you are." He stares at the simple gold medal his father once proudly wore, and Andy begins to cry.
Even though he's only ten, Andy knows the truth. There was no answer to his simple question yesterday. There is no answer today. And there will be no answer tomorrow. But Andy'll be here tomorrow. And the day after. And the week after. And...
PLEASE FIND OUR DADDY
Andy remembers his Dad's stories about serving in Vietnam. He'd only been there six weeks when he was shot saving two men in his platoon. They gave him this medal and sent him home, but he was so proud to have served his country. And now...
"It's not fair," Andy cries. Ben Adigun would have laughed if he had heard that. "Life's not here to be fair," he used to tell the boy when things didn't go his way, which, to a ten-year-old, is most of the time. "You just gotta make the best of it, is all."
Raven is what is called an empath. She senses and feels what others feel, and she is drawn to alleviate pain and suffering because that is what she is, and because that is what she must do. She takes Andy's hands in her own and gently smiles at him.
This, too, shall pass.
STORY MARV WOLFMAN
ART BARRY KITSON AND RICH FABER
LETTERS KEN LOPEZ
COLOR WILDSTORM

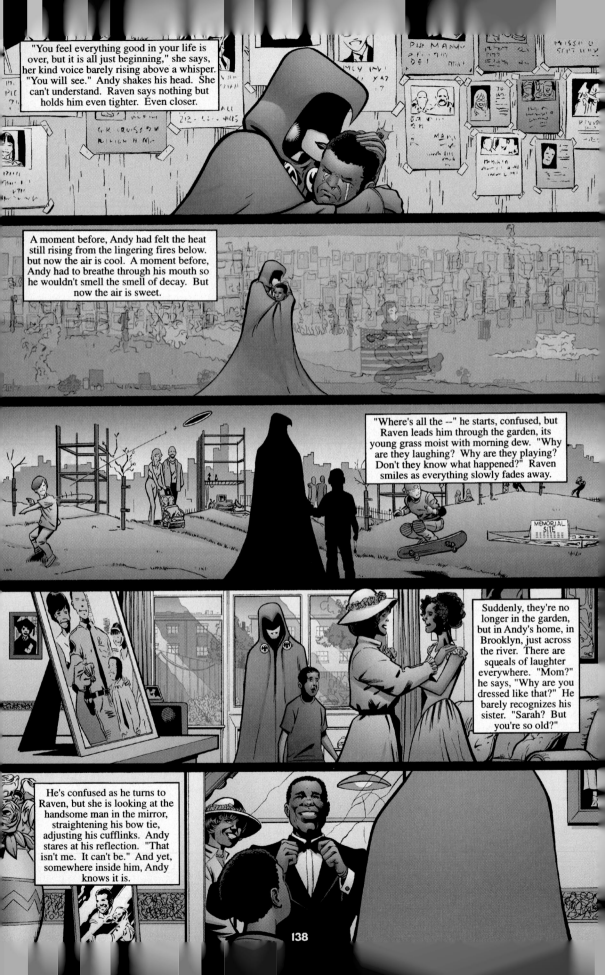

"You feel everything good in your life is over, but it is all just beginning," she says, her kind voice barely rising above a whisper. "You will see." Andy shakes his head. She can't understand. Raven says nothing but holds him even tighter. Even closer.

A moment before, Andy had felt the heat still rising from the lingering fires below. but now the air is cool. A moment before, Andy had to breathe through his mouth so he wouldn't smell the smell of decay. But now the air is sweet.

"Where's all the --" he starts, confused, but Raven leads him through the garden, its young grass moist with morning dew. "Why are they laughing? Why are they playing? Don't they know what happened?" Raven smiles as everything slowly fades away.

Suddenly, they're no longer in the garden, but in Andy's home, in Brooklyn, just across the river. There are squeals of laughter everywhere. "Mom?" he says, "Why are you dressed like that?" He barely recognizes his sister. "Sarah? But you're so old?"

He's confused as he turns to Raven, but she is looking at the handsome man in the mirror, straightening his bow tie, adjusting his cufflinks. Andy stares at his reflection. "That isn't me. It can't be." And yet, somewhere inside him, Andy knows it is.

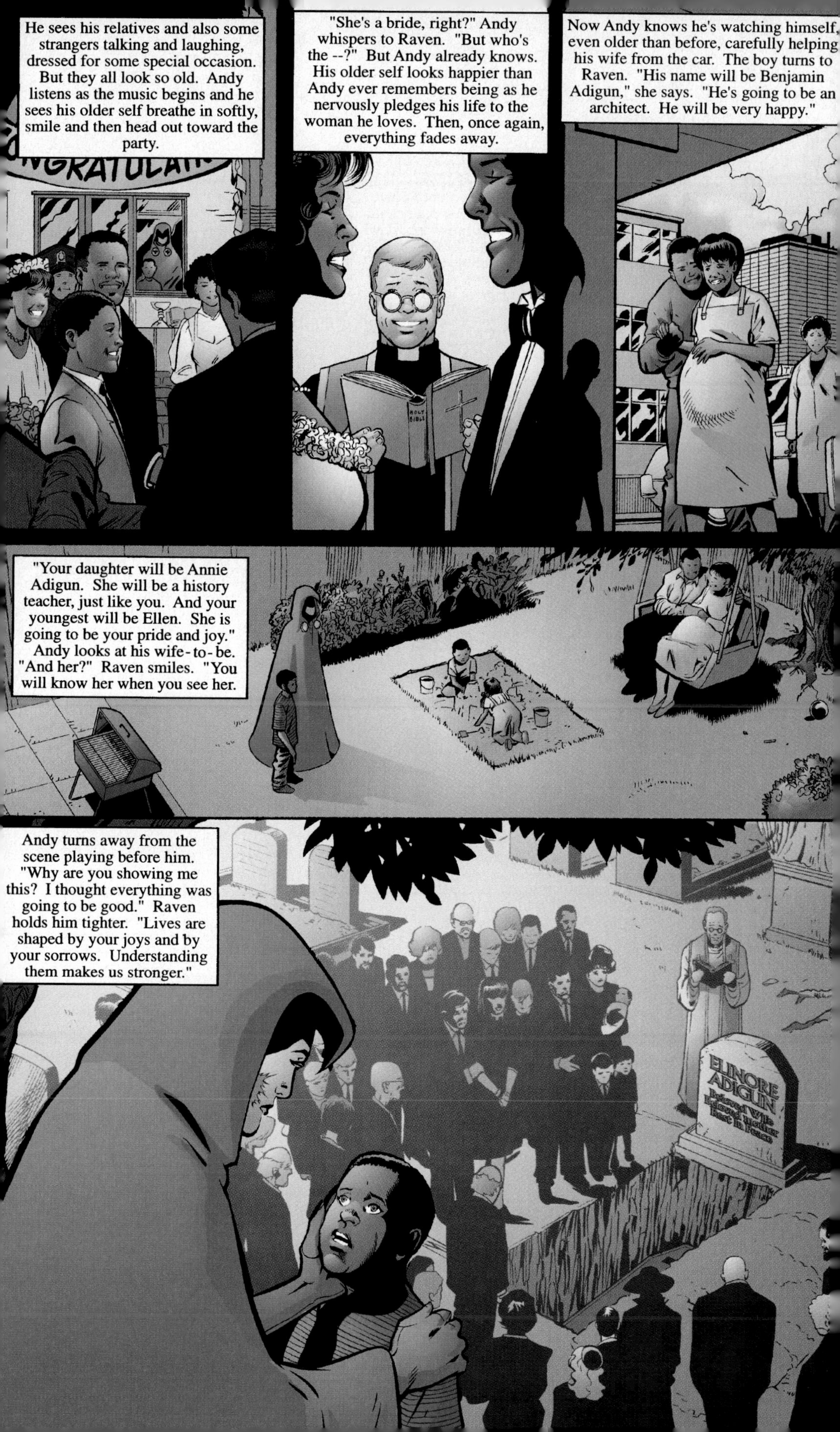
He sees his relatives and also some strangers talking and laughing, dressed for some special occasion. But they all look so old. Andy listens as the music begins and he sees his older self breathe in softly, smile and then head out toward the party.
"She's a bride, right?" Andy whispers to Raven. "But who's the --?" But Andy already knows. His older self looks happier than Andy ever remembers being as he nervously pledges his life to the woman he loves. Then, once again, everything fades away.
Now Andy knows he's watching himself, even older than before, carefully helping his wife from the car. The boy turns to Raven. "His name will be Benjamin Adigun," she says. "He's going to be an architect. He will be very happy."
"Your daughter will be Annie Adigun. She will be a history teacher, just like you. And your youngest will be Ellen. She is going to be your pride and joy." Andy looks at his wife-to-be. "And her?" Raven smiles. "You will know her when you see her.
Andy turns away from the scene playing before him. "Why are you showing me this? I thought everything was going to be good." Raven holds him tighter. "Lives are shaped by your joys and by your sorrows. Understanding them makes us stronger."
ELINORE ADIGUN

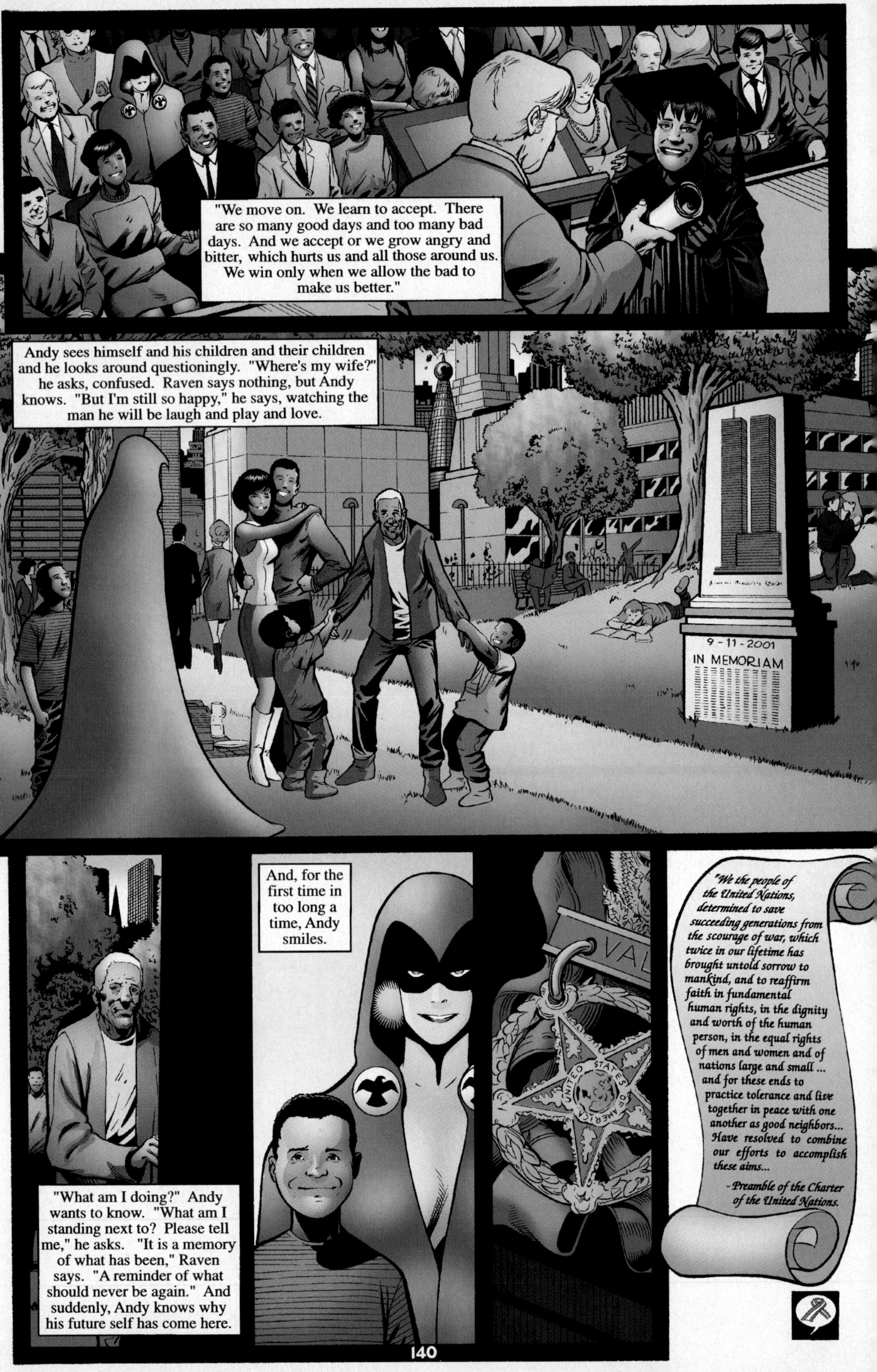
"We move on. We learn to accept. There are so many good days and too many bad days. And we accept or we grow angry and bitter, which hurts us and all those around us. We win only when we allow the bad to make us better."
Andy sees himself and his children and their children and he looks around questioningly. "Where's my wife?" he asks, confused. Raven says nothing, but Andy knows. "But I'm still so happy," he says, watching the man he will be laugh and play and love.
9-11-2001
IN MEMORIAM
"What am I doing?" Andy wants to know. "What am I standing next to? Please tell me," he asks. "It is a memory of what has been," Raven says. "A reminder of what should never be again." And suddenly, Andy knows why his future self has come here.
And, for the first time in too long a time, Andy smiles.
UNITED STATES OF AMERICA
"We the people of the United Nations, determined to save succeeding generations from the scourge of war, which twice in our lifetime has brought untold sorrow to mankind, and to reaffirm faith in fundamental human rights, in the dignity and worth of the human person, in the equal rights of men and women and of nations large and small ... and for these ends to practice tolerance and live together in peace with one another as good neighbors... Have resolved to combine our efforts to accomplish these aims...
-Preamble of the Charter of the United Nations.

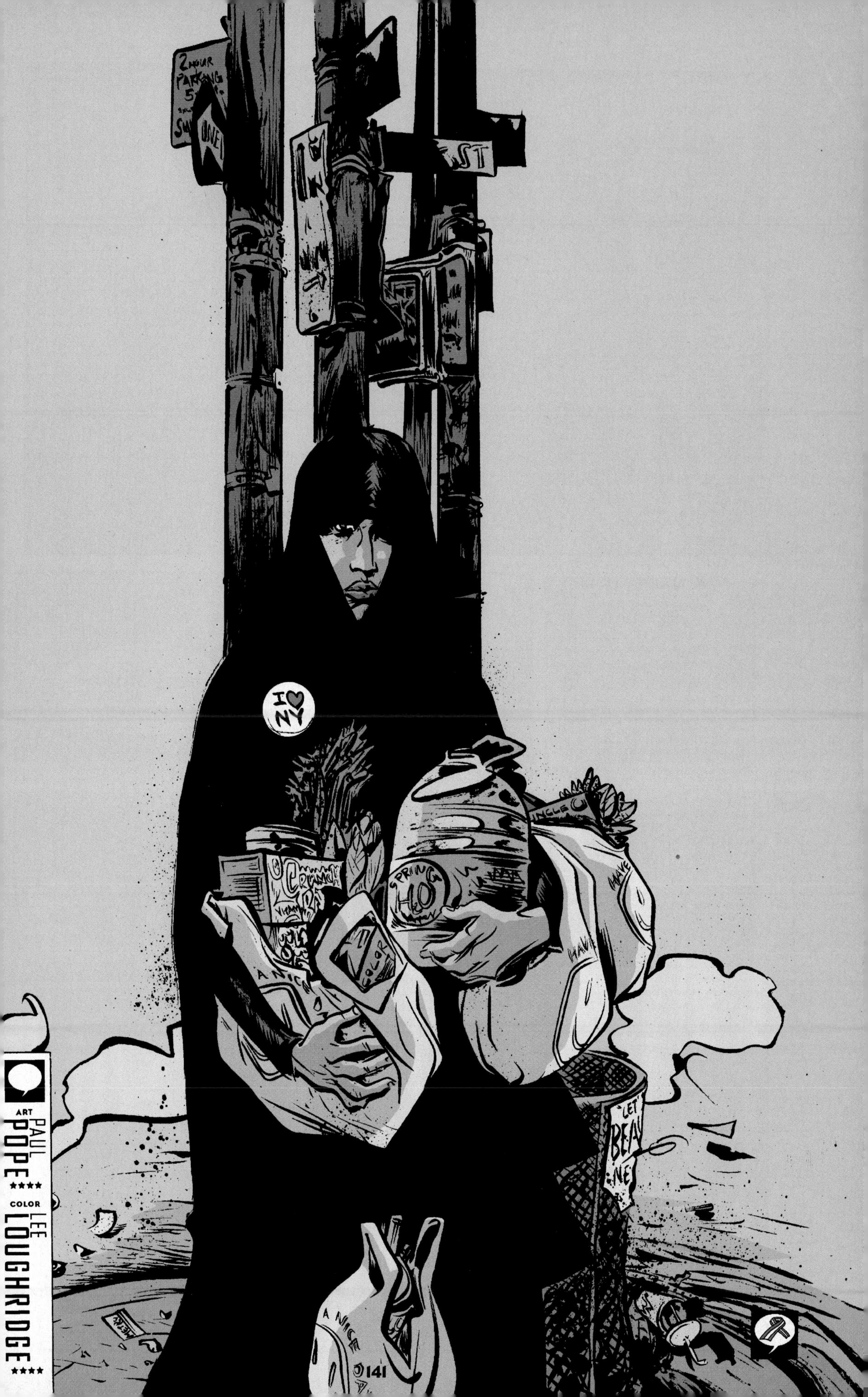

2 HOUR PARKING
ST
I ♥ NY
SPRING H2O
A NICE
COLOR
ART PAUL POPE ★★★★
COLOR LEE LOUGHRIDGE ★★★★
141

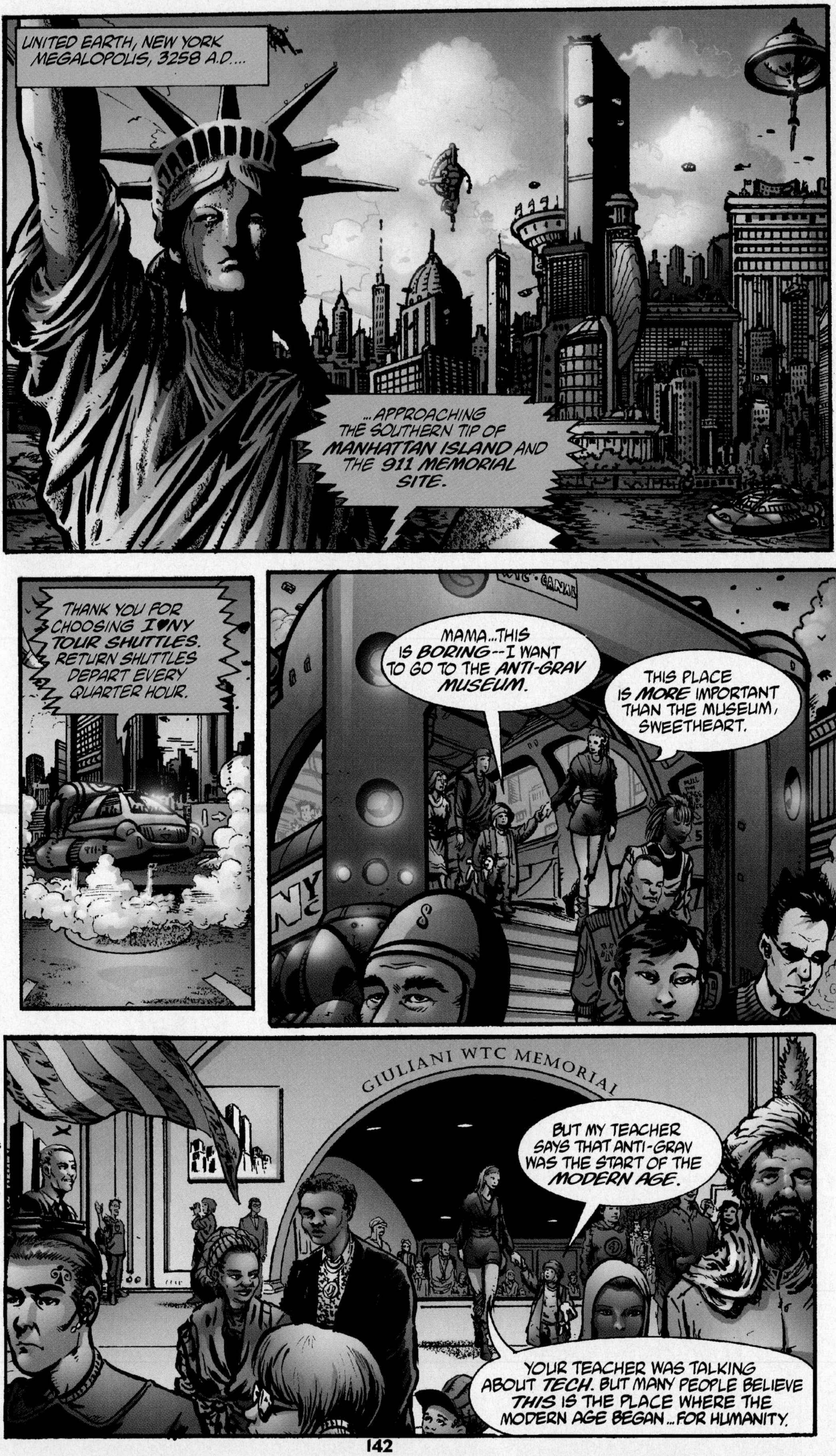
UNITED EARTH, NEW YORK MEGALOPOLIS, 3258 A.D....
...APPROACHING THE SOUTHERN TIP OF MANHATTAN ISLAND AND THE 911 MEMORIAL SITE.
THANK YOU FOR CHOOSING I♥NY TOUR SHUTTLES. RETURN SHUTTLES DEPART EVERY QUARTER HOUR.
MAMA...THIS IS BORING--I WANT TO GO TO THE ANTI-GRAV MUSEUM.
THIS PLACE IS MORE IMPORTANT THAN THE MUSEUM, SWEETHEART.
GIULIANI WTC MEMORIAI
BUT MY TEACHER SAYS THAT ANTI-GRAV WAS THE START OF THE MODERN AGE.
YOUR TEACHER WAS TALKING ABOUT TECH. BUT MANY PEOPLE BELIEVE THIS IS THE PLACE WHERE THE MODERN AGE BEGAN...FOR HUMANITY.

STORY PETER GROSS
ART DARICK ROBERTSON
LETTERS CLEM ROBINS
COLOR WILDSTORM

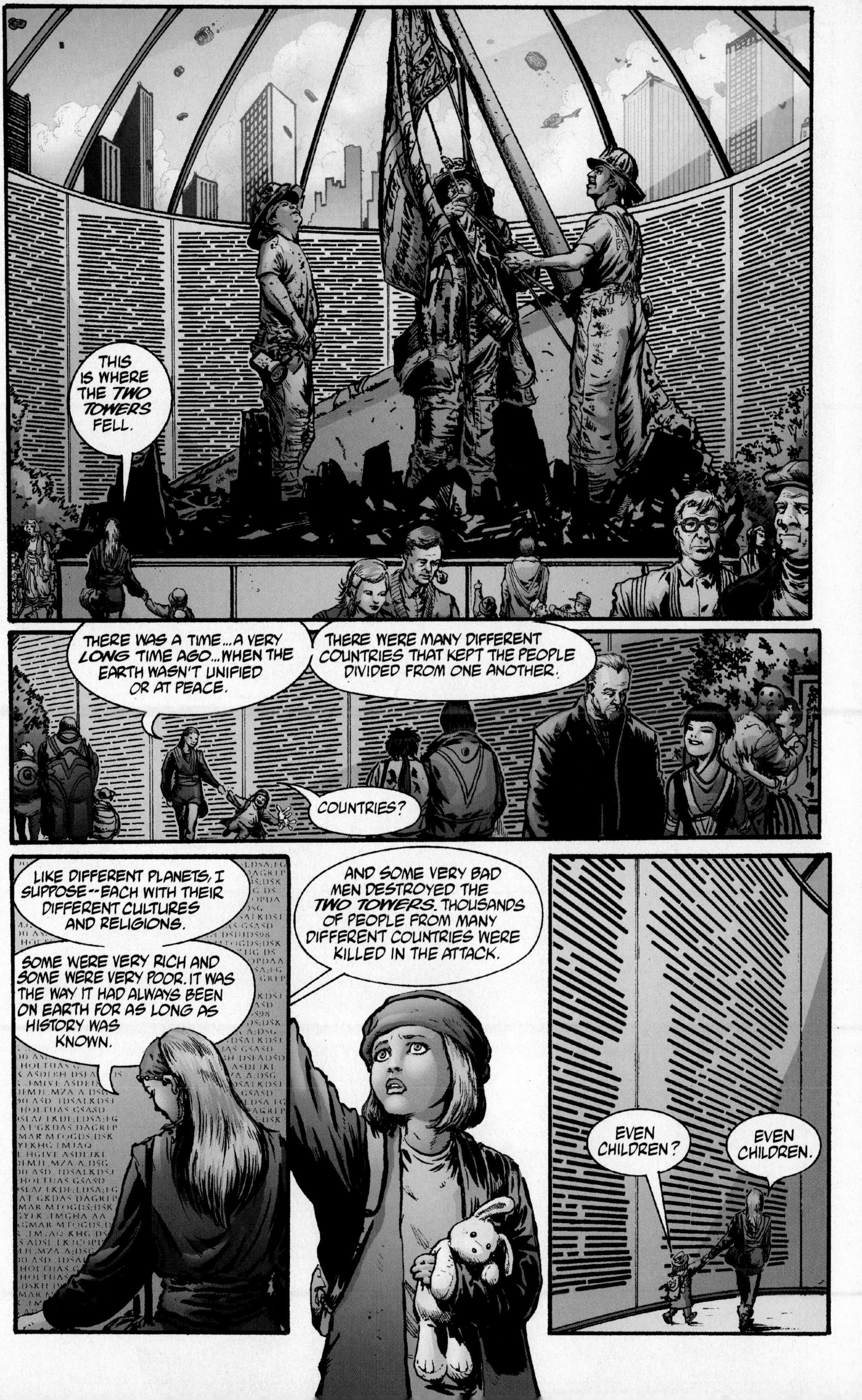
THIS IS WHERE THE TWO TOWERS FELL.
THERE WAS A TIME...A VERY LONG TIME AGO...WHEN THE EARTH WASN'T UNIFIED OR AT PEACE.
THERE WERE MANY DIFFERENT COUNTRIES THAT KEPT THE PEOPLE DIVIDED FROM ONE ANOTHER.
COUNTRIES?
LIKE DIFFERENT PLANETS, I SUPPOSE--EACH WITH THEIR DIFFERENT CULTURES AND RELIGIONS.
SOME WERE VERY RICH AND SOME WERE VERY POOR. IT WAS THE WAY IT HAD ALWAYS BEEN ON EARTH FOR AS LONG AS HISTORY WAS KNOWN.
AND SOME VERY BAD MEN DESTROYED THE TWO TOWERS. THOUSANDS OF PEOPLE FROM MANY DIFFERENT COUNTRIES WERE KILLED IN THE ATTACK.
EVEN CHILDREN?
EVEN CHILDREN.

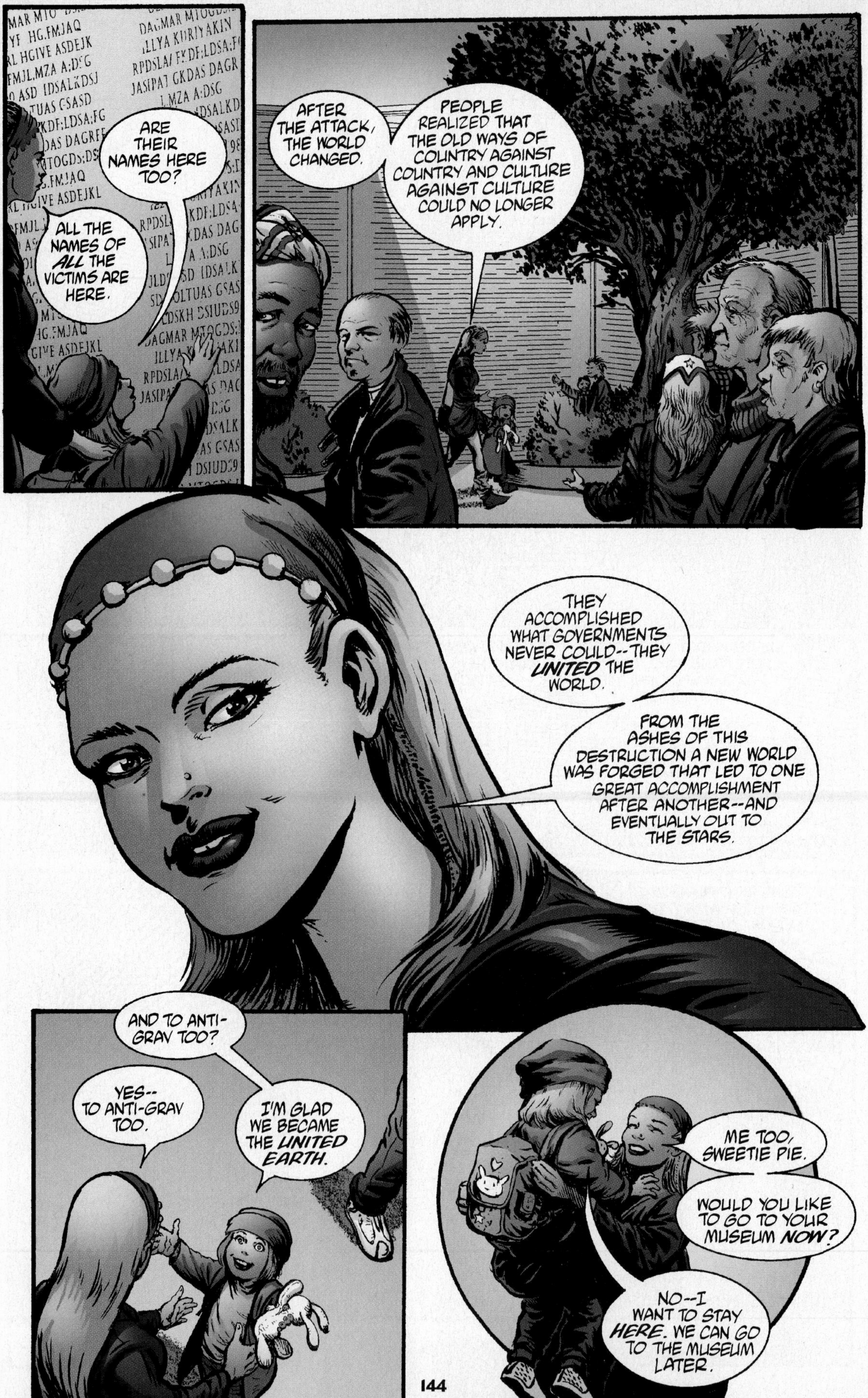
ARE THEIR NAMES HERE TOO?
ALL THE NAMES OF ALL THE VICTIMS ARE HERE.
AFTER THE ATTACK, THE WORLD CHANGED.
PEOPLE REALIZED THAT THE OLD WAYS OF COUNTRY AGAINST COUNTRY AND CULTURE AGAINST CULTURE COULD NO LONGER APPLY.
THEY ACCOMPLISHED WHAT GOVERNMENTS NEVER COULD--THEY UNITED THE WORLD.
FROM THE ASHES OF THIS DESTRUCTION A NEW WORLD WAS FORGED THAT LED TO ONE GREAT ACCOMPLISHMENT AFTER ANOTHER--AND EVENTUALLY OUT TO THE STARS.
AND TO ANTI-GRAV TOO?
YES--TO ANTI-GRAV TOO.
I'M GLAD WE BECAME THE UNITED EARTH.
ME TOO, SWEETIE PIE.
WOULD YOU LIKE TO GO TO YOUR MUSEUM NOW?
NO--I WANT TO STAY HERE. WE CAN GO TO THE MUSEUM LATER.

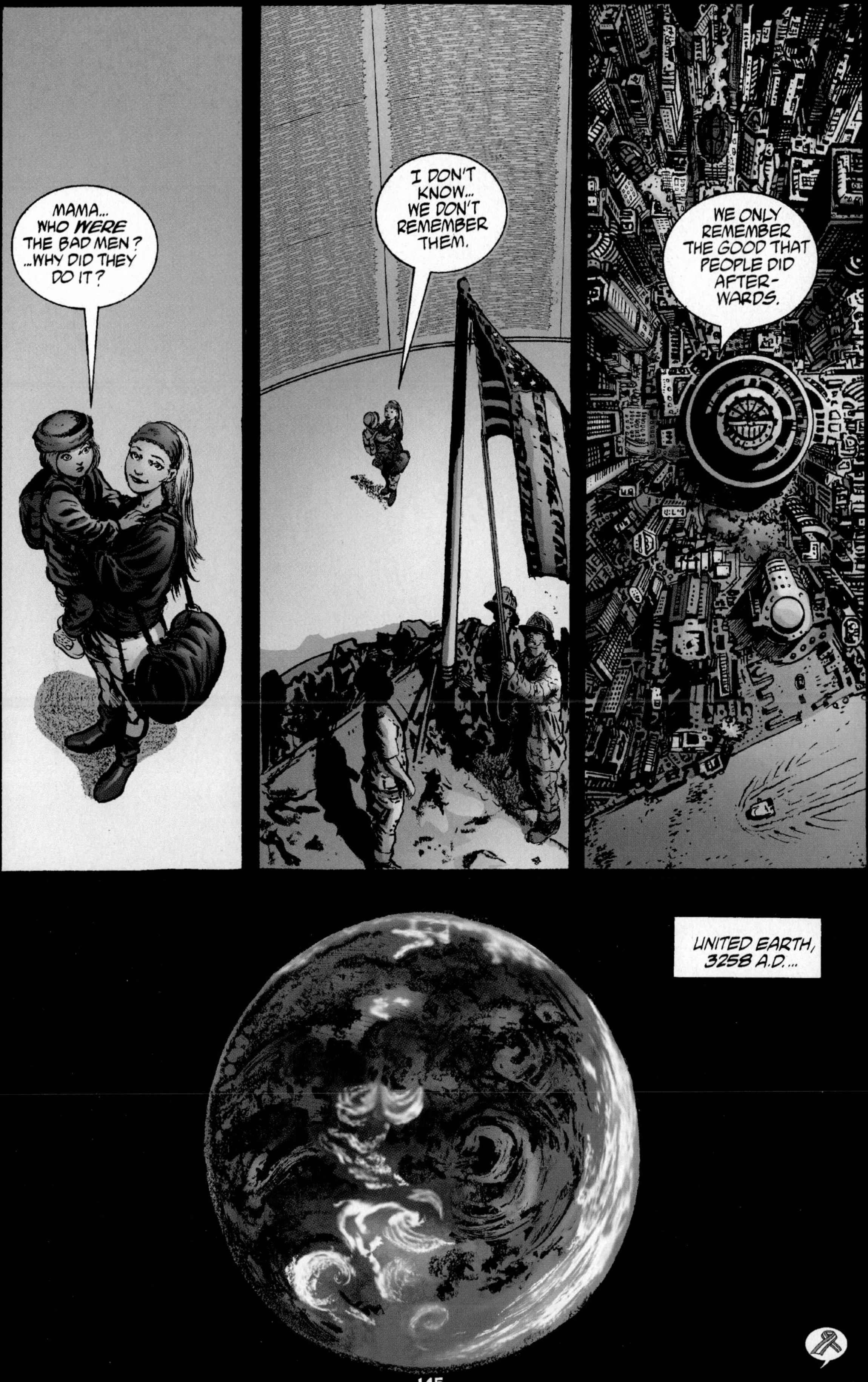
MAMA... WHO WERE THE BAD MEN? ...WHY DID THEY DO IT?
I DON'T KNOW... WE DON'T REMEMBER THEM.
WE ONLY REMEMBER THE GOOD THAT PEOPLE DID AFTER-WARDS.
UNITED EARTH, 3258 A.D....

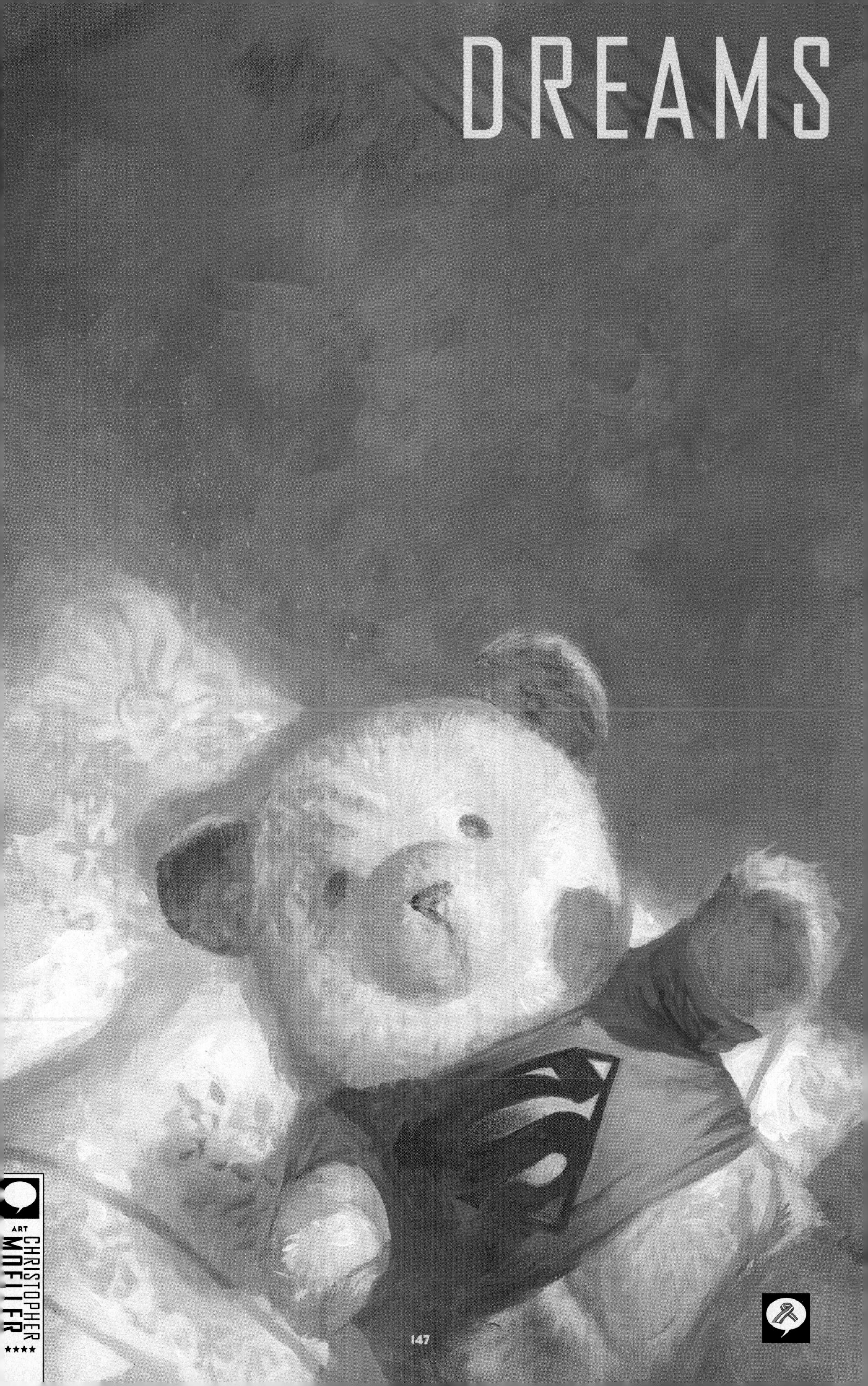
DREAMS
ART
CHRISTOPHER
MOELLER

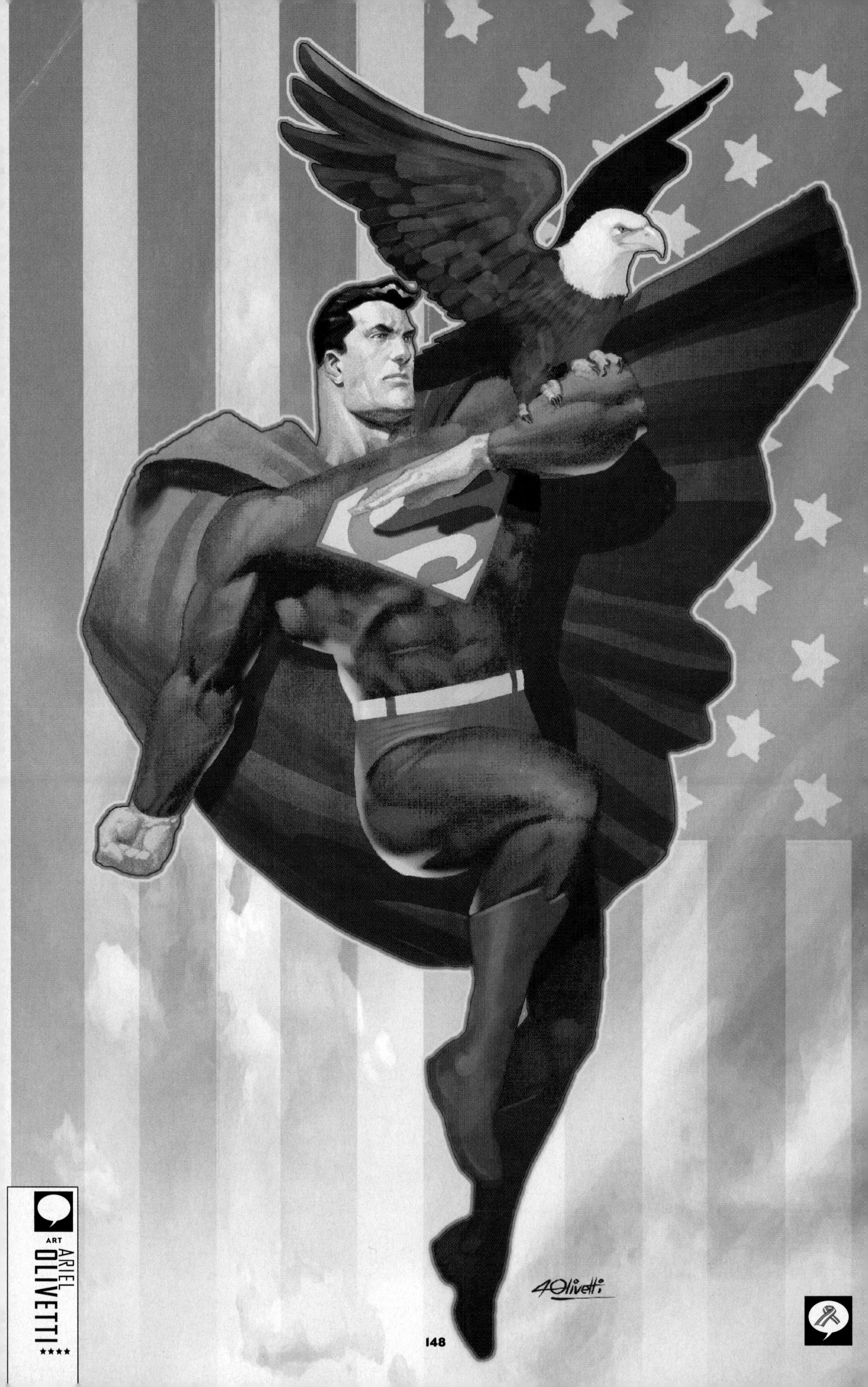
ART
ARIEL
OLIVETTI
AOlivetti

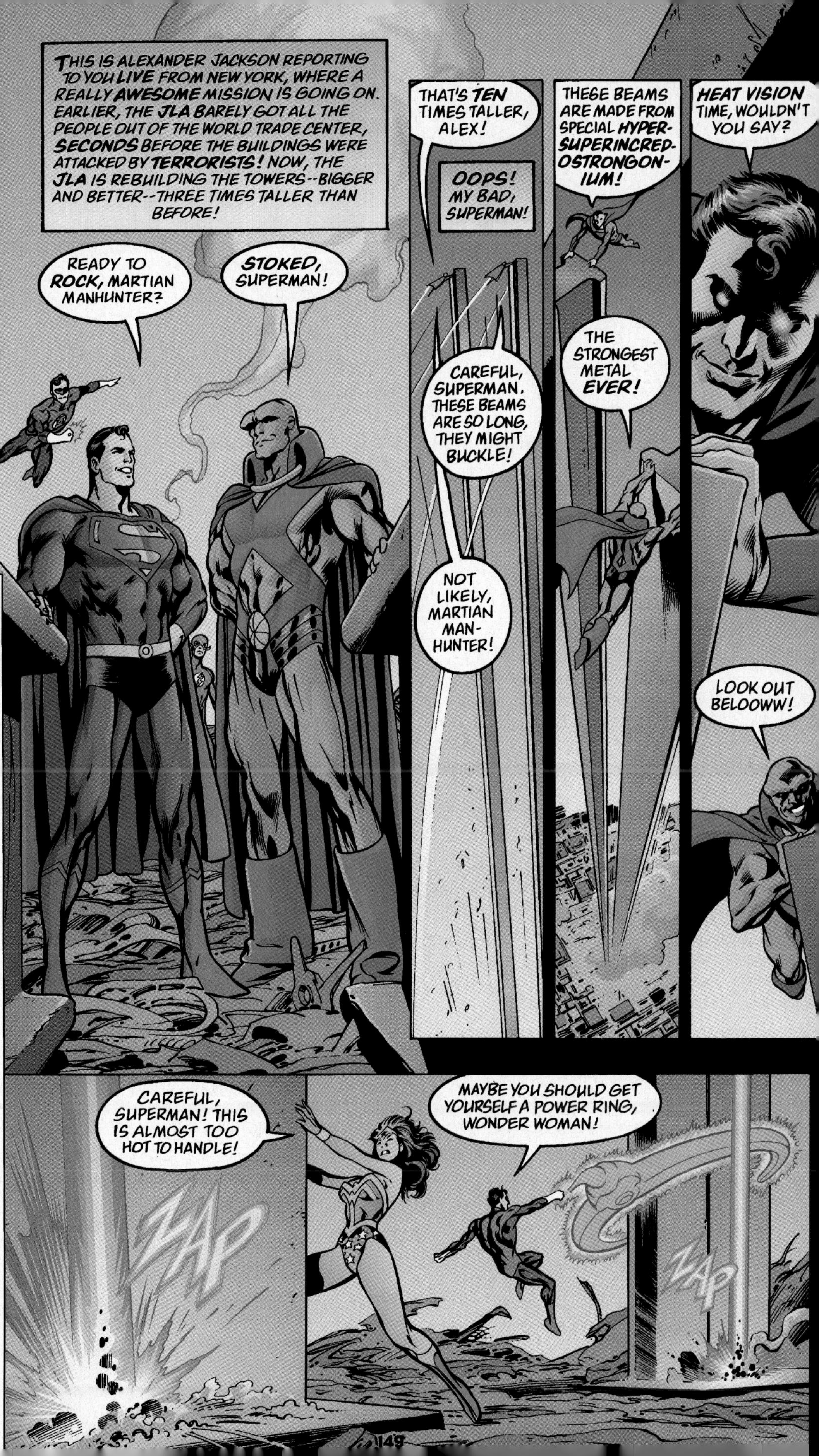
THIS IS ALEXANDER JACKSON REPORTING TO YOU LIVE FROM NEW YORK, WHERE A REALLY AWESOME MISSION IS GOING ON. EARLIER, THE JLA BARELY GOT ALL THE PEOPLE OUT OF THE WORLD TRADE CENTER, SECONDS BEFORE THE BUILDINGS WERE ATTACKED BY TERRORISTS! NOW, THE JLA IS REBUILDING THE TOWERS--BIGGER AND BETTER--THREE TIMES TALLER THAN BEFORE!
READY TO ROCK, MARTIAN MANHUNTER?
STOKED, SUPERMAN!
THAT'S TEN TIMES TALLER, ALEX!
OOPS! MY BAD, SUPERMAN!
CAREFUL, SUPERMAN. THESE BEAMS ARE SO LONG, THEY MIGHT BUCKLE!
NOT LIKELY, MARTIAN MANHUNTER!
THESE BEAMS ARE MADE FROM SPECIAL HYPER-SUPERINCRED-OSTRONGON-IUM!
THE STRONGEST METAL EVER!
HEAT VISION TIME, WOULDN'T YOU SAY?
LOOK OUT BELOOWW!
CAREFUL, SUPERMAN! THIS IS ALMOST TOO HOT TO HANDLE!
MAYBE YOU SHOULD GET YOURSELF A POWER RING, WONDER WOMAN!
ZAP
ZAP
149

STORY DAN JURGENS ART ALAN DAVIS, ROBIN RIGGS, MIKE COLLINS AND MARK FARMER LETTERS TODD KLEIN COLOR LEE LOUGHRIDGE

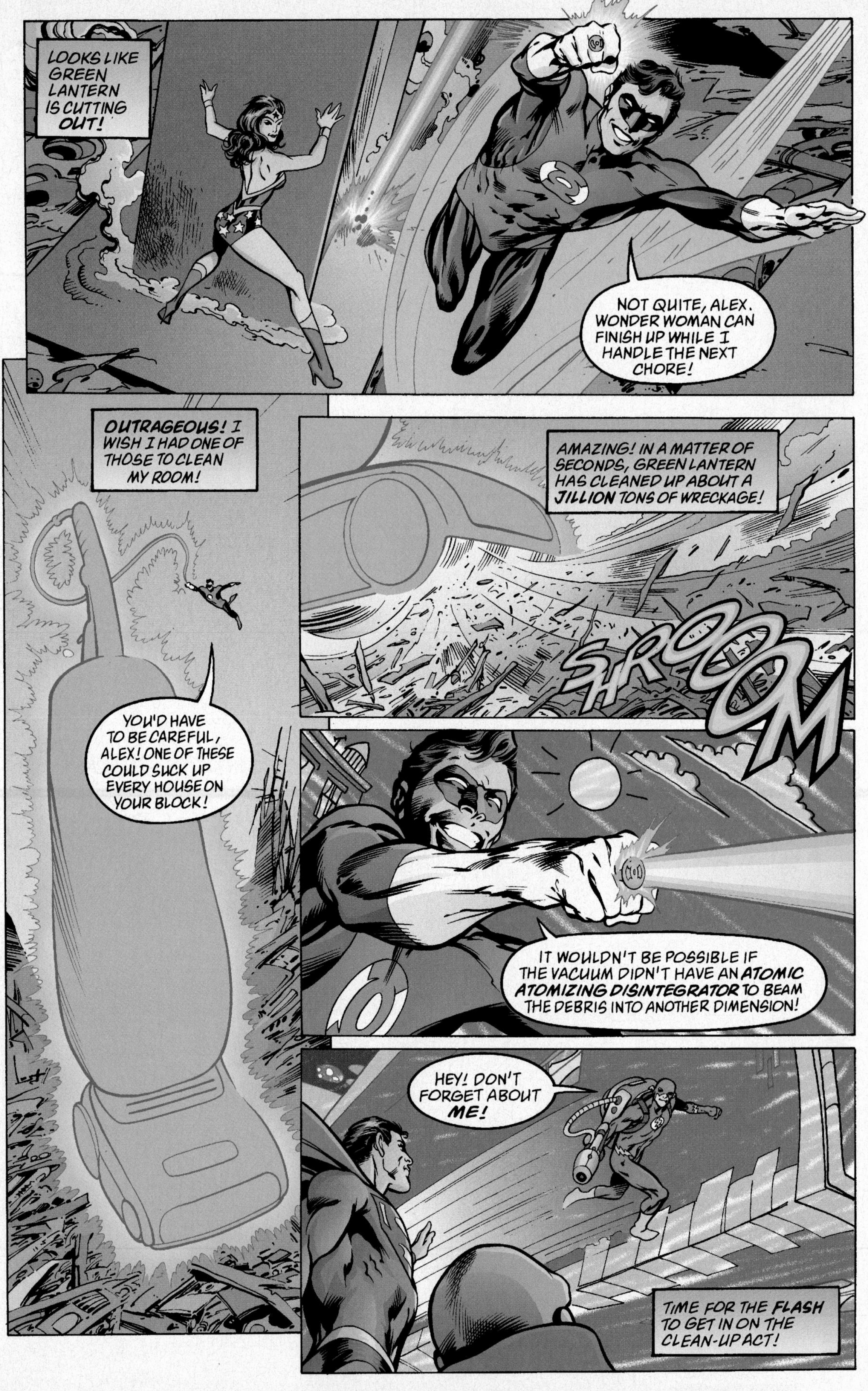
LOOKS LIKE GREEN LANTERN IS CUTTING OUT!
NOT QUITE, ALEX. WONDER WOMAN CAN FINISH UP WHILE I HANDLE THE NEXT CHORE!
OUTRAGEOUS! I WISH I HAD ONE OF THOSE TO CLEAN MY ROOM!
YOU'D HAVE TO BE CAREFUL, ALEX! ONE OF THESE COULD SUCK UP EVERY HOUSE ON YOUR BLOCK!
AMAZING! IN A MATTER OF SECONDS, GREEN LANTERN HAS CLEANED UP ABOUT A JILLION TONS OF WRECKAGE!
SHROOOOM
IT WOULDN'T BE POSSIBLE IF THE VACUUM DIDN'T HAVE AN ATOMIC ATOMIZING DISINTEGRATOR TO BEAM THE DEBRIS INTO ANOTHER DIMENSION!
HEY! DON'T FORGET ABOUT ME!
TIME FOR THE FLASH TO GET IN ON THE CLEAN-UP ACT!

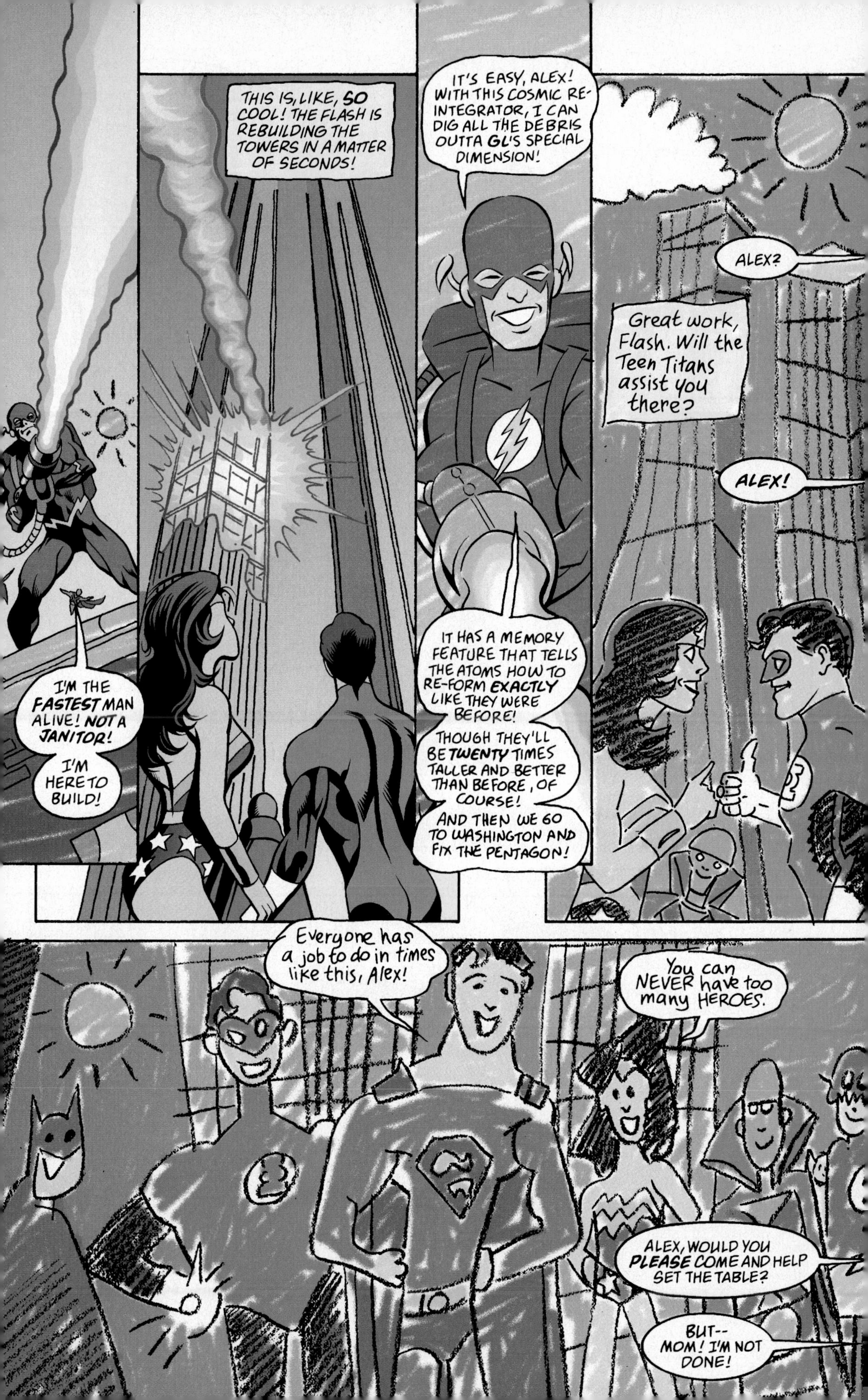
I'M THE FASTEST MAN ALIVE! NOT A JANITOR!
I'M HERE TO BUILD!
THIS IS, LIKE, SO COOL! THE FLASH IS REBUILDING THE TOWERS IN A MATTER OF SECONDS!
IT'S EASY, ALEX! WITH THIS COSMIC RE-INTEGRATOR, I CAN DIG ALL THE DEBRIS OUTTA GL'S SPECIAL DIMENSION!
IT HAS A MEMORY FEATURE THAT TELLS THE ATOMS HOW TO RE-FORM EXACTLY LIKE THEY WERE BEFORE!
THOUGH THEY'LL BE TWENTY TIMES TALLER AND BETTER THAN BEFORE, OF COURSE!
AND THEN WE GO TO WASHINGTON AND FIX THE PENTAGON!
ALEX?
Great work, Flash. Will the Teen Titans assist you there?
ALEX!
Everyone has a job to do in times like this, Alex!
You can NEVER have too many HEROES.
ALEX, WOULD YOU PLEASE COME AND HELP SET THE TABLE?
BUT-- MOM! I'M NOT DONE!

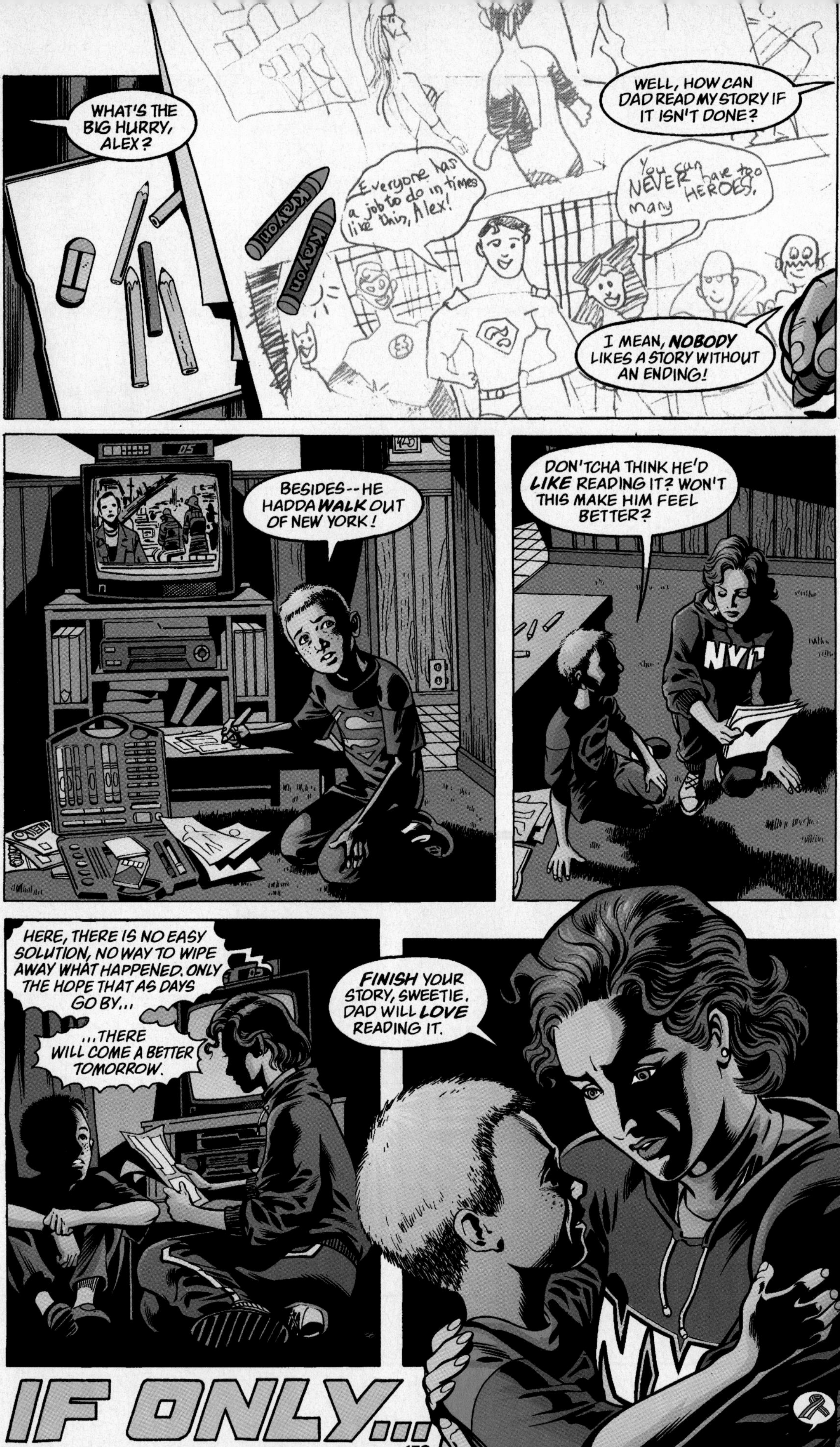
WHAT'S THE BIG HURRY, ALEX?
WELL, HOW CAN DAD READ MY STORY IF IT ISN'T DONE?
Everyone has a job to do in times like this, Alex!
You can NEVER have too many HEROES!
I MEAN, NOBODY LIKES A STORY WITHOUT AN ENDING!
BESIDES--HE HADDA WALK OUT OF NEW YORK!
DON'TCHA THINK HE'D LIKE READING IT? WON'T THIS MAKE HIM FEEL BETTER?
HERE, THERE IS NO EASY SOLUTION, NO WAY TO WIPE AWAY WHAT HAPPENED. ONLY THE HOPE THAT AS DAYS GO BY...
...THERE WILL COME A BETTER TOMORROW.
FINISH YOUR STORY, SWEETIE. DAD WILL LOVE READING IT.
IF ONLY...

I dreamed there was a Hole in the sky, where Two Towers once stood.

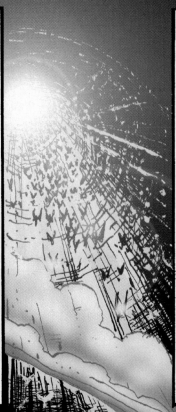

And through that Hole the Angels flew--down from Eternity...

...spreading wings of compassion.

Wings of grief.

STORY
J.M. DeMATTEIS ★★★★

ART
MICHAEL ZULLI ★★★★

LETTERS
JOHN WORKMAN ★★★★

COLOR
WILDSTORM ★★★★

Ascending

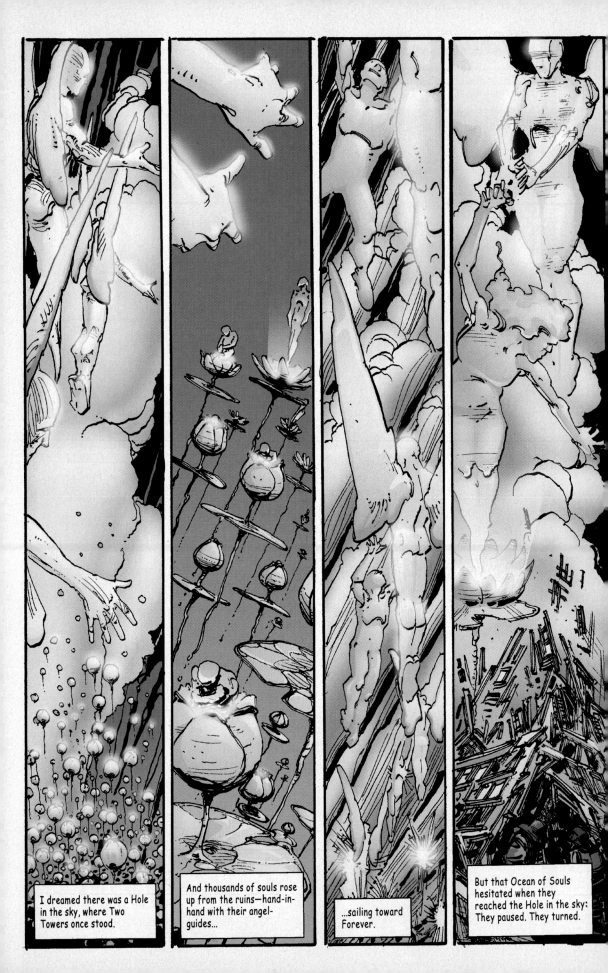

I dreamed there was a Hole in the sky, where Two Towers once stood.

And thousands of souls rose up from the ruins—hand-in-hand with their angel-guides...

...sailing toward Forever.

But that Ocean of Souls hesitated when they reached the Hole in the sky: They paused. They turned.

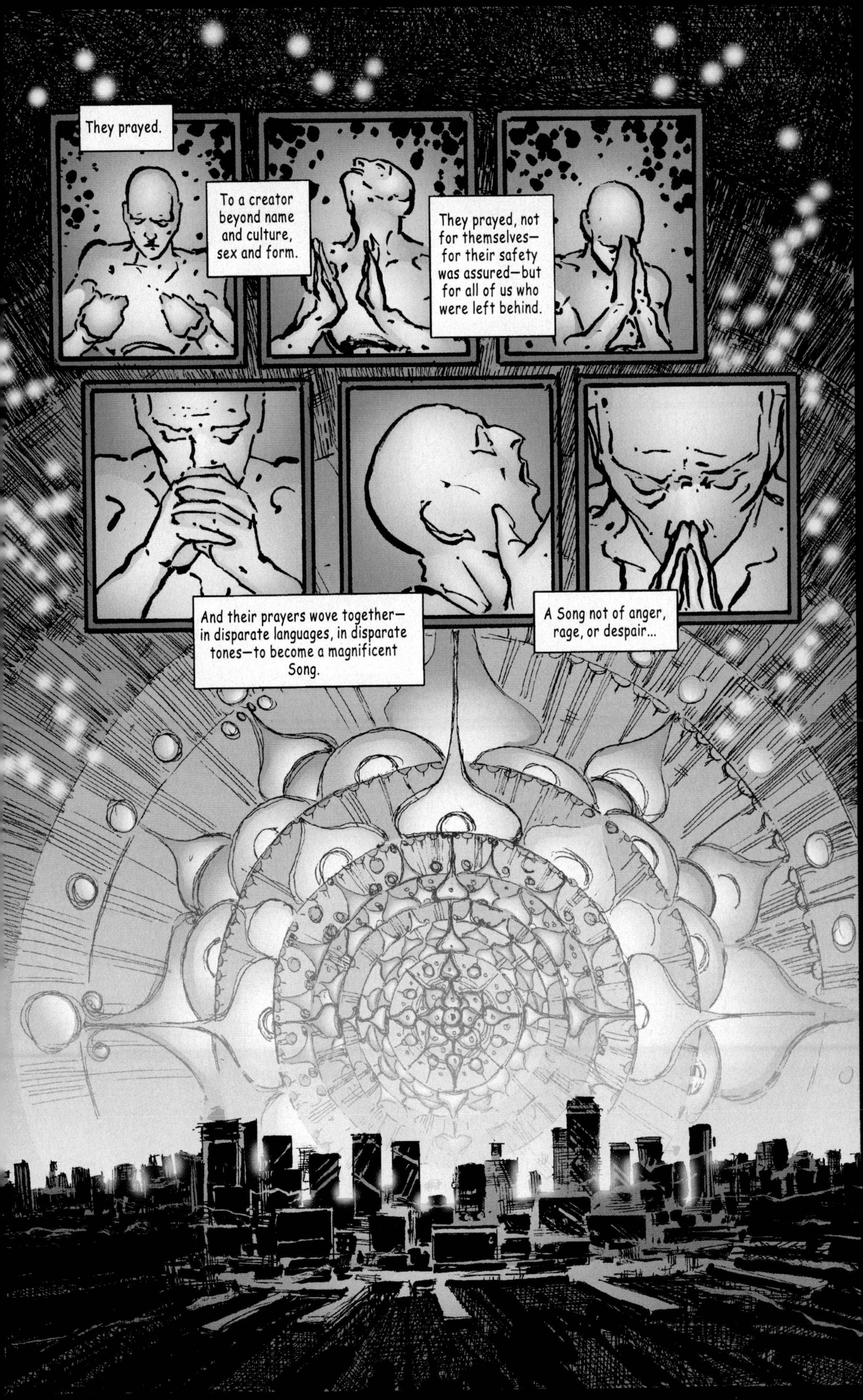

They prayed.
To a creator beyond name and culture, sex and form.
They prayed, not for themselves—for their safety was assured—but for all of us who were left behind.
And their prayers wove together—in disparate languages, in disparate tones—to become a magnificent Song.
A Song not of anger, rage, or despair...

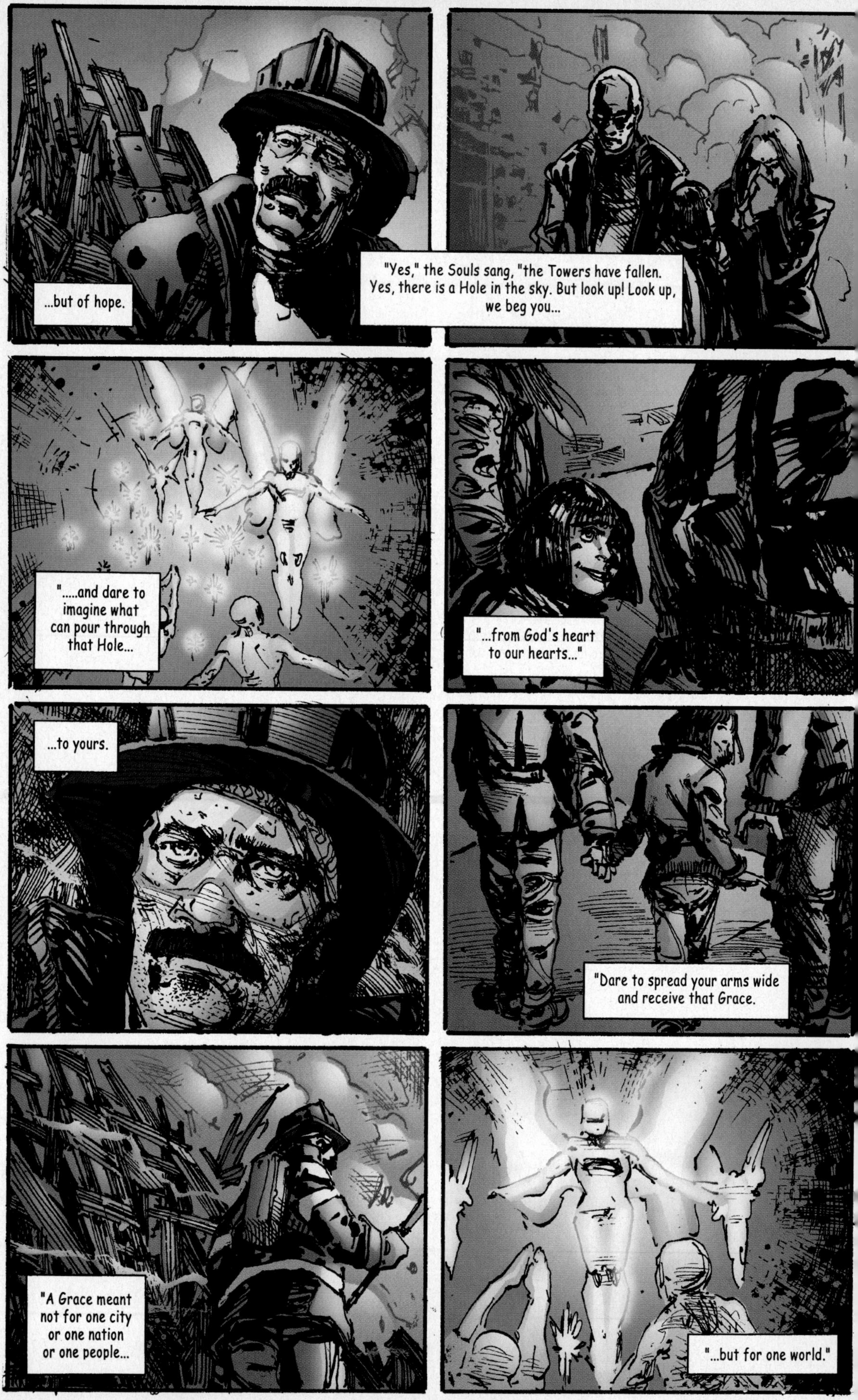
...but of hope.
"Yes," the Souls sang, "the Towers have fallen. Yes, there is a Hole in the sky. But look up! Look up, we beg you...
".....and dare to imagine what can pour through that Hole...
"...from God's heart to our hearts..."
...to yours.
"Dare to spread your arms wide and receive that Grace.
"A Grace meant not for one city or one nation or one people...
"...but for one world."

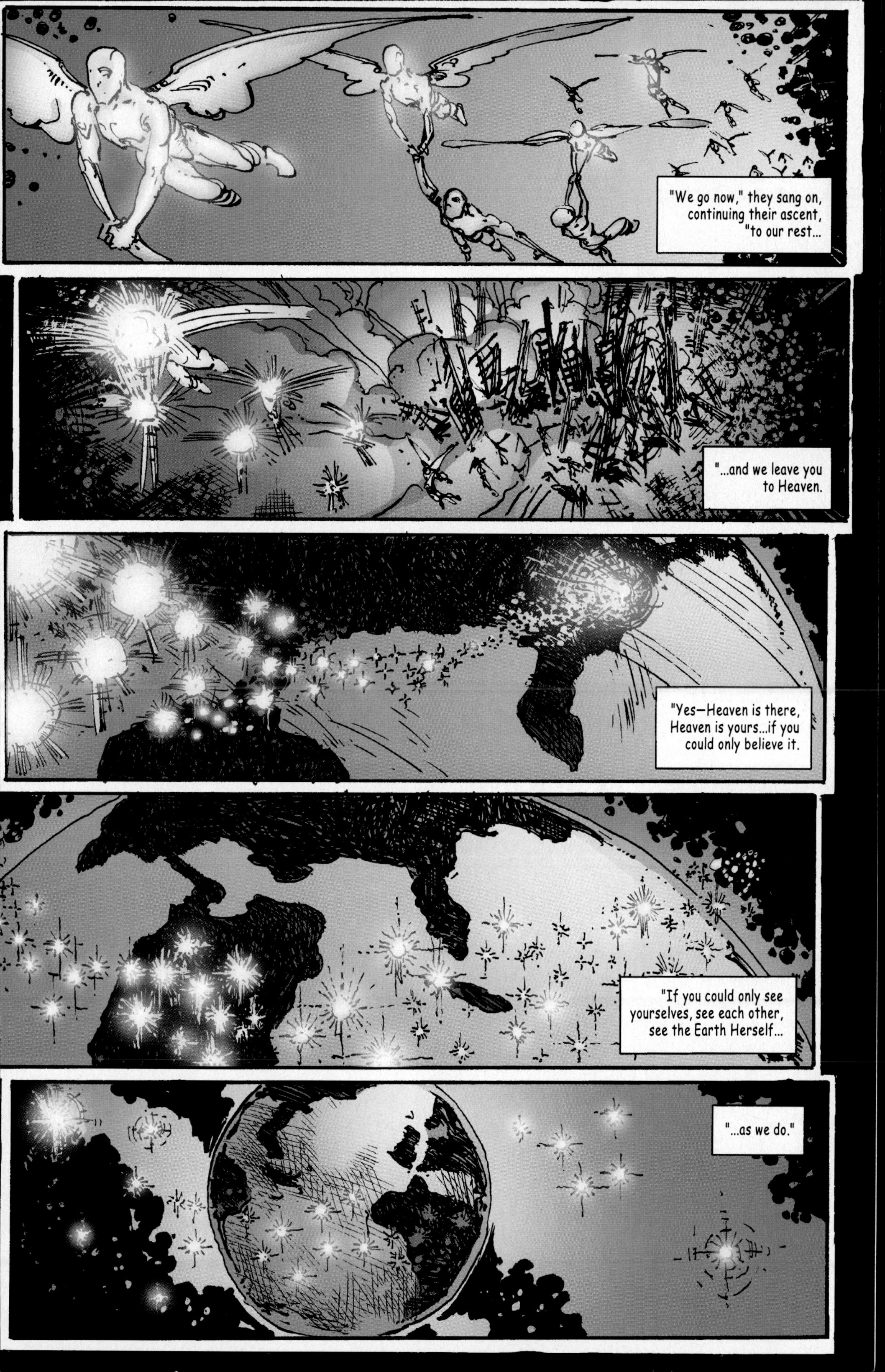
"We go now," they sang on, continuing their ascent, "to our rest...
"...and we leave you to Heaven.
"Yes—Heaven is there, Heaven is yours...if you could only believe it.
"If you could only see yourselves, see each other, see the Earth Herself...
"...as we do."

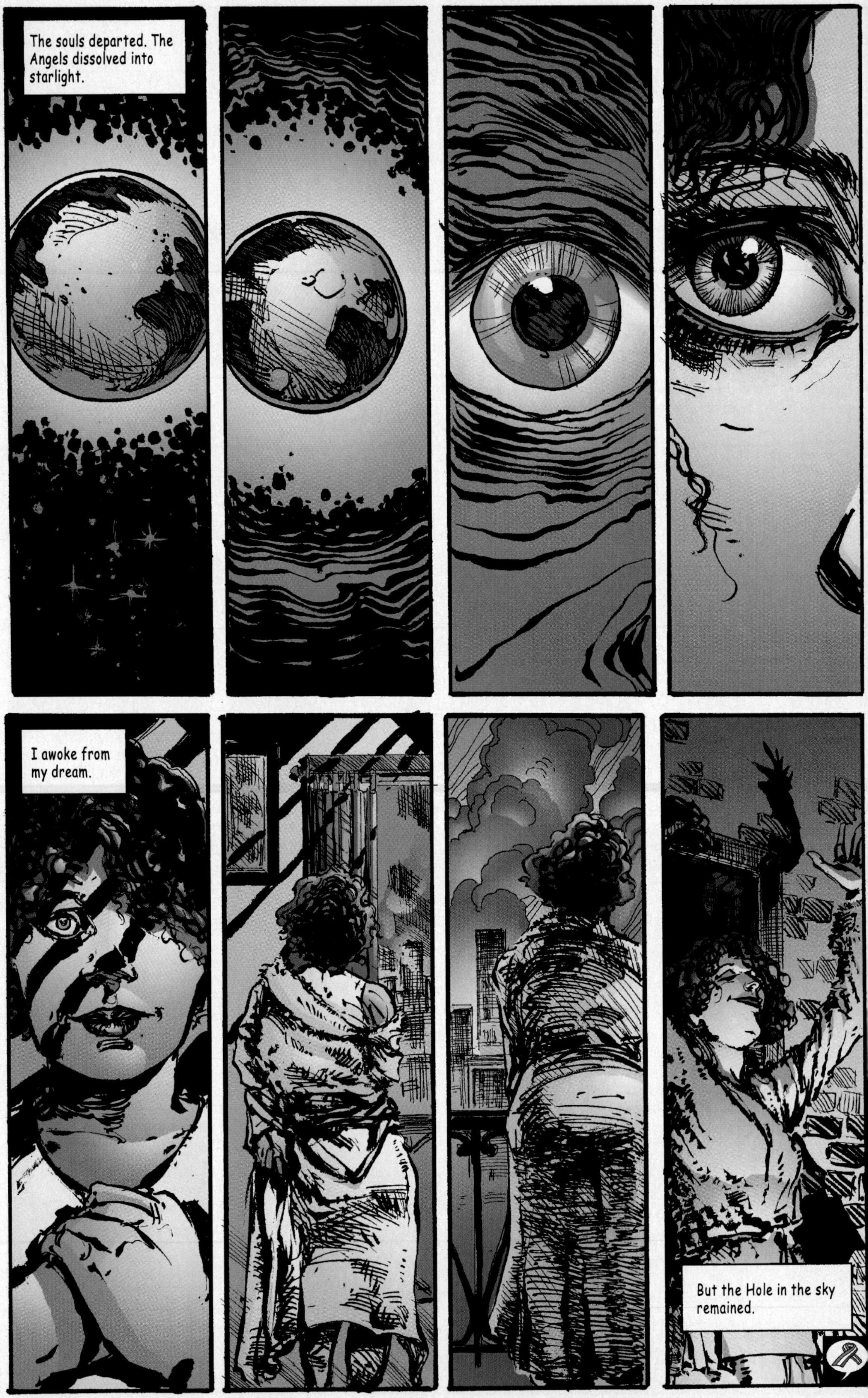
The souls departed. The Angels dissolved into starlight.
I awoke from my dream.
But the Hole in the sky remained.

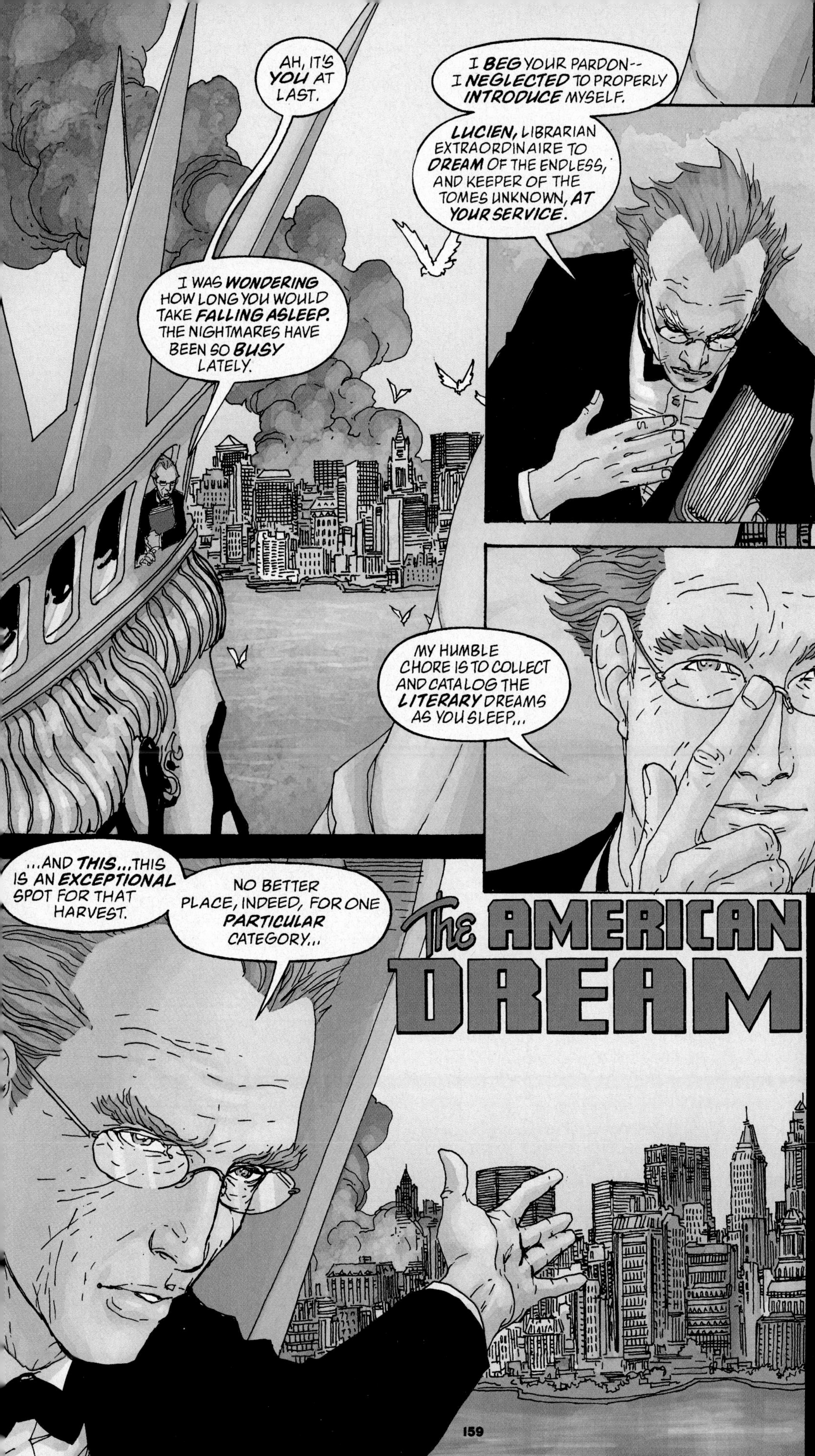
AH, IT'S YOU AT LAST.
I BEG YOUR PARDON-- I NEGLECTED TO PROPERLY INTRODUCE MYSELF.
LUCIEN, LIBRARIAN EXTRAORDINAIRE TO DREAM OF THE ENDLESS, AND KEEPER OF THE TOMES UNKNOWN, AT YOUR SERVICE.
I WAS WONDERING HOW LONG YOU WOULD TAKE FALLING ASLEEP. THE NIGHTMARES HAVE BEEN SO BUSY LATELY.
MY HUMBLE CHORE IS TO COLLECT AND CATALOG THE LITERARY DREAMS AS YOU SLEEP...
...AND THIS...THIS IS AN EXCEPTIONAL SPOT FOR THAT HARVEST.
NO BETTER PLACE, INDEED, FOR ONE PARTICULAR CATEGORY...
THE AMERICAN DREAM

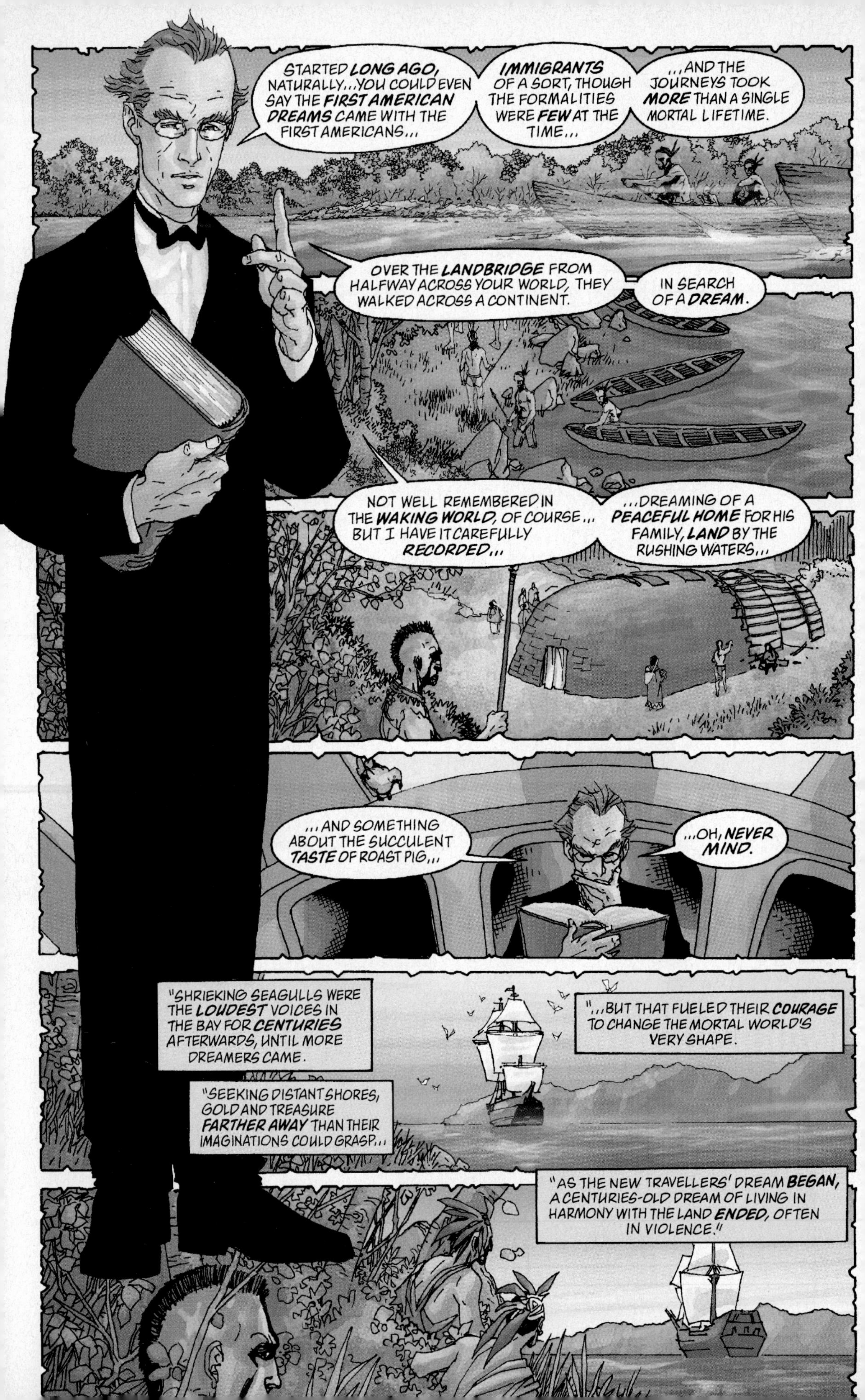
STARTED LONG AGO, NATURALLY... YOU COULD EVEN SAY THE FIRST AMERICAN DREAMS CAME WITH THE FIRST AMERICANS...
IMMIGRANTS OF A SORT, THOUGH THE FORMALITIES WERE FEW AT THE TIME...
...AND THE JOURNEYS TOOK MORE THAN A SINGLE MORTAL LIFETIME.
OVER THE LANDBRIDGE FROM HALFWAY ACROSS YOUR WORLD, THEY WALKED ACROSS A CONTINENT.
IN SEARCH OF A DREAM.
NOT WELL REMEMBERED IN THE WAKING WORLD, OF COURSE... BUT I HAVE IT CAREFULLY RECORDED...
...DREAMING OF A PEACEFUL HOME FOR HIS FAMILY, LAND BY THE RUSHING WATERS...
...AND SOMETHING ABOUT THE SUCCULENT TASTE OF ROAST PIG...
...OH, NEVER MIND.
"SHRIEKING SEAGULLS WERE THE LOUDEST VOICES IN THE BAY FOR CENTURIES AFTERWARDS, UNTIL MORE DREAMERS CAME.
"SEEKING DISTANT SHORES, GOLD AND TREASURE FARTHER AWAY THAN THEIR IMAGINATIONS COULD GRASP...
"...BUT THAT FUELED THEIR COURAGE TO CHANGE THE MORTAL WORLD'S VERY SHAPE.
"AS THE NEW TRAVELLERS' DREAM BEGAN, A CENTURIES-OLD DREAM OF LIVING IN HARMONY WITH THE LAND ENDED, OFTEN IN VIOLENCE."

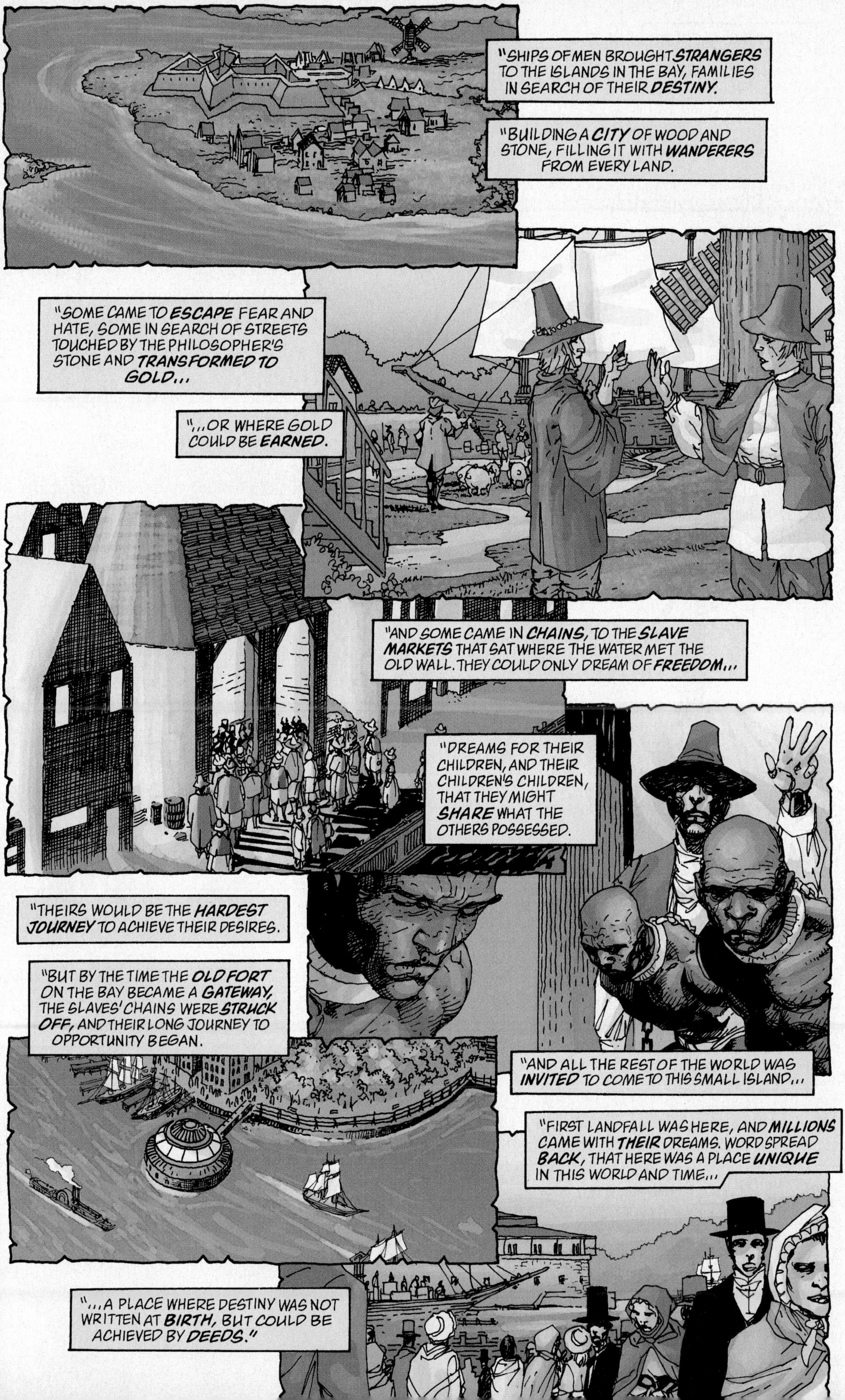
"SHIPS OF MEN BROUGHT STRANGERS TO THE ISLANDS IN THE BAY, FAMILIES IN SEARCH OF THEIR DESTINY.
"BUILDING A CITY OF WOOD AND STONE, FILLING IT WITH WANDERERS FROM EVERY LAND.
"SOME CAME TO ESCAPE FEAR AND HATE, SOME IN SEARCH OF STREETS TOUCHED BY THE PHILOSOPHER'S STONE AND TRANSFORMED TO GOLD...
"...OR WHERE GOLD COULD BE EARNED.
"AND SOME CAME IN CHAINS, TO THE SLAVE MARKETS THAT SAT WHERE THE WATER MET THE OLD WALL. THEY COULD ONLY DREAM OF FREEDOM...
"DREAMS FOR THEIR CHILDREN, AND THEIR CHILDREN'S CHILDREN, THAT THEY MIGHT SHARE WHAT THE OTHERS POSSESSED.
"THEIRS WOULD BE THE HARDEST JOURNEY TO ACHIEVE THEIR DESIRES.
"BUT BY THE TIME THE OLD FORT ON THE BAY BECAME A GATEWAY, THE SLAVES' CHAINS WERE STRUCK OFF, AND THEIR LONG JOURNEY TO OPPORTUNITY BEGAN.
"AND ALL THE REST OF THE WORLD WAS INVITED TO COME TO THIS SMALL ISLAND...
"FIRST LANDFALL WAS HERE, AND MILLIONS CAME WITH THEIR DREAMS. WORD SPREAD BACK, THAT HERE WAS A PLACE UNIQUE IN THIS WORLD AND TIME...
"...A PLACE WHERE DESTINY WAS NOT WRITTEN AT BIRTH, BUT COULD BE ACHIEVED BY DEEDS."

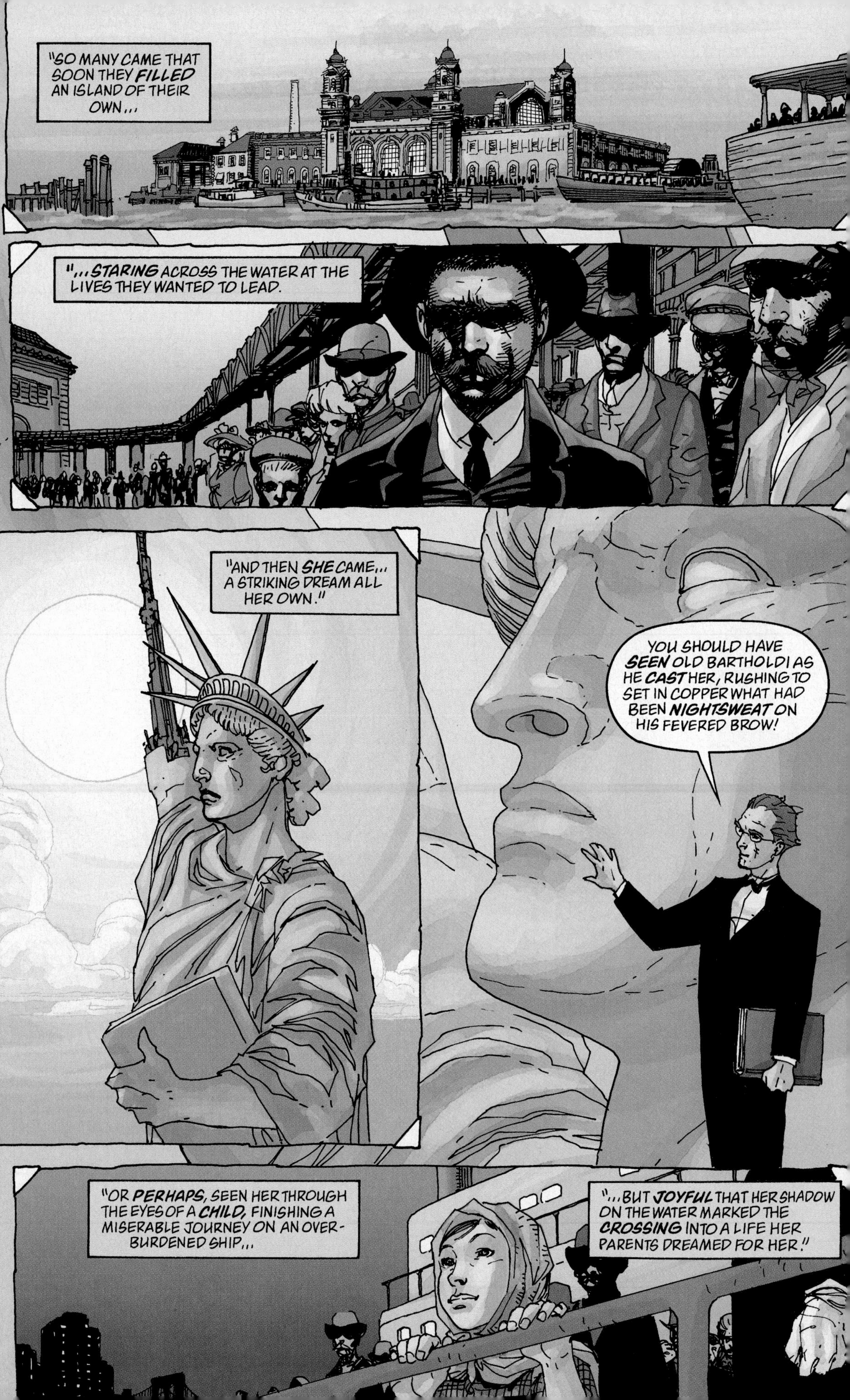
"SO MANY CAME THAT SOON THEY FILLED AN ISLAND OF THEIR OWN...
"...STARING ACROSS THE WATER AT THE LIVES THEY WANTED TO LEAD.
"AND THEN SHE CAME... A STRIKING DREAM ALL HER OWN."
YOU SHOULD HAVE SEEN OLD BARTHOLDI AS HE CAST HER, RUSHING TO SET IN COPPER WHAT HAD BEEN NIGHTSWEAT ON HIS FEVERED BROW!
"OR PERHAPS, SEEN HER THROUGH THE EYES OF A CHILD, FINISHING A MISERABLE JOURNEY ON AN OVER-BURDENED SHIP...
"...BUT JOYFUL THAT HER SHADOW ON THE WATER MARKED THE CROSSING INTO A LIFE HER PARENTS DREAMED FOR HER."

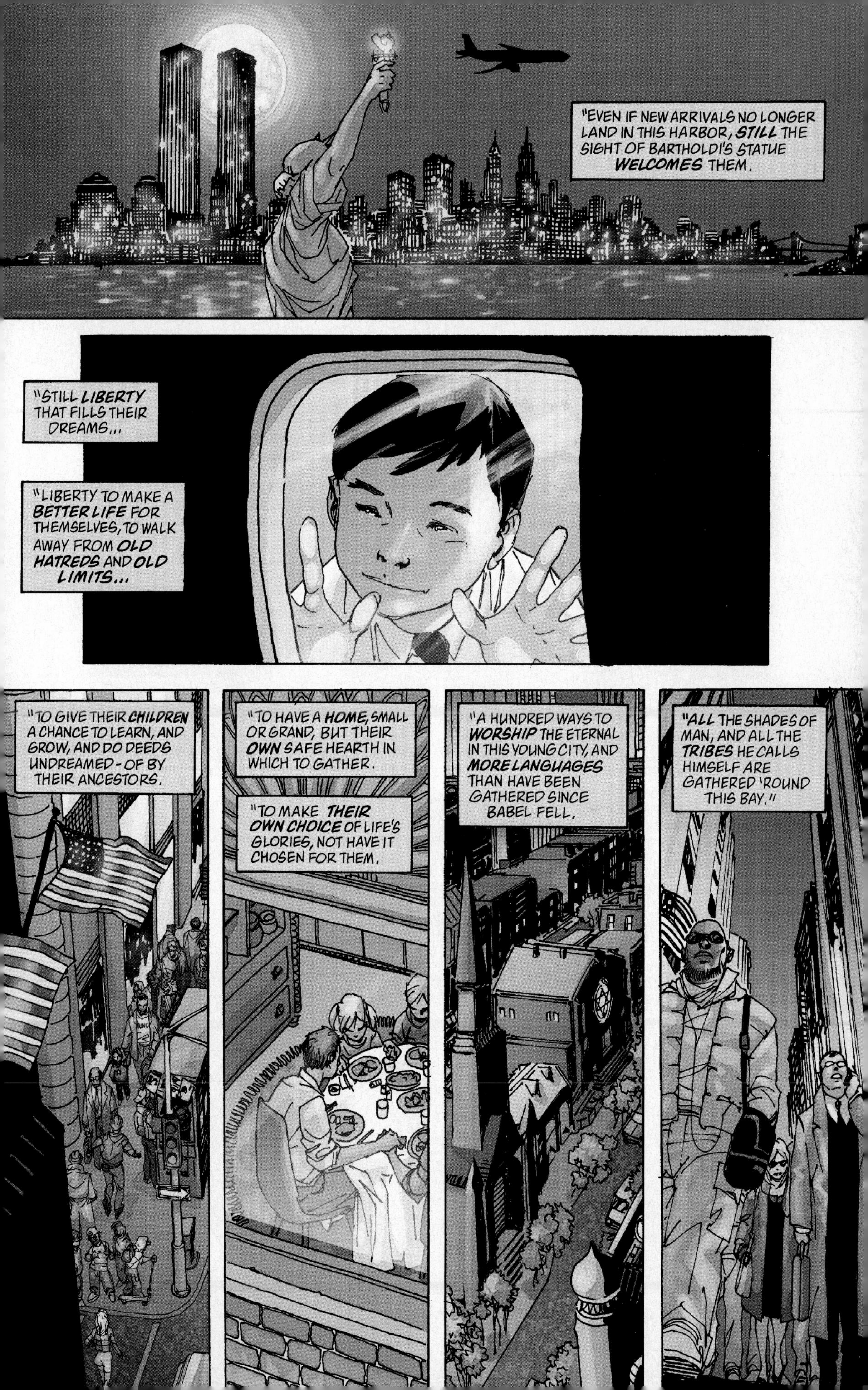
"EVEN IF NEW ARRIVALS NO LONGER LAND IN THIS HARBOR, STILL THE SIGHT OF BARTHOLDI'S STATUE WELCOMES THEM.
"STILL LIBERTY THAT FILLS THEIR DREAMS...
"LIBERTY TO MAKE A BETTER LIFE FOR THEMSELVES, TO WALK AWAY FROM OLD HATREDS AND OLD LIMITS...
"TO GIVE THEIR CHILDREN A CHANCE TO LEARN, AND GROW, AND DO DEEDS UNDREAMED-OF BY THEIR ANCESTORS.
"TO HAVE A HOME, SMALL OR GRAND, BUT THEIR OWN SAFE HEARTH IN WHICH TO GATHER.
"TO MAKE THEIR OWN CHOICE OF LIFE'S GLORIES, NOT HAVE IT CHOSEN FOR THEM.
"A HUNDRED WAYS TO WORSHIP THE ETERNAL IN THIS YOUNG CITY, AND MORE LANGUAGES THAN HAVE BEEN GATHERED SINCE BABEL FELL.
"ALL THE SHADES OF MAN, AND ALL THE TRIBES HE CALLS HIMSELF ARE GATHERED 'ROUND THIS BAY."

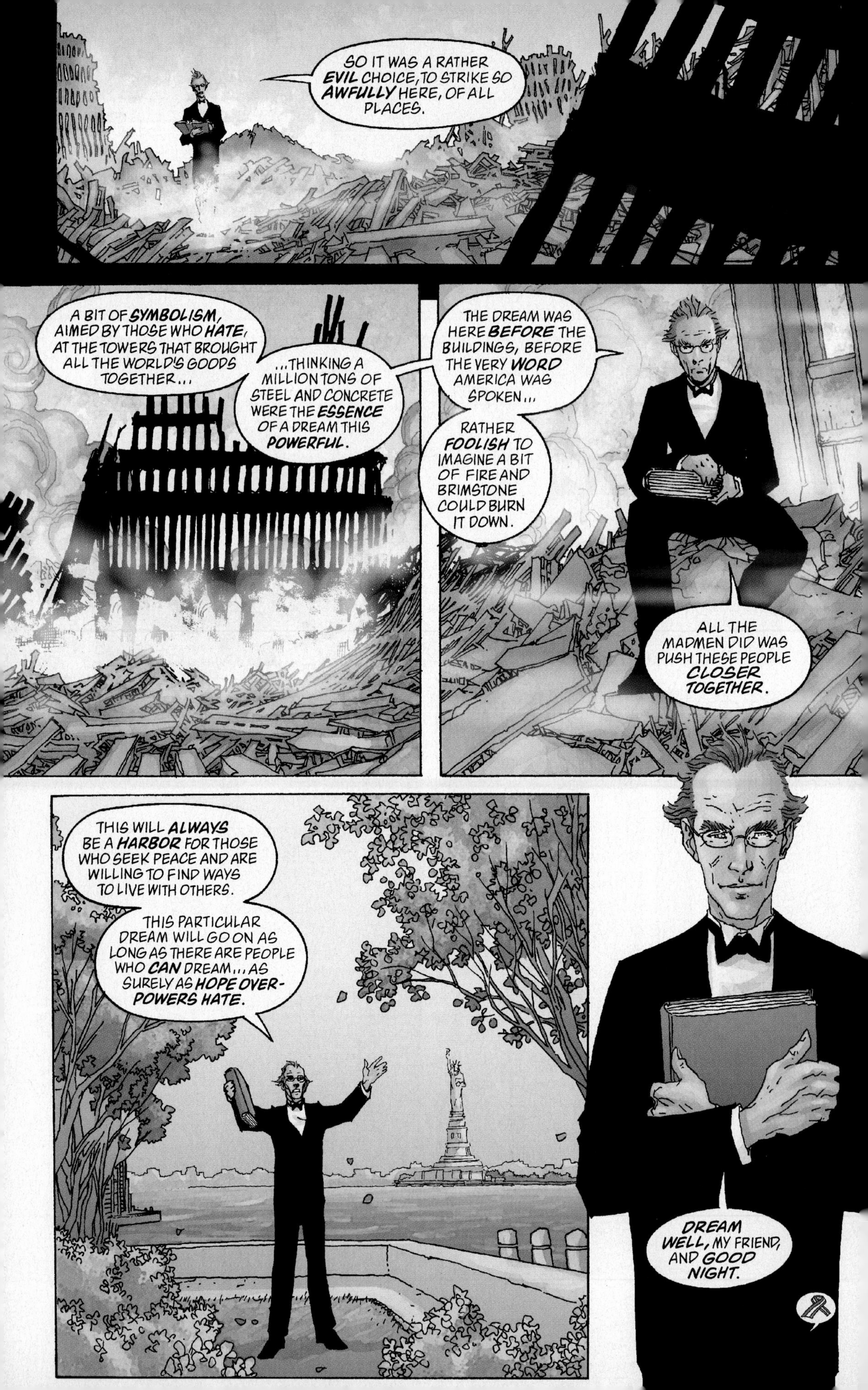
SO IT WAS A RATHER EVIL CHOICE, TO STRIKE SO AWFULLY HERE, OF ALL PLACES.
A BIT OF SYMBOLISM, AIMED BY THOSE WHO HATE, AT THE TOWERS THAT BROUGHT ALL THE WORLD'S GOODS TOGETHER...
...THINKING A MILLION TONS OF STEEL AND CONCRETE WERE THE ESSENCE OF A DREAM THIS POWERFUL.
THE DREAM WAS HERE BEFORE THE BUILDINGS, BEFORE THE VERY WORD AMERICA WAS SPOKEN...
RATHER FOOLISH TO IMAGINE A BIT OF FIRE AND BRIMSTONE COULD BURN IT DOWN.
ALL THE MADMEN DID WAS PUSH THESE PEOPLE CLOSER TOGETHER.
THIS WILL ALWAYS BE A HARBOR FOR THOSE WHO SEEK PEACE AND ARE WILLING TO FIND WAYS TO LIVE WITH OTHERS.
THIS PARTICULAR DREAM WILL GO ON AS LONG AS THERE ARE PEOPLE WHO CAN DREAM... AS SURELY AS HOPE OVER-POWERS HATE.
DREAM WELL, MY FRIEND, AND GOOD NIGHT.

SPIRIT

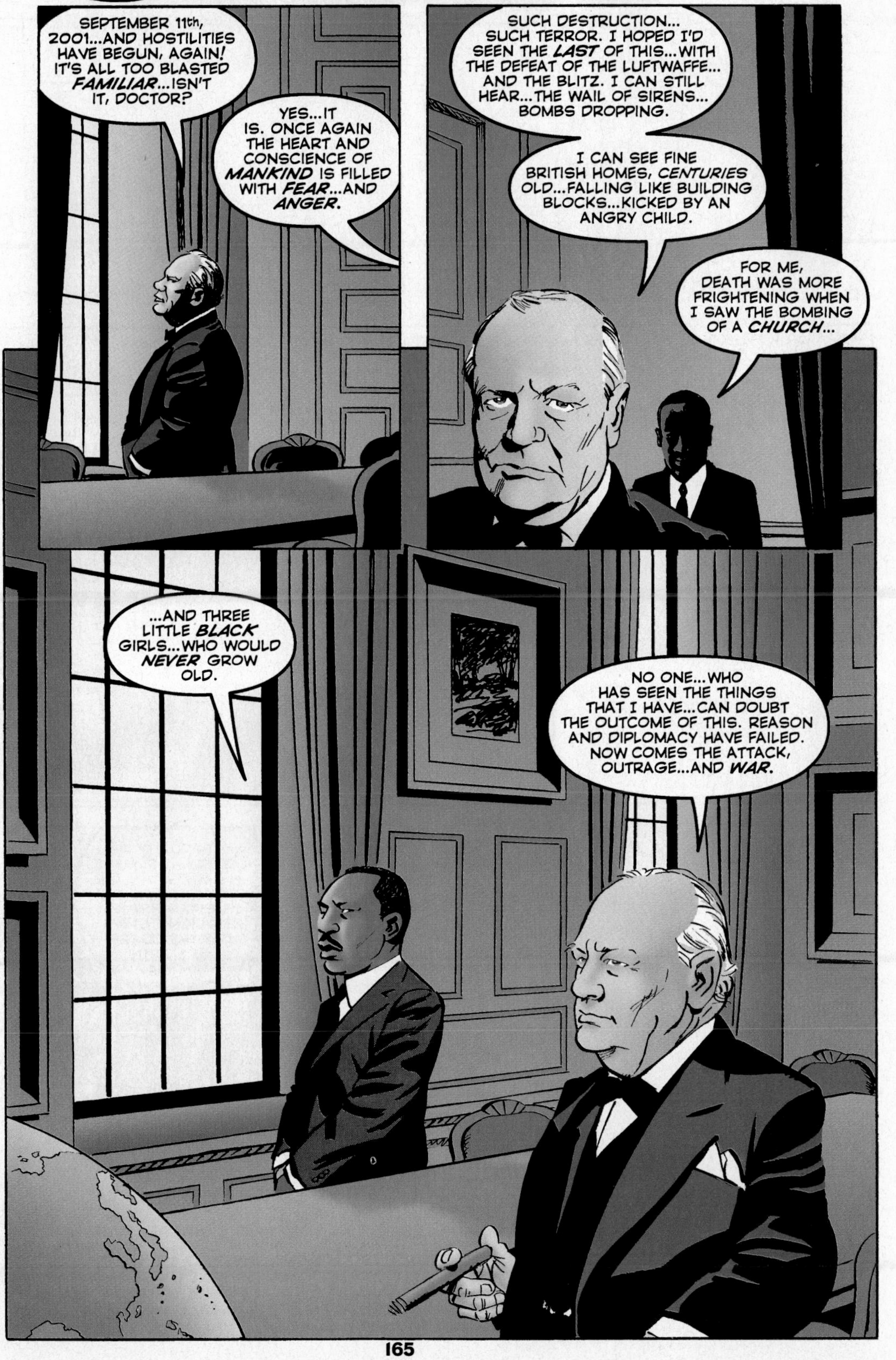
SEPTEMBER 11th, 2001...AND HOSTILITIES HAVE BEGUN, AGAIN! IT'S ALL TOO BLASTED FAMILIAR...ISN'T IT, DOCTOR?
YES...IT IS. ONCE AGAIN THE HEART AND CONSCIENCE OF MANKIND IS FILLED WITH FEAR...AND ANGER.
SUCH DESTRUCTION... SUCH TERROR. I HOPED I'D SEEN THE LAST OF THIS...WITH THE DEFEAT OF THE LUFTWAFFE... AND THE BLITZ. I CAN STILL HEAR...THE WAIL OF SIRENS... BOMBS DROPPING.
I CAN SEE FINE BRITISH HOMES, CENTURIES OLD...FALLING LIKE BUILDING BLOCKS...KICKED BY AN ANGRY CHILD.
FOR ME, DEATH WAS MORE FRIGHTENING WHEN I SAW THE BOMBING OF A CHURCH...
...AND THREE LITTLE BLACK GIRLS...WHO WOULD NEVER GROW OLD.
NO ONE...WHO HAS SEEN THE THINGS THAT I HAVE...CAN DOUBT THE OUTCOME OF THIS. REASON AND DIPLOMACY HAVE FAILED. NOW COMES THE ATTACK, OUTRAGE...AND WAR.

STORY ALEX SIMMONS ★★★★
ART ANGELO TORRES ★★★★
LETTERS WILDSTORM ★★★★
COLOR DAVE TANGUAY ★★★★

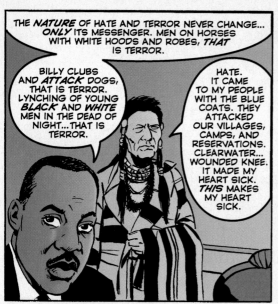

THE *NATURE* OF HATE AND TERROR NEVER CHANGE... *ONLY* ITS MESSENGER. MEN ON HORSES WITH WHITE HOODS AND ROBES, *THAT* IS TERROR.

BILLY CLUBS AND *ATTACK* DOGS, THAT IS TERROR. LYNCHING OF YOUNG *BLACK* AND *WHITE* MEN IN THE DEAD OF NIGHT...THAT IS TERROR.

HATE. IT CAME TO MY PEOPLE WITH THE BLUE COATS. THEY ATTACKED OUR VILLAGES, CAMPS, AND RESERVATIONS. CLEARWATER... WOUNDED KNEE. IT MADE MY HEART SICK. *THIS* MAKES MY HEART SICK.

WAIT A MINUTE, *CHIEF* JOSEPH. WERE THOSE CAVALRY'S ATTACKS ANY DIFFERENT FROM THE MASSACRE CRAZY HORSE LED AT *LITTLE BIG HORN?*

AND FOR THAT SLAUGHTER, DOUGLAS... THE CAVALRY RELENTLESSLY HUNTED THE INDIANS FOR MANY MONTHS THEREAFTER. NOT UNLIKE THE UNION SOLDIERS WHO PURSUED THE CONFEDERATES, AFTER THE WAR. IS *ANY* OF IT DIFFERENT, GENERAL?

WANT FOR *VENGEANCE* IS STRONG IN PEOPLE. DEFENDING LAND IS STRONG. SIXTY THOUSAND ZULUS DIED WHEN BRITISH *INVADED* OUR LAND.

IF MEMORY SERVES...YOU WERE DOING REMARKABLY WELL IN THE ARTS OF WAR...*PRIOR* TO OUR ARRIVAL. FOR SOME TWENTY-ONE YEARS...AM I CORRECT, CHIEF SHAKA?

PRIOR TO THE 1870s, HOW MANY *ZULU* VILLAGES AWOKE TO THE BATTLE CRIES... OF *YOUR* MEN?

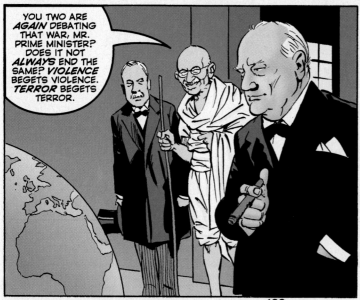

YOU TWO ARE *AGAIN* DEBATING THAT WAR, MR. PRIME MINISTER? DOES IT NOT *ALWAYS* END THE SAME? *VIOLENCE* BEGETS VIOLENCE. *TERROR* BEGETS TERROR.

TERROR IS A CONSTANT PLAGUE IN HISTORY. IN THE 1500s, IT WAS THE BARBARY PIRATES ATTACKING SHIPS OFF THE COAST OF NORTH AFRICA.

IN 1865...IT WAS A *SINGLE SHOT* FROM BEHIND, WHEN *I* SHOULD HAVE FINALLY FOUND LAUGHTER AND PEACE.

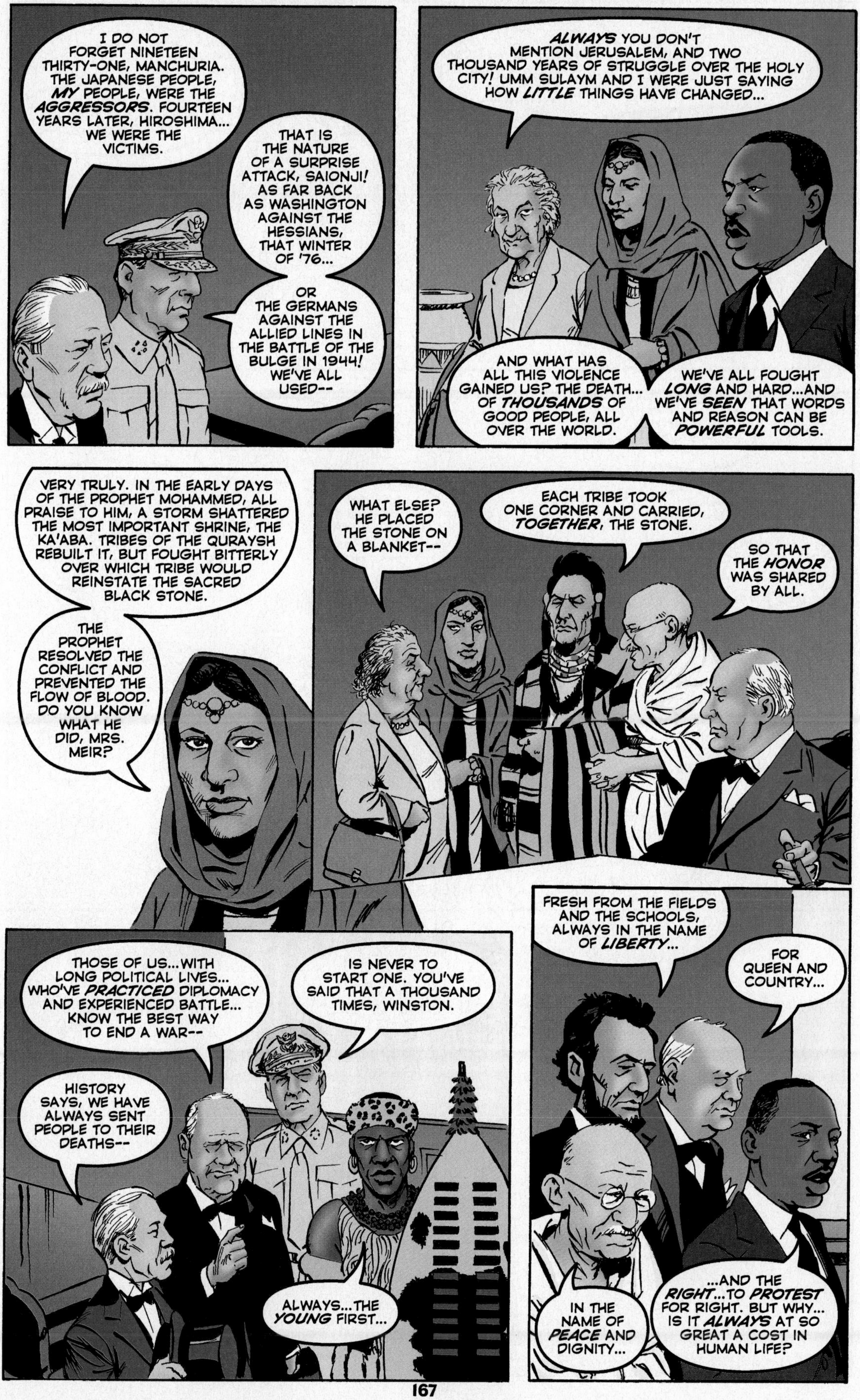
I DO NOT FORGET NINETEEN THIRTY-ONE, MANCHURIA. THE JAPANESE PEOPLE, *MY* PEOPLE, WERE THE *AGGRESSORS*. FOURTEEN YEARS LATER, HIROSHIMA... WE WERE THE VICTIMS.
THAT IS THE NATURE OF A SURPRISE ATTACK, SAIONJI! AS FAR BACK AS WASHINGTON AGAINST THE HESSIANS, THAT WINTER OF '76...
OR THE GERMANS AGAINST THE ALLIED LINES IN THE BATTLE OF THE BULGE IN 1944! WE'VE ALL USED--
ALWAYS YOU DON'T MENTION JERUSALEM, AND TWO THOUSAND YEARS OF STRUGGLE OVER THE HOLY CITY! UMM SULAYM AND I WERE JUST SAYING HOW *LITTLE* THINGS HAVE CHANGED...
AND WHAT HAS ALL THIS VIOLENCE GAINED US? THE DEATH... OF *THOUSANDS* OF GOOD PEOPLE, ALL OVER THE WORLD.
WE'VE ALL FOUGHT *LONG* AND HARD...AND WE'VE *SEEN* THAT WORDS AND REASON CAN BE *POWERFUL* TOOLS.
VERY TRULY. IN THE EARLY DAYS OF THE PROPHET MOHAMMED, ALL PRAISE TO HIM, A STORM SHATTERED THE MOST IMPORTANT SHRINE, THE KA'ABA. TRIBES OF THE QURAYSH REBUILT IT, BUT FOUGHT BITTERLY OVER WHICH TRIBE WOULD REINSTATE THE SACRED BLACK STONE.
THE PROPHET RESOLVED THE CONFLICT AND PREVENTED THE FLOW OF BLOOD. DO YOU KNOW WHAT HE DID, MRS. MEIR?
WHAT ELSE? HE PLACED THE STONE ON A BLANKET--
EACH TRIBE TOOK ONE CORNER AND CARRIED, *TOGETHER*, THE STONE.
SO THAT THE *HONOR* WAS SHARED BY ALL.
THOSE OF US...WITH LONG POLITICAL LIVES... WHO'VE *PRACTICED* DIPLOMACY AND EXPERIENCED BATTLE... KNOW THE BEST WAY TO END A WAR--
IS NEVER TO START ONE. YOU'VE SAID THAT A THOUSAND TIMES, WINSTON.
HISTORY SAYS, WE HAVE ALWAYS SENT PEOPLE TO THEIR DEATHS--
ALWAYS...THE *YOUNG* FIRST...
FRESH FROM THE FIELDS AND THE SCHOOLS, ALWAYS IN THE NAME OF *LIBERTY*...
FOR QUEEN AND COUNTRY...
IN THE NAME OF *PEACE* AND DIGNITY...
...AND THE *RIGHT*...TO *PROTEST* FOR RIGHT. BUT WHY... IS IT *ALWAYS* AT SO GREAT A COST IN HUMAN LIFE?

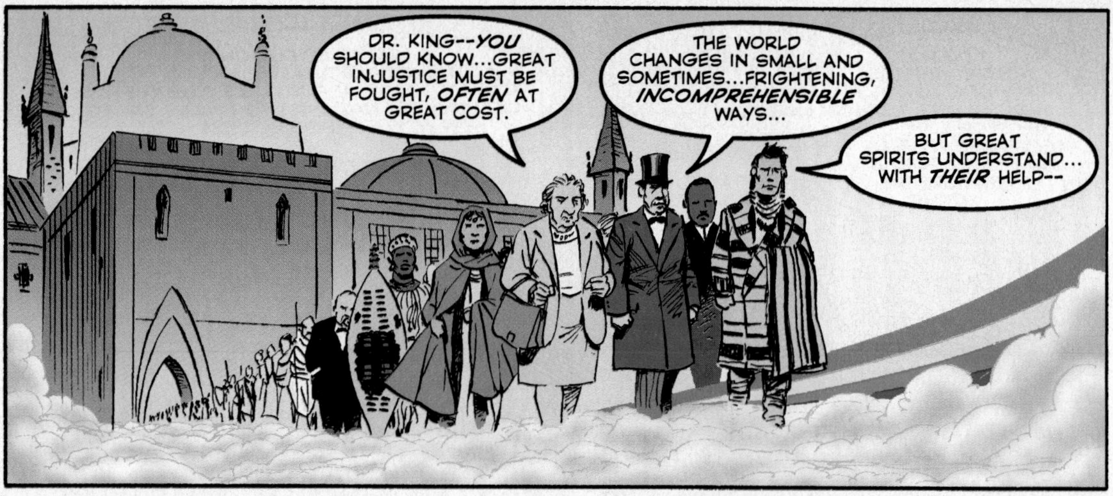
DR. KING--YOU SHOULD KNOW...GREAT INJUSTICE MUST BE FOUGHT, OFTEN AT GREAT COST.
THE WORLD CHANGES IN SMALL AND SOMETIMES...FRIGHTENING, INCOMPREHENSIBLE WAYS...
BUT GREAT SPIRITS UNDERSTAND... WITH THEIR HELP--

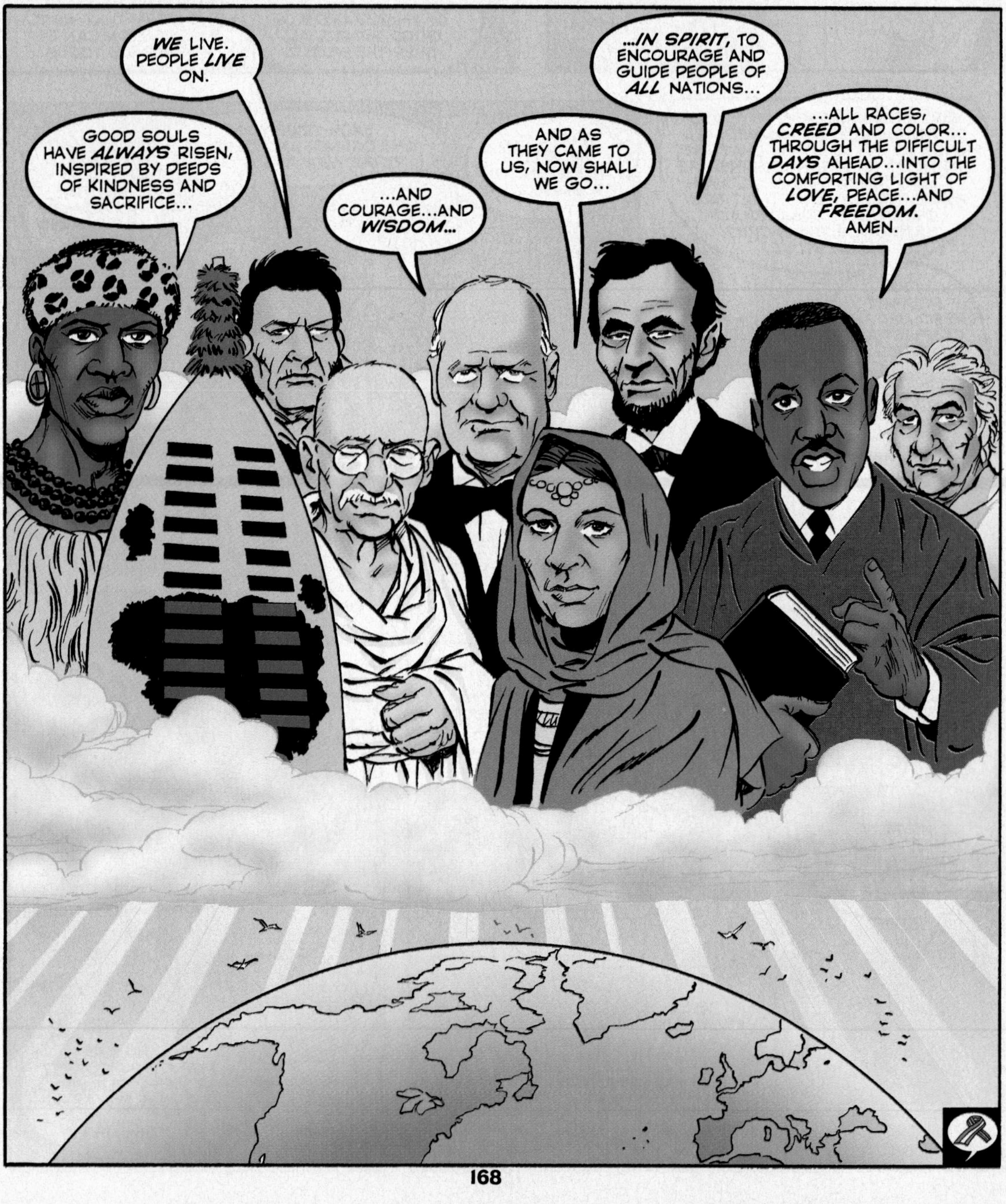
GOOD SOULS HAVE ALWAYS RISEN, INSPIRED BY DEEDS OF KINDNESS AND SACRIFICE...
WE LIVE. PEOPLE LIVE ON.
...AND COURAGE...AND WISDOM...
AND AS THEY CAME TO US, NOW SHALL WE GO...
...IN SPIRIT, TO ENCOURAGE AND GUIDE PEOPLE OF ALL NATIONS...
...ALL RACES, CREED AND COLOR... THROUGH THE DIFFICULT DAYS AHEAD...INTO THE COMFORTING LIGHT OF LOVE, PEACE...AND FREEDOM. AMEN.

TALL BUILDINGS

IN A SINGLE BOUND I WAS BACK IN 1995.

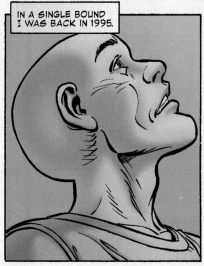

TALLEST BUILDINGS IN THE MOST CELE-BRATED CITY IN THE WORLD, BUT THAT'S NOT WHAT MADE ME STOP AND STARE AT THEM.

IT WAS THE SENSE OF WHAT IT'D TAKEN TO GET THEM UP THERE. PEOPLE HAD GAZED SKYWARD, THE WAY THEY'D LOOKED UP FROM THE MUD, MILLENNIA AGO, AND SAID 'WE CAN RISE, SO WE SHOULD'.

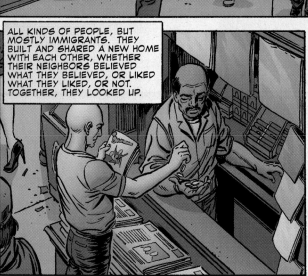

STORY
CHRIS SEQUIERA ★★★★

ART
TOM GRUMMETT AND TOM PALMER ★★★★

LETTERS
KURT HATHAWAY ★★★★

COLOR
MOOSE BAUMANN ★★★★

ALL KINDS OF PEOPLE, BUT MOSTLY IMMIGRANTS. THEY BUILT AND SHARED A NEW HOME WITH EACH OTHER, WHETHER THEIR NEIGHBORS BELIEVED WHAT THEY BELIEVED, OR LIKED WHAT THEY LIKED, OR NOT. TOGETHER, THEY LOOKED UP.

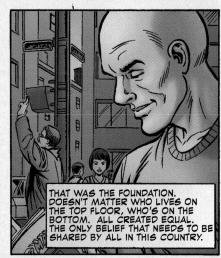

THAT WAS THE FOUNDATION. DOESN'T MATTER WHO LIVES ON THE TOP FLOOR, WHO'S ON THE BOTTOM. ALL CREATED EQUAL. THE ONLY BELIEF THAT NEEDS TO BE SHARED BY ALL IN THIS COUNTRY.

THAT WAS SIX YEARS AGO.

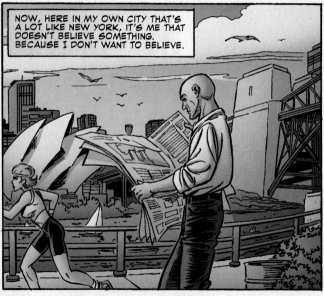

NOW, HERE IN MY OWN CITY THAT'S A LOT LIKE NEW YORK, IT'S ME THAT DOESN'T BELIEVE SOMETHING. BECAUSE I DON'T WANT TO BELIEVE.

I DON'T WANT TO BELIEVE THAT THE TOWERS ARE BURNING, THE TOWERS ARE FALLING, THE TOWERS ARE GONE. EVERY HALF HOUR, ON THE HOUR.

VISIONS BLUDGEON MY EYES, FROM FLICKERING TV SETS, FROM THE GREY-SCALE DOTTED COVERS OF NEWSPAPERS AND THE LOW-RES PICS ON MAGAZINES.

I DON'T WANT TO BELIEVE THAT THE TOWERS AND THE THOUSANDS OF PEOPLE IN THEM HAVE BEEN TORN FROM THAT CITY AND SHOVED INTO A PHOSPHOR-DOT, SHAKY-CAM GRAVEYARD.

CONDEMNED TO MISERY IN A VIDEO NEWS-FLASH AND TABLOID-COVER PHANTOM ZONE.

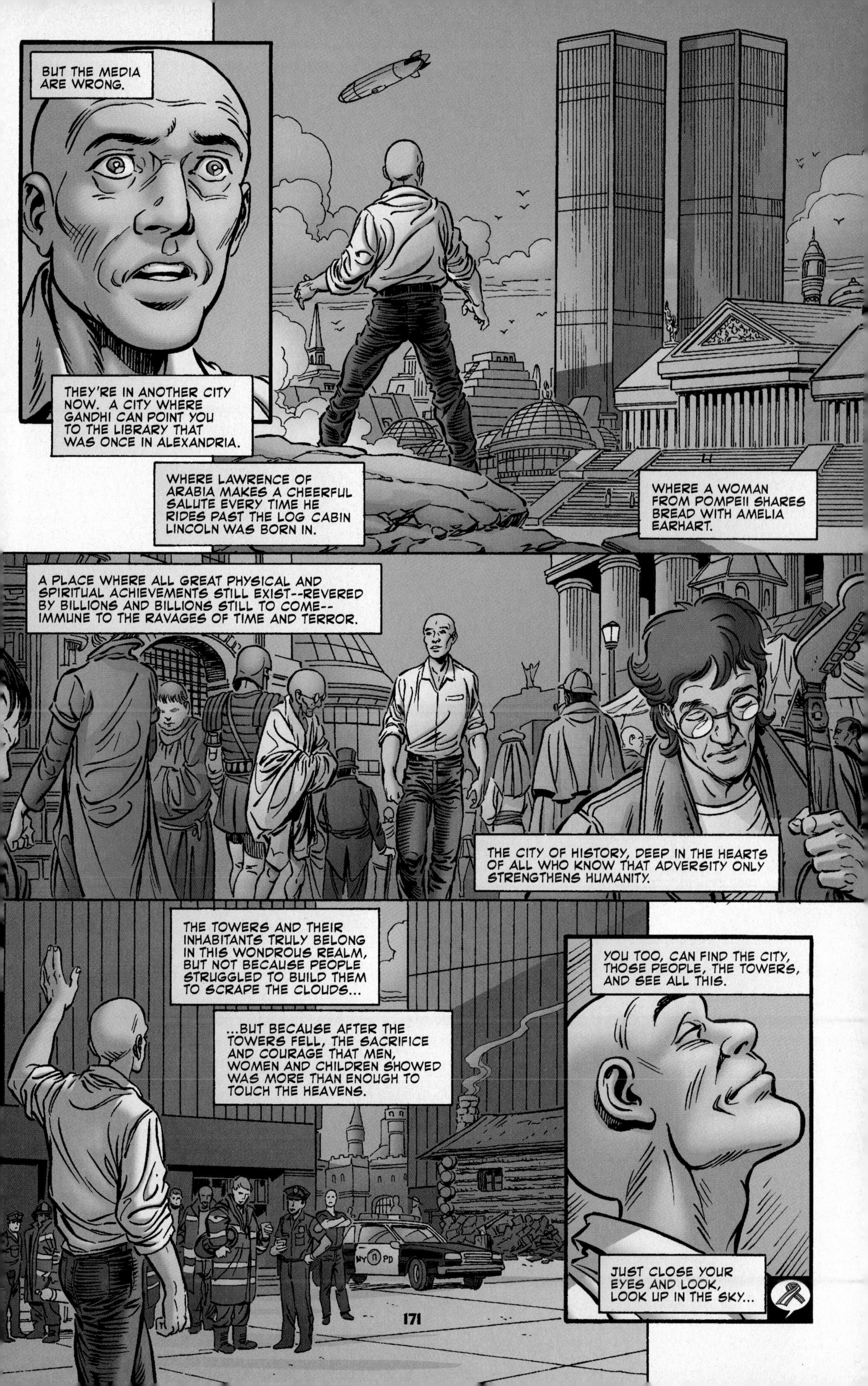
BUT THE MEDIA ARE WRONG.
THEY'RE IN ANOTHER CITY NOW. A CITY WHERE GANDHI CAN POINT YOU TO THE LIBRARY THAT WAS ONCE IN ALEXANDRIA.
WHERE LAWRENCE OF ARABIA MAKES A CHEERFUL SALUTE EVERY TIME HE RIDES PAST THE LOG CABIN LINCOLN WAS BORN IN.
WHERE A WOMAN FROM POMPEII SHARES BREAD WITH AMELIA EARHART.
A PLACE WHERE ALL GREAT PHYSICAL AND SPIRITUAL ACHIEVEMENTS STILL EXIST--REVERED BY BILLIONS AND BILLIONS STILL TO COME--IMMUNE TO THE RAVAGES OF TIME AND TERROR.
THE CITY OF HISTORY, DEEP IN THE HEARTS OF ALL WHO KNOW THAT ADVERSITY ONLY STRENGTHENS HUMANITY.
THE TOWERS AND THEIR INHABITANTS TRULY BELONG IN THIS WONDROUS REALM, BUT NOT BECAUSE PEOPLE STRUGGLED TO BUILD THEM TO SCRAPE THE CLOUDS...
...BUT BECAUSE AFTER THE TOWERS FELL, THE SACRIFICE AND COURAGE THAT MEN, WOMEN AND CHILDREN SHOWED WAS MORE THAN ENOUGH TO TOUCH THE HEAVENS.
YOU TOO, CAN FIND THE CITY, THOSE PEOPLE, THE TOWERS, AND SEE ALL THIS.
JUST CLOSE YOUR EYES AND LOOK, LOOK UP IN THE SKY...

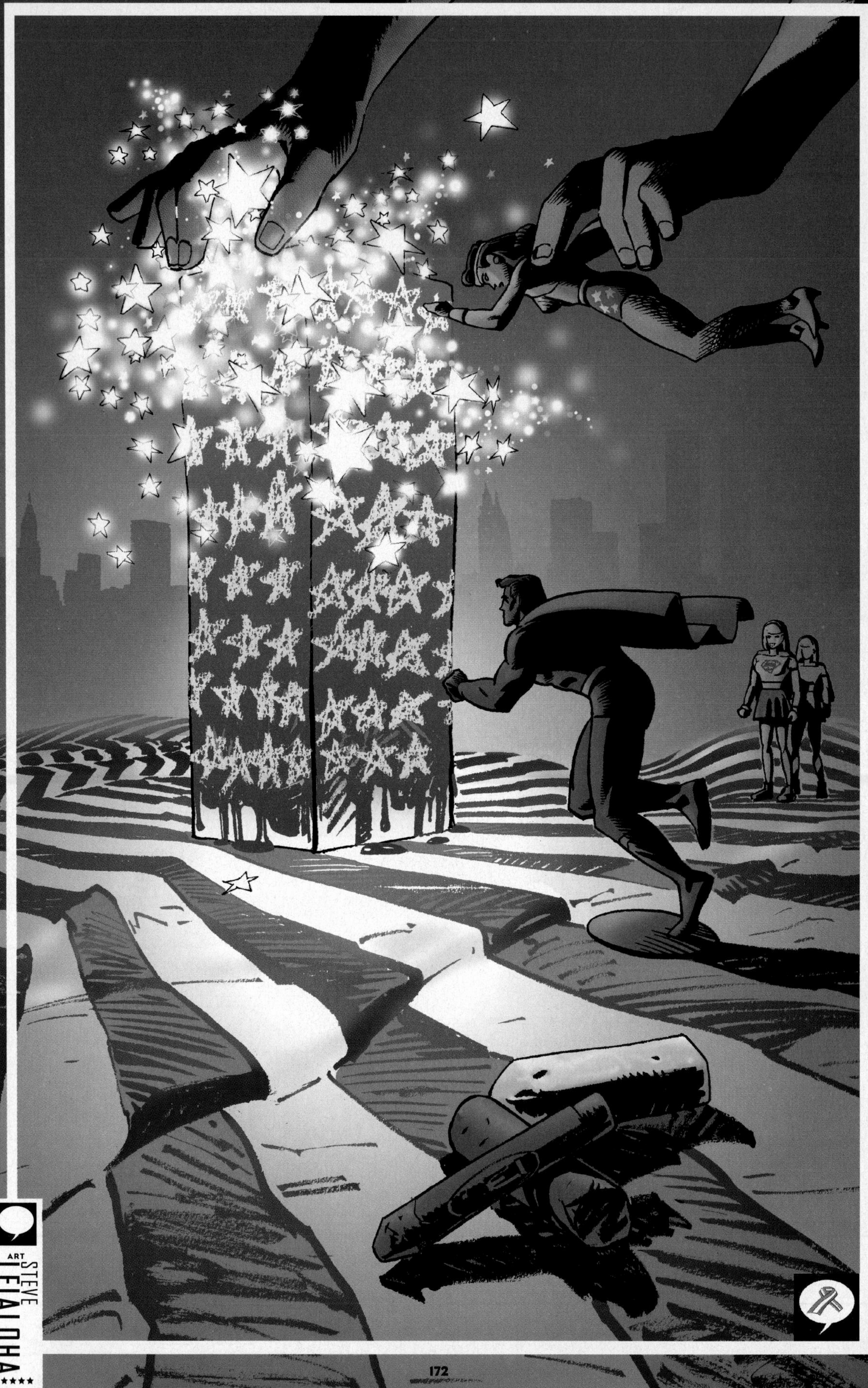

ART STEVE LEIALOHA

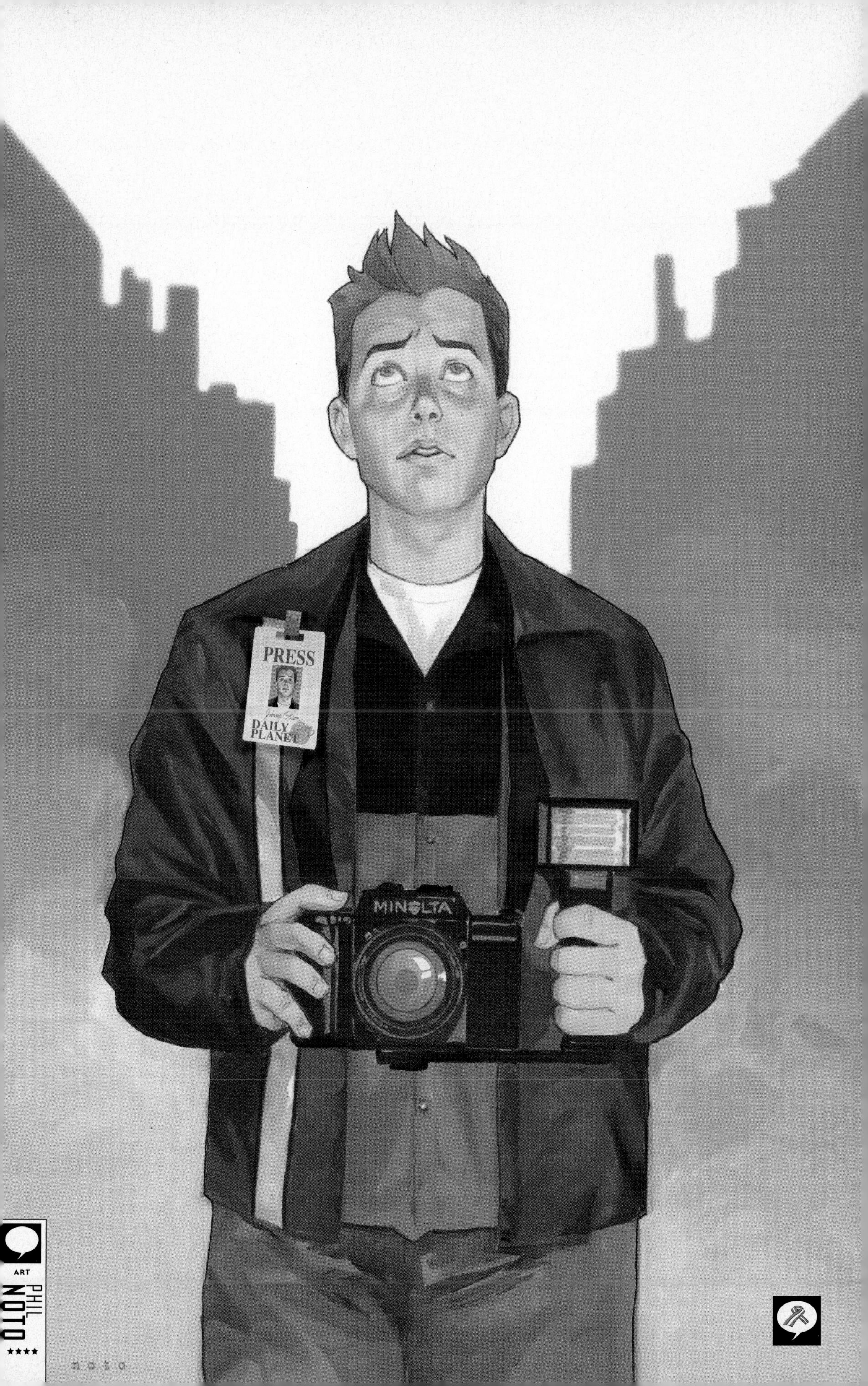
PRESS
DAILY PLANET
MINOLTA
noto
ART
PHIL NOTO

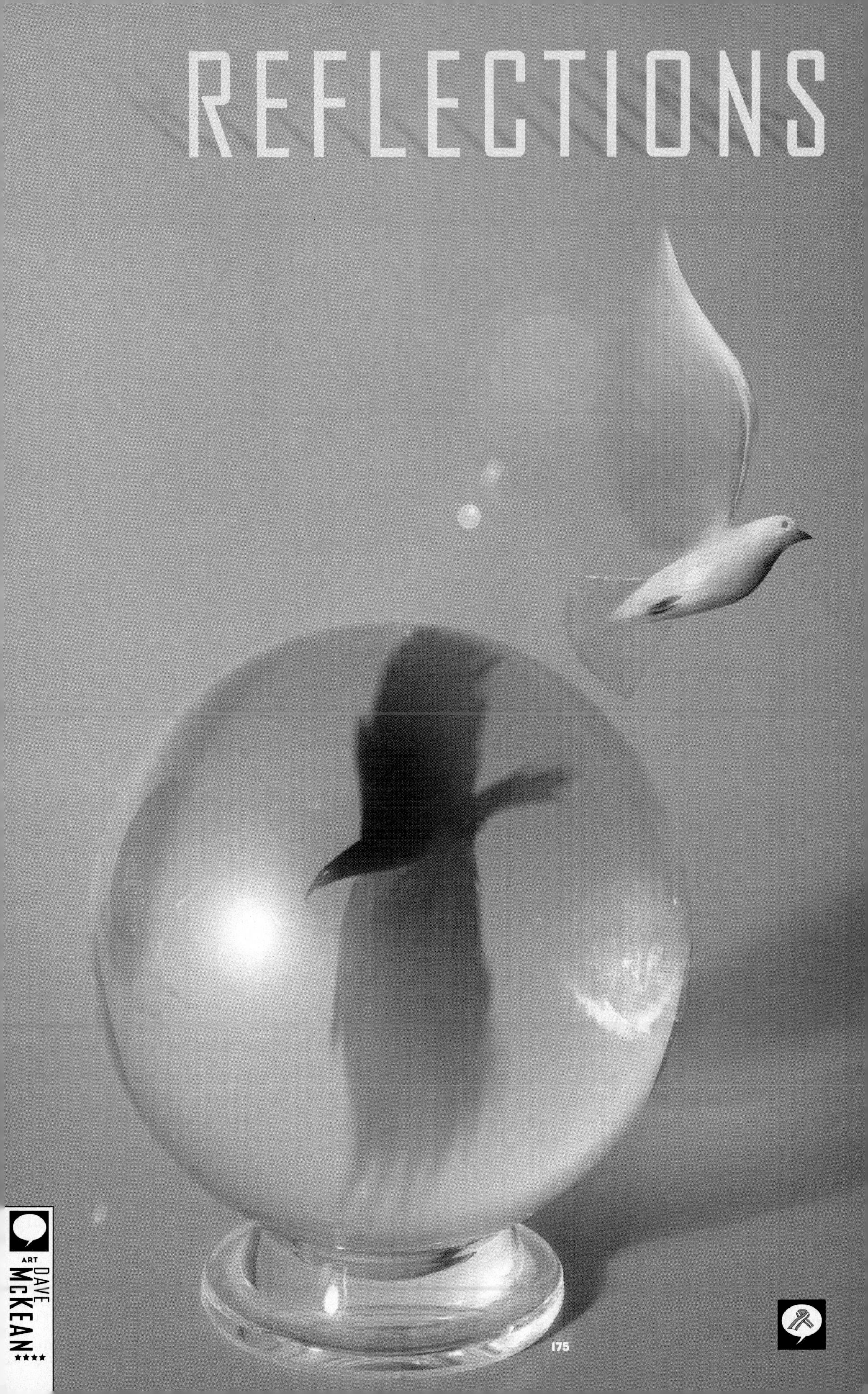
REFLECTIONS
ART DAVE McKEAN

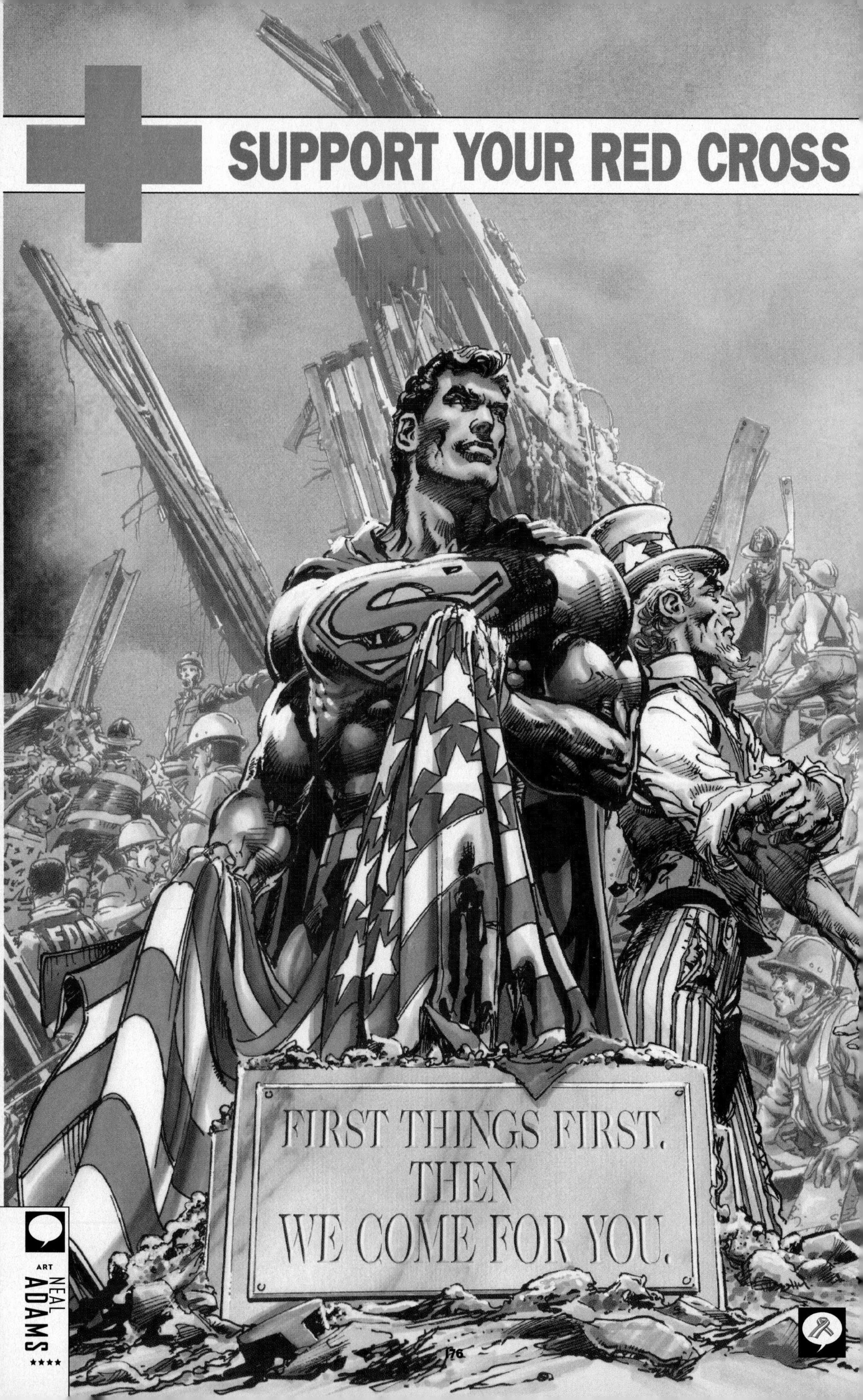
SUPPORT YOUR RED CROSS
FIRST THINGS FIRST.
THEN
WE COME FOR YOU.
FDN
ART
NEAL ADAMS

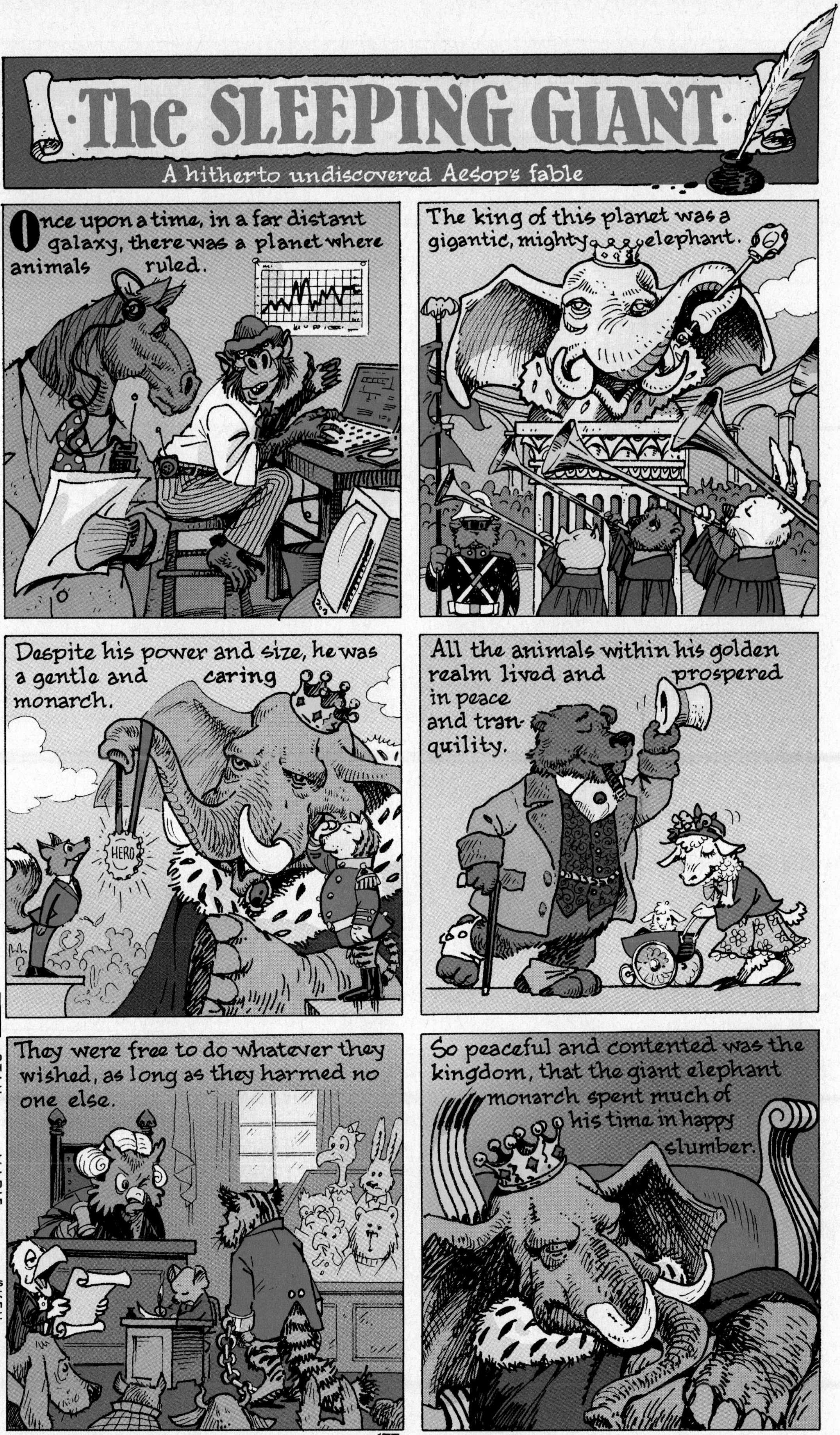

·The SLEEPING GIANT·
A hitherto undiscovered Aesop's fable
Once upon a time, in a far distant galaxy, there was a planet where animals ruled.
The king of this planet was a gigantic, mighty elephant.
Despite his power and size, he was a gentle and caring monarch.
HERO
All the animals within his golden realm lived and prospered in peace and tranquility.
They were free to do whatever they wished, as long as they harmed no one else.
So peaceful and contented was the kingdom, that the giant elephant monarch spent much of his time in happy slumber.

STORY STAN LEE
ART & COLOR MARIE SEVERIN
LETTERS KEN BRUZENAK

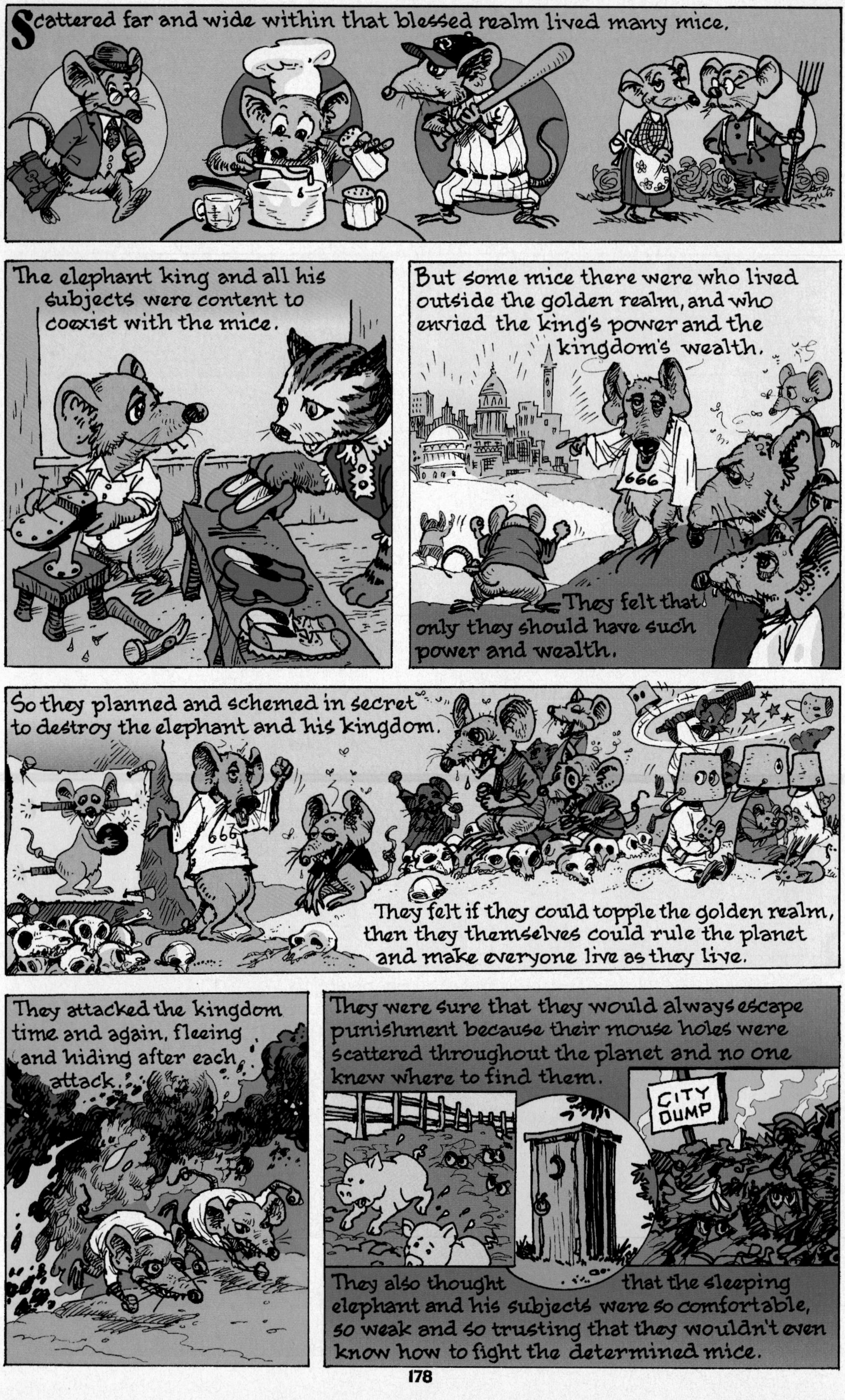
Scattered far and wide within that blessed realm lived many mice.
The elephant king and all his subjects were content to coexist with the mice.
But some mice there were who lived outside the golden realm, and who envied the king's power and the kingdom's wealth.
666
They felt that only they should have such power and wealth.
So they planned and schemed in secret to destroy the elephant and his kingdom.
666
They felt if they could topple the golden realm, then they themselves could rule the planet and make everyone live as they live.
They attacked the kingdom time and again, fleeing and hiding after each attack.
They were sure that they would always escape punishment because their mouse holes were scattered throughout the planet and no one knew where to find them.
CITY DUMP
They also thought that the sleeping elephant and his subjects were so comfortable, so weak and so trusting that they wouldn't even know how to fight the determined mice.

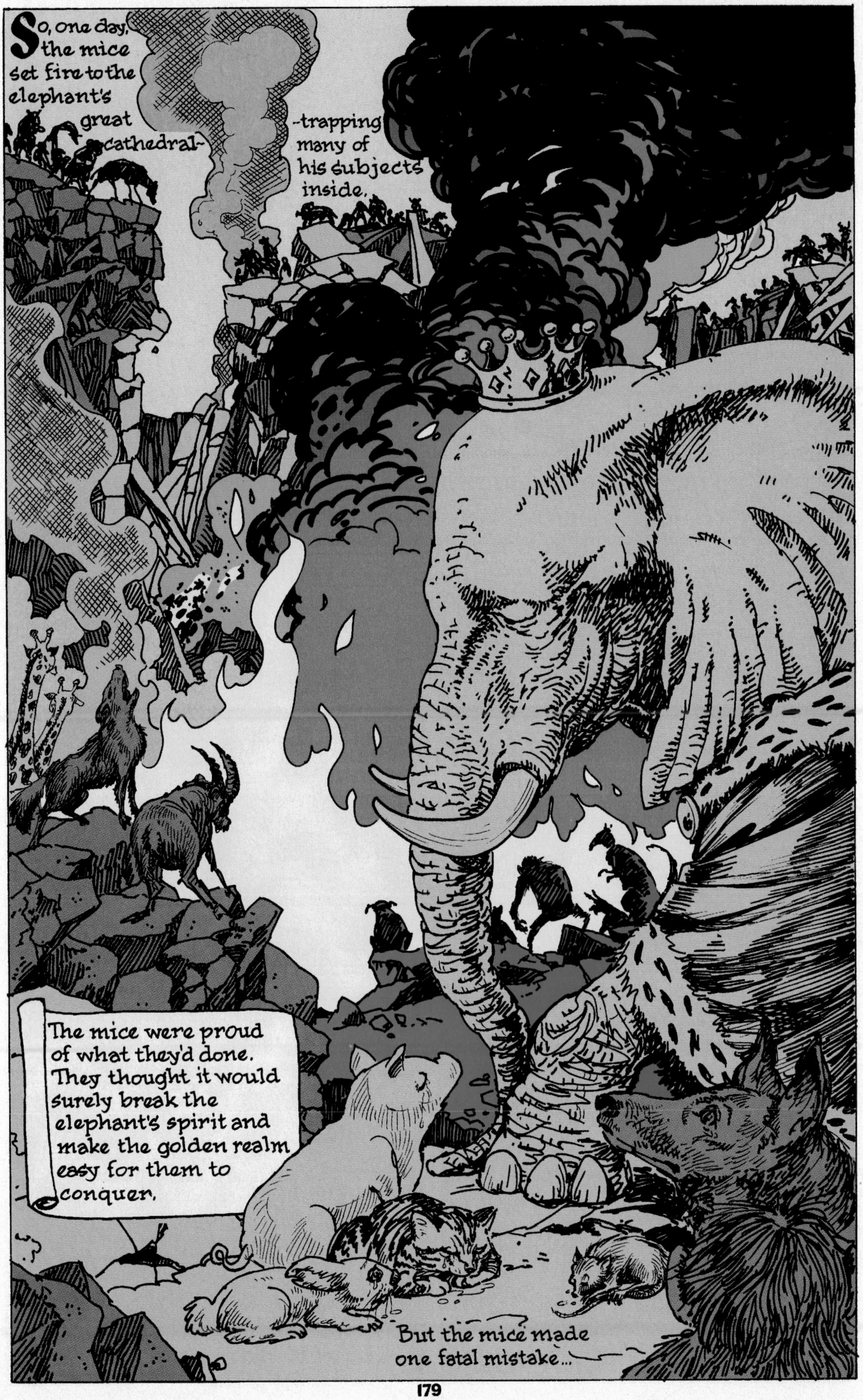
So, one day, the mice set fire to the elephant's great cathedral-
-trapping many of his subjects inside.
The mice were proud of what they'd done. They thought it would surely break the elephant's spirit and make the golden realm easy for them to conquer.
But the mice made one fatal mistake...

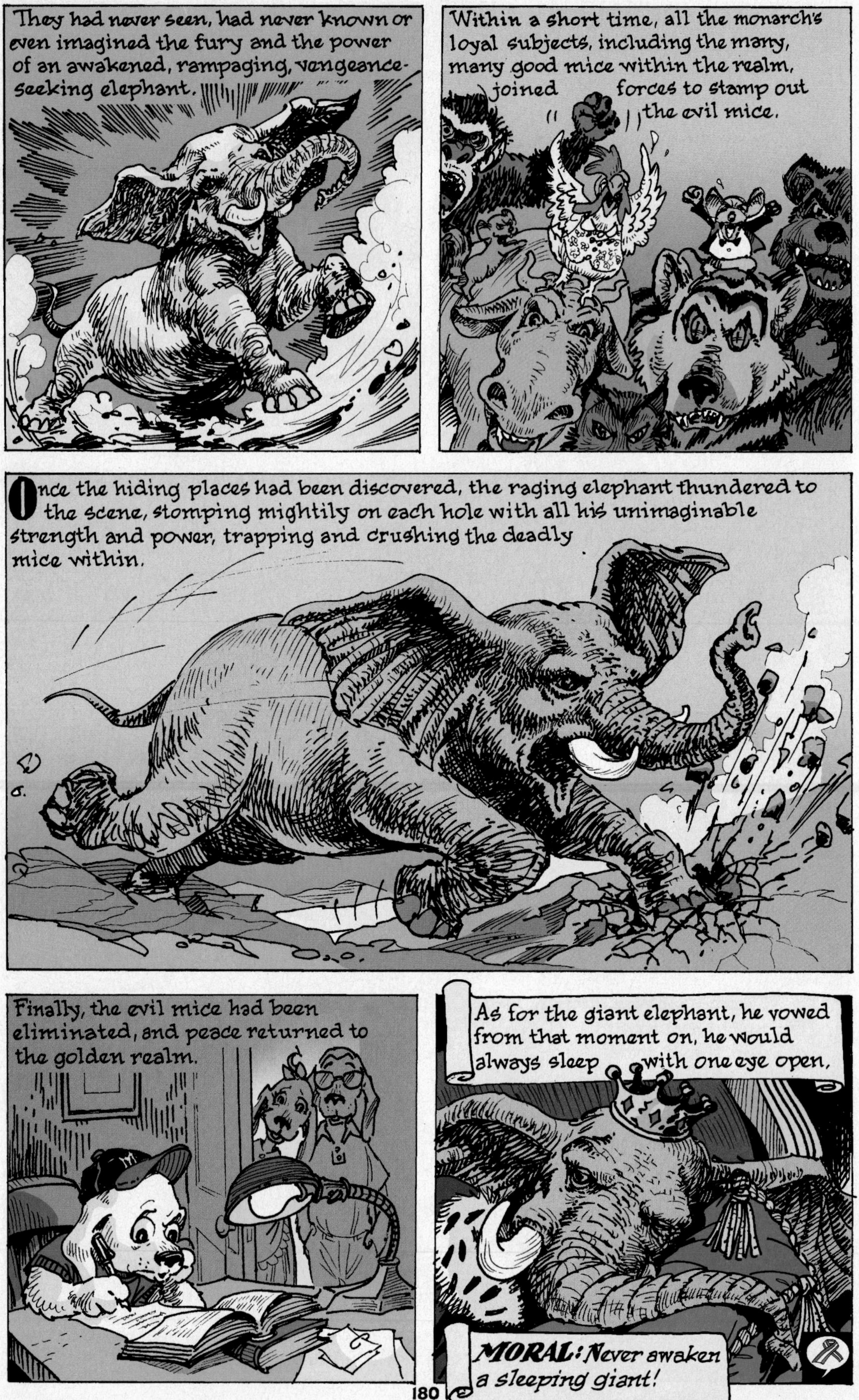
They had never seen, had never known or even imagined the fury and the power of an awakened, rampaging, vengeance-seeking elephant.
Within a short time, all the monarch's loyal subjects, including the many, many good mice within the realm, joined forces to stamp out the evil mice.
Once the hiding places had been discovered, the raging elephant thundered to the scene, stomping mightily on each hole with all his unimaginable strength and power, trapping and crushing the deadly mice within.
Finally, the evil mice had been eliminated, and peace returned to the golden realm.
As for the giant elephant, he vowed from that moment on, he would always sleep with one eye open.
MORAL: Never awaken a sleeping giant!

THE WHEEL

STORY
NEIL GAIMAN
★★★★

ART
CHRIS BACHALO
★★★★

LETTERS
TODD KLEIN
★★★★

COLOR
ROB
AND ALEX
BLEYAERT
★★★★

I made this story up to make me feel better. Now I'm writing it down. It's not true.

It's about how, one day in late October when everything was gray and there was nobody about, I climbed over a wire fence, and then I climbed over another wire fence.

There were signs on the fences, saying the place was patrolled by security and by dogs, but I didn't see anyone. Just an empty fairground, and the wheel.

When I got to the big wheel I started to climb. I'm a good climber. At school I can climb better than anybody.

One time I slipped, and I nearly fell, but I grabbed a strut and I caught myself. My heart was thumping in my chest.

Now, the crazy thing is this: I was only climbing the wheel to jump off. So you'd think that falling off would be something I'd want.

But I wanted to do this right. I had to do everything right. I kept climbing. And eventually, I got to the top of the wheel.

So I'm at the top. I tore a finger when I fell, and it's bleeding, and I suck it.

Apart from that, it's all pretty much as I expected. The light is fading fast, but I can see everything from here.

When I was a kid, about six months ago, I came here in the summer and I could see the towers, and I'd wave at my mom. I knew she couldn't see me, but I'd still wave.

It's strange how some things just vanish.

And I freeze, and I think it's security, with dogs, now I'm really in trouble and I figure I'll duck down low and keep real still and maybe he'll move on.

But I can hear a clambering, and then a huge thud as somebody drops into the car I'm in, and this big guy with a beard is saying--

HEY! YOU! UP THERE!

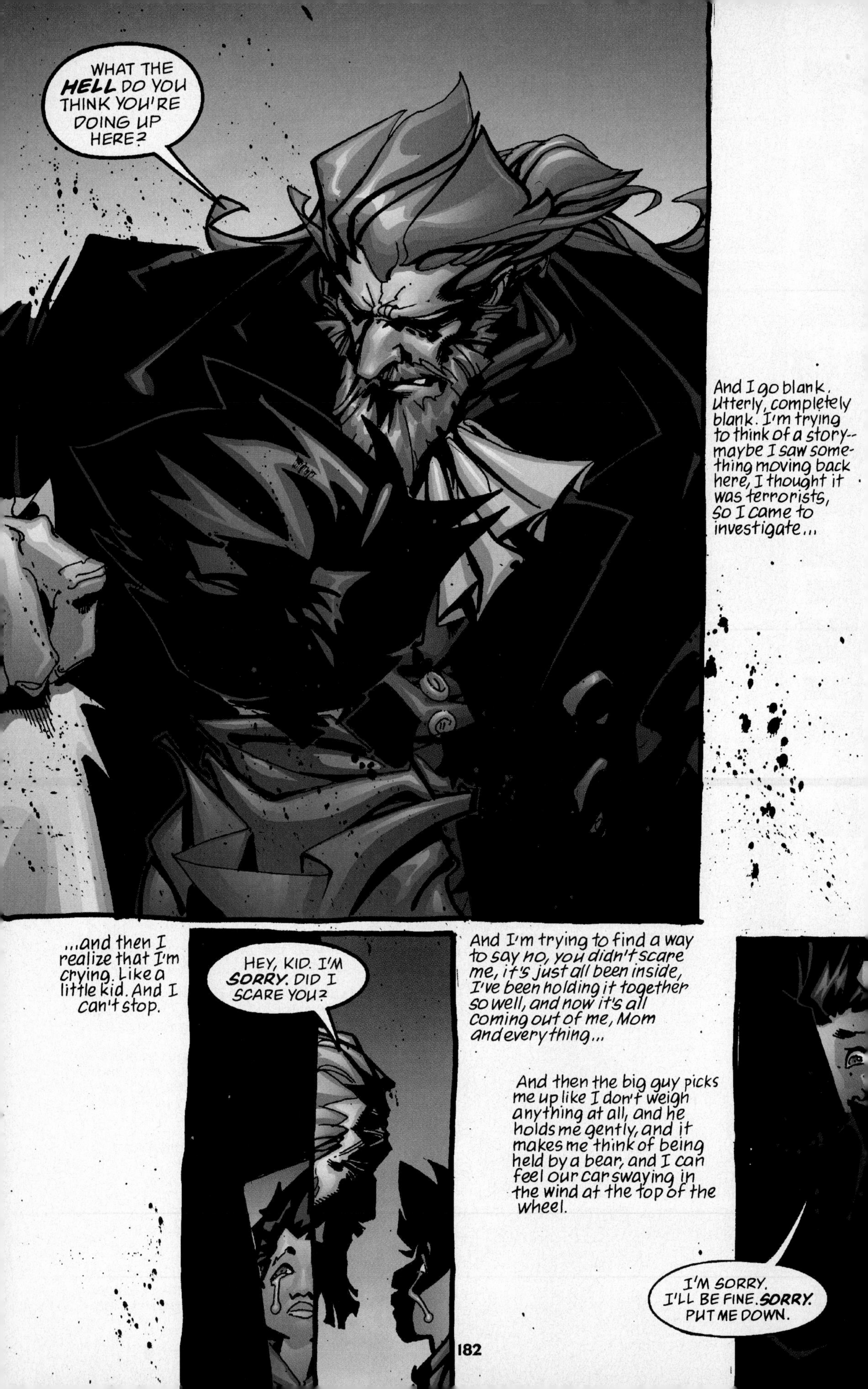
WHAT THE HELL DO YOU THINK YOU'RE DOING UP HERE?
And I go blank. Utterly, completely blank. I'm trying to think of a story-- maybe I saw something moving back here, I thought it was terrorists, so I came to investigate...
...and then I realize that I'm crying. Like a little kid. And I can't stop.
HEY, KID. I'M SORRY. DID I SCARE YOU?
And I'm trying to find a way to say no, you didn't scare me, it's just all been inside, I've been holding it together so well, and now it's all coming out of me, Mom and everything...
And then the big guy picks me up like I don't weigh anything at all, and he holds me gently, and it makes me think of being held by a bear, and I can feel our car swaying in the wind at the top of the wheel.
I'M SORRY. I'LL BE FINE. SORRY. PUT ME DOWN.

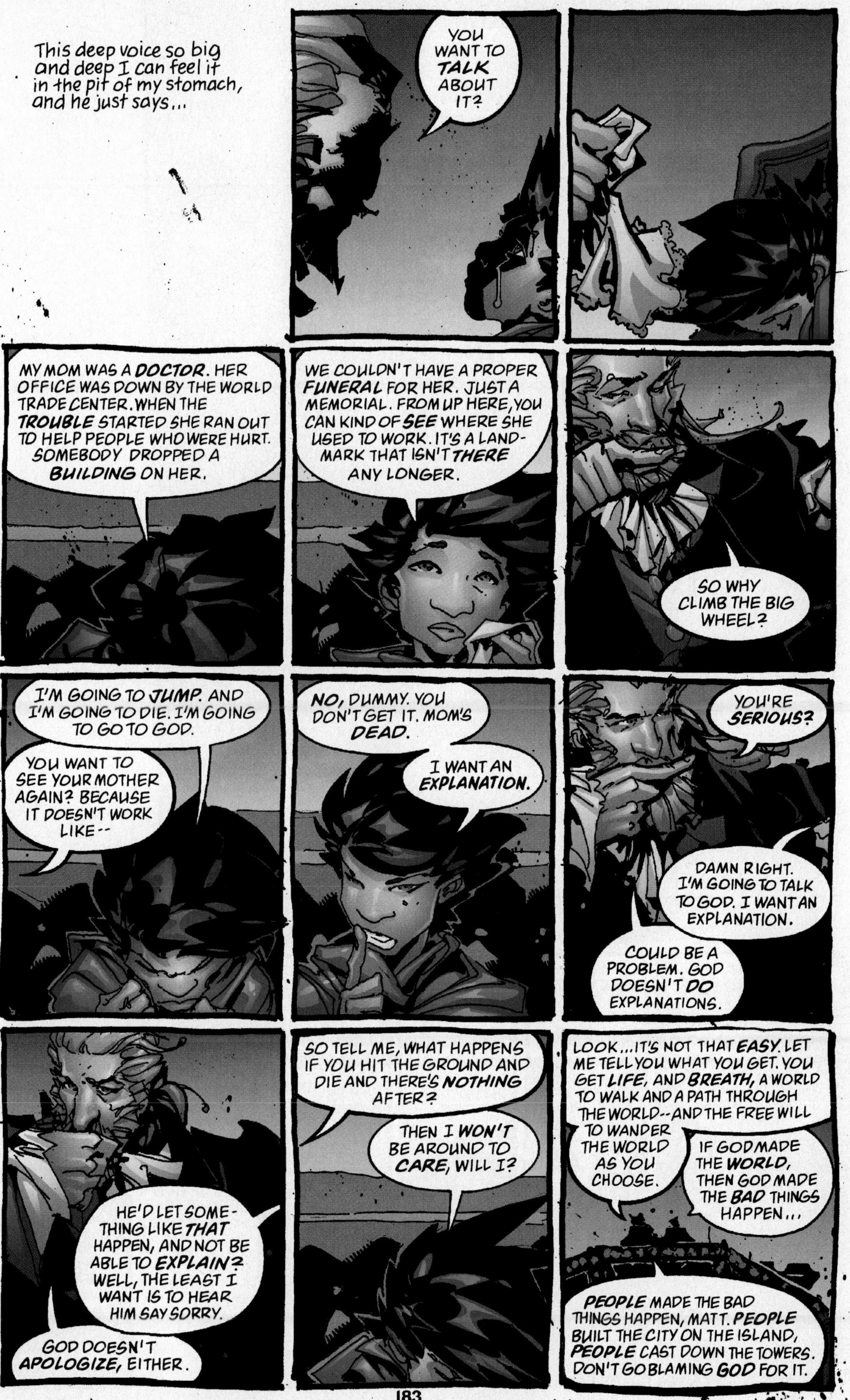
This deep voice so big and deep I can feel it in the pit of my stomach, and he just says...
YOU WANT TO TALK ABOUT IT?
MY MOM WAS A DOCTOR. HER OFFICE WAS DOWN BY THE WORLD TRADE CENTER. WHEN THE TROUBLE STARTED SHE RAN OUT TO HELP PEOPLE WHO WERE HURT. SOMEBODY DROPPED A BUILDING ON HER.
WE COULDN'T HAVE A PROPER FUNERAL FOR HER. JUST A MEMORIAL. FROM UP HERE, YOU CAN KIND OF SEE WHERE SHE USED TO WORK. IT'S A LAND-MARK THAT ISN'T THERE ANY LONGER.
SO WHY CLIMB THE BIG WHEEL?
I'M GOING TO JUMP. AND I'M GOING TO DIE. I'M GOING TO GO TO GOD.
YOU WANT TO SEE YOUR MOTHER AGAIN? BECAUSE IT DOESN'T WORK LIKE--
NO, DUMMY. YOU DON'T GET IT. MOM'S DEAD.
I WANT AN EXPLANATION.
YOU'RE SERIOUS?
DAMN RIGHT. I'M GOING TO TALK TO GOD. I WANT AN EXPLANATION.
COULD BE A PROBLEM. GOD DOESN'T DO EXPLANATIONS.
HE'D LET SOME-THING LIKE THAT HAPPEN, AND NOT BE ABLE TO EXPLAIN? WELL, THE LEAST I WANT IS TO HEAR HIM SAY SORRY.
GOD DOESN'T APOLOGIZE, EITHER.
SO TELL ME, WHAT HAPPENS IF YOU HIT THE GROUND AND DIE AND THERE'S NOTHING AFTER?
THEN I WON'T BE AROUND TO CARE, WILL I?
LOOK... IT'S NOT THAT EASY. LET ME TELL YOU WHAT YOU GET. YOU GET LIFE, AND BREATH, A WORLD TO WALK AND A PATH THROUGH THE WORLD--AND THE FREE WILL TO WANDER THE WORLD AS YOU CHOOSE.
IF GOD MADE THE WORLD, THEN GOD MADE THE BAD THINGS HAPPEN...
PEOPLE MADE THE BAD THINGS HAPPEN, MATT. PEOPLE BUILT THE CITY ON THE ISLAND, PEOPLE CAST DOWN THE TOWERS. DON'T GO BLAMING GOD FOR IT.

This is how you know I'm making this up. I'm not telling you it's true. I wouldn't try to convince anybody. Because now there were three of us in the car, at the top of the dark wheel.

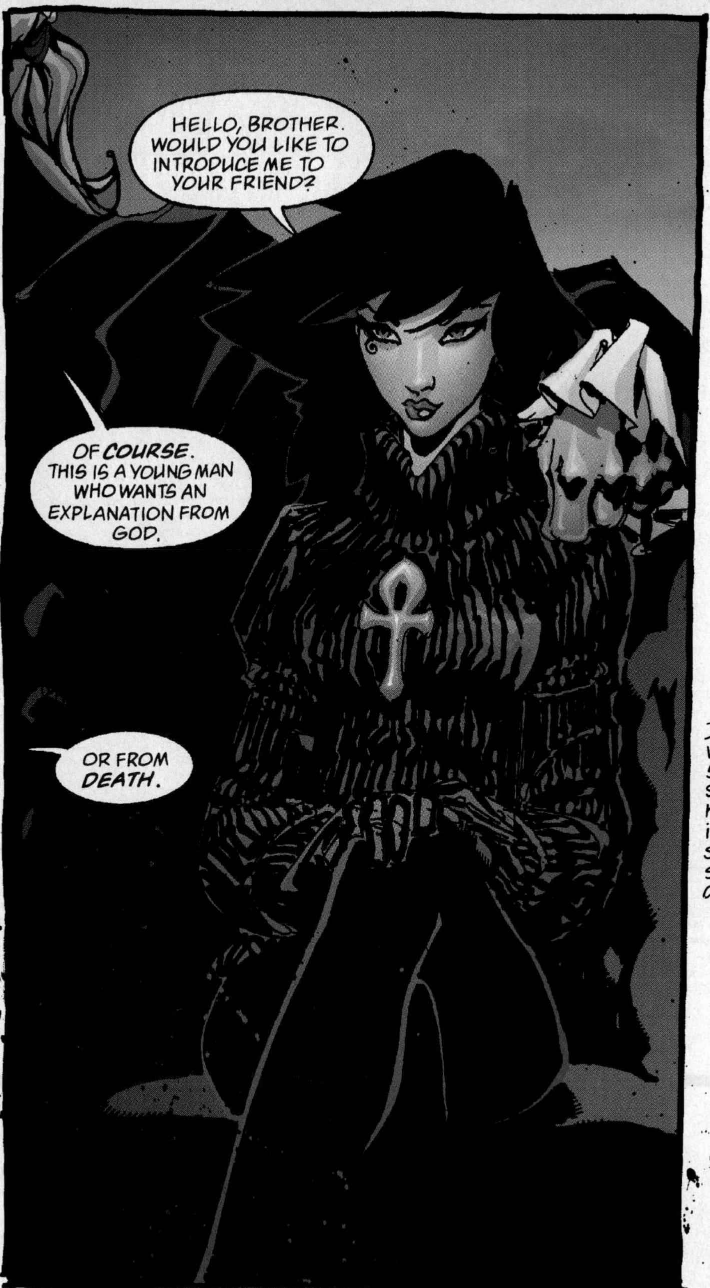
HELLO, BROTHER. WOULD YOU LIKE TO INTRODUCE ME TO YOUR FRIEND?
OF COURSE. THIS IS A YOUNG MAN WHO WANTS AN EXPLANATION FROM GOD.
OR FROM DEATH.

I don't know what made me say that. But she just nodded, as if I had said something sensible after all.

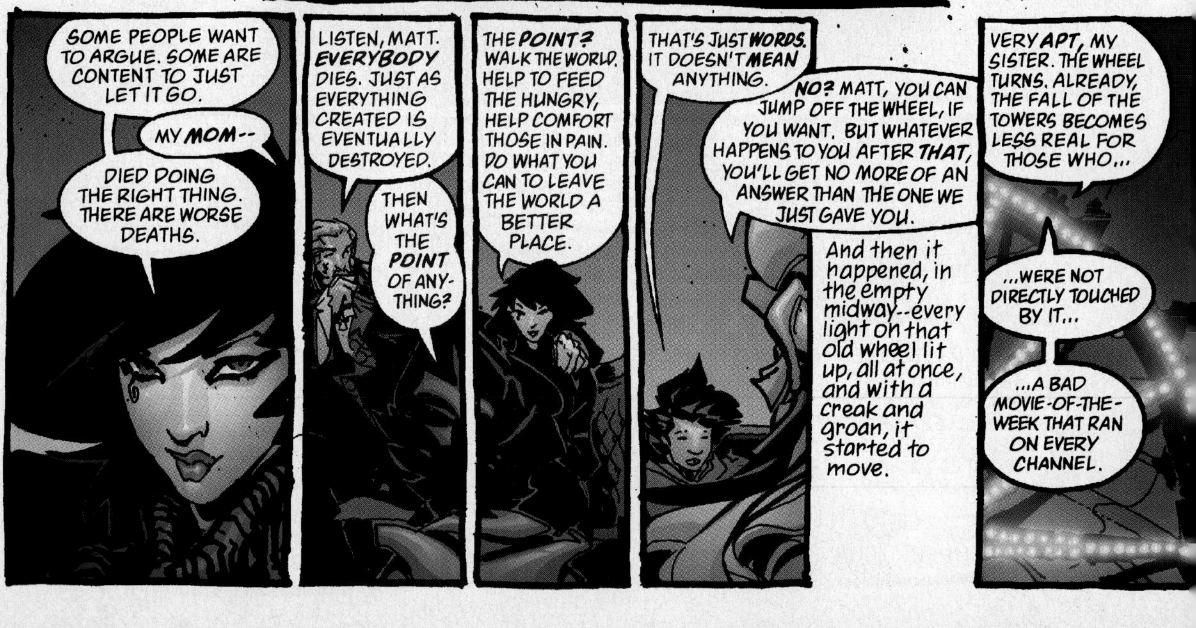
SOME PEOPLE WANT TO ARGUE. SOME ARE CONTENT TO JUST LET IT GO.
MY MOM--
DIED DOING THE RIGHT THING. THERE ARE WORSE DEATHS.
LISTEN, MATT. EVERYBODY DIES. JUST AS EVERYTHING CREATED IS EVENTUALLY DESTROYED.
THEN WHAT'S THE POINT OF ANYTHING?
THE POINT? WALK THE WORLD. HELP TO FEED THE HUNGRY, HELP COMFORT THOSE IN PAIN. DO WHAT YOU CAN TO LEAVE THE WORLD A BETTER PLACE.
THAT'S JUST WORDS. IT DOESN'T MEAN ANYTHING.
NO? MATT, YOU CAN JUMP OFF THE WHEEL, IF YOU WANT. BUT WHATEVER HAPPENS TO YOU AFTER THAT, YOU'LL GET NO MORE OF AN ANSWER THAN THE ONE WE JUST GAVE YOU.
And then it happened, in the empty midway--every light on that old wheel lit up, all at once, and with a creak and groan, it started to move.
VERY APT, MY SISTER. THE WHEEL TURNS. ALREADY, THE FALL OF THE TOWERS BECOMES LESS REAL FOR THOSE WHO...
...WERE NOT DIRECTLY TOUCHED BY IT...
...A BAD MOVIE-OF-THE-WEEK THAT RAN ON EVERY CHANNEL.

IT'S JUST SO HARD.

IT'S ALWAYS HARD. RIDE THE WHEEL, MATT.

And she squeezed my hand.

When I grow up, I thought, I'll have a girlfriend like you.

Which meant, I guessed, that I wasn't going to be jumping off the top of the wheel.

So, no, I don't know who turned on the wheel, who turned on the lights. I guess I must have made up the people in the car, because if they had ever been there, they weren't anymore.

So I was all alone in the car, riding the wonder wheel, and then the music began to play. Corny carnival music. Mom said it always made her remember what it was to be a kid again, and just for a moment, I knew what she meant.

And the music was playing, and the lights were burning, and when I got to the top of the wheel it felt like I could see forever.

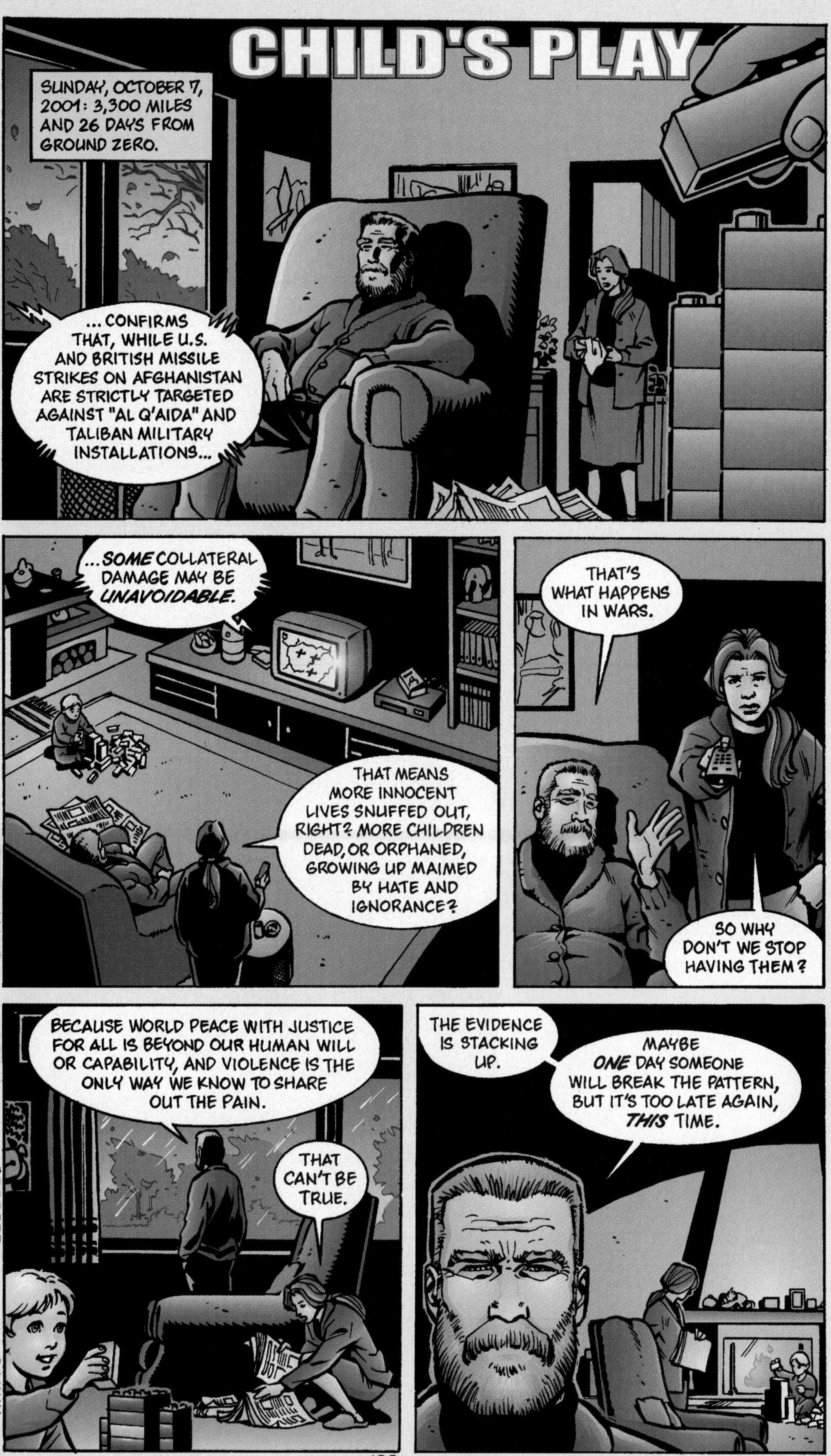
CHILD'S PLAY
SUNDAY, OCTOBER 7, 2001: 3,300 MILES AND 26 DAYS FROM GROUND ZERO.
...CONFIRMS THAT, WHILE U.S. AND BRITISH MISSILE STRIKES ON AFGHANISTAN ARE STRICTLY TARGETED AGAINST "AL Q'AIDA" AND TALIBAN MILITARY INSTALLATIONS...
...*SOME* COLLATERAL DAMAGE MAY BE *UNAVOIDABLE*.
THAT MEANS MORE INNOCENT LIVES SNUFFED OUT, RIGHT? MORE CHILDREN DEAD, OR ORPHANED, GROWING UP MAIMED BY HATE AND IGNORANCE?
THAT'S WHAT HAPPENS IN WARS.
SO WHY DON'T WE STOP HAVING THEM?
BECAUSE WORLD PEACE WITH JUSTICE FOR ALL IS BEYOND OUR HUMAN WILL OR CAPABILITY, AND VIOLENCE IS THE ONLY WAY WE KNOW TO SHARE OUT THE PAIN.
THAT CAN'T BE TRUE.
THE EVIDENCE IS STACKING UP.
MAYBE *ONE* DAY SOMEONE WILL BREAK THE PATTERN, BUT IT'S TOO LATE AGAIN, *THIS* TIME.

STORY JAMIE DELANO
ART GORAN SEDŽUKA
LETTERS ROBERT SOLANOVIĆ
COLOR DANNY VOZZO

WE SPREAD THE GASOLINE, THEY DROPPED THE MATCH, AND NOW THE WILDFIRE HAS TO BURN ITSELF OUT.

WE HAVE TO HAVE *HOPE*. THE FUTURE'S NOT *OURS* TO ABANDON.

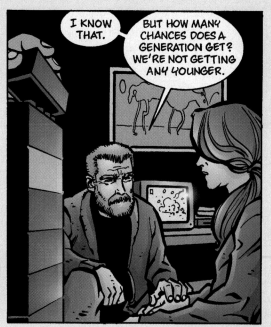

I KNOW THAT.

BUT HOW MANY CHANCES DOES A GENERATION GET? WE'RE NOT GETTING ANY *YOUNGER*.

RIGHT. SO PLAY WITH YOUR GRANDSON WHILE I GET HIS TEA. THE KIDS'LL BE BACK FOR HIM SOON.

SURE.

GOES ON.

LIFE GOES ON, I GUESS.

TOWER.

LEWIS *BUILD* IT. *BIG* TOWER.

YEAH. GOOD JOB, BOY.

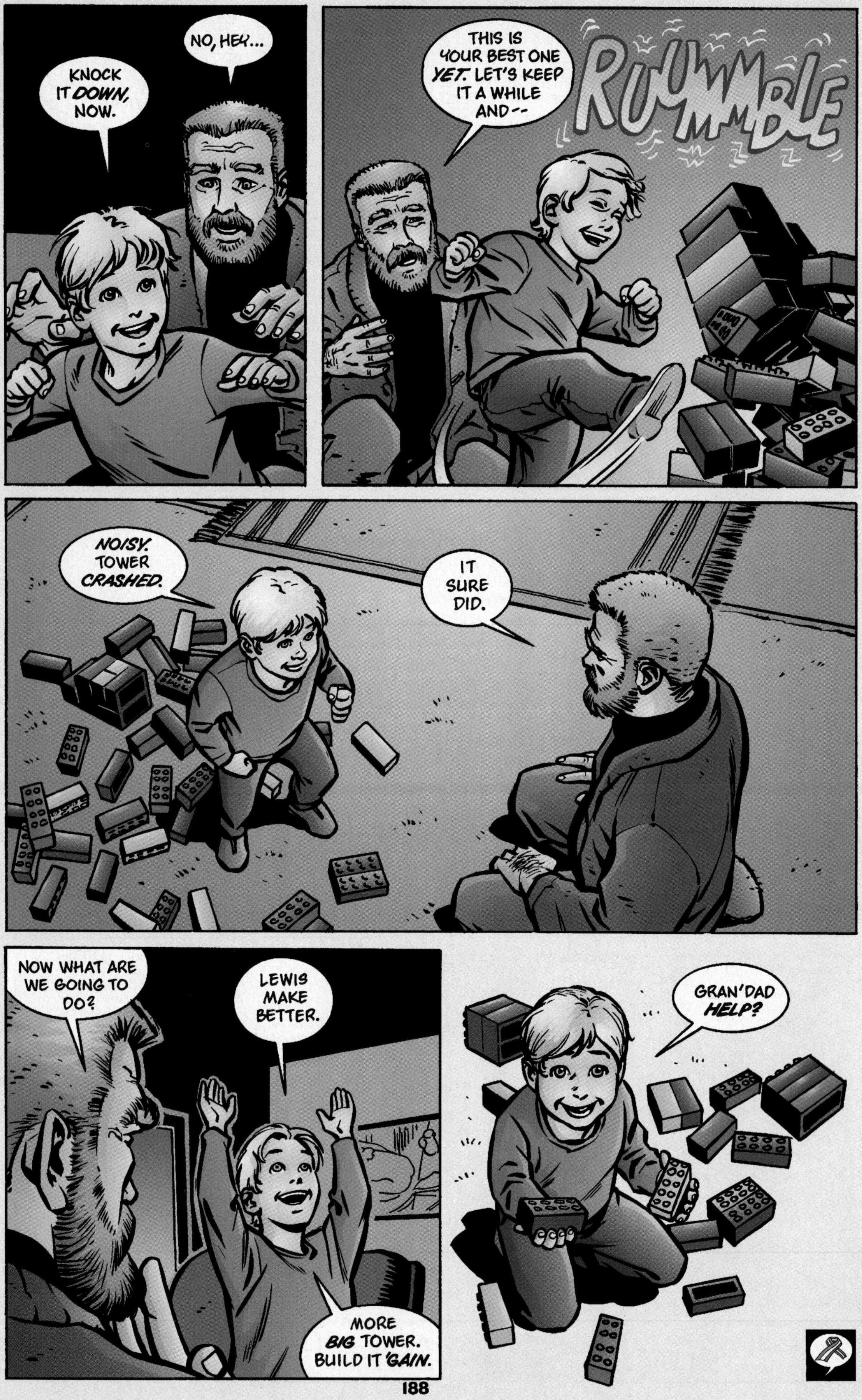
KNOCK IT *DOWN,* NOW.
NO, HEY...
THIS IS YOUR BEST ONE *YET.* LET'S KEEP IT A WHILE AND--
RUUMMBLE
NOISY. TOWER *CRASHED.*
IT SURE DID.
NOW WHAT ARE WE GOING TO DO?
LEWIS MAKE BETTER.
MORE *BIG* TOWER. BUILD IT *'GAIN.*
GRAN'DAD *HELP?*

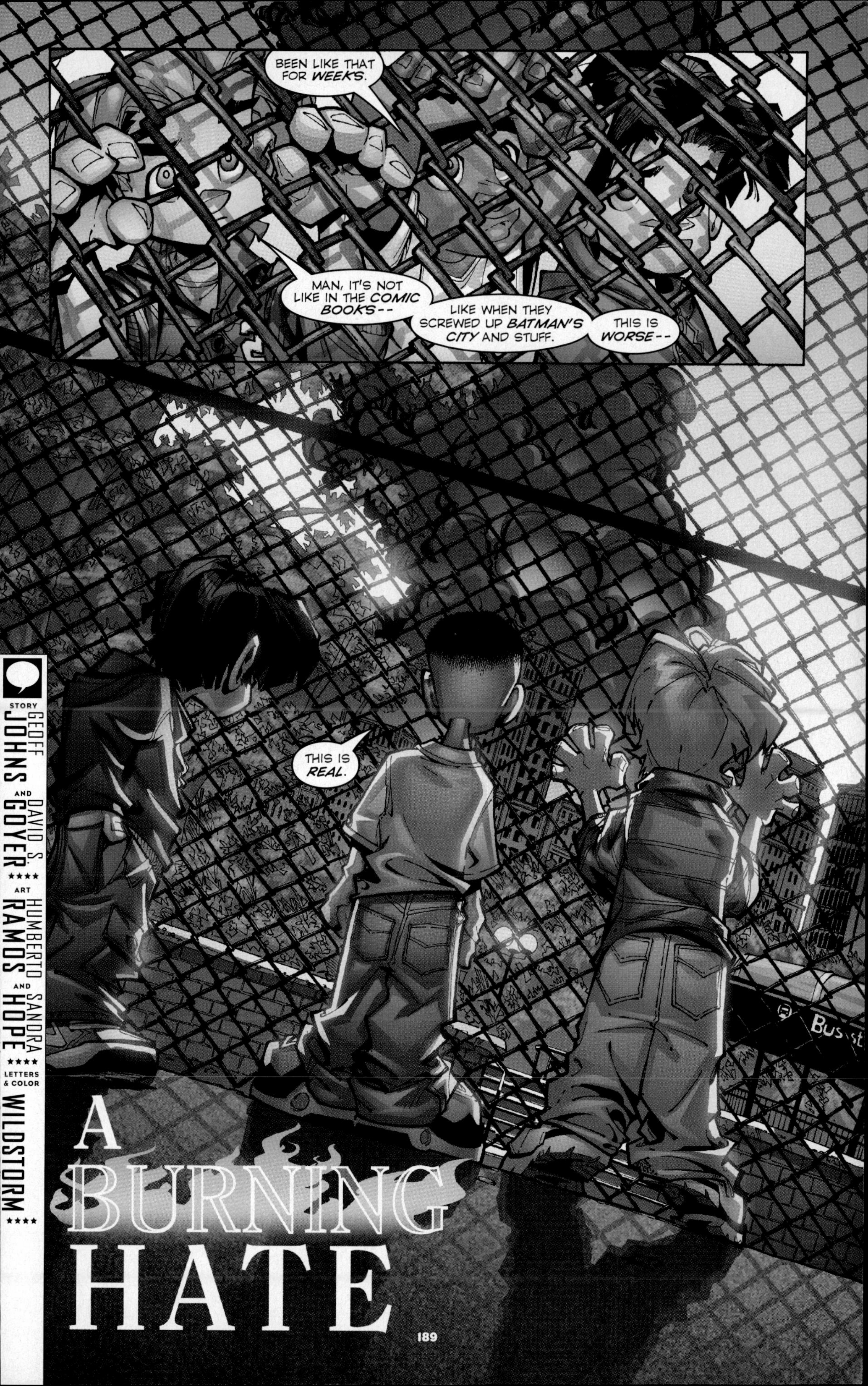
BEEN LIKE THAT FOR WEEKS.
MAN, IT'S NOT LIKE IN THE COMIC BOOKS--
LIKE WHEN THEY SCREWED UP BATMAN'S CITY AND STUFF.
THIS IS WORSE--
THIS IS REAL.
Bus st
STORY GEOFF JOHNS AND DAVID S. GOYER
ART HUMBERTO RAMOS AND SANDRA HOPE
LETTERS & COLOR WILDSTORM
A BURNING HATE

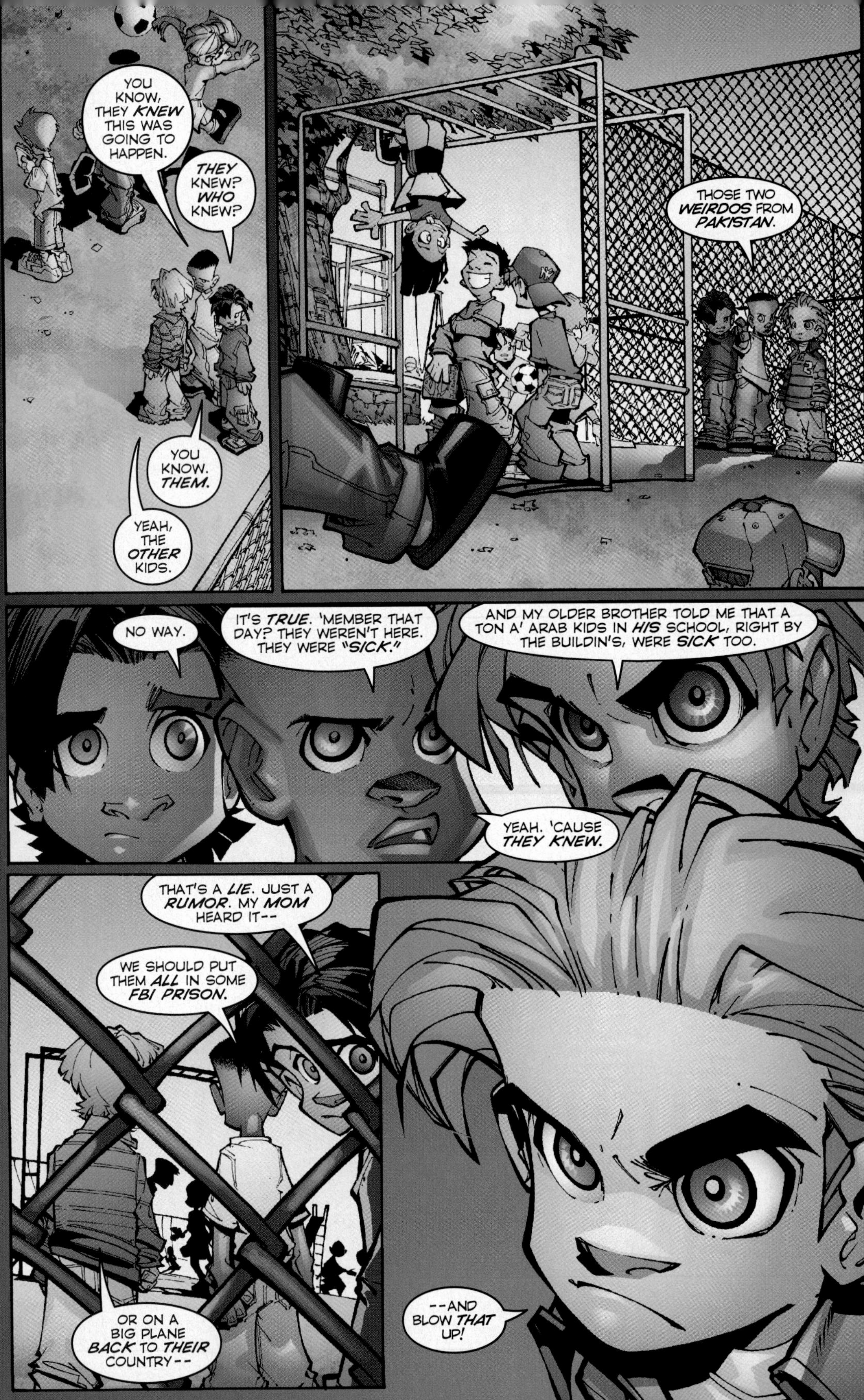

YOU KNOW, THEY KNEW THIS WAS GOING TO HAPPEN.
THEY KNEW? WHO KNEW?
YOU KNOW. THEM.
YEAH, THE OTHER KIDS.
THOSE TWO WEIRDOS FROM PAKISTAN.
NO WAY.
IT'S TRUE. 'MEMBER THAT DAY? THEY WEREN'T HERE. THEY WERE "SICK."
AND MY OLDER BROTHER TOLD ME THAT A TON A' ARAB KIDS IN HIS SCHOOL, RIGHT BY THE BUILDIN'S, WERE SICK TOO.
YEAH. 'CAUSE THEY KNEW.
THAT'S A LIE. JUST A RUMOR. MY MOM HEARD IT--
WE SHOULD PUT THEM ALL IN SOME FBI PRISON.
OR ON A BIG PLANE BACK TO THEIR COUNTRY--
--AND BLOW THAT UP!

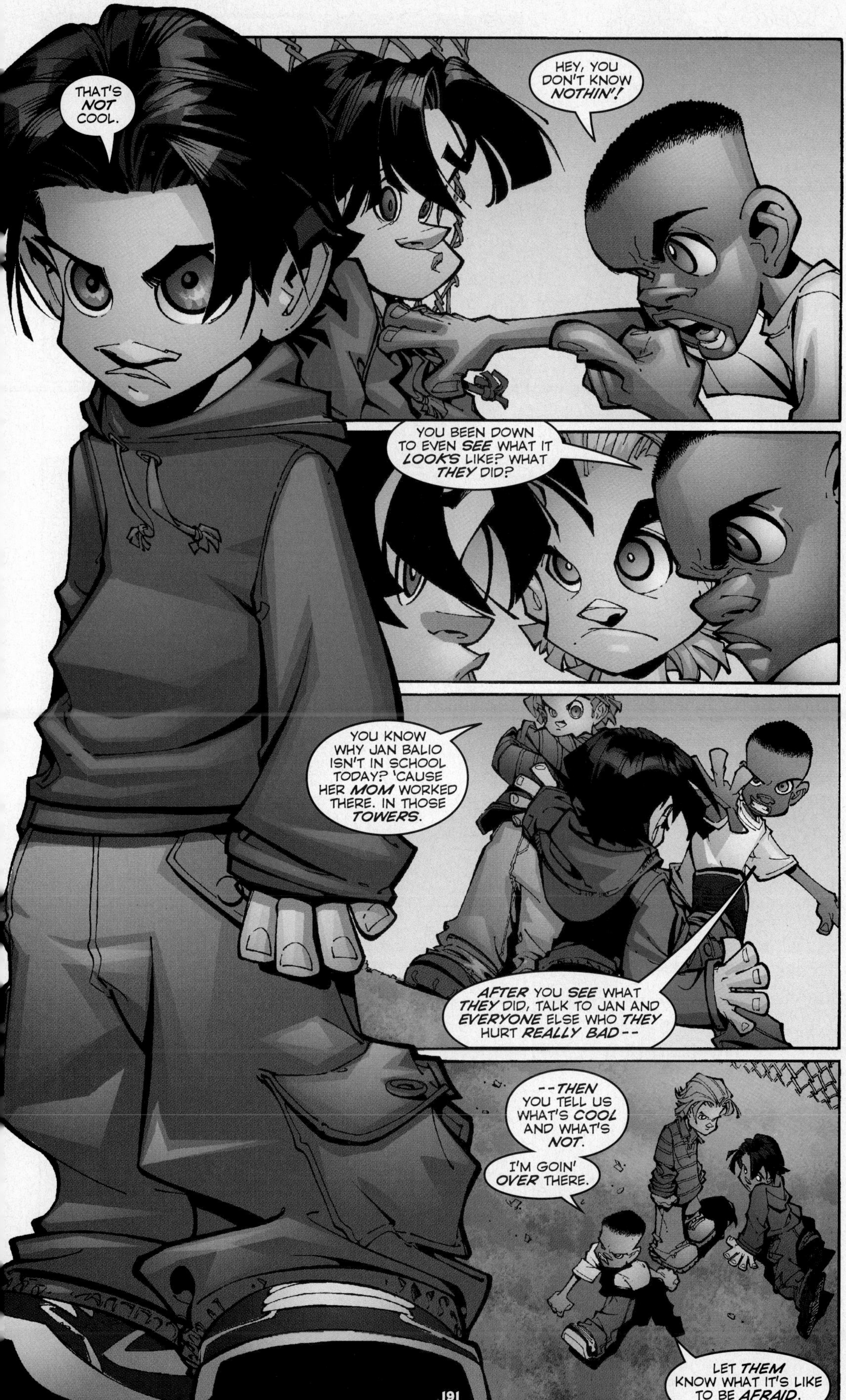
THAT'S NOT COOL.
HEY, YOU DON'T KNOW NOTHIN'!
YOU BEEN DOWN TO EVEN SEE WHAT IT LOOKS LIKE? WHAT THEY DID?
YOU KNOW WHY JAN BALIO ISN'T IN SCHOOL TODAY? 'CAUSE HER MOM WORKED THERE. IN THOSE TOWERS.
AFTER YOU SEE WHAT THEY DID, TALK TO JAN AND EVERYONE ELSE WHO THEY HURT REALLY BAD--
--THEN YOU TELL US WHAT'S COOL AND WHAT'S NOT.
I'M GOIN' OVER THERE.
LET THEM KNOW WHAT IT'S LIKE TO BE AFRAID.

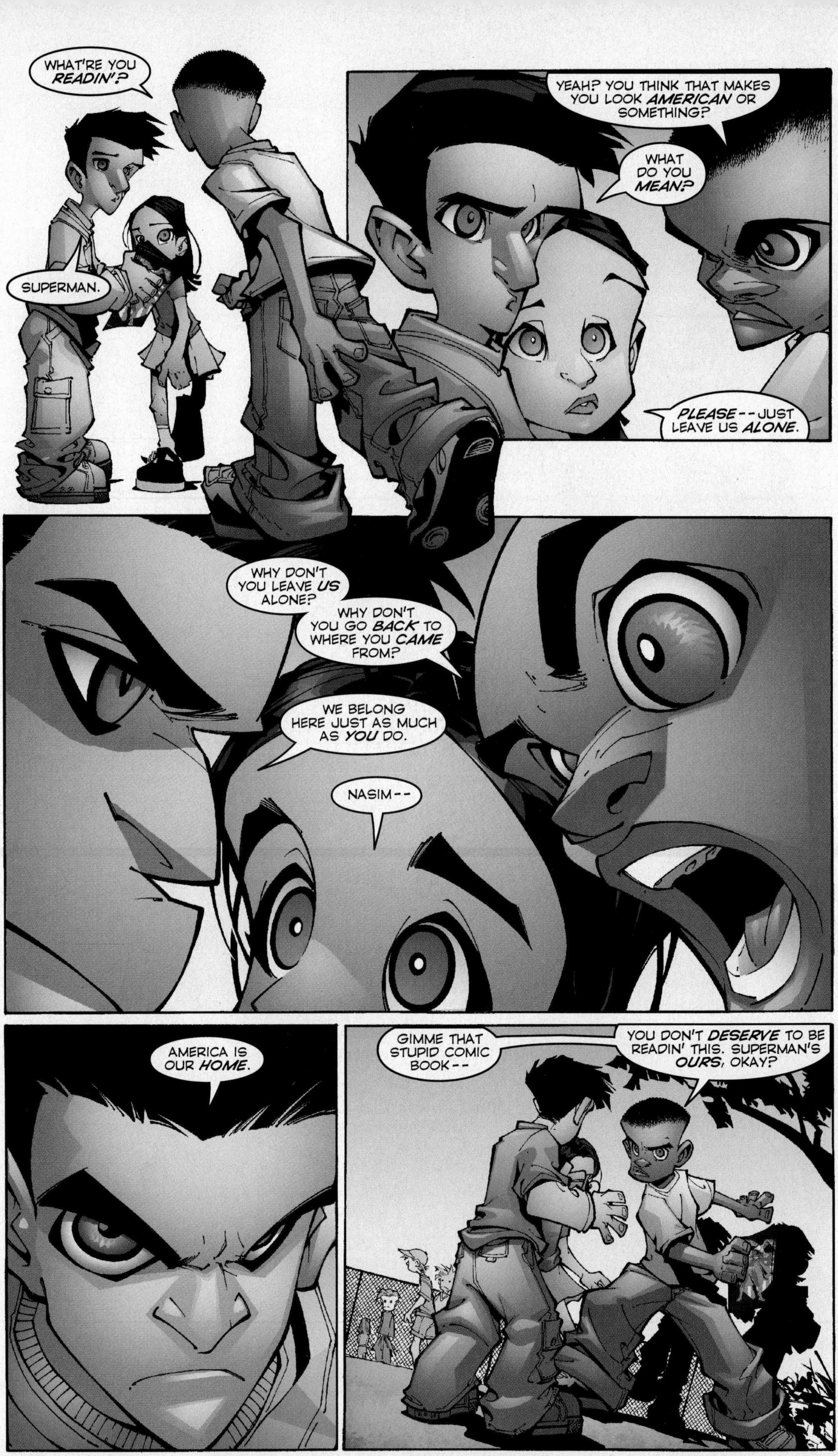
WHAT'RE YOU *READIN'?*
SUPERMAN.
YEAH? YOU THINK THAT MAKES YOU LOOK *AMERICAN* OR SOMETHING?
WHAT DO YOU *MEAN?*
PLEASE--JUST LEAVE US *ALONE*.
WHY DON'T YOU LEAVE *US* ALONE?
WHY DON'T YOU GO *BACK* TO WHERE YOU *CAME* FROM?
WE BELONG HERE JUST AS MUCH AS *YOU* DO.
NASIM--
AMERICA IS OUR *HOME*.
GIMME THAT STUPID COMIC BOOK--
YOU DON'T *DESERVE* TO BE READIN' THIS. SUPERMAN'S *OURS*, OKAY?

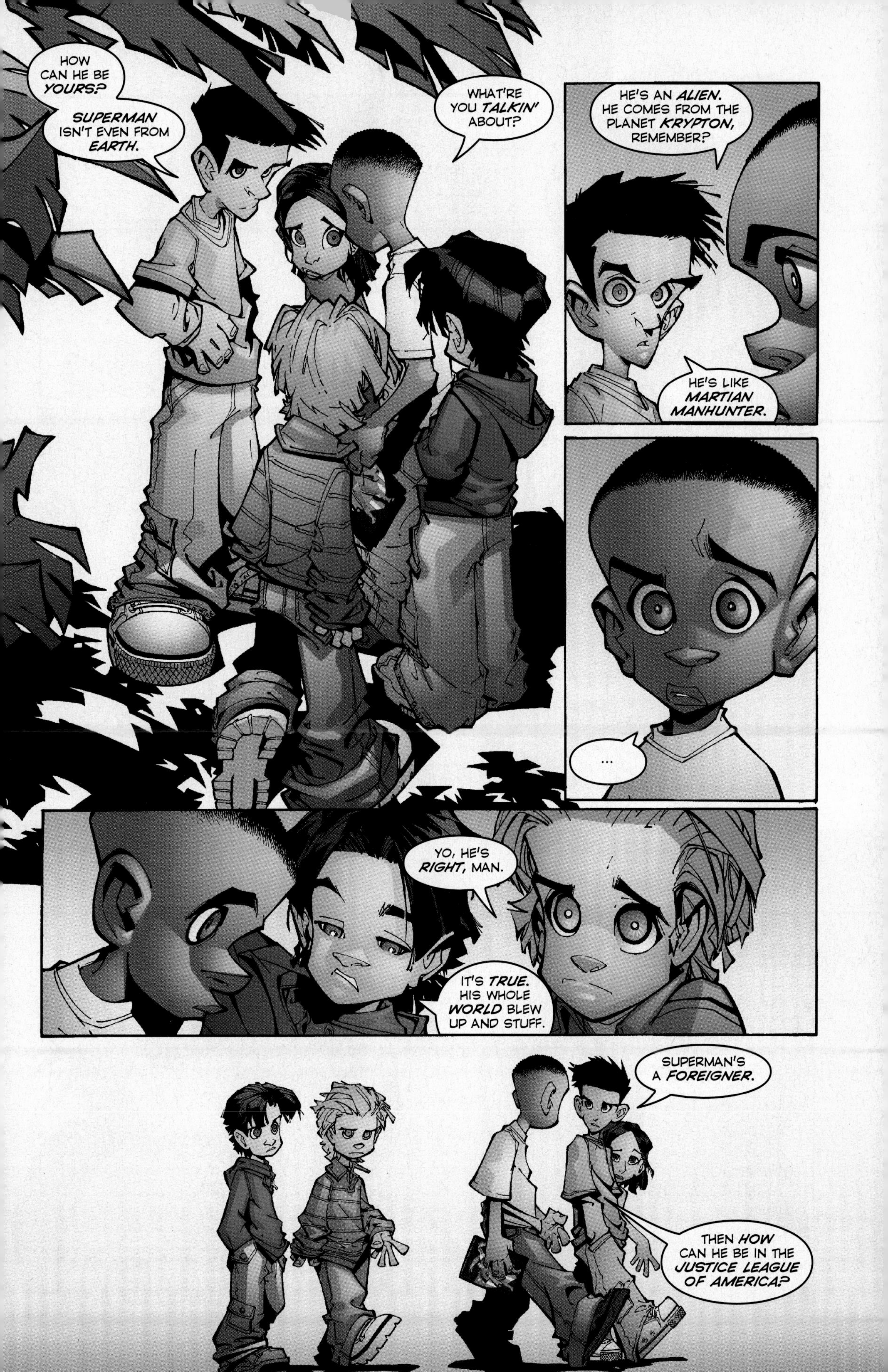
HOW CAN HE BE YOURS?
SUPERMAN ISN'T EVEN FROM EARTH.
WHAT'RE YOU TALKIN' ABOUT?
HE'S AN ALIEN. HE COMES FROM THE PLANET KRYPTON, REMEMBER?
HE'S LIKE MARTIAN MANHUNTER.
...
YO, HE'S RIGHT, MAN.
IT'S TRUE. HIS WHOLE WORLD BLEW UP AND STUFF.
SUPERMAN'S A FOREIGNER.
THEN HOW CAN HE BE IN THE JUSTICE LEAGUE OF AMERICA?

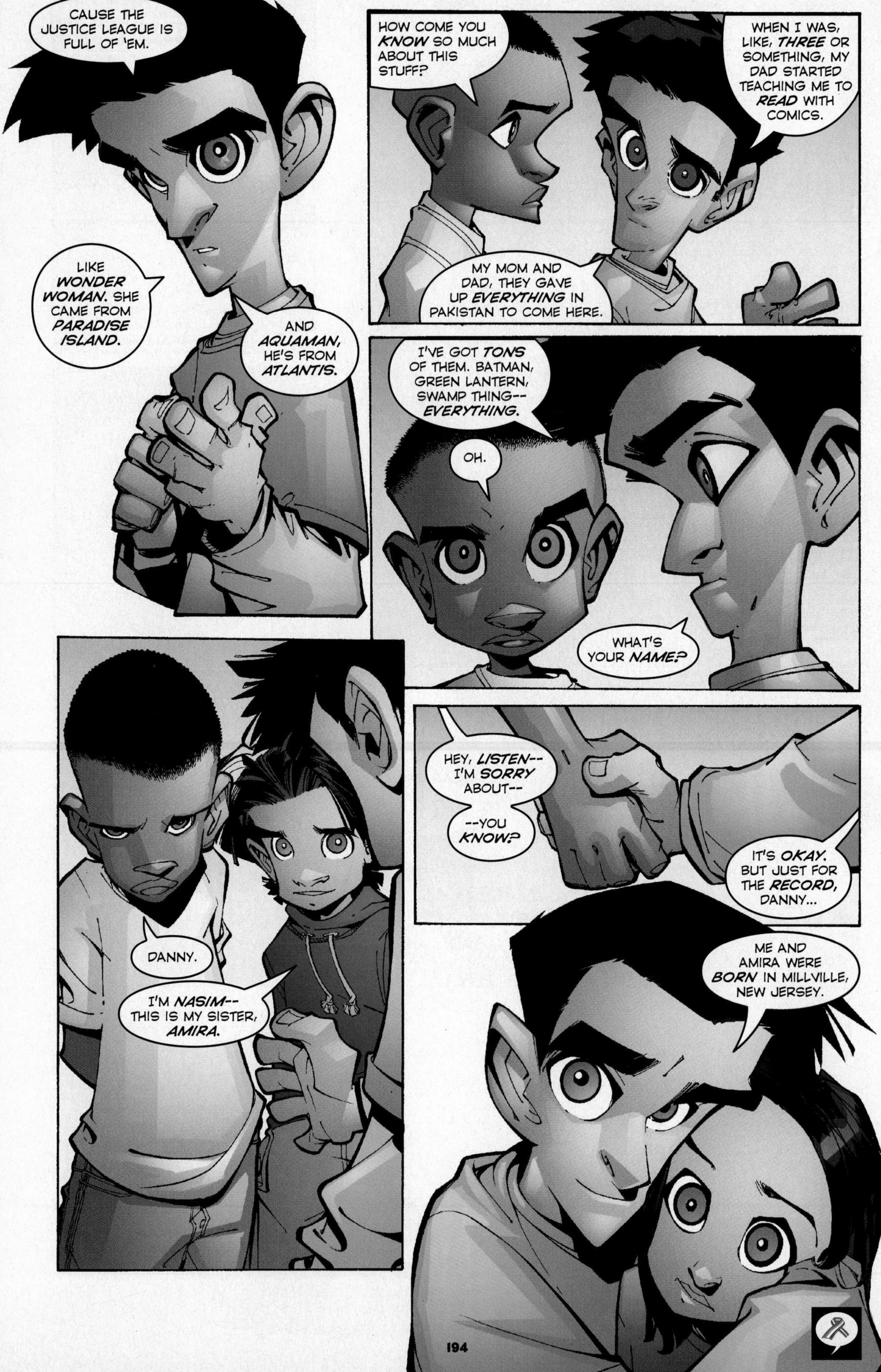
CAUSE THE JUSTICE LEAGUE IS FULL OF 'EM.
LIKE WONDER WOMAN. SHE CAME FROM PARADISE ISLAND.
AND AQUAMAN, HE'S FROM ATLANTIS.
HOW COME YOU KNOW SO MUCH ABOUT THIS STUFF?
WHEN I WAS, LIKE, THREE OR SOMETHING, MY DAD STARTED TEACHING ME TO READ WITH COMICS.
MY MOM AND DAD, THEY GAVE UP EVERYTHING IN PAKISTAN TO COME HERE.
I'VE GOT TONS OF THEM. BATMAN, GREEN LANTERN, SWAMP THING-- EVERYTHING.
OH.
WHAT'S YOUR NAME?
DANNY.
I'M NASIM-- THIS IS MY SISTER, AMIRA.
HEY, LISTEN-- I'M SORRY ABOUT--
--YOU KNOW?
IT'S OKAY. BUT JUST FOR THE RECORD, DANNY...
ME AND AMIRA WERE BORN IN MILLVILLE, NEW JERSEY.

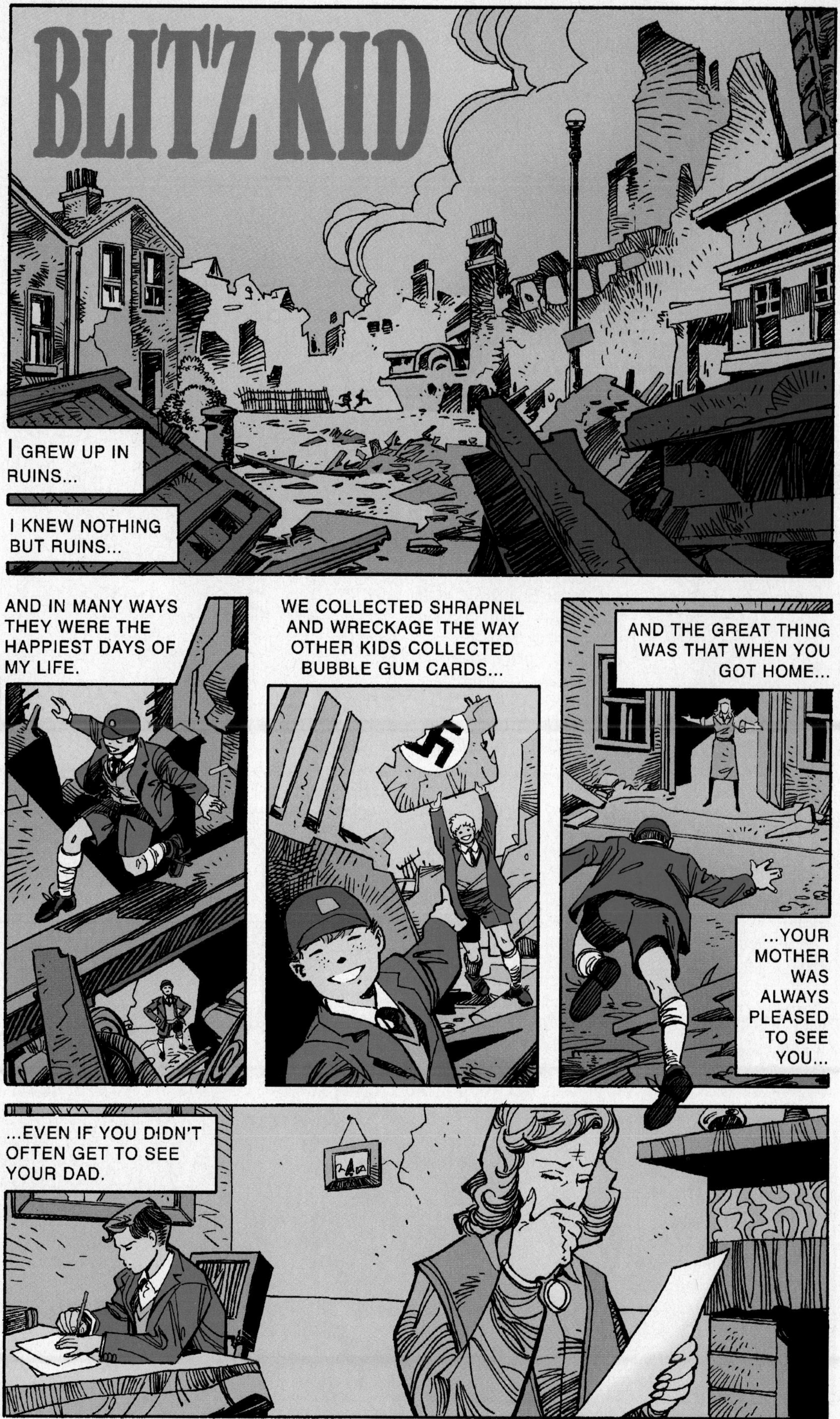
BLITZ KID
I GREW UP IN RUINS...
I KNEW NOTHING BUT RUINS...
AND IN MANY WAYS THEY WERE THE HAPPIEST DAYS OF MY LIFE.
WE COLLECTED SHRAPNEL AND WRECKAGE THE WAY OTHER KIDS COLLECTED BUBBLE GUM CARDS...
AND THE GREAT THING WAS THAT WHEN YOU GOT HOME...
...YOUR MOTHER WAS ALWAYS PLEASED TO SEE YOU...
...EVEN IF YOU DIDN'T OFTEN GET TO SEE YOUR DAD.

STORY MICHAEL MOORCOCK
ART WALTER SIMONSON AND BOB WIACEK
LETTERS JOHN WORKMAN
COLOR TATJANA WOOD

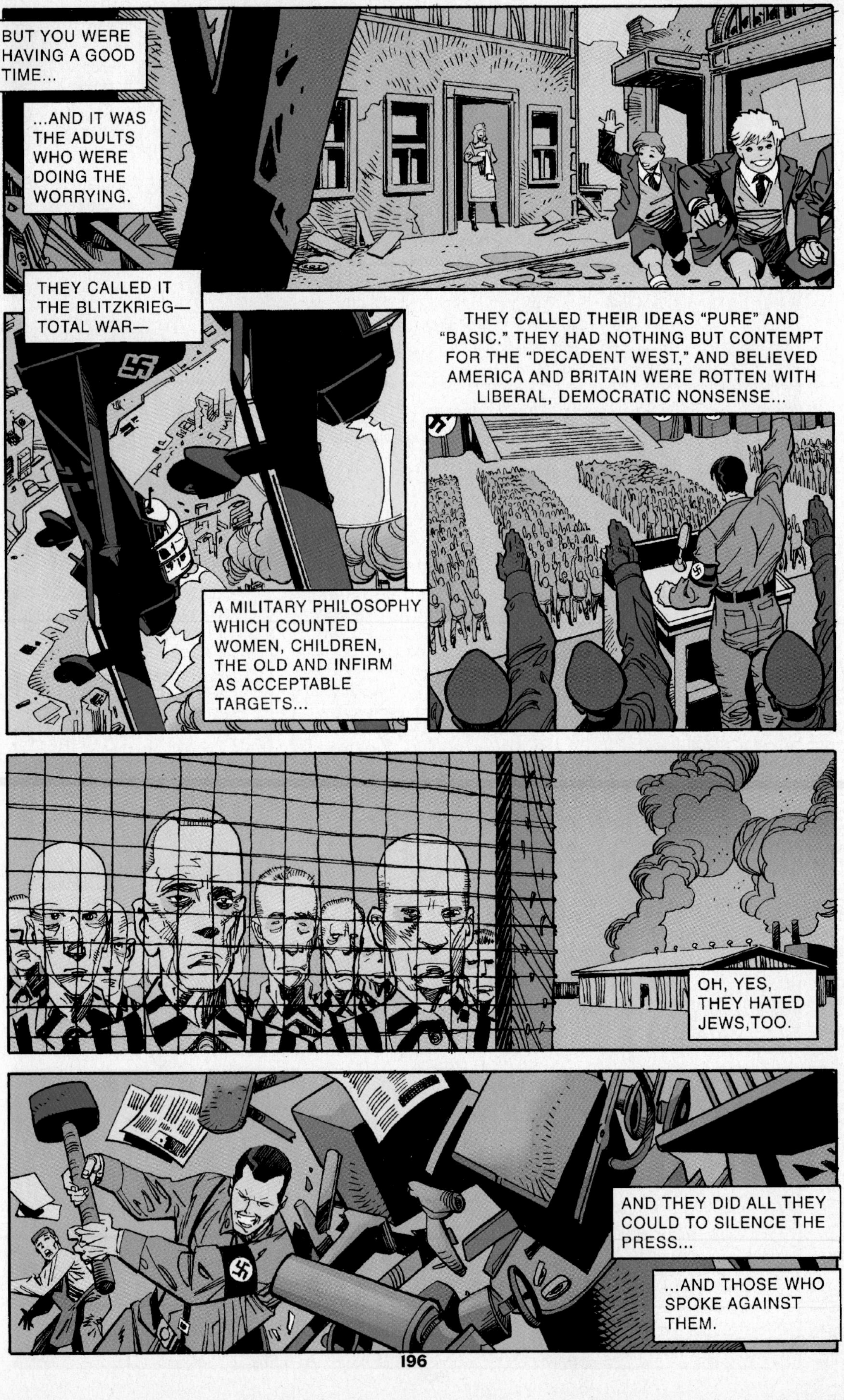
BUT YOU WERE HAVING A GOOD TIME...
...AND IT WAS THE ADULTS WHO WERE DOING THE WORRYING.
THEY CALLED IT THE BLITZKRIEG— TOTAL WAR—
A MILITARY PHILOSOPHY WHICH COUNTED WOMEN, CHILDREN, THE OLD AND INFIRM AS ACCEPTABLE TARGETS...
THEY CALLED THEIR IDEAS "PURE" AND "BASIC." THEY HAD NOTHING BUT CONTEMPT FOR THE "DECADENT WEST," AND BELIEVED AMERICA AND BRITAIN WERE ROTTEN WITH LIBERAL, DEMOCRATIC NONSENSE...
OH, YES, THEY HATED JEWS,TOO.
AND THEY DID ALL THEY COULD TO SILENCE THE PRESS...
...AND THOSE WHO SPOKE AGAINST THEM.

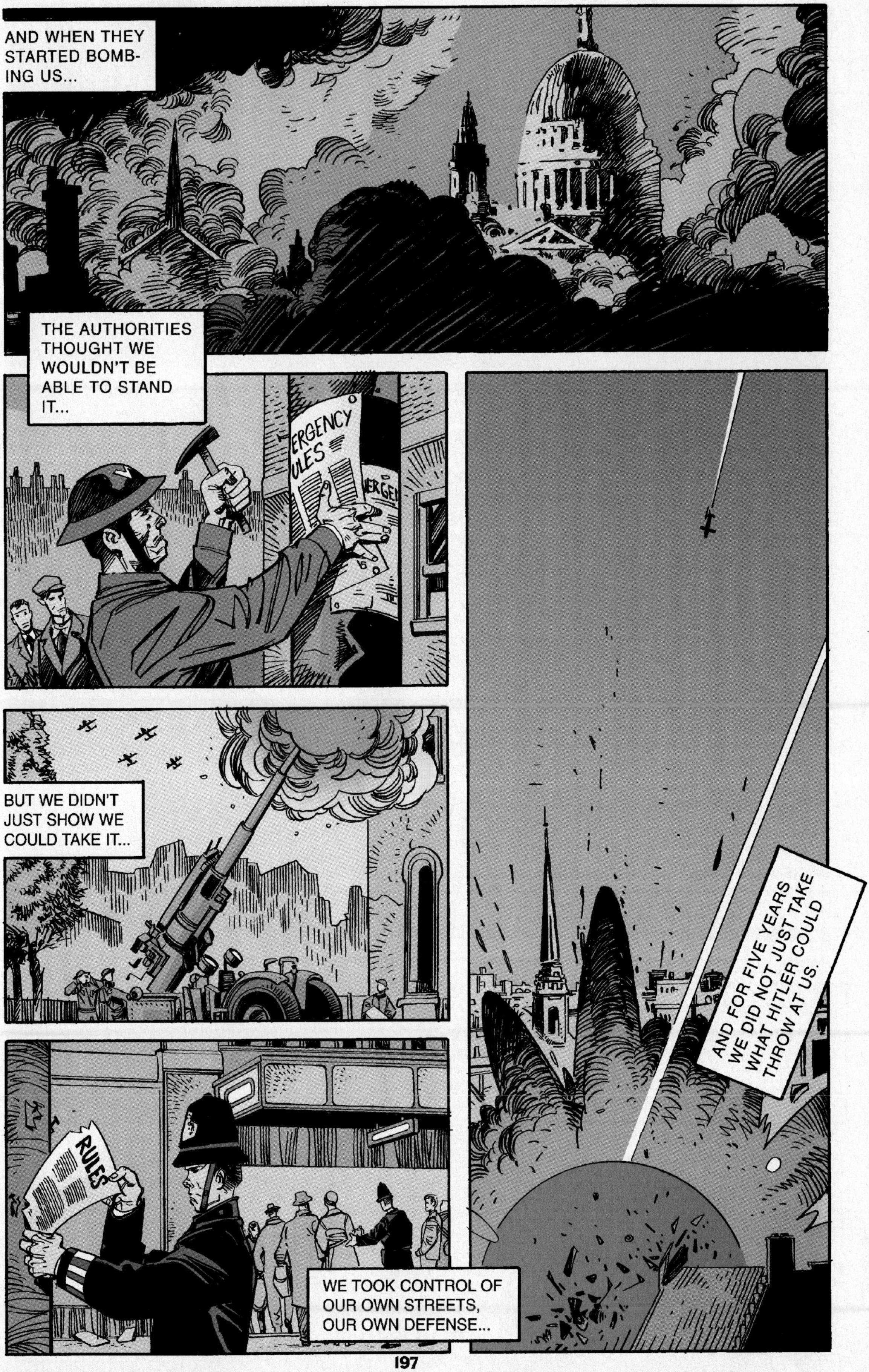

AND WHEN THEY STARTED BOMB-ING US...
THE AUTHORITIES THOUGHT WE WOULDN'T BE ABLE TO STAND IT...
ERGENCY
ULES
BUT WE DIDN'T JUST SHOW WE COULD TAKE IT...
RULES
WE TOOK CONTROL OF OUR OWN STREETS, OUR OWN DEFENSE...
AND FOR FIVE YEARS WE DID NOT JUST TAKE WHAT HITLER COULD THROW AT US.

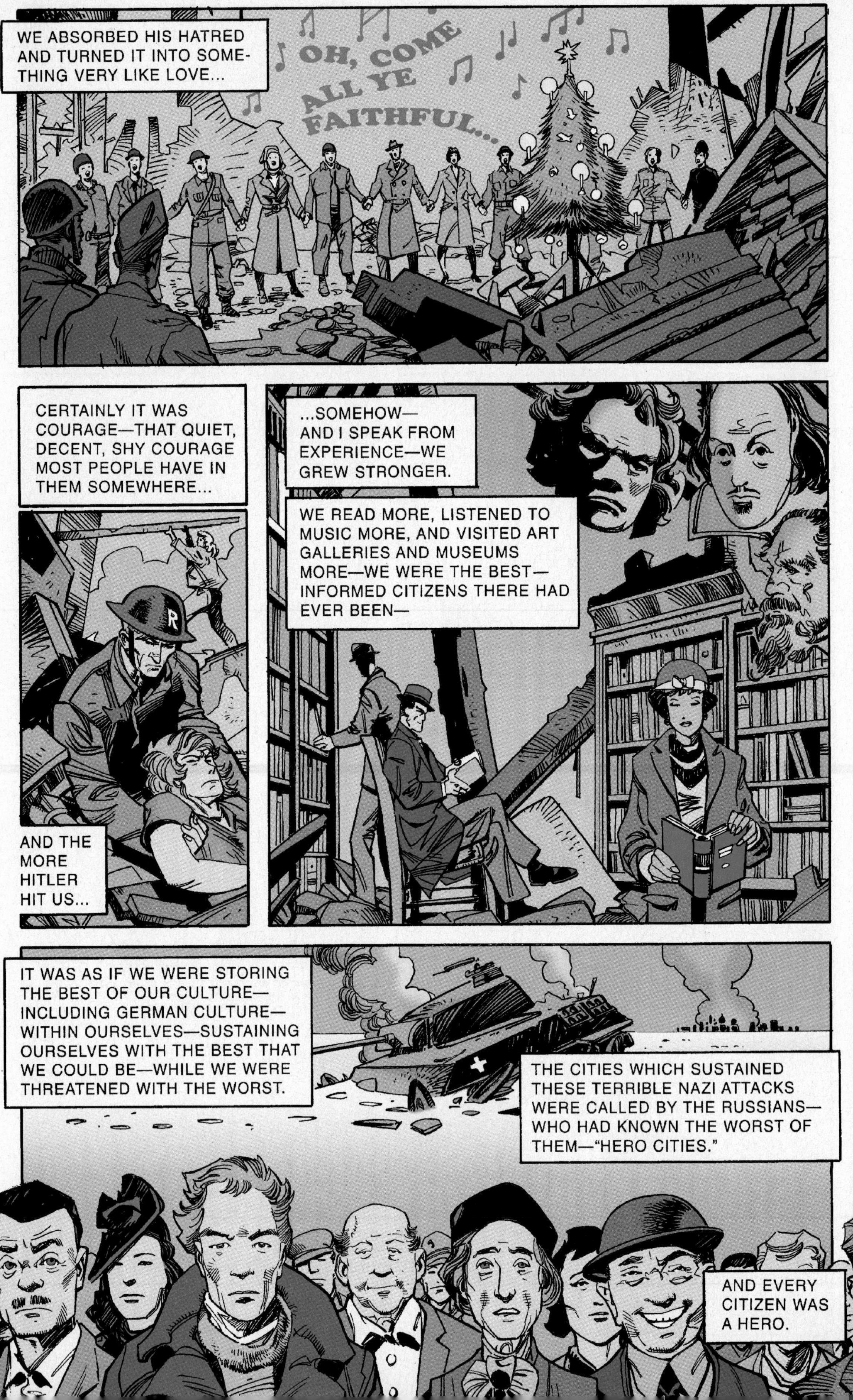
WE ABSORBED HIS HATRED AND TURNED IT INTO SOMETHING VERY LIKE LOVE...
OH, COME ALL YE FAITHFUL...
CERTAINLY IT WAS COURAGE—THAT QUIET, DECENT, SHY COURAGE MOST PEOPLE HAVE IN THEM SOMEWHERE...
AND THE MORE HITLER HIT US...
...SOMEHOW—AND I SPEAK FROM EXPERIENCE—WE GREW STRONGER.
WE READ MORE, LISTENED TO MUSIC MORE, AND VISITED ART GALLERIES AND MUSEUMS MORE—WE WERE THE BEST-INFORMED CITIZENS THERE HAD EVER BEEN—
IT WAS AS IF WE WERE STORING THE BEST OF OUR CULTURE—INCLUDING GERMAN CULTURE—WITHIN OURSELVES—SUSTAINING OURSELVES WITH THE BEST THAT WE COULD BE—WHILE WE WERE THREATENED WITH THE WORST.
THE CITIES WHICH SUSTAINED THESE TERRIBLE NAZI ATTACKS WERE CALLED BY THE RUSSIANS—WHO HAD KNOWN THE WORST OF THEM—"HERO CITIES."
AND EVERY CITIZEN WAS A HERO.

MY OPTIMISM, MY FAITH IN THE COMMON SENSE OF ORDINARY PEOPLE, MY UNDERSTANDING OF THE GOODNESS AND THE EXTRAORDINARY COURAGE WHICH EXISTS IN THE MAJORITY OF US, INFORMS MY WORK AND KEEPS ME WRITING—

THAT OPTIMISM IS BASED ON SOLID EXPERIENCE—OF SEEING PEOPLE AT THEIR VERY BEST, DAY IN AND DAY OUT.

PEOPLE WERE AT THEIR VERY BEST IN OKLAHOMA CITY AND NEW YORK AND I FOR ONE EXPECTED NOTHING LESS—BECAUSE I ALREADY KNEW HOW WELL PEOPLE BEHAVE WHEN FACED WITH UNIMAGINABLE HORROR AND A THREAT TO EVERYTHING THEY VALUE—

MOST OF THE TIME, THEY GO ABOUT THEIR ORDINARY BUSINESS, MAKING A LIVING, HAVING POLITICAL ARGUMENTS, GETTING EXCITED ABOUT BALLGAMES—

PEOPLE SAY IT'S A SHAME THAT IT TAKES A CRISIS TO BRING OUT THE BEST IN THEM, MAKE US FORGET OUR PETTY DIFFERENCES...

BUT I SAY WE ARE USUALLY NOT AT OUR VERY BEST BECAUSE IT WOULD BE INHUMAN TO BE FOREVER AT OUR VERY BEST...

I WAS BORN AND RAISED IN RUINS, AND I KNEW PEOPLE AT THEIR VERY BEST. I SUSPECT THAT FRANKLIN D. ROOSEVELT, A GOOD FRIEND TO BRITAIN WHEN WE WERE BEING TERRORIZED, KNEW WHAT HE WAS SAYING WHEN HE TOLD US WE HAD NOTHING TO FEAR BUT FEAR ITSELF.

THROUGHOUT A LONG AND ENJOYABLE LIFE I'VE BEEN SUSTAINED BY THOSE LIBERAL HUMANIST CULTURAL VALUES, WHICH ALL BIGOTS HATE, BUT WHICH I SHARE WITH FRIENDS OF EVERY RELIGIOUS PERSUASION.

AND I ALSO KNOW THAT NOBODY'S PERFECT. YET IT IS THOSE VALUES WE CALL UPON IN CRISES LIKE THE RECENT ONE AND IT IS THOSE VALUES WHICH SOMEHOW DO SUSTAIN US. I KNOW FROM EXPERIENCE, AND FROM WHAT HAPPENED A WHILE AGO IN NEW YORK, THAT MY FELLOW HUMAN BEINGS CAN ALWAYS BE RELIED UPON IN A CRUNCH.

AND BETWEEN OURSELVES, PARDS, THAT'S GOOD ENOUGH FOR ME.

—MICHAEL MOORCOCK

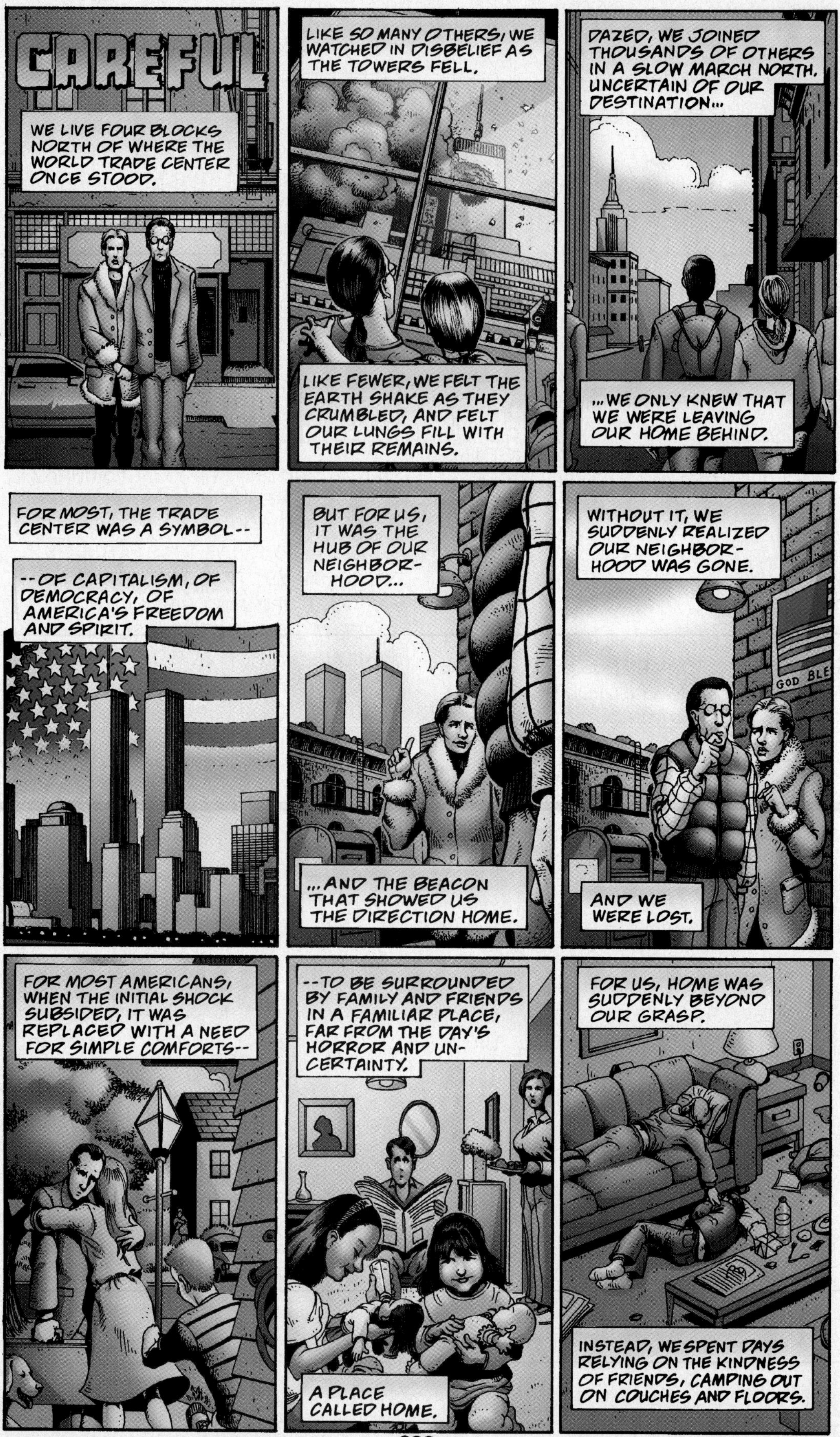
CAREFUL
WE LIVE FOUR BLOCKS NORTH OF WHERE THE WORLD TRADE CENTER ONCE STOOD.
LIKE SO MANY OTHERS, WE WATCHED IN DISBELIEF AS THE TOWERS FELL.
LIKE FEWER, WE FELT THE EARTH SHAKE AS THEY CRUMBLED, AND FELT OUR LUNGS FILL WITH THEIR REMAINS.
DAZED, WE JOINED THOUSANDS OF OTHERS IN A SLOW MARCH NORTH, UNCERTAIN OF OUR DESTINATION...
...WE ONLY KNEW THAT WE WERE LEAVING OUR HOME BEHIND.
FOR MOST, THE TRADE CENTER WAS A SYMBOL--
--OF CAPITALISM, OF DEMOCRACY, OF AMERICA'S FREEDOM AND SPIRIT.
BUT FOR US, IT WAS THE HUB OF OUR NEIGHBOR-HOOD...
...AND THE BEACON THAT SHOWED US THE DIRECTION HOME.
WITHOUT IT, WE SUDDENLY REALIZED OUR NEIGHBOR-HOOD WAS GONE.
GOD BLE
AND WE WERE LOST.
FOR MOST AMERICANS, WHEN THE INITIAL SHOCK SUBSIDED, IT WAS REPLACED WITH A NEED FOR SIMPLE COMFORTS--
--TO BE SURROUNDED BY FAMILY AND FRIENDS IN A FAMILIAR PLACE, FAR FROM THE DAY'S HORROR AND UN-CERTAINTY.
A PLACE CALLED HOME.
FOR US, HOME WAS SUDDENLY BEYOND OUR GRASP.
INSTEAD, WE SPENT DAYS RELYING ON THE KINDNESS OF FRIENDS, CAMPING OUT ON COUCHES AND FLOORS.

STORY ANDREW HELFER
ART JOHN C. CEBOLLERO
LETTERS PHIL FELIX
COLOR WILDSTORM

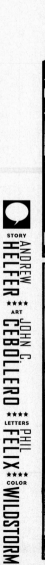

WE WATCHED AS OUR LEADERS SCRAMBLED TO REASSEMBLE OUR SHATTERED COUNTRY. HEROES WERE PROCLAIMED. FLAGS WERE RAISED. SUSPECTS WERE ARRESTED.

SOLIDARITY AND SECURITY WERE THE SOLE CONCERNS OF THE NATION.

PATIENTLY WE WAITED FOR NEWS OF OUR NEIGHBORHOOD. BUT NO WORD CAME.

A WEEK PASSED BEFORE WE DECIDED FOR OURSELVES: IT WAS TIME TO GO HOME.

A FENCE HAD BEEN ERECTED TO ESTABLISH THE PERIMETER OF THE "HOT ZONE" A BLOCK NORTH OF OUR HOUSE.

POLICE AND ARMED NATIONAL GUARDSMAN STOOD AT THE GATES. NO ONE WOULD BE ALLOWED THROUGH.

NO INFORMATION, NO EXPLANATIONS, NO TIME-TABLES FOR OUR RETURN WERE AVAILABLE. THE AIR ITSELF MIGHT BE POISONOUS, BUT NO ONE WAS CERTAIN.

THE ONLY THING CERTAIN WAS THAT THERE WAS A FENCE.

BLOCKING US FROM OUR HOME.

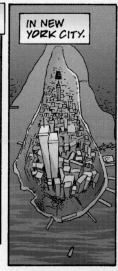

IN NEW YORK CITY.

IN AMERICA.

FOR A MOMENT, WE FELT AS IF WE WERE LIVING SOMEPLACE ELSE. SOMEPLACE NOT AMERICA.

THE MOMENT PASSED. BUT WE THINK ABOUT IT STILL. ABOUT HOW PRECIOUS OUR FREEDOMS ARE. AND HOW FRAGILE.

BE CAREFUL.

FIVE WEEKS LATER WE MOVED BACK HOME.

BUT ON THAT DAY, AS TOURISTS TOOK SNAPSHOTS OF THE EMPTY SPACE WHERE THE TOWERS ONCE STOOD, WE TURNED AND BEGAN THE LONG WALK UPTOWN.

"THEY THAT CAN GIVE UP ESSENTIAL LIBERTY TO OBTAIN A LITTLE TEMPORARY SAFETY DESERVE NEITHER LIBERTY NOR SAFETY."

-- BENJAMIN FRANKLIN

HISTORICAL REVIEW OF PENNSYLVANIA, 1759

WARNINGS

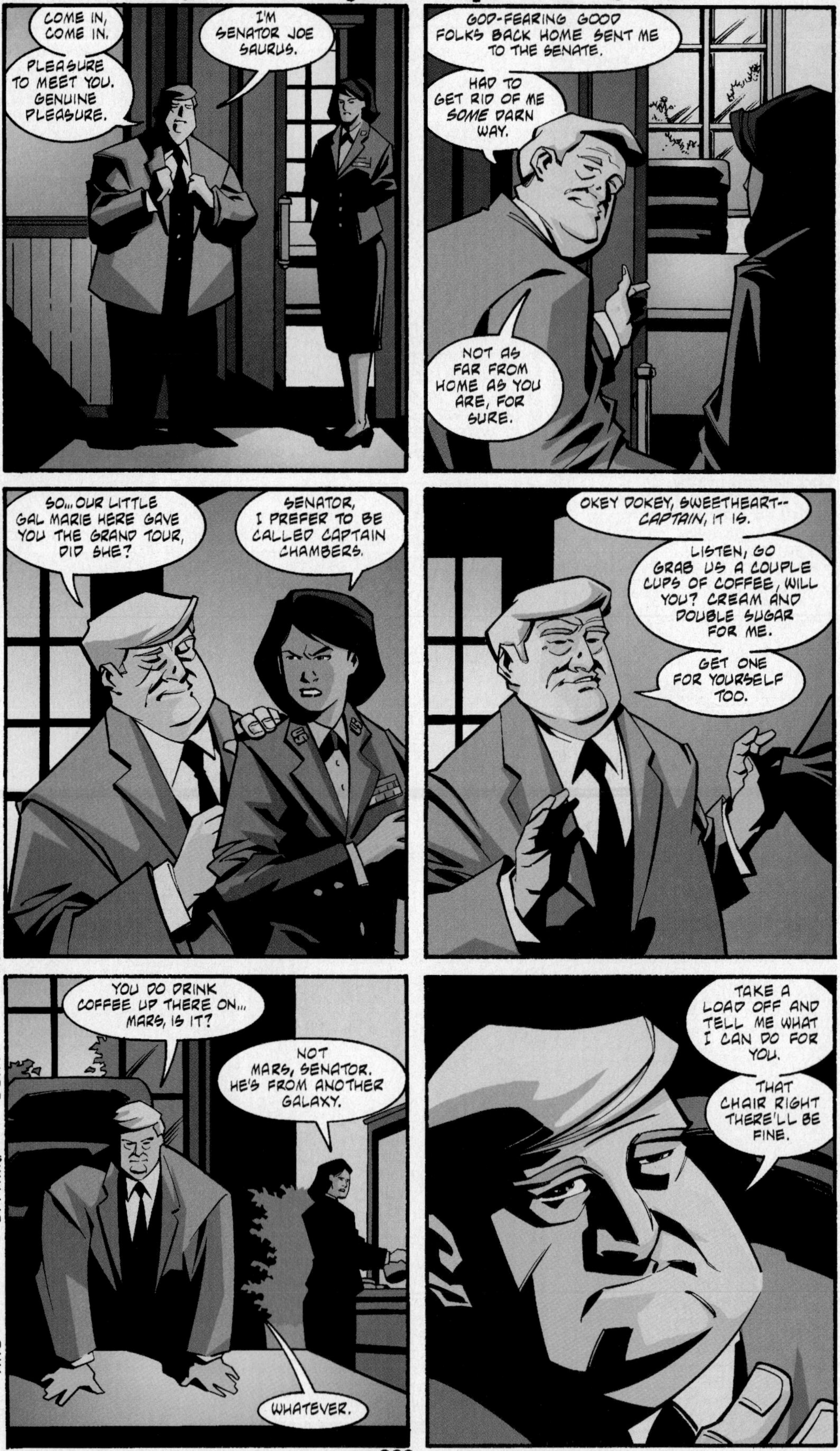
COME IN, COME IN.
I'M SENATOR JOE SAURUS.
PLEASURE TO MEET YOU. GENUINE PLEASURE.
GOD-FEARING GOOD FOLKS BACK HOME SENT ME TO THE SENATE.
HAD TO GET RID OF ME *SOME* DARN WAY.
NOT AS FAR FROM HOME AS YOU ARE, FOR SURE.
SO...OUR LITTLE GAL MARIE HERE GAVE YOU THE GRAND TOUR, DID SHE?
SENATOR, I PREFER TO BE CALLED CAPTAIN CHAMBERS.
OKEY DOKEY, SWEETHEART-- *CAPTAIN*, IT IS.
LISTEN, GO GRAB US A COUPLE CUPS OF COFFEE, WILL YOU? CREAM AND DOUBLE SUGAR FOR ME.
GET ONE FOR YOURSELF TOO.
YOU DO DRINK COFFEE UP THERE ON... MARS, IS IT?
NOT MARS, SENATOR. HE'S FROM ANOTHER GALAXY.
WHATEVER.
TAKE A LOAD OFF AND TELL ME WHAT I CAN DO FOR YOU.
THAT CHAIR RIGHT THERE'LL BE FINE.

STORY DENNY O'NEIL (WITH THANKS TO LARRY O'NEIL AND JORDAN GORFINKEL)

ART PHIL HESTER AND ANDE PARKS

LETTERS WILLIE SCHUBERT

COLOR GUY MAJOR

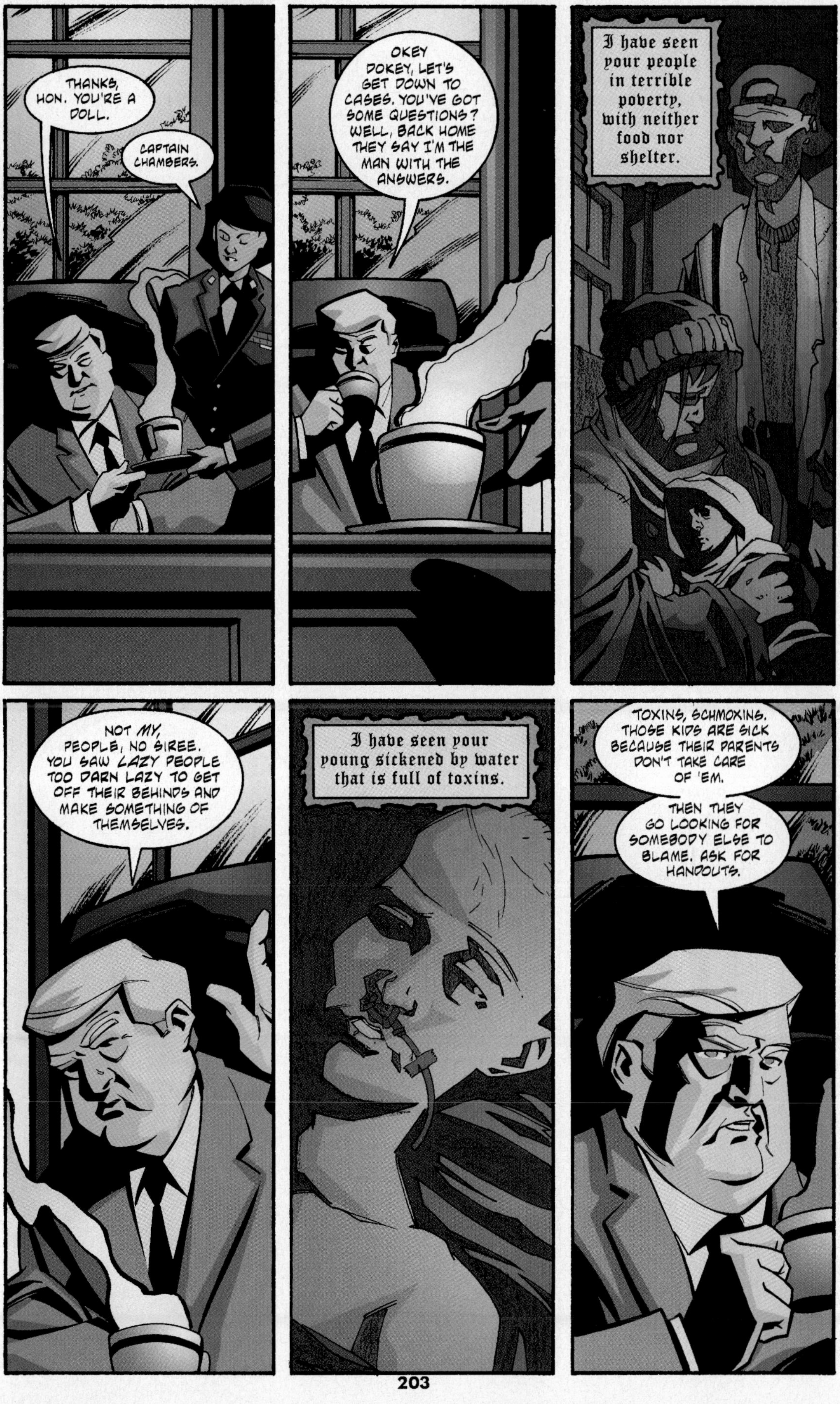
THANKS, HON. YOU'RE A DOLL.
CAPTAIN CHAMBERS.
OKEY DOKEY, LET'S GET DOWN TO CASES. YOU'VE GOT SOME QUESTIONS? WELL, BACK HOME THEY SAY I'M THE MAN WITH THE ANSWERS.
I have seen your people in terrible poverty, with neither food nor shelter.
NOT *MY* PEOPLE, NO SIREE. YOU SAW *LAZY* PEOPLE TOO DARN LAZY TO GET OFF THEIR BEHINDS AND MAKE SOMETHING OF THEMSELVES.
I have seen your young sickened by water that is full of toxins.
TOXINS, SCHMOXINS. THOSE KIDS ARE SICK BECAUSE THEIR PARENTS DON'T TAKE CARE OF 'EM.
THEN THEY GO LOOKING FOR SOMEBODY ELSE TO BLAME. ASK FOR HANDOUTS.

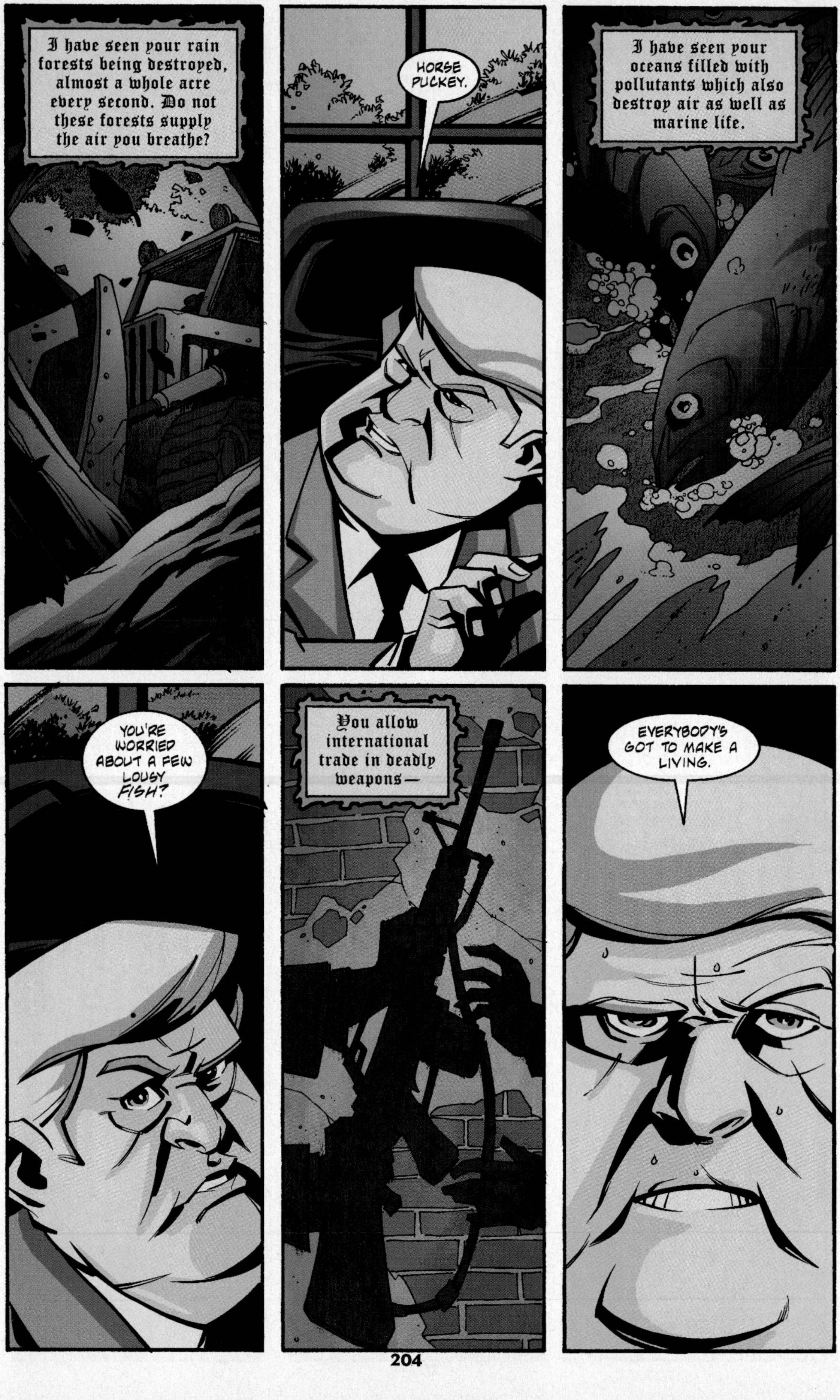

I have seen your rain forests being destroyed, almost a whole acre every second. Do not these forests supply the air you breathe?
HORSE PUCKEY.
I have seen your oceans filled with pollutants which also destroy air as well as marine life.
YOU'RE WORRIED ABOUT A FEW LOUSY FISH?
You allow international trade in deadly weapons—
EVERYBODY'S GOT TO MAKE A LIVING.

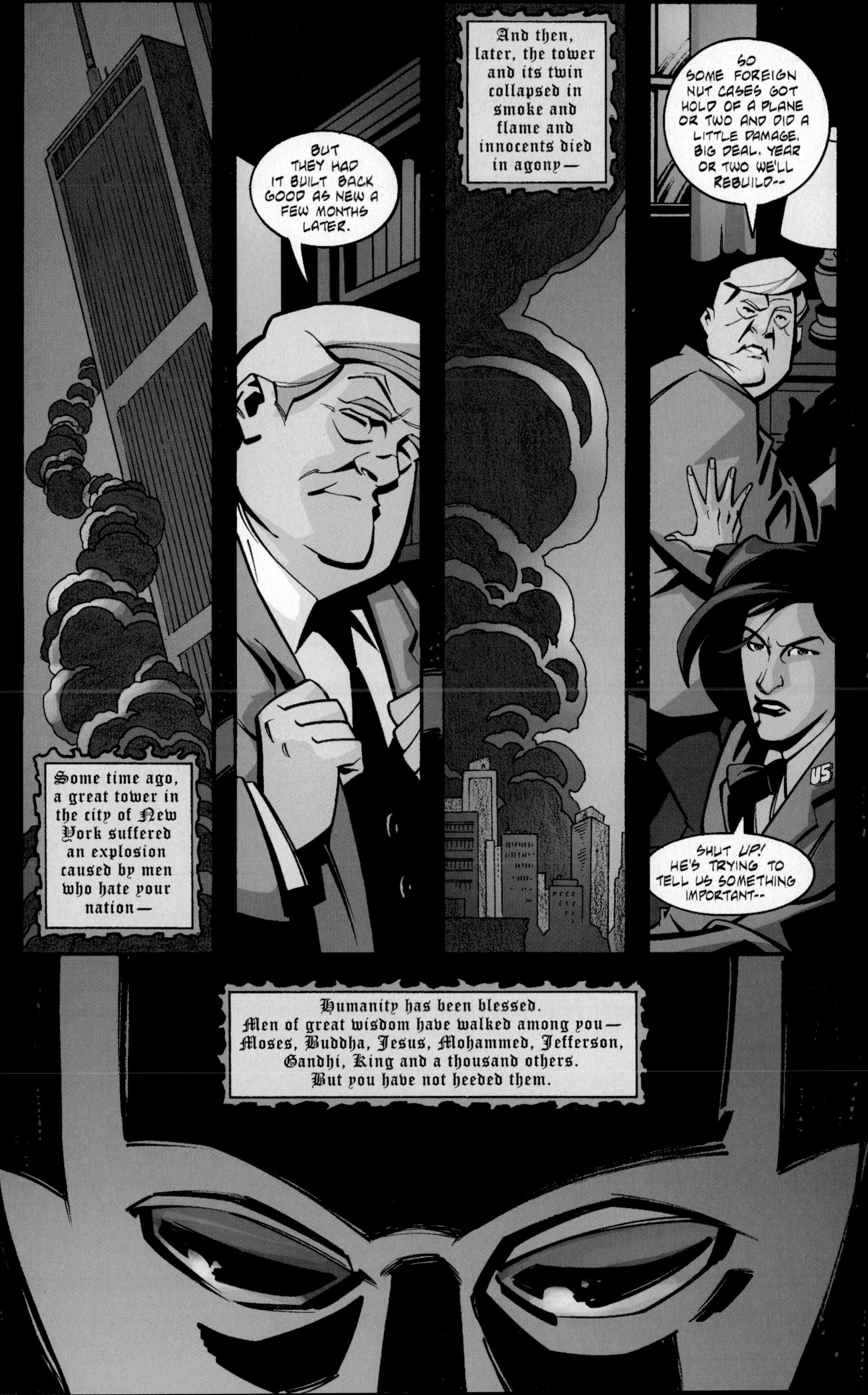
Some time ago, a great tower in the city of New York suffered an explosion caused by men who hate your nation—
BUT THEY HAD IT BUILT BACK GOOD AS NEW A FEW MONTHS LATER.
And then, later, the tower and its twin collapsed in smoke and flame and innocents died in agony—
SO SOME FOREIGN NUT CASES GOT HOLD OF A PLANE OR TWO AND DID A LITTLE DAMAGE. BIG DEAL. YEAR OR TWO WE'LL REBUILD--
SHUT UP! HE'S TRYING TO TELL US SOMETHING IMPORTANT--
US
Humanity has been blessed. Men of great wisdom have walked among you—Moses, Buddha, Jesus, Mohammed, Jefferson, Gandhi, King and a thousand others. But you have not heeded them.

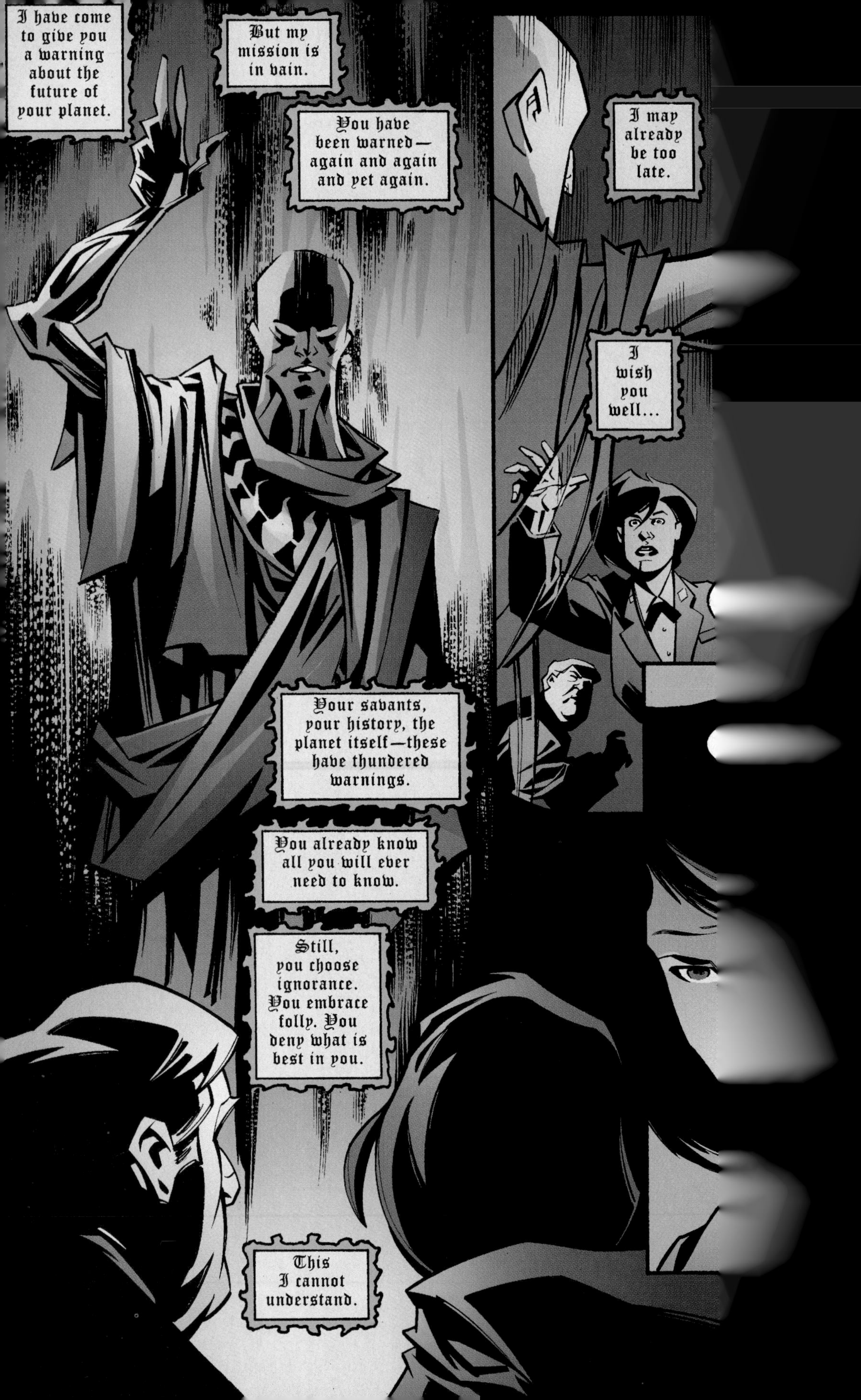
I have come to give you a warning about the future of your planet.
But my mission is in vain.
You have been warned—again and again and yet again.
I may already be too late.
I wish you well...
Your savants, your history, the planet itself—these have thundered warnings.
You already know all you will ever need to know.
Still, you choose ignorance. You embrace folly. You deny what is best in you.
This I cannot understand.

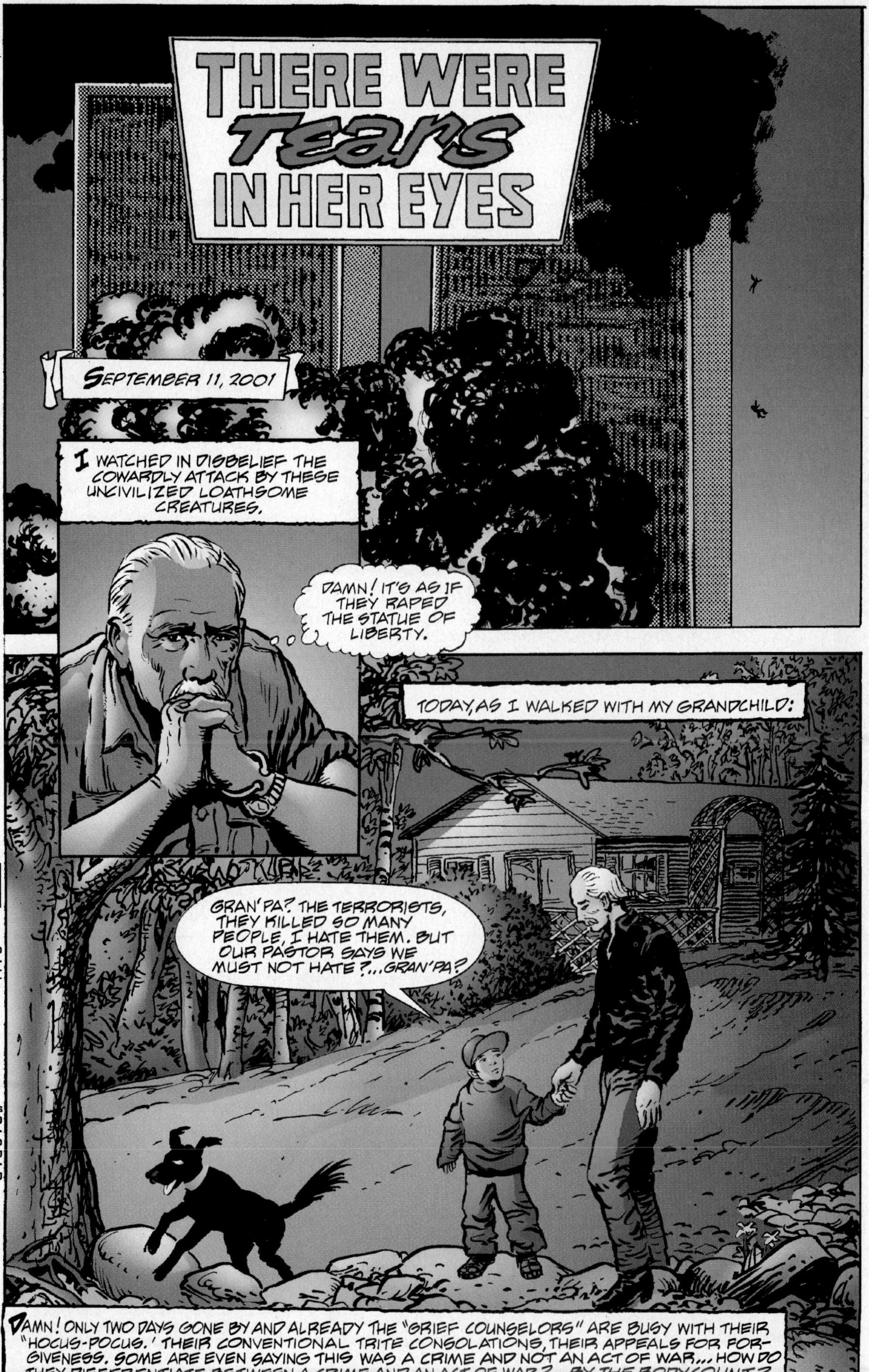
THERE WERE TEARS IN HER EYES
SEPTEMBER 11, 2001
I WATCHED IN DISBELIEF THE COWARDLY ATTACK BY THESE UNCIVILIZED LOATHSOME CREATURES.
DAMN! IT'S AS IF THEY RAPED THE STATUE OF LIBERTY.
TODAY, AS I WALKED WITH MY GRANDCHILD:
GRAN'PA? THE TERRORISTS, THEY KILLED SO MANY PEOPLE, I HATE THEM. BUT OUR PASTOR SAYS WE MUST NOT HATE?... GRAN'PA?
DAMN! ONLY TWO DAYS GONE BY AND ALREADY THE "GRIEF COUNSELORS" ARE BUSY WITH THEIR "HOCUS-POCUS." THEIR CONVENTIONAL TRITE CONSOLATIONS, THEIR APPEALS FOR FORGIVENESS. SOME ARE EVEN SAYING THIS WAS A CRIME AND NOT AN ACT OF WAR... HOW DO THEY DIFFERENTIATE BETWEEN A CRIME AND AN ACT OF WAR?... BY THE BODYCOUNT?
SJG

STORY & ART SAM GLANZMAN
LETTERS GASPAR SALADINO
COLOR WILDSTORM

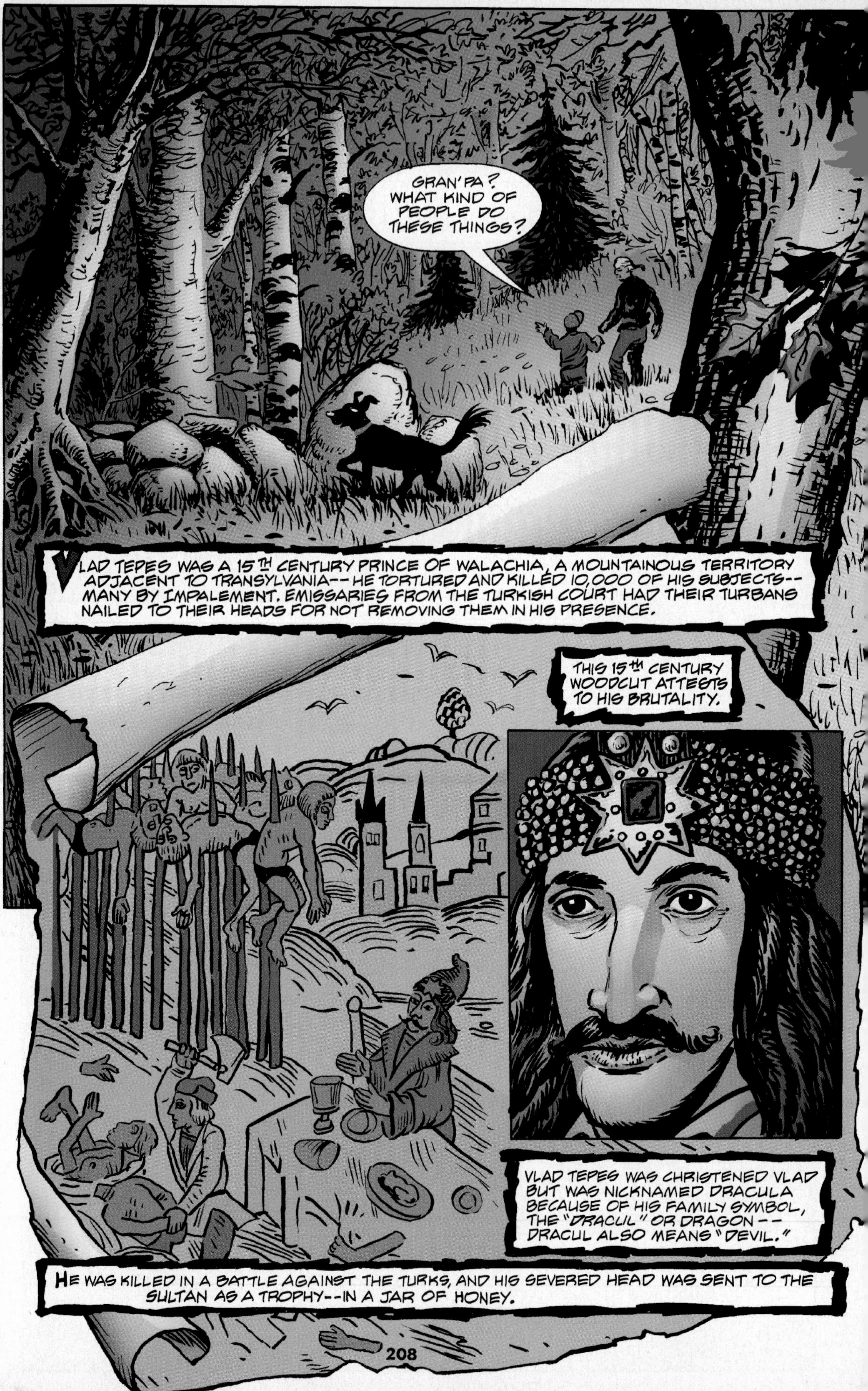
GRAN'PA? WHAT KIND OF PEOPLE DO THESE THINGS?
VLAD TEPES WAS A 15TH CENTURY PRINCE OF WALACHIA, A MOUNTAINOUS TERRITORY ADJACENT TO TRANSYLVANIA-- HE TORTURED AND KILLED 10,000 OF HIS SUBJECTS-- MANY BY IMPALEMENT. EMISSARIES FROM THE TURKISH COURT HAD THEIR TURBANS NAILED TO THEIR HEADS FOR NOT REMOVING THEM IN HIS PRESENCE.
THIS 15TH CENTURY WOODCUT ATTESTS TO HIS BRUTALITY.
VLAD TEPES WAS CHRISTENED VLAD BUT WAS NICKNAMED DRACULA BECAUSE OF HIS FAMILY SYMBOL, THE "DRACUL" OR DRAGON-- DRACUL ALSO MEANS "DEVIL."
HE WAS KILLED IN A BATTLE AGAINST THE TURKS, AND HIS SEVERED HEAD WAS SENT TO THE SULTAN AS A TROPHY--IN A JAR OF HONEY.

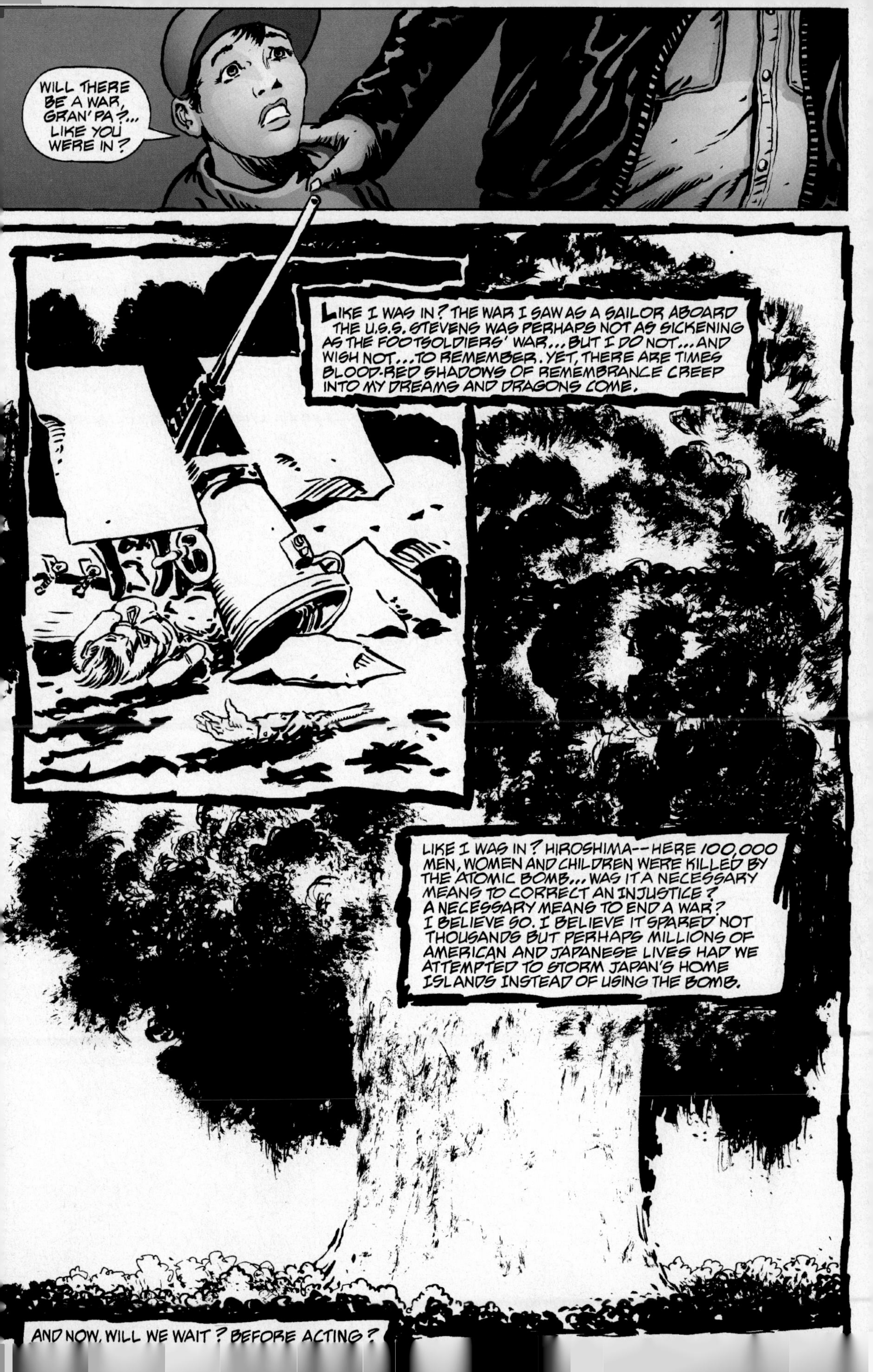
WILL THERE BE A WAR, GRAN'PA?... LIKE YOU WERE IN?
LIKE I WAS IN? THE WAR I SAW AS A SAILOR ABOARD THE U.S.S. STEVENS WAS PERHAPS NOT AS SICKENING AS THE FOOTSOLDIERS' WAR... BUT I DO NOT... AND WISH NOT... TO REMEMBER. YET, THERE ARE TIMES BLOOD-RED SHADOWS OF REMEMBRANCE CREEP INTO MY DREAMS AND DRAGONS COME.
LIKE I WAS IN? HIROSHIMA-- HERE 100,000 MEN, WOMEN AND CHILDREN WERE KILLED BY THE ATOMIC BOMB... WAS IT A NECESSARY MEANS TO CORRECT AN INJUSTICE? A NECESSARY MEANS TO END A WAR? I BELIEVE SO. I BELIEVE IT SPARED NOT THOUSANDS BUT PERHAPS MILLIONS OF AMERICAN AND JAPANESE LIVES HAD WE ATTEMPTED TO STORM JAPAN'S HOME ISLANDS INSTEAD OF USING THE BOMB.
AND NOW, WILL WE WAIT? BEFORE ACTING?

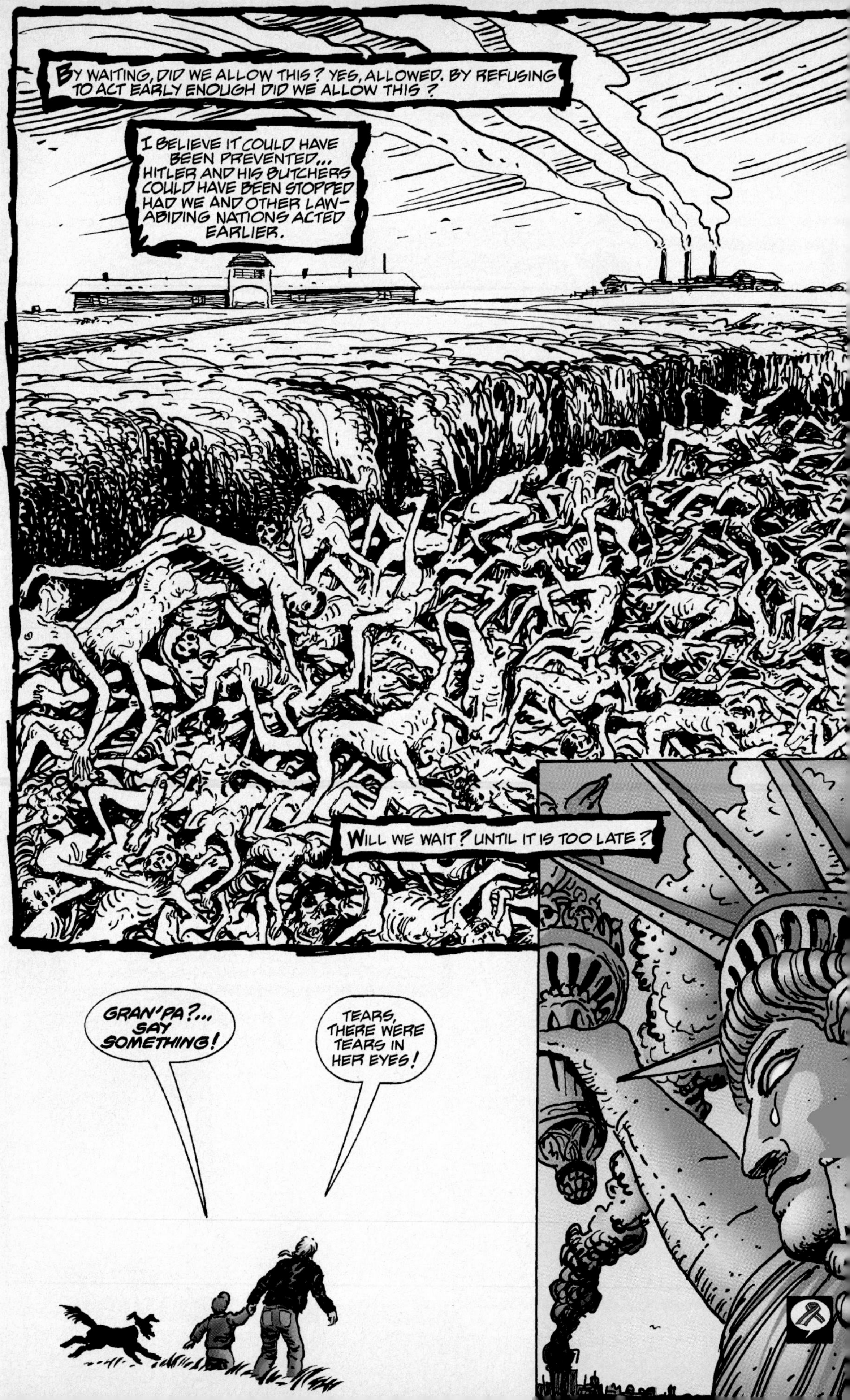

BY WAITING, DID WE ALLOW THIS? YES, ALLOWED. BY REFUSING TO ACT EARLY ENOUGH DID WE ALLOW THIS?
I BELIEVE IT COULD HAVE BEEN PREVENTED... HITLER AND HIS BUTCHERS COULD HAVE BEEN STOPPED HAD WE AND OTHER LAW-ABIDING NATIONS ACTED EARLIER.
WILL WE WAIT? UNTIL IT IS TOO LATE?
GRAN'PA?... SAY SOMETHING!
TEARS, THERE WERE TEARS IN HER EYES!

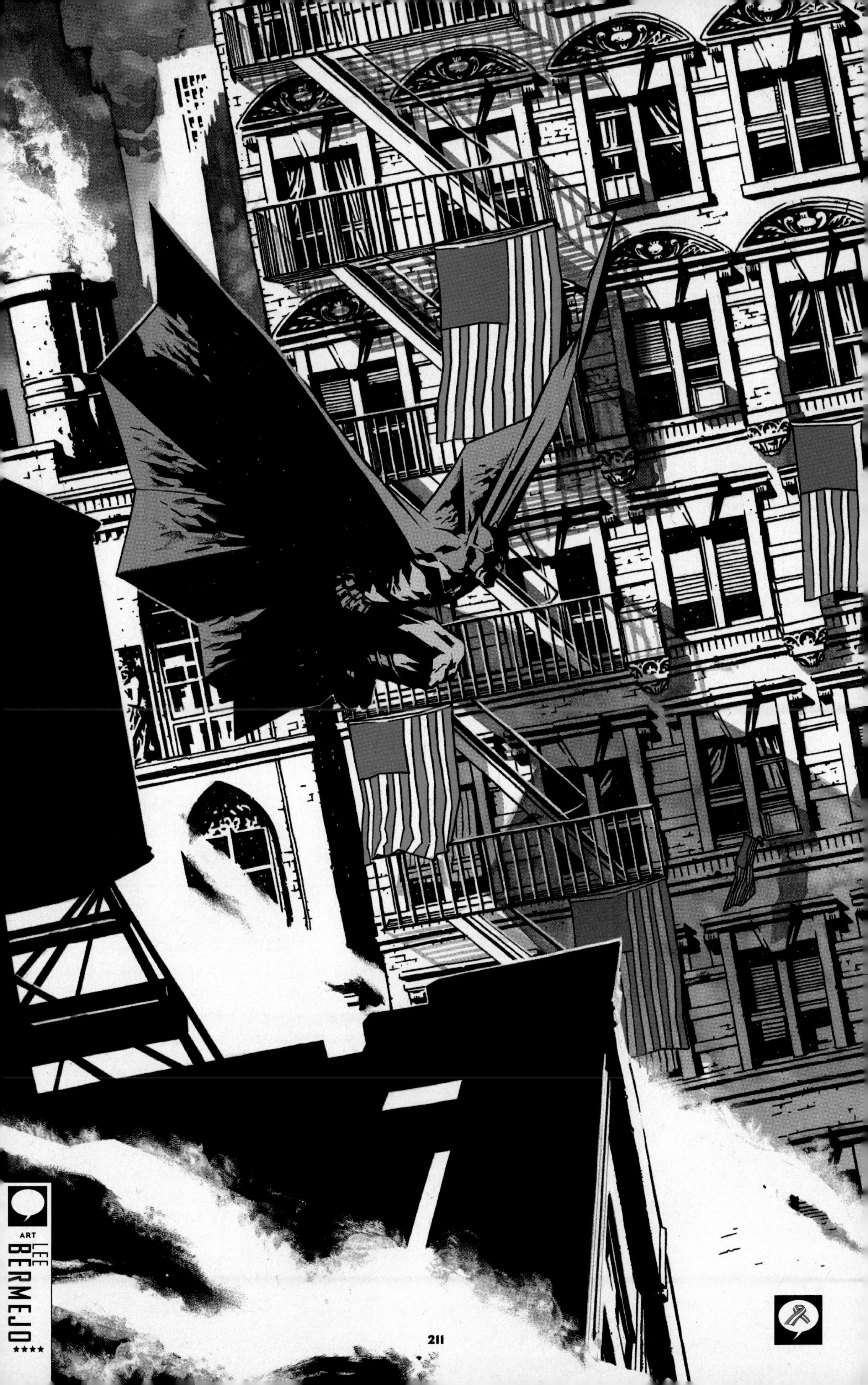

ART
LEE
BERMEJO

What of Tomorrow?

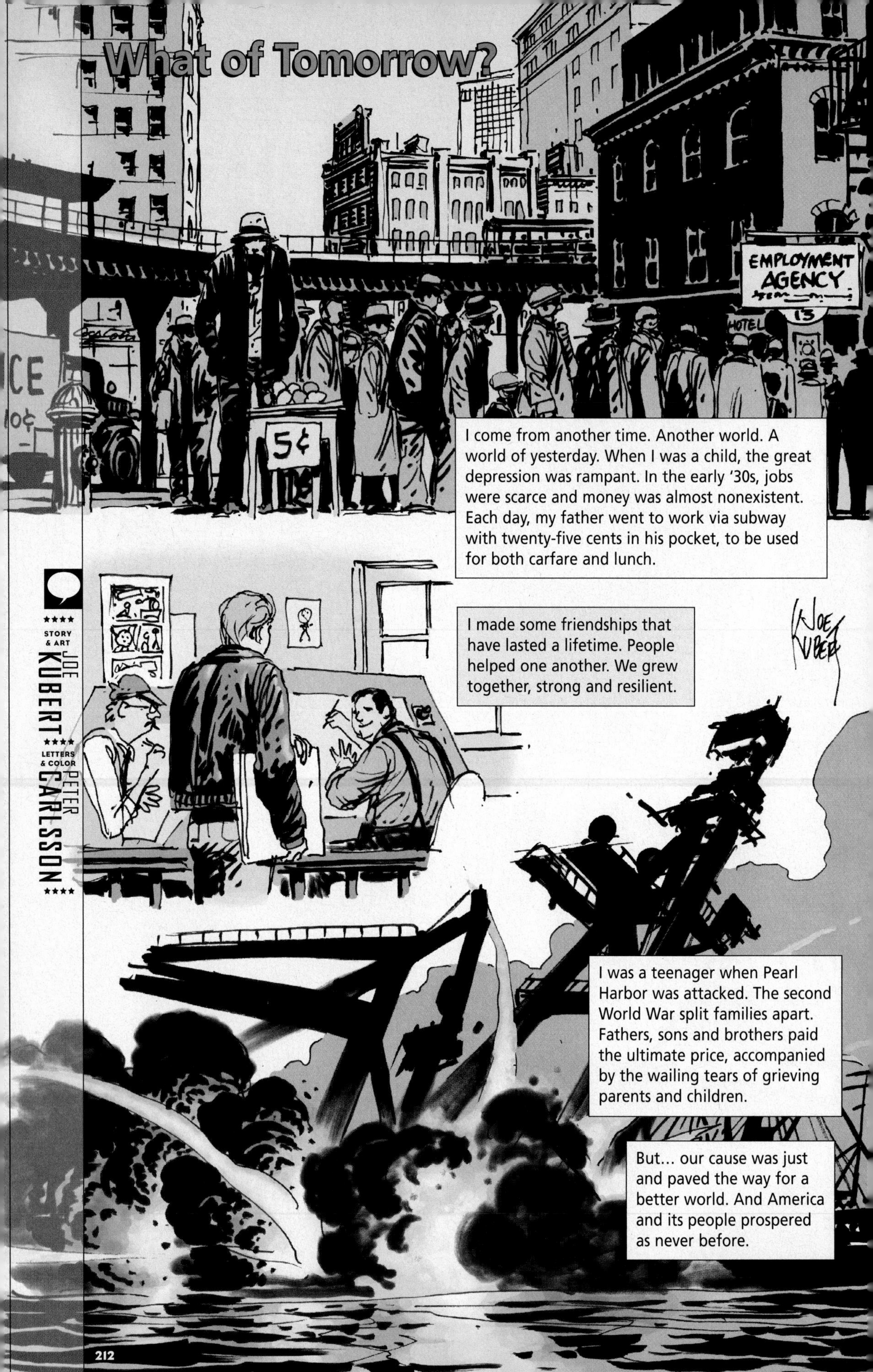
EMPLOYMENT AGENCY
13
HOTEL
5¢
I come from another time. Another world. A world of yesterday. When I was a child, the great depression was rampant. In the early '30s, jobs were scarce and money was almost nonexistent. Each day, my father went to work via subway with twenty-five cents in his pocket, to be used for both carfare and lunch.
I made some friendships that have lasted a lifetime. People helped one another. We grew together, strong and resilient.
JOE KUBERT
I was a teenager when Pearl Harbor was attacked. The second World War split families apart. Fathers, sons and brothers paid the ultimate price, accompanied by the wailing tears of grieving parents and children.
But... our cause was just and paved the way for a better world. And America and its people prospered as never before.
STORY & ART JOE KUBERT
LETTERS & COLOR PETER CARLSSON

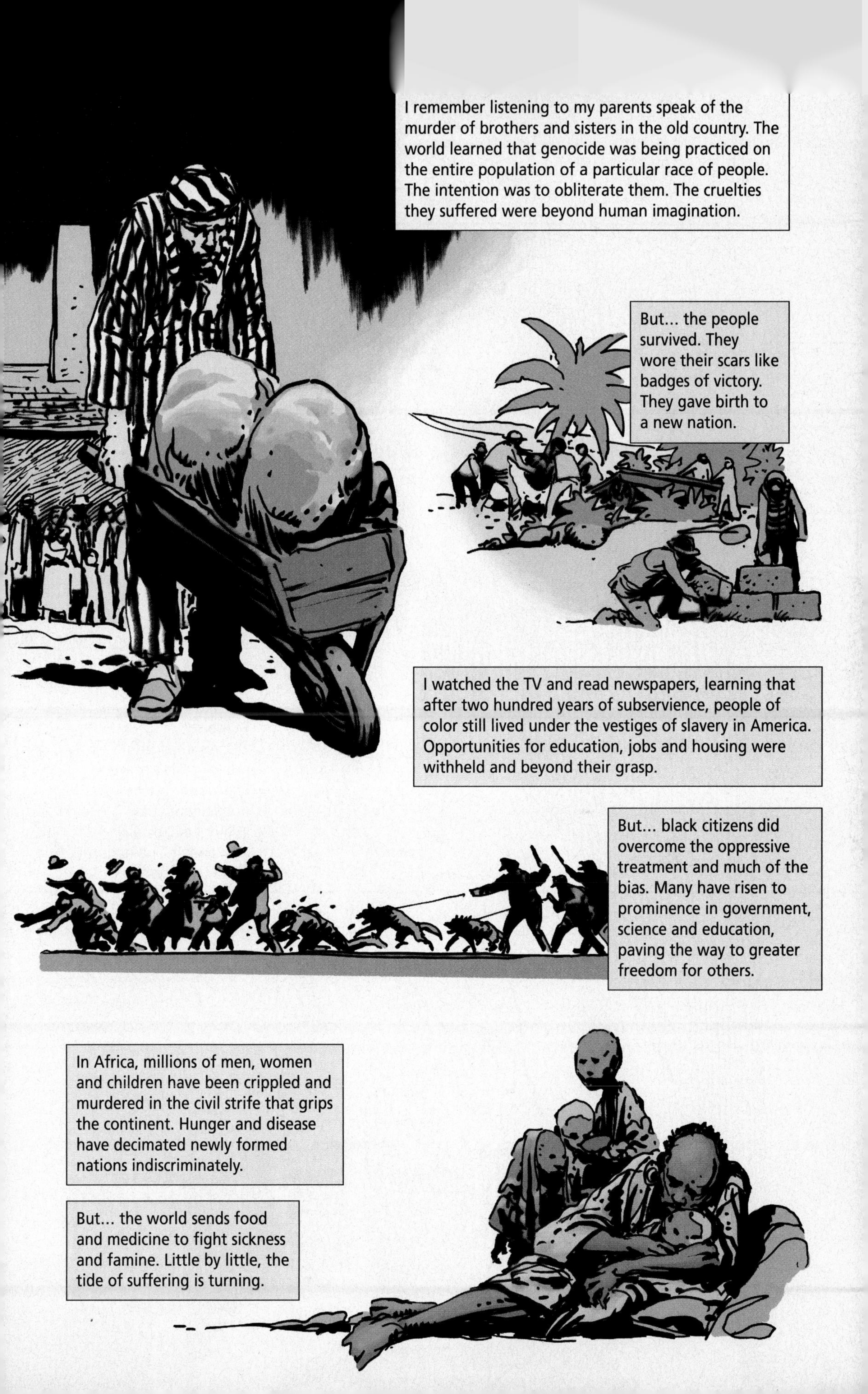
I remember listening to my parents speak of the murder of brothers and sisters in the old country. The world learned that genocide was being practiced on the entire population of a particular race of people. The intention was to obliterate them. The cruelties they suffered were beyond human imagination.
But... the people survived. They wore their scars like badges of victory. They gave birth to a new nation.
I watched the TV and read newspapers, learning that after two hundred years of subservience, people of color still lived under the vestiges of slavery in America. Opportunities for education, jobs and housing were withheld and beyond their grasp.
But... black citizens did overcome the oppressive treatment and much of the bias. Many have risen to prominence in government, science and education, paving the way to greater freedom for others.
In Africa, millions of men, women and children have been crippled and murdered in the civil strife that grips the continent. Hunger and disease have decimated newly formed nations indiscriminately.
But... the world sends food and medicine to fight sickness and famine. Little by little, the tide of suffering is turning.

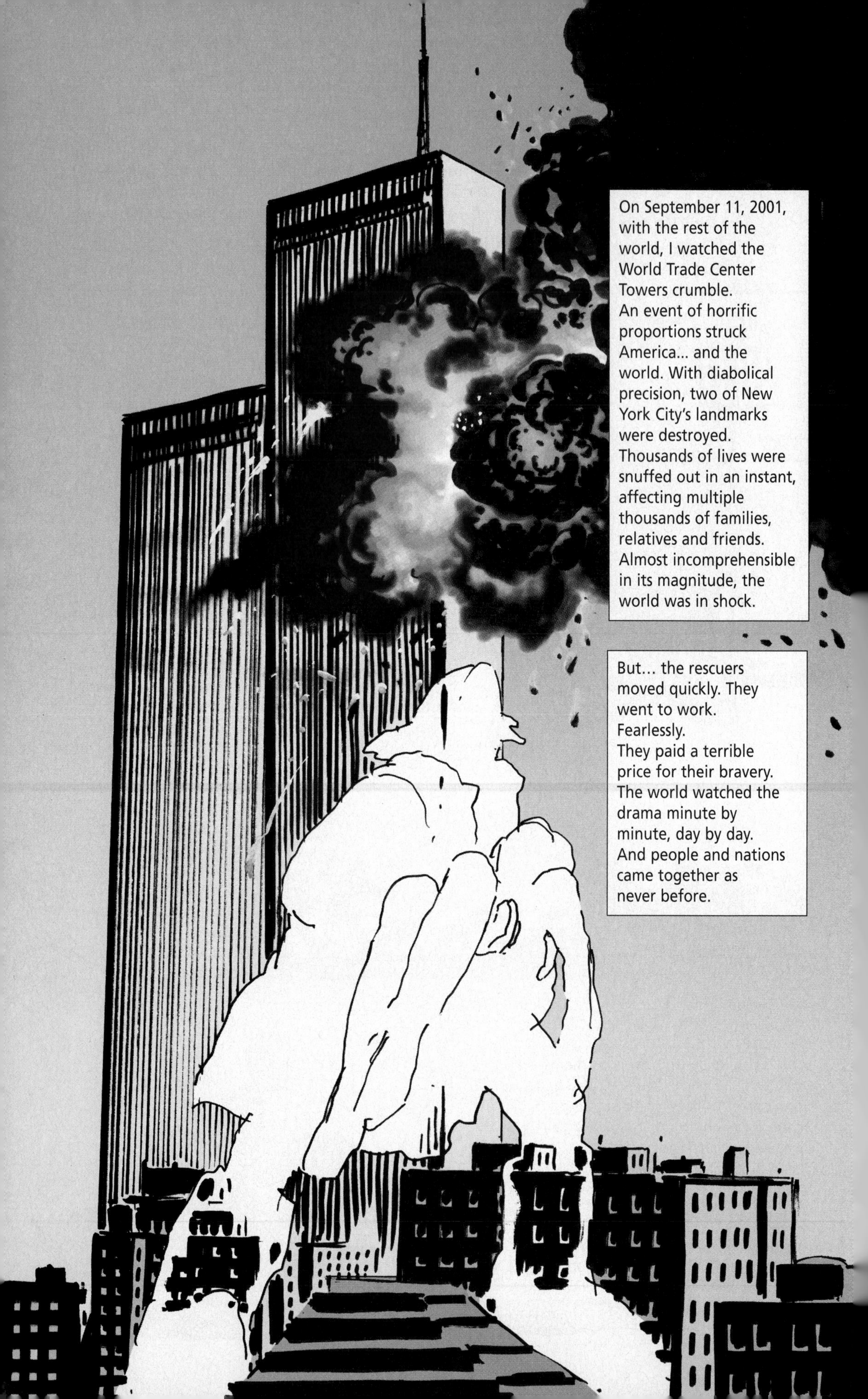
On September 11, 2001, with the rest of the world, I watched the World Trade Center Towers crumble. An event of horrific proportions struck America... and the world. With diabolical precision, two of New York City's landmarks were destroyed. Thousands of lives were snuffed out in an instant, affecting multiple thousands of families, relatives and friends. Almost incomprehensible in its magnitude, the world was in shock.
But... the rescuers moved quickly. They went to work. Fearlessly. They paid a terrible price for their bravery. The world watched the drama minute by minute, day by day. And people and nations came together as never before.

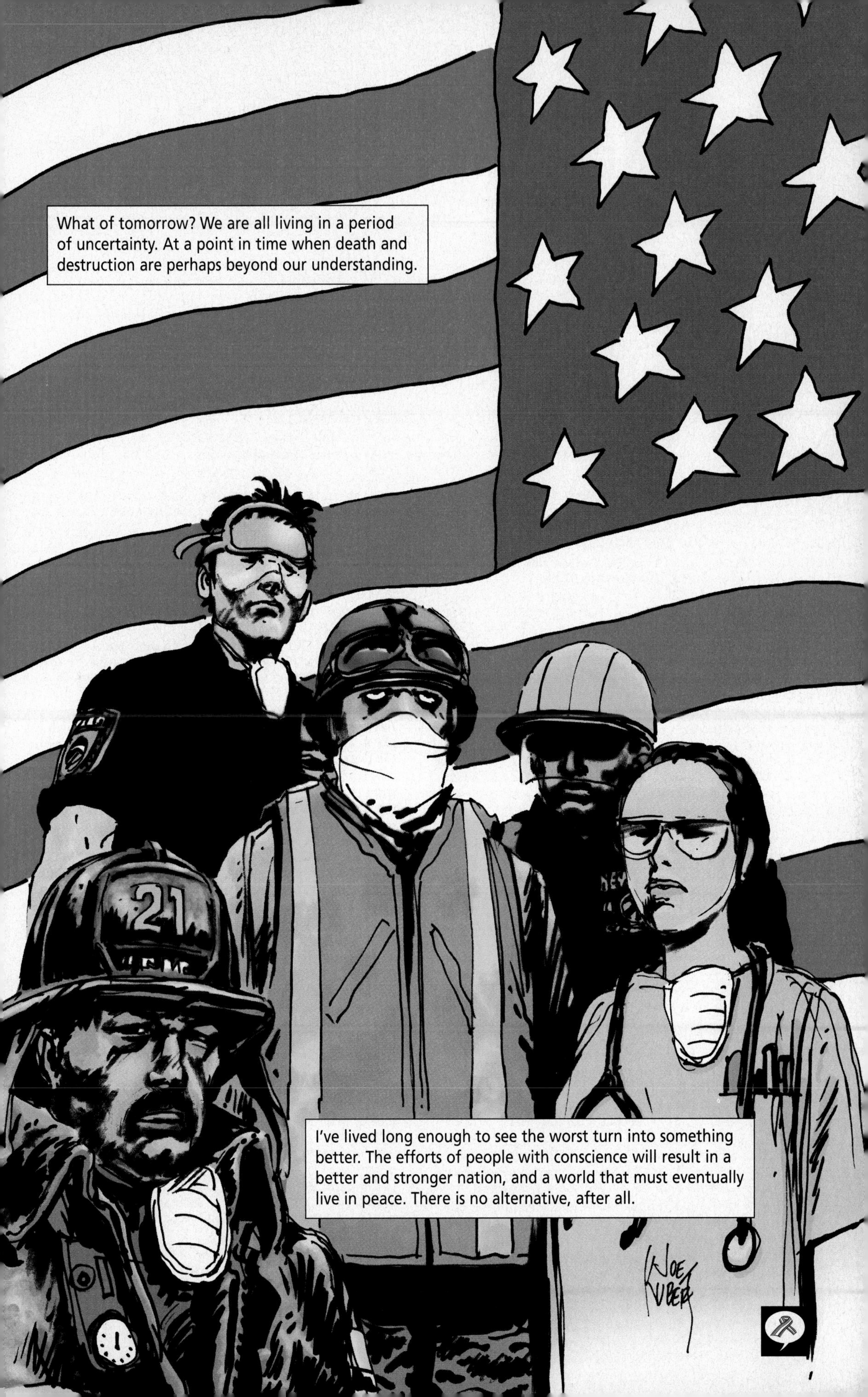
What of tomorrow? We are all living in a period of uncertainty. At a point in time when death and destruction are perhaps beyond our understanding.
21
I've lived long enough to see the worst turn into something better. The efforts of people with conscience will result in a better and stronger nation, and a world that must eventually live in peace. There is no alternative, after all.
JOE KUBERT

CONTRIBUTORS

Hundreds of creative people who contribute to DC Comics, Vertigo, WildStorm Productions and MAD Magazine volunteered their time to participate in this project. We gratefully acknowledge their efforts, whether published in this volume, exhibited, auctioned or not included due to the limitations of space and time. In addition, we thank our collaborators at Quebecor World Montréal, Diamond Comic Distributors, AOL Time Warner Trade Publishing Group, Dark Horse Comics, Image Comics, Chaos! Comics, Oni Press, and Top Shelf Productions for their donations to this project.

The following brief biographies do not do justice to the accomplishments of our contributors, who include winners of the Alley, Bram Stoker, Eagle, Eisner, Emmy, Harvey, Hugo, Reuben, Shazam and *Wizard* Awards, among many other honors. If you would like to read more of their work, it is available in DC Comics or MAD Books editions at comics shops and bookstores everywhere. To locate a comics shop near you, call 1-888-COMICBOOK. To find out more about us, check online at DCComics.com or AOL Keyword DC Comics.

DAN ABNETT is British and lives and works in Maidstone, England. He has been writing children's books, comics, and novels for nearly fifteen years and is currently co-writer of THE LEGION for DC Comics.

NEAL ADAMS is a privileged American who's never met a policeman or fireman that he didn't like.

AMERICAN COLOR is one of the largest premedia companies in the U.S. and Canada and a pioneer of digital prepress and photography. Founded in 1975, American Color has been at the forefront of the evolution of digital prepress technology.

BRENT ERIC ANDERSON is a co-founder of ASTRO CITY, has been helping construct comic books for 25 years, and will continue to do so well into the future. Peace.

SERGIO ARAGONES is one of the most prolific artists in the comics industry and is best known for drawing thousands of cartoons in the margins of MAD MAGAZINE since 1962. He has won numerous awards for his work, including the prestigious Reuben Award.

BRIAN AZZARELLO is an Eisner Award-winning writer best known as the co-creator and writer of 100 BULLETS. His other DC credits include HELLBLAZER, JOHNNY DOUBLE, and EL DIABLO. He lives in Chicago.

CHRIS BACHALO is trapped along with his wife, Helen, and his son, Dylan, in a world they never made. Chris has been known to enjoy the experiences of drinking glug, eating tea cakes, and having visited the top of the World Trade Center in 1992...once upon a time. Chris has spent time drawing and creating the likes of SHADE, DEATH, GENERATION X, X-MEN and his current escapism, STEAMPUNK. God Bless America!!

HILARY BADER grew up in Bay Ridge, Brooklyn. She is a writer of TV shows *(Xena, Star Trek, Lois and Clark)* and spent 5 years on the staff of the animated *Batman, Superman* and *Batman Beyond* TV shows. She has written for a number of DC titles and was the writer of the BATMAN BEYOND monthly comic.

KYLE BAKER is the author of the graphic novels YOU ARE HERE, THE COWBOY WALLY SHOW, WHY I HATE SATURN, and KING DAVID.

MOOSE BAUMANN currently colors ACTION COMICS and GREEN LANTERN for DC Comics. How he's managed to stay employed this long is a question for the ages.

EDDIE BERGANZA is the current Superman editor. He has written SUPERBOY in the past, and hopes his children read the story in this book.

LEE BERMEJO has created art for many comics including GEN 13, SUPERMAN/GEN 13, and STARMAN. He's also done illustrations for the *Star Wars* role-playing game.

ALEX BLEYAERT and **ROB RO** met while working for WildStorm FX. They opened up their own studio, Bad@ss, in 1996 and have provided color art for STEAMPUNK and CRIMSON, both from WildStorm. Currently their work can be found in AZRAEL and GREEN LANTERN: LEGACY—THE LAST WILL AND TESTAMENT OF HAL JORDAN.

JOHN BOLTON lives and works in London, the city of his birth. He is an award-winning artist who has worked on graphic novels and Prestige Format books with Clive Barker, Chris Claremont, Neil Gaiman, Sam Raimi, Anne Rice and many others.

ENRIQUE BRECCIA was born in the Republic of Argentina. He is a comics artist, an illustrator and a plastic artist. He has been working on these three disciplines for more than 30 years for European and Latin American audiences. Two years ago, he joined the American market, first working for Marvel Comics and now for DC Comics.

AMIE BROCKWAY-METCALF happily designs funnybooks for DC Comics. She was nominated for the Eisner Award for Best Publication Design twice in 2000, and was previously Art Director at the sorely missed Kitchen Sink Press.

ED BRUBAKER spends as much time as possible trying not to think about the horrendous things people do to each other in this world. He is a cartoonist and a writer working on such books as BATMAN and CATWOMAN, as well as the Eisner Award-nominated SCENE OF THE CRIME. He is married and lives in the middle of nowhere.

RICHARD BRUNING has been a graphic designer for 25 years and has also written, illustrated, edited and read comics for a long time. He is employed very full-time as DC's VP-Creative Director.

KEN BRUZENAK is currently lettering AZRAEL and AMERICAN CENTURY for DC.

RICK BURCHETT is a 20-year veteran of the comics industry, working as both a penciller and an inker. His work includes BLACKHAWK, JUSTICE LEAGUE, and a long run on DC's animated tie-in books. Rick lives in Missouri with his wife and two sons.

KURT BUSIEK has been a professional comics writer since 1982, working on such series as AVENGERS, THUNDERBOLTS, and THE POWER COMPANY. This story marks the return to print of his award-winning ASTRO CITY series. Kurt lives in the Pacific Northwest, with his wife and two daughters.

MIKE CAREY was born in Liverpool but lives and works in London. He currently writes LUCIFER for DC Vertigo, as well as for TV and film. Neil Gaiman has described him as "easily one of the half-dozen best writers of mainstream comics."

SERGIO CARIELLO has drawn many of the major comics characters, from Daredevil and Batman to Spawn and Superman. He recently drew the MAGE KNIGHT role-playing game mini-comic and has been the regular artist on AZRAEL for DC.

PETER CARLSSON is the art director at Tell-A-Graphics. He lives and works in New Jersey.

JOHN C. CEBOLLERO's career in comics started over 10 years ago. His work can be seen in such DC titles as BATMAN: LEGENDS OF THE DARK KNIGHT, REALWORLDS: BATMAN, and the BIG BOOK series. John was born, raised, and still lives in New York City and is profoundly proud to be an American.

KEITH CHAMPAGNE, a Connecticut-based inker, is proud to be able to contribute to this book.

CLIFF WU CHIANG was born in New York and will always consider it home. He is currently drawing Josie Mac, a backup feature in DETECTIVE COMICS, and an upcoming Elseworlds, THE GOLDEN STREETS OF GOTHAM.

MARK CHIARELLO is currently DC's Editorial Art Director. As a freelance illustrator, he has received the comic book industry's Eisner, Harvey and cartooning's Reuben Awards.

CHRISTOPHER CHUCKRY lives in Winnipeg, Manitoba with his wife, Cheryl. He has been coloring comics for the past 11 years and can easily say that this is the best job he has ever had.

MIKE COLLINS has been working in the industry for 15 years, mainly for DC, but has also spent time at Marvel, penciling the X-MEN. Back on his side of the pond, he's contributed to 2000 AD. He comes from Cardiff, Wales.

AMANDA CONNER, comic book artist and creator, lives in Brooklyn. Currently her work can be seen on CODENAME: KNOCKOUT, MAD MAGAZINE and the upcoming PRO graphic novel from Image Comics. She started drawing at age three and wants to be a superhero when she grows up.

DARWYN COOKE is the penciller on the new CAT-WOMAN series and writer/artist of BATMAN: EGO. Highlights from the Toronto native's illustrious career in animation include 3 years working for Bruce Timm on *The Batman/Superman Adventures* and designing the main title for *Batman Beyond*.

RICHARD CORBEN has over 30 years' experience drawing comics. His work is a study in light, modeling, movement and interesting composition. For him, it's about movies on pages.

JOHN COSTANZA, a cartoonist in his own right, is an award-winning comic book letterer for such books as BIZARRO COMICS.

DENYS COWAN was born and raised in New York City and loves his hometown. He has illustrated numerous comic books and in 1991 founded Milestone Comics. He has directed and storyboarded both feature and television animation. Denys is very proud of his son, Miles.

ALAN DAVIS's first U.S. work was BATMAN AND THE OUTSIDERS for DC Comics. Since then he's worked on everything from THE AVENGERS to the X-MEN. He created his own group of superheroes called THE CLANDESTINE and wrote and pencilled the acclaimed JLA: THE NAIL. Alan is currently working on KILLRAVEN for Marvel Comics.

GUY DAVIS is probably best known for his work on the Vertigo series SANDMAN MYSTERY THEATRE and the independent comic BAKER STREET. He currently lives in Michigan and continues to draw away for DC/ Vertigo.

JAMIE DELANO was born in 1954. He is a British writer/creator of many diverse works including WORLD WITHOUT END, GHOSTDANCING, 2020 VISIONS, HELL ETERNAL, CRUEL & UNUSUAL, and OUTLAW NATION.

J.M. DeMATTEIS has written for newspapers, magazines, television, movies, and of course comics, where his work has taken him from the super-heroics of Spider-Man, Superman, and the Justice League to the more personal universes of MOONSHADOW, BROOKLYN DREAMS, and SEEKERS INTO THE MYSTERY.

JAMES DENNING writes for LOONEY TUNES and DEXTER'S LABORATORY comics. He has also written for the *Los Angeles Times Sunday Magazine,* the *Magic School Bus* CD-rom and Hub City Spoke Repair. He lived in New York for eight years before moving to Los Angeles.

DIAMOND COMIC DISTRIBUTORS is proud to assist in the promotion and distribution of this fine effort. In our 20 years of business, we have worked on many charity projects and have donated countless times to good causes, but no cause could be more important or more worthy than this one. We are honored to be able to be a part of helping the victims of September 11 in any way we can.

DIGITAL CHAMELEON is a group of artists working under the stewardship of Lovern Kindzierski, himself a master colorist and award-winning writer.

COLLEEN DORAN is the granddaughter of a deputy sheriff. Her father is a police chief and former marine who specializes in bomb disposal, anti-terrorism, and dignitary protection. Her brother is a retired undercover vice cop and also a former marine. Her parents met and married while in the Civil Air Patrol. She is the creator of the fantasy series A DISTANT SOIL and is currently working on ORBITER with Warren Ellis for Vertigo (due to be released in 2002). She's drawn and written about a lot of heroes, but the most amazing heroes she's ever known are in her family.

JO DUFFY has been a longtime writer and editor in the field of comics. She had a long run as the writer of CAT-WOMAN and will soon be co-writing THE DEFENDERS for Marvel.

KIERON DWYER is the current artist of THE AVENGERS from Marvel Comics. His work has appeared in ACTION COMICS, SUPERMAN: THE DARK SIDE and his creator-owned series, LCD: LOWEST COMMON DENOMINATOR. He dedicates his piece in this book to the memory of those who died and the spirit of those who survive.

WILL EISNER is a graphic novelist who has written and drawn copiously about New York City, his hometown. Most notably, his THE SPIRIT is set in the New York milieu.

NATHAN EYRING is currently the colorist of TRANS-METROPOLITAN for Vertigo.

RICH FABER has worked on STEEL, GREEN LANTERN, and currently, TITANS, among many other jobs. Until recently, he was a lifelong resident of New York, and the tragic events of 9-11 have profoundly affected his life. He now lives in Pennsylvania with his lovely wife Traci and their two cats.

GLENN FABRY has been working in and around comics since 1984. He is married to Nikki, has two children (Kitty and Tom) and lives in Brighton, England.

MARK FARMER has inked many books over the years. FANTASTIC FOUR, JLA: THE NAIL, CLANDESTINE, X-MEN to name just a few. He comes from England and is usually found collaborating with his fellow Brit Alan Davis.

PHIL FELIX lettered many episodes of Harvey Kurtzman and Will Elder's Little Annie Fanny in *Playboy* before striking out on his own to become one of comics' most prolific letterers. He teaches at the Joe Kubert School of Cartoon and Graphic Art.

GARY FIELDS had been a freelance cartoonist and illustrator since 1985. He has worked for/on a variety of original and licensed comic books, magazines, comic strips, children's books, websites, toy companies, and animation studios. He has one beautiful wife, three wonderful children, and one stubborn dog.

MARCELO FRUSIN is a 33-year-old Argentinean. Before working for DC Comics, he drew for different publishers in the U.S. (Marvel, Acclaim), Italy (Universo), and Argentina (Columba). He is currently the regular artist in HELLBLAZER for Vertigo.

NEIL GAIMAN came to America almost a decade ago. His most recent novel is *American Gods.* He's English.

DAVE GIBBONS, whilst a native and resident of the United Kingdom, has drawn and written many of DC Comics' major characters over the past twenty years. He is perhaps best known as the artist of WATCHMEN.

NOELLE GIDDINGS is a New Yorker as well as a NYC Marathon runner. She has also worked as an illustrator of children's books and an animator on many video cartoon projects including the ABC television show *Doug.* She loves working on comics—a new adventure every day.

KEITH GIFFEN has had a long, varied career at DC Comics with a successful run as the penciller of LEGION OF SUPER-HEROES, a book he would go on to write as well. He is also known for his writing/plotting of JUSTICE LEAGUE and currently of SUICIDE SQUAD.

SAM GLANZMAN served in the U.S. Navy during World War Two and has written and drawn comics since 1940. His credits also include the acclaimed autobiographical series U.S.S. STEVENS, JUNGLE TALES OF TARZAN, and THE HAUNTED TANK.

DAVID S. GOYER is a screenwriter-producer (Blade, Blade II, Dark City). Paying homage to his fanboy roots, he also co-writes JSA for DC Comics. At the age of 15 he had a letter printed in SWAMP THING.

PETER GROSS broke into comics with his self-published series EMPIRE LANES and is best known for his work on BOOKS OF MAGIC, BOOKS OF FAERIE, and the ongoing series LUCIFER. He also developed and directs the comic art program at the Minneapolis College of Art and Design (MCAD) where he currently teaches when he isn't drawing. Peter lives in Minneapolis with his partner, Jeanne and their daughter, Alice.

TOM GRUMMETT has been a professional penciller since 1988, his first ongoing assignment being the NEW TITANS for DC. He is currently pencilling THE POWER COMPANY for DC. He lives in Canada with his wife and two children, and he loves them very much.

PAUL GULACY is well known for his graphic cinematic approach to such titles as BATMAN, MASTER OF KUNG FU, and many others. His work with writer Don McGregor on SABRE produced one of the first American graphic novels.

KURT HATHAWAY has been lettering, writing and editing comics for almost 18 years. Someday he'd like to be the King of Mars, but apparently it hasn't much of an atmosphere. Perhaps Venus, then. What?

ANDREW HELFER and his fiancée, Jaimie, live four blocks north of the World Trade Center. The rest of his family resides in Battery Park City, two blocks west of Ground Zero. He dedicates his contribution to this volume to them.

HEROIC AGE is one of the most requested separators in the business, providing their services on many books including JSA, SUICIDE SQUAD and JLA: INCARNATIONS.

PHIL HESTER is an Eisner Award-nominated artist born in Iowa. His pencilling credits include SWAMP THING, ULTIMATE MARVEL TEAM-UP, THE COFFIN, CLERKS: THE LOST SCENE, THE WRETCH, and GREEN ARROW. He continues to reside in Iowa with his wife, Christine, and their two children, Dean and Emma.

GREG AND TIM HILDEBRANDT's career has spanned 40 years. These award-winning artists have produced paintings for films such as Star Wars, and magazines such as Omni, and games such as Dungeons and Dragons. Their epic novel Urshurak reached the New York Times best-seller list.

SANDRA HOPE has earned critical acclaim on her work inking Humberto Ramos on CRIMSON and is continuing to win accolades working with him on their current series, OUT THERE. She is also inking Gary Frank on JUST IMAGINE STAN LEE WITH GARY FRANK CREATING SHAZAM! Hope lives in San Diego.

RICHARD AND TANYA HORIE began working in comics in 1992. They have colored titles such as AQUAMAN, BATMAN, BATMAN: HARLEY QUINN, SUPERBOY'S LEGION, SUPERMAN: THE MAN OF STEEL, ADVENTURES OF SUPERMAN and are currently working on SUPERMAN with Jeph Loeb and Ed McGuiness.

ALEX HORLEY was born on the outskirts of Milan, Italy and has drawn and painted for both DC Comics and Vertigo on such projects as LOBO, BATTLEAXES, and the recent JLA: RIDDLE OF THE BEAST.

DENNIS JANKE is currently inking an issue of THE SPECTRE; before that Superman books through the '90s; before that CAPTAIN AMERICA at Marvel. Comics trivia: first published work was a two-pager written by Paul Levitz.

KLAUS JANSON has been in comics for over 25 years and in that time has pencilled or inked virtually every major character at DC and Marvel, but he is proudest of fulfilling his childhood dream: being a New Yorker.

PHIL JIMENEZ moved to New York City from his native Los Angeles when he was 19. He cannot imagine living anywhere else, now more so than ever.

GEOFF JOHNS has written comics, including JSA and THE FLASH, for the last 3 years and is currently living in Hollywood where he is producing and writing for television. His sister, Courtney Johns, was one of the passengers killed on TWA Flight 800 in 1996.

DAVE JOHNSON has worked in comics going on 10 years. He draws covers for 100 BULLETS among others and has been known to have other people impersonate him at awards banquets.

DAN JURGENS has written and drawn virtually every character in DC's rich history, most notably a long run on SUPERMAN. The Minnesota resident currently writes THE MIGHTY THOR and LARA CROFT: TOMB RAIDER.

JOHN KALISZ worked in the Marvel bullpen in the early '90s doing art corrections before embarking on a career as a freelancer. Currently he is the colorist of JSA, SUICIDE SQUAD, and JLA ADVENTURES.

MICHAEL Wm. KALUTA is best known by DC Comics and Vertigo fans for his painted covers for BOOKS OF MAGIC and WITCHCRAFT as well as his designs for JLA: RIDDLE OF THE BEAST. He has just released a large book of his illustrations called Wings of Twilight.

JOE KELLY is a writer, blessed to be the father of two Fantastic Kids, the husband of one Radiant Wife, and the son of an Old School Cop and the Hard Core Housemom who kept him in line.

CHUCK KIM lived in New York City for 9 years and misses it every day. He is currently a writer in Los Angeles but will always consider the Big Apple his home.

BARRY KITSON has been an artist and writer in the comics field since the 1980s. His credits include regular work on many of DC's major characters including Batman, Superman and the JLA. He is currently the penciller on TITANS and EMPIRE. He lives in the wilds of Norfolk in Great Britain.

TODD KLEIN has been lettering for DC Comics since 1977. He's won numerous awards for his work.

SCOTT KOLINS has loved comics and uplifting stories ever since he was 6 years old. He's been living his "dream job" by drawing SPIDER-MAN, GREEN LANTERN, THE LEGION OF SUPER-HEROES, WONDER WOMAN and currently THE FLASH. Scott now lives in Arizona with his beautiful wife, Kim.

JOSH KRACH, the son of a former EMT, co-wrote DC's one-shot JLA: GODS AND MONSTERS. He lives in Texas with his wife and two cats.

KRUGER INC. donated the Rebax 45# interior stock. Sustainable forest management, recycling, newsprint, supercalendered, coated grades and other publication papers, tissue, linerboard, packaging, lumber and other forest products. Dedicated to serving you better! www.kruger.com

JOE KUBERT has been a professional cartoonist for over 60 years and has drawn almost every comic book character in existence. In addition to drawing, he has been an editor, publisher, writer and letterer. He is the founder of the Joe Kubert School of Cartoon and Graphic Art, Inc., which opened its doors in 1976 and has turned out many of the prominent cartoonists working today.

ANDY LANNING lives and works in the U.K., just outside of London. He has been writing, drawing and inking comics since leaving art college in 1985, and currently co-writes and inks THE LEGION and inks WONDER WOMAN.

MICHAEL LARK has illustrated several comics series since 1989, including the critically acclaimed miniseries TERMINAL CITY and SCENE OF THE CRIME. His imagery for "Still Life" was inspired by the work of the many photojournalists who, often at the risk of their own lives, united the country by bringing the horror and emotion of September 11th home to the entire nation.

JIM LEE was born in Seoul, South Korea and is the creator of such popular comic book titles as WILDC.A.T.S and GEN 13. When not at the drawing board, he acts as the Editorial Director of WildStorm Productions, overseeing the creation and development of new titles and publishing imprints.

STAN LEE has been a comic book writer and creator for five decades. As a sergeant in World War II his specialty was training and instructing our GI's. Today, he feels every American is a GI in the fight against terrorism.

STEVE LEIALOHA has been a comics artist since the mid seventies for all the major comics companies and many of the minor ones as well. Before that he was a firefighter for the State of California.

PAUL LEVITZ is a first-generation American and a native New Yorker. He has written comics, including a notable run on LEGION OF SUPER-HEROES, and has been on DC's staff for almost three decades, currently as its publisher.

DAVID LLOYD is responsible for many comics including V FOR VENDETTA, THE HORRORIST, NIGHT RAVEN: HOUSE OF CARDS, and several issues of HELLBLAZER among many, many others.

JEPH LOEB is a New York boy who currently lives in Los Angeles where he produces and writes movies and television. His comic book credits include BATMAN: THE LONG HALLOWEEN and SUPERMAN.

JOSE LUIS GARCIA-LOPEZ was born in Spain, raised in Argentina and currently resides in New York City. In a career that has spanned three decades, he has drawn hundreds of DC characters and is currently drawing for DC's licensing department as well as upcoming issues of DEADMAN.

KEN LOPEZ entered comics in 1980 as a high school intern at Marvel Comics. He is currently the letterer of JLA, JSA, YOUNG JUSTICE, SUPERMAN: THE MAN OF STEEL and HARLEY QUINN.

LEE LOUGHRIDGE is the proprietor of Zylonol, the separation house that has separated such books as LEGEND OF THE HAWKMAN, ROBIN: YEAR ONE, and the Vertigo graphic novel HOUSE ON THE BORDERLANDS. He resides in Savannah, Georgia.

JOHN LUCAS is currently drawing THE LIFE AND TIMES OF FOREVER MAELSTROM, a 6-issue miniseries written by Howard Chaykin and David Tischman.

GUY MAJOR has lent his coloring skills to several companies in the comics industry. He is the regular colorist and separator on GREEN ARROW.

TOM MANDRAKE has worked in comics over 20 years pencilling and inking projects including THE SPECTRE, MARTIAN MANHUNTER, THE KENTS, GRIMJACK and BATMAN. Currently he is working on JLA: DESTINY for DC and his creator-owned project, CREEPS, with Dan Mishkin.

SUSAN MANGAN was reared in Western New York and currently lives and works in Baltimore. Trained by the devoted professors at SUNY Oswego as a printmaker and painter, she now indulges her love of ink on a page in the graphic design field.

SCOTT McDANIEL is a Pittsburgh native and former electrical engineer whose microfilmed name once soared above the planet Venus on the Magellan spacecraft. Now firmly planted back on planet Earth, his name has appeared on comics like DAREDEVIL, GREEN GOBLIN, NIGHTWING, and currently BATMAN.

DWAYNE McDUFFIE is a co-founder of Milestone Media, Inc. He is the co-creator of STATIC SHOCK, DAMAGE CONTROL and the "Milestone Universe" of multicultural comic book characters.

PAT McGREAL is the writer of I, PAPARAZZI, a photographic novel set in New York that went to press just as terrorists struck on September 11. The WTC can be glimpsed in the book, making I, PAPARAZZI an unintentional reminder of the city that was.

DON McGREGOR is writer/creator of SABRE, DETECTIVES INC., a comic series for which he has also written and directed a film version, and RAGAMUFFINS, about children growing up in the 1950s. He has also written two prose books, Dragonflame and The Variable Syndrome.

DAVE McKEAN lives and works in Kent, England. He has illustrated several award-winning comics including ARKHAM ASYLUM and MR. PUNCH, has written and illustrated two books, Cages and Pictures That Tick, and has created hundreds of comic and book covers (including THE SANDMAN), ad campaigns (Nike, Kodak, Mini) and CD packages. He is currently directing and designing films and running the jazz record label Feral.

JAIME MENDOZA has inked such diverse books as SUPERMAN, ACTION COMICS, YOUNG JUSTICE, BATMAN, and X-MEN among many others. Currently he is working on the YOUNG JUSTICE/ SPYBOY crossover for Dark Horse comics and is also writing and inking the miniseries MOON RUSH.

JESUS MERINO has worked on FANTASTIC FOUR and is inking the upcoming JLA/JSA hardcover.

CHRISTOPHER MOELLER has been writing and painting since 1990. He is best known for his IRON EMPIRES graphic novels and the recent JLA hardcover A LEAGUE OF ONE.

MICHAEL MOORCOCK, at age 16, lived in London and edited Tarzan Adventures while writing for most British comics. As editor of New Worlds, he spearheaded the "New Wave" of science-fiction writers. Known for his fantasy sequences, which introduced the idea of the multiverse, and for novels like Mother London, he still performs periodically with Hawkwind and The Deep Fix, has a platinum record, and currently lives near Austin, Texas.

JENNIFER MOORE's work (with writing partner Sean Carolan) can be most recently found in the pages of THE POWERPUFF GIRLS and LOONEY TUNES and will appear in the form of a story concept credit in an upcoming Powerpuff Girls episode on Cartoon Network.

PAUL MOUNTS is currently coloring S.C.I.-SPY for Vertigo and has colored GATE CRASHER for Black Bull Comics.

PATRICIA MULVIHILL is a colorist who lives in Soho, New York City, where she rides her bike and keeps watch for bad guys. She drinks too much tea and is pretty formidable at skeeball.

TODD NAUCK began working in comics in April 1994. He is currently the regular penciller of YOUNG JUSTICE. Todd lives in Orange County, California with his lovely wife, Dawn.

ASHLEY-JAYNE NICOLAUS is a native Californian and co-writes HAVEN: THE BROKEN CITY. Ashley also has a short story published in Bento (Alan Spiegel Fine Arts 2001). She is currently an art student and spends most of her time writing and painting.

PHIL NOTO is the cover artist for BIRDS OF PREY and currently is an assistant animator at Walt Disney Feature Animation.

BILL OAKLEY is one of our field's best and most sought-after lettering talents. His work can be found in THE LEAGUE OF EXTRAORDINARY GENTLEMEN, THE SPECTRE, BATMAN: NINE LIVES and the upcoming HAWKMAN series.

ARIEL OLIVETTI was born in Buenos Aires and has worked on THE AVENGERS, LOBO, JLA: HAVEN and THE KINGDOM. Hundreds of young Argentinean artists have studied under his guidance, and some of them are working professionally for publishing houses all over the world.

DENNY O'NEIL put the "dark" in "Dark Knight" for over 20 years as a writer and editor of BATMAN. A best-selling novelist and screenwriter, he has taught writing at the School of Visual Arts in New York City and lectures at numerous colleges.

CARLOS PACHECO was born in Spain and began working in comics a decade ago for Marvel UK. He went on to draw THE FLASH at DC and the X-MEN, AVENGERS, INHUMANS and FANTASTIC FOUR at Marvel. Currently he is pencilling a JLA/JSA graphic novel.

TOM PALMER is a freelance artist with numerous comic book and advertising credits to his name. He currently resides in northern New Jersey.

JIMMY PALMIOTTI is a native Brooklynite. He has co-founded Event Comics, Marvel Knights and inked just about every artist in the field. His current projects are writing SUPERBOY for DC and 21 DOWN for WildStorm, and inking S.C.I.-SPY and MIDNIGHT MASS for Vertigo.

DANIEL DUKE PANOSIAN has pencilled and inked a variety of books including CAPTAIN AMERICA, SPIDER-MAN, THE HULK and THE X-MEN. Most recently he started his own advertising agency providing design work for DreamWorks, Universal and Warner Bros., but nothing thrills him more than his continued career in the comic book industry.

YANICK PAQUETTE intended to write classical music, but fate chose otherwise. Involved in comics since 1995, his work includes WONDER WOMAN, SUPERMAN, GAMBIT and CODENAME: KNOCKOUT. He lives in Montreal with his girlfriend Marie-pier.

STEVEN PARKE is a former art director and designer for the artist currently known as Prince. I, PAPARAZZI from Vertigo was Steven's first foray into the DC Universe.

ANDE PARKS was born and raised in Kansas and has been employed in the world of comic book inking for over a decade, on such titles as SUPERMAN, WONDER WOMAN and CATWOMAN. He is currently teamed with his long-time friend Phil Hester on GREEN ARROW. He lives in

Kansas with his lovely wife and daughter.

JAMES PASCOE is a freelance artist and has worked in the comics field, primarily with DC, for the last 9 years.

STEPHEN JOHN PHILLIPS's photographs have been published both nationally and internationally and are included in the permanent collection of the National Museum of American Art. He is best known in comics for his work on the graphic novels VEILS and I, PAPARAZZI.

PAUL POPE is a New Yorker. His new book 100% will be published by Vertigo in summer 2002.

QUEBECOR WORLD MONTREAL is the largest printer worldwide, committed to printing comic books. We thank the comics industry for the opportunity of being a partner in such an important mission.

BENJAMIN RAAB still considers himself a New Yorker despite his current Los Angeles address. During his career, he's had the good fortune of entertaining readers at home in the U.S. as well as abroad in countries such as Sweden and Australia. He is the proud author of DC's upcoming JLA: SHOGUN OF STEEL.

PAM RAMBO is currently coloring WAR STORIES and GRIP: THE STRANGE WORLD OF MEN for Vertigo.

HUMBERTO RAMOS co-created IMPULSE for DC and is the writer and artist of his creator-owned series OUT THERE and CRIMSON.

ROBIN RIGGS is an Englishman in New York who has been inking comics for DC and Marvel for over a decade. This is his first pencilling work for DC.

EDUARDO RISSO is proud of descending from the Argentinean Comic School. He´s been working in the European market for about 15 years and currently in the American market drawing his own monthly comic, 100 BULLETS for Vertigo.

DARICK ROBERTSON could see the World Trade Center fall from the window in his home in Brooklyn. Artist and co-creator of TRANSMETROPOLITAN, a book wherein a sprawling city is a major character, it affected him profoundly. Born in California, New York became his adopted home in 2000.

CLEM ROBINS has a hip, happening lettering style that has adorned far too many DC Comics to enumerate here. He is an adjunct professor of anatomy at the Art Academy of Cincinnati, and his book The Art of Figure Drawing will be released in May 2002.

ROGER ROBINSON is the former artist on AZRAEL and the current penciller for BATMAN: GOTHAM KNIGHTS, both for DC.

PRENTIS ROLLINS grew up in and around Washington, D.C. and now lives in New York. He and his wife Jackie recently self-published their daughter, Scotia Ray.

ALEX ROSS is an acclaimed, award-winning painter whose work over the past decade has helped broaden the medium of comic books. His most recent project for DC Comics is the graphic novel WONDER WOMAN: SPIRIT OF TRUTH.

DUNCAN ROULEAU is the artist on ACTION COMICS. He feels privileged to contribute to this benefit book. He hopes that in a small way it helps ease those suffering and shine a light on the true heroes of the hour.

JIM ROYAL has inked such titles as LAZARUS 5, SPECTRE, STAR WARS: CHEWBACCA and the upcoming CITIZEN V AND THE V-BATTALION. He resides in Georgia or California (he's not quite sure yet).

GASPAR SALADINO has been in the comics business for many years and is currently the letterer on THE FLASH.

TIM SALE is the artist of BATMAN: DARK VICTORY, BATMAN: THE LONG HALLOWEEN, SUPERMAN FOR ALL SEASONS, GRENDEL: DEVIL CHILD, BILLI 99 and THE AMAZON. He lives in southern California with his family.

WILLIE SCHUBERT illuminates comics manuscripts in the shadow of Pikes Peak while his wife, Kathy, teaches elementary school art and his daughter, Marika, is in kindergarten. A vagabond letterer since 1984, he nowadays does most of his work for DC. His work appears in NIGHTWING, ROBIN, and several other assorted DC titles.

STEVE SCOTT has pencilled for many publishers and is currently working for DC Comics. His work has been seen in the pages of HOURMAN and various JLA projects including the upcoming

JLA: OMNIVORES. In addition to working in the comics industry, he is a professional firefighter of nearly 12 years.

STEVEN T. SEAGLE is part of the Man Of Action idea studio and has created and written for film, television, animation, and comics including HOUSE OF SECRETS, UNCANNY X-MEN, SANDMAN MYSTERY THEATRE, and currently THE CRUSADES and SUPERMAN: IT'S A BIRD.

VAL SEMEIKS is a 15-year comics industry veteran. His recent career highlights include DC ONE MILLION and JLA: INCARNATIONS

CHRISTOPHER SEQUEIRA is an Australian writer who was born, raised, and still lives in Sydney. He has been published mostly in his home country but recently made his first foray into the mainstream U.S. comics arena with a script for a forthcoming issue of JUSTICE LEAGUE ADVENTURES.

MARIE SEVERIN, a native New Yorker, started in comics at E.C. Comics in the 1950's and was on staff for about 30 years at Marvel. Retired and currently enjoys freelancing at DC. She runs with scissors.

BILL SIENKIEWICZ lives and works in Connecticut and is a writer and artist of many different comics including STRAY TOASTERS. He also does book and CD covers, advertising and editorial illustration, as well as film and television work. The recipient of many industry awards, he was twice nominated for an Emmy for his character designs on Where In The World Is Carmen Sandiego?

ALEX SIMMONS is a writer who has spent all his life in New York City. In his career he's written articles, plays, children's books, novels, and his comic book creation, BLACKJACK. All of his work reflects his appreciation of the similarity and infinite variety of the human experience ... sinners and saviors, all.

WALTER SIMONSON was born in Tennessee, grew up in Maryland, went to school in New England, lived for years in New York City, and has done a lot of comic books. He hasn't worked on anything he's felt more deeply about than "Blitz Kid."

ALEX SINCLAIR has been coloring comics since joining the gang at WildStorm in 1993. His current projects include HARLEY QUINN, TOP 10, POWER COMPANY, and a couple of JUST IMAGINE titles. He lives in San Diego with his wife, Rebecca, and their (count them) four daughters: Grace, Blythe, Meredith, and Harley.

JAMES SINCLAIR has done coloring work for DC Comics for the last 8 years. He is currently the regular colorist on THE FLASH.

BOB SMITH lived in New York for 13 years. In 20 years of working for DC he inked everything from AQUAMAN to ZATANNA. He currently inks for Archie and Bongo Comics.

BEAU SMITH has written many comic books, including BATMAN/WILDCAT, CATWOMAN/WILDCAT, GUY GARDNER: WARRIOR and the upcoming WONDER WOMAN vs. XENA. He is also the former Vice President of Marketing and Promotions for Eclipse Comics, Image Comics and Todd McFarlane Productions.

ROBERT SOLANOVIC is the letterer of OUTLAW NATION from Vertigo.

AARON SOWD has inked many DC titles including BATMAN, THE FLASH, and NIGHTWING: THE TARGET. Based in Los Angeles, Aaron has also worked on films such as Austin Powers 3, Virus and Anastasia. He served as art director for Stan Lee Media and is currently art director for StatCard Entertainment.

RICHARD STARKINGS has worked in the comic book industry as a cartoonist, writer, colorist, production manager and publisher but is primarily known for his work as a lettering artist. He founded the Comicraft Design and Lettering studio with John "JG" Roshell in 1992. The Comicraftsmen who also contributed work to this book include Wes Abbott and Saida Temofonte.

JOE STATON has drawn comic books for more than 30 years. With some interruptions, he has worked for DC for 25 years. He currently pencils SCOOBY-DOO for DC's Cartoon Network line.

BRIAN STELFREEZE is the artist for WildStorm's MATADOR, as well as for several X-Men projects and the upcoming DOMINO miniseries. The Eisner Award-winning artist is part of the Atlanta-based Gaijin Studios.

DAVID STEWART began his coloring career on the staff of Dark Horse Comics. After 5 years there, he now freelances full-time on projects like HELLBOY, FRAY and DOOM PATROL. When not coloring, he might be found trying to keep his basement from flooding.

GORAN SUDZUKA was born in Zagreb, Croatia in 1969 and his comics and illustrations have been published for over 10 years. He began working with Jamie Delano on OUTLAW NATION in 1999. He won the Russ Manning Award for the most promising newcomer in 2001.

SUN CHEMICAL INC. is proud to be associated with the comic book industry and thankful to be given the opportunity to participate in this 9/11 benefit project.

ROMEO C. TANGHAL, a native of the Philippines, migrated to the U.S. in 1976 and began illustrating for DC Comics pencilling various short stories and inking THE NEW TEEN TITANS and GREEN LANTERN. He has three children.

DAVE TANGUAY started his own comic company in the early '80s. This led to a position with DC Comics where he worked as color separator, assistant editor, colorist and computer guru. Now a freelancer, he currently colors both POWERPUFF GIRLS and LOONEY TUNES.

RICK TAYLOR is the former Director of Graphic Services and Senior Editor of Collected Editions for DC Comics. He's also been the colorist on BATMAN ADVENTURES, TERMINAL CITY, FINALS, IMPULSE and BIZARRO COMICS.

JILL THOMPSON has drawn lots of titles for Vertigo. She is Will Pfeifer's collaborator on the series FINALS and is the artist and writer of the SCARY GODMOTHER series of graphic novels.

EMAN R. TORRE is the creator, writer, and inker of THE DARK FRINGE, a noir miniseries. His most recent work can be found in the DC Roleplaying Game books *Directive on Superpowers* and *JLA Sourcebook*.

ANGELO TORRES was born in Puerto Rico and grew up in New York City. In the early '50s he served with the Army in Korea, after which he attended the School of Visual Arts and broke into comics. Since 1968 he has been a regular contributor to MAD MAGAZINE.

UPM-KYMMENE. Paper proudly supplied for the cause.

JOHN VAN FLEET's painted work includes the recent BATMAN: THE CHALICE and BATMAN: THE ANKH.

BRIAN K. VAUGHAN lives in Brooklyn, where from the roof of his apartment he watched the World Trade Center fall. He is a writer for DC Comics and an auxiliary police officer in Manhattan's 10th Precinct. He is writing an upcoming creator-owned series for Vertigo, Y.

GLORIA VASQUEZ was born in Cali, Colombia and grew up in New York City. She studied in the Art Students' League and began working in comics in 1987. She is married and is the mother of two children.

RICK VEITCH has written and illustrated a number of graphic novels including THE ONE, BRATPACK, THE MAXIMORTAL, and ABRAXAS AND THE EARTHMAN. He is currently working on GREYSHIRT: INDIGO SUNSET for ABC Comics.

DANIEL VOZZO was born and raised in Brooklyn. He has had the privilege of coloring such books as THE SANDMAN, THE DOOM PATROL, and THE INVISIBLES. He is currently the colorist on THE CRUSADES and LUCIFER for Vertigo. He now lives in northern New Jersey with his wife and daughter.

BOB WIACEK attended The School of Visual Arts, learning from such teachers as Will Eisner and Harvey Kurtzman. He then apprenticed at Continuity Associates under Neal Adams and Dick Giordano. He's inked many comics,

including THE LEGION OF SUPER-HEROES and THE GUARDIANS OF THE GALAXY. Currently he works with Walt Simonson on ORION. WILDSTORM FX was founded in 1993 to color the comics produced by Jim Lee's WildStorm Productions. Since WildStorm Productions joined DC, WildStorm FX has been responsible for coloring a number of DC Comics titles as well as WildStorm titles. The current roster of colorists includes Wendy Fouts, Carrie Strachan, Tony Avina, Randy Mayor, Larry Molinar, D-Rod, and Darlene Royer.

MO WILLEMS is a four-time Emmy-winning *Sesame Street* writer/animator and is the creator/writer of Cartoon Network's *Sheep in the Big City* as well as the head writer of the network's upcoming *Code Name: Kids Next Door.*

MARV WOLFMAN was born in Brooklyn and has been writing comics, TV and movies for more than 30 years. He's created hundreds of characters and books, from Marvel's Black Cat, Bullseye and Blade, the Vampire Hunter to DC Comics' businessman version of Lex Luthor, THE NEW TEEN TITANS and CRISIS ON INFINITE EARTHS, which won the CBG Award for second-best comic book story of the 20th century.

TATJANA WOOD has colored comics since 1969, including a long stint on DC's SWAMP THING, MICHAEL MOORCOCK'S MULTIVERSE and ORION. She emigrated to the United States from Europe, but considers New York to be her true home.

PETE WOODS lives in Portland, Oregon with his wife, Rebecca, and their daughter. He says "Hi."

JOHN WORKMAN is known primarily for his lettering, but he has, over a period of 30-plus years, been an editor, writer, designer, art director, penciller, inker, colorist, and production director. He has great respect for the unique storytelling medium called comics.

BILL WRAY lived for 9 years in lower Manhattan, freelancing for DC Comics and studying at the Art Students' League. Moving back to Los Angeles in 1991 to work on the *Ren and Stimpy Show*, Bill is still freelancing for DC, Cartoon Network and MAD MAGAZINE.

DANIJEL ZEZELJ was born in Zagreb, Croatia where he began publishing comics during his first year at the Academy of Fine Arts. Since then he has drawn for *The New York Times Book Review* and in comics such as CONGORILLA, EL DIABLO, and FLINCH.

MICHAEL ZULLI is a resident of New England, wears his heart on his sleeve and is damn proud of it. He also works with the radio on. His great grandparents came from Italy through Ellis Island like a lot of dreamers. The tradition continues.

CAUSES

This volume is dedicated to the victims of the September 11th attacks, their families, and the heroes who aided them that day and in the difficult days that have followed, with sympathy and respect from all of us at DC Comics.

All of the creative talent in this volume have donated their efforts, as have the suppliers, printer, and distributors of the book. All of the publisher's profits from the sale of this book will be donated to organizations for the benefit and relief of the victims of the September 11, 2001 attack on America, their families and affected communities, including:

New York State World Trade Center Relief Fund

Survivors Fund of the National Capital Region

The September 11th Fund of The New York Community Trust and the United Way of New York City

Twin Towers Fund

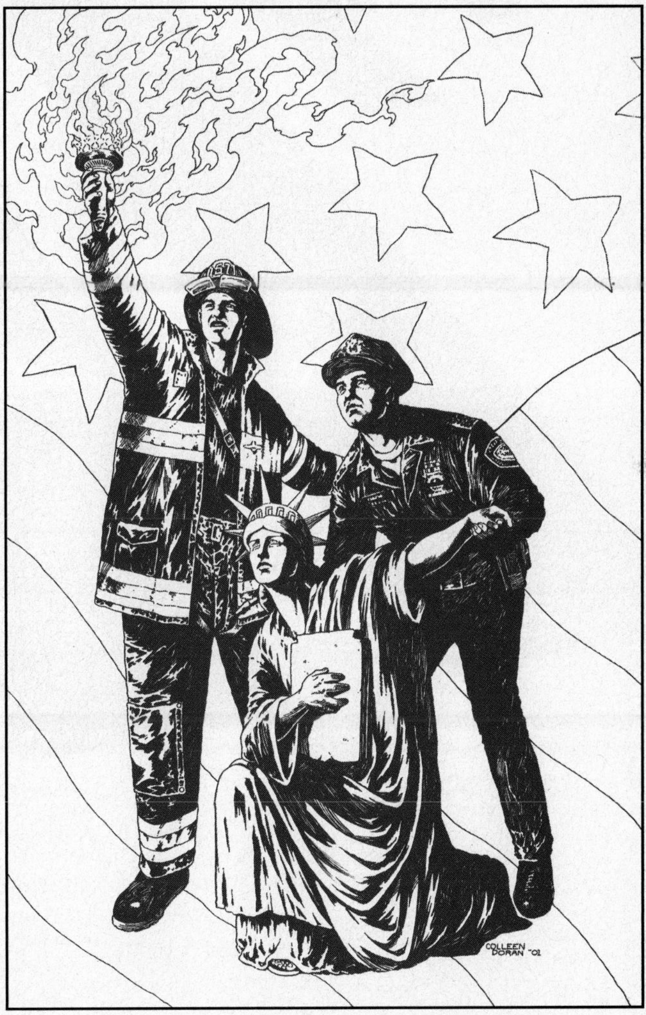
COLLEEN DORAN '01

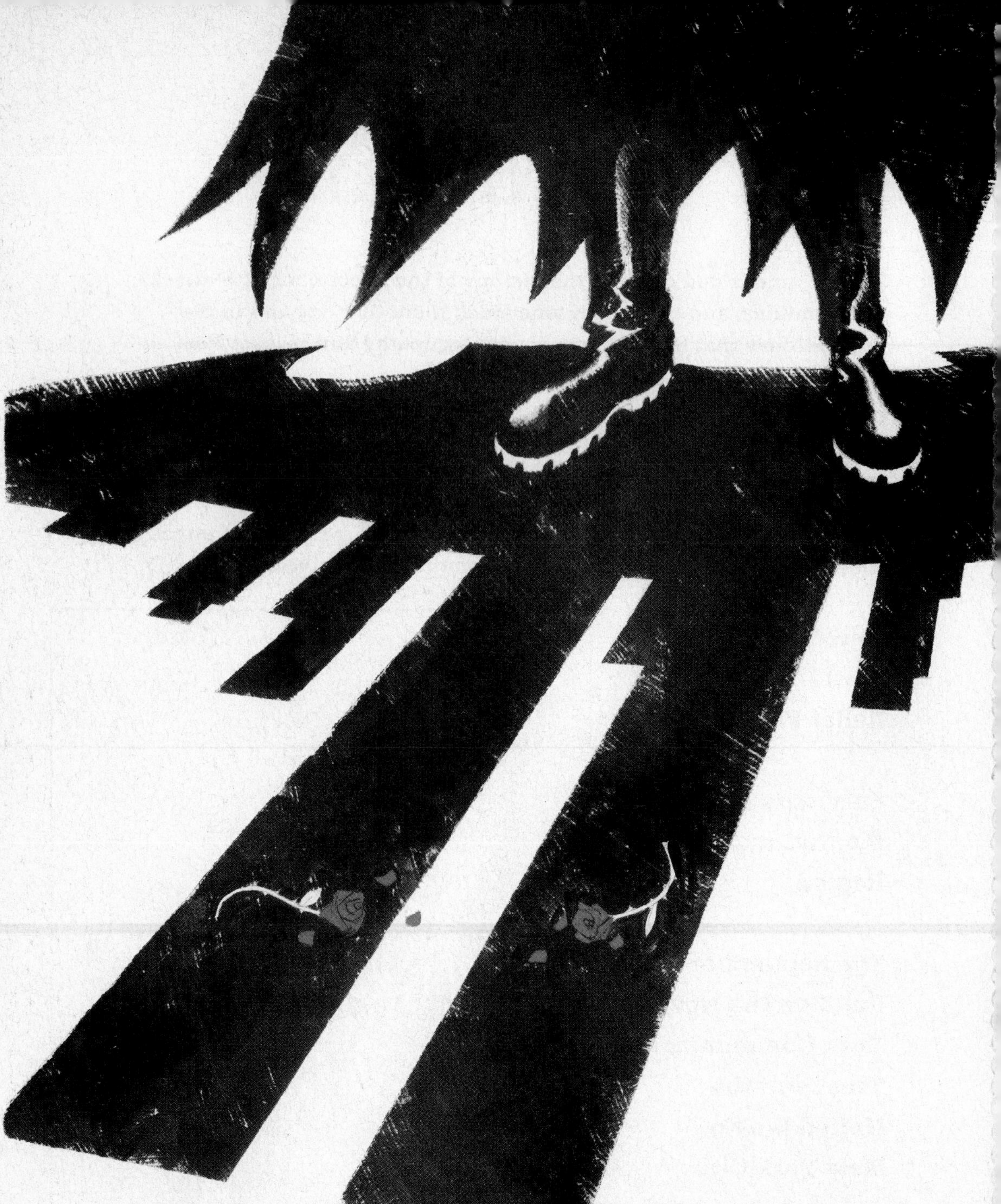
JOHNSON
2001

ART
DAVE
JOHNSON

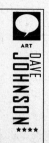